THE WAY OF THE BARBARIANS

The Way of the Barbarians

Redrawing Ethnic Boundaries
in Tang and Song China

Shao-yun Yang

UNIVERSITY OF WASHINGTON PRESS
Seattle

The Way of the Barbarians was made possible in part by a grant from the Chiang Ching-kuo Foundation for International Scholarly Exchange.

Copyright © 2019 by the University of Washington Press
Composed in Minion Pro, typeface designed by Robert Slimbach

23 22 21 20 19   5 4 3 2 1

Printed and bound in the United States of America

All rights reserved. No part of this publication may be reproduced or transmitted in any form or by any means, electronic or mechanical, including photocopy, recording, or any information storage or retrieval system, without permission in writing from the publisher.

UNIVERSITY OF WASHINGTON PRESS
uwapress.uw.edu

LIBRARY OF CONGRESS CATALOGING-IN-PUBLICATION DATA
Names: Yang, Shao-yun, author.
Title: The way of the barbarians : redrawing ethnic boundaries in Tang and Song China / Shao-yun Yang.
Description: Seattle : University of Washington Press, [2019] | Includes bibliographical references and index. |
Identifiers: LCCN 2019014020 (print) | LCCN 2019019537 (ebook) | ISBN 9780295746012 (ebook) | ISBN 9780295746029 (hardcover : alk. paper) | ISBN 9780295746036 (pbk. : alk. paper)
Subjects: LCSH: China—Ethnic relations—History—To 1500. | Minorities—China—History—To 1500. | National characteristics, Chinese—History—To 1500. | China—Civilization—221 B.C.-960 A.D. | China—Civilization—960-1644. | China—History—Tang dynasty, 618-907. | China—History—Song dynasty, 960-1279.
Classification: LCC DS730 (ebook) | LCC DS730 .Y428 2019 (print) | DDC 305.800951/09021—dc23
LC record available at https://lccn.loc.gov/2019014020

COVER ILLUSTRATION: Traditionally attributed to Zhao Guangfu (ca. 923–976), *Barbarian Royalty Worshiping the Buddha*, detail. Handscroll, ink, and color on silk; H 28.6 cm, L 103.5 cm. Cleveland Museum of Art.

The paper used in this publication is acid free and meets the minimum requirements of American National Standard for Information Sciences—Permanence of Paper for Printed Library Materials, ANSI Z39.48–1984.∞

Contents

Acknowledgments vii
Chronology of Dynasties xi

INTRODUCTION 3
1. Han Yu, the *Annals*, and the Origins of Ethnicized Orthodoxy 24
2. Han Yu, Liu Zongyuan, and the Debate over Buddhism and Barbarism 43
3. Ethnocentric Moralism in Two Late Tang Essays 57
4. Ethnicized Orthodoxy in the Northern Song Guwen Revival 74
5. Ideas of Barbarization in Eleventh-Century *Annals* Exegesis 98
6. Chineseness and Barbarism in Early Daoxue Philosophy 119
CONCLUSION 141

Glossary 155
Notes 163
Bibliography 201
Index 219

Acknowledgments

It seems appropriate here to "begin at the beginning" by thanking Yu Pingguang, who used stories to introduce me to premodern Chinese history in the mid-1990s, and Fong Say Fong (Hong Xuefang), my first teacher in Classical Chinese. At the National University of Singapore, Huang Jianli urged me to find a historical question that really mattered to me. I owe it to his wise and patient tutelage that the question I stumbled upon has taken me this far. I am deeply grateful also to David Johnson, Nicolas Tackett, Robert Ashmore, and especially Michael Nylan at the University of California, Berkeley. Each of them has enriched my understanding of China's past and of the historian's craft, increasing my willingness to look at my sources with fresh, objective eyes and my ability to interpret what I see.

At various stages of writing, I have benefited from the encouragement and advice of Barry Keenan, Ruth Dunnell, Richard J. Smith, Yuri Pines, Charles Holcombe, András Róna-Tas, Javier Caramés Sánchez, Moritz Huber, and Sharon Sanderovitch. My thanks also to Tineke D'Haeseleer, Charles Hartman, Liu Chengguo, Hoyt Tillman, and Melissa Brown for their candid and perceptive critiques of early versions of the argument. I have presented ideas and arguments from the book at Harvard University, Yale University, and Kenyon College, and would like to thank Mark C. Elliott, James Robson, Valerie Hansen, François Louis, and Ruth Dunnell for these opportunities, as well as Li Wai-yee, Hue-Tam Ho Tai, Peter Bol, Daniel Kane, Naomi Standen, Pierre Marsone, Wen Xin, Kim Youn-mi, Joseph Adler, Yang Xiao, and Anna Sun for their interest and helpful comments on those occasions. I thank Higashi Hidetoshi, whose scholarship on Northern Song Guwen writers has been vital to my work, and who generously answered a key question in detail via e-mail. I gained useful perspectives on current Chinese historiography surrounding identity and empire from extended conversations with Yao Dali, Ge Zhaoguang, Wen Haiqing, Qiu Yihao, and Zhang Jia at Fudan University in the summer of 2018, and appreciate their generosity in sharing their time and ideas.

Special thanks go to two anonymous readers for the University of Washington Press who improved the book considerably through detailed feedback on the finished manuscript. Executive editor Lorri Hagman also provided valuable stylistic recommendations and persuaded me that it was possible to make the book both significantly shorter *and* better—a task she clearly has had to accomplish with many academic writers. Responsibility for the final shape that the book has taken, including errors and omissions, is mine alone.

The research for this book was conducted using sources held in the C. V. Starr East Asian Library at the University of California, Berkeley, and the Thompson Library at the Ohio State University, as well as books obtained from other universities through the remarkably efficient interlibrary loan service at Denison University's Doane Library. For their invaluable assistance, I would like to express my appreciation to librarians He Jianye (Berkeley) and Susan Rice (Denison). I was able to begin writing in 2015 during a semester of parental leave following the birth of my son Daniel, and engaged in the penultimate stage of revision to the manuscript during a semester-long sabbatical in 2018. I am grateful to my colleagues in the Department of History and the East Asian Studies program at Denison University for accommodating my absence during these precious periods of time away from my regular teaching duties. I am even more grateful for their collegiality and support, which have made those regular duties a joy throughout the five years of working on the book.

My wife, Estelle—both my toughest critic and my biggest cheerleader—has had to keep the house running and dish out healthy doses of real-world perspective (in addition to healthy *and* delicious food) while I labored and brooded over this project. For her daily acts of selflessness over the years, I owe her more gratitude than words can express. Our children Ying Ling, Huimin, and Daniel have cheered me up innumerable times with smiles and hugs and laughter, reminding me what all this work is for in the end. Our parents, siblings, and various kin in Singapore, Australia, China, and the United States have been sources of support and advice that we can always count on, even over great distances. I am particularly indebted and grateful to my father, Yang Lih Shyng, and my mother, Chen Chorng Ru, to William and Amy Chan, and to Lin Jingyi for their years of timely help on matters big and small.

Some twelve years of studying the long history of Chinese ethnocentrism have made me acutely aware that few ideas are as universal, and as impermeable to reason, as the idea that one's culture or nation is inherently better than all others in the world. This book is thus dedicated to all who have worked, or are now working, to bring peoples and cultures together in understanding, mutual respect, friendship, and peace.

Chronology of Dynasties

Names of the Sixteen Kingdoms between 304 and 439 and the Ten Kingdoms between 907 and 979 are omitted for brevity.

Xia   mythical?
Shang   ca. 1600–1046 BCE
Zhou   ca. 1046–256 BCE
    Western Zhou   ca. 1046–771 BCE
    Eastern Zhou   770–256 BCE
        Annals ("Spring and Autumn") period   770–476 BCE
        Warring States period   476–221 BCE
Qin   221–206 BCE
Han   206 BCE–220 CE
    Western Han   206 BCE–9 CE
    Xin   9–23 CE
    Eastern Han   25–220 CE
Three Kingdoms   220–280
    Cao-Wei   220–266
    Shu-Han   221–263
    Wu   222/229–280
Jin   266–420
    Western Jin   266–316
    Eastern Jin   317–420
Sixteen Kingdoms   304–439
Southern Dynasties   420–589
    Liu-Song   420–479
    Southern Qi   479–502
    Liang   502–557
    Chen   557–589

Northern Dynasties   386/399–581
    Northern Wei   386/399–534
    Eastern Wei   534–550   Western Wei   534–557
    Northern Qi   550–577   Northern Zhou   557–581
Sui   581–618
Tang   618–907
Five Dynasties   907–960
    Later Liang   907–923
    Later Tang   923–936
    Later Jin   936–947
    Later Han   947–951
    Later Zhou   951–960
Ten Kingdoms   907–979
Liao (Kitan)   907/916–1125
Song   960–1276
    Northern Song   960–1127
    Southern Song   1127–1276
Xi Xia (Tangut)   1038–1227
Jin (Jurchen)   1115–1234
Yuan (Mongol)   1206/1271–1368/1388
Ming   1368–1644
Qing (Manchu)   1616/1636–1911

THE WAY OF THE BARBARIANS

Introduction

IN Chinese history, the Tang-Song transition of circa 755–1127 CE was a watershed period of wide-ranging social, economic, demographic, and intellectual change.¹ Since the mid-twentieth century, two grand narratives that bookend the Tang-Song transition have also strongly influenced studies of premodern Chinese attitudes regarding ethnocultural identity and difference. The first of these postulates a ninth-century shift from a spirit of "cosmopolitanism," which welcomed foreign peoples and integrated them and their cultures into Chinese society, to one of "xenophobia," which called for their exclusion or expulsion. The second narrative speaks of an eleventh-century or twelfth-century shift from a traditional notion of "culturalism" or "cultural universalism" to a new ethnic "nationalism"; foreign peoples were formerly treated as as-yet uncivilized "barbarians" who could, and should, become civilized and Chinese through a process of acculturation, but were now viewed as dangerous invaders to (again) be kept or driven out from Chinese territory.

These narratives use different terms and concepts but share the assumption that traumatic geopolitical events, for which foreigners were held responsible, triggered a drastic transformation in how the Chinese defined themselves as a people and understood their relationship to the rest of the world. In the case of the cosmopolitanism-to-xenophobia narrative, the key event is the powerful Turco-Sogdian general An Lushan's (703–757) rebellion against the Tang imperial court, which began in 755 and dragged on until 763, through various changes in leadership. In the case of the culturalism-to-nationalism narrative, it is either the tenth-century emergence of the Kitan people's Liao empire as a powerful rival to the post-Tang Chinese dynasties, or the Jurchen people's invasion and conquest of north China in 1125–30 that marks the divide between the Northern Song and Southern Song periods.[2] In both cases, one can discern the influence of twentieth-century historiographical perspectives on the gradual rise of modern Chinese nationalism as a response to foreign imperialist encroachment, beginning with the Opium War of 1839–42 and culminating in the war of resistance against Japan in 1937–45. In other words, the historians who have used Tang-period and Song-period texts to support both narratives have interpreted these texts through the lens of more recent historical experience, assuming that throughout Chinese history the natural reaction to political crises originating in foreign threats has been a stronger emphasis on ethnic solidarity and greater hostility toward ethnocultural others.

The alternative view presented in this volume better reflects the rhetorical, ideological, and philosophical agendas that motivated new interpretations of Chineseness and its supposed antithesis, "barbarism," during the late Tang and Northern Song periods. Intellectual change during this period was not a straightforward product of political change or crisis but rather had its own developmental logic, driving forces, intertextual influences, and internal debates surrounding two broad intellectual shifts among the Chinese literati elite—shifts affected, but neither initiated nor determined, by the impact of political-military events like the An Lushan Rebellion, the rise of the Kitan Liao, and the Jurchen invasion. The first shift, beginning in the ninth century and culminating in the middle of the eleventh, was the rise of a new, exclusively "Confucian" or Classicist (Ru) conception of ideological and intellectual orthodoxy, expressed through the medium of a self-consciously plain literary style known as Guwen (Ancient-Style Prose) and purportedly modeled on the language of the "Confucian" Classics.[3] The second shift, spanning the last decades of the eleventh century and all of the twelfth, was the emergence and widening appeal of the Daoxue (Learning of the Way) form of Classicism, better known to the Western world as "Neo-Confucianism." This new philosophical school replaced the complex cosmological system of correlations and cycles inherited from Han-dynasty thought with a new, simpler cosmology defined by an integral relationship between metaphysics and morality, thus supplying an accessible explanation for why human moral perfection is both vitally important and attainable.

Leading figures in the emergence of Guwen and Daoxue played key roles in the rise of two new and distinct interpretations of the boundary between Chineseness and barbarism: an ideology-centered interpretation of

Chineseness, which I term "ethnicized orthodoxy," and a morality-centered interpretation of the same, which I term "ethnocentric moralism." Rather than reflecting a hardening of ethnocultural boundaries in response to foreign threats, these new discourses on the Chinese-barbarian dichotomy emphasized its fluidity in a manner that subverted the traditional centrality of cultural or ritual practices to Chinese identity, in an attempt at redefining the essence of Chinese civilization and its purported superiority. The key issues and debates at stake concerned the acceptability of intellectual pluralism in a Chinese society and the importance of Classicist ("Confucian") moral values to the integrity and continuity of the Chinese state. In addition, users of both discourses often articulated them through another notable development in the intellectual history of the Tang-Song transition: namely, an interest in reassessing and correcting past interpretations of the *Annals* (Chunqiu; literally, "Spring and Autumn"), a historical chronicle traditionally attributed to Confucius (Kongzi; 551–479 BCE) and seen as a repository of insights into the ancient sage's thinking.[4] This made the *Annals* a central text for Classicist interpretations of the Chinese-barbarian dichotomy for the first time in history, influencing subsequent readings of the chronicle to such an extent that many scholars now treat it as an archetypal example of the "traditional" Chinese approach to ethnocultural identity.

HAN YU AND THE MYTH OF LATE TANG XENOPHOBIA

The late Tang Guwen writer Han Yu (768–824) and his intellectual legacy are central to this book. Since the middle of the twentieth century, numerous historians have interpreted Han Yu's famous anti-Buddhist polemics—especially "Memorial on the Buddha Relic" (Lun fogu biao) of 819—as reflecting a trend toward "xenophobia," "nativism," or "cultural nationalism" in late Tang society, a reaction to the sociopolitical upheaval caused by the Turco-Sogdian An Lushan's rebellion against the empire.[5] It is not difficult to discern in this interpretation the shadow of modern events in relations between China and the Western world, including eruptions of anti-foreign violence like the Boxer Uprising of 1900. Certainly, the nature of Chinese foreign relations changed significantly after the An Lushan Rebellion, as the Tang found itself in a position of distinct weakness relative to the Tibetan empire (an aggressive enemy) and the Uighur empire (an often overbearing ally) for some eighty years until both empires collapsed in 840–48. However, the evidence for late Tang hostility and violence toward foreigners and their ways is extremely thin and, when put in context, can be seen as atypical rather than representative. Claims about post-rebellion prejudice against Sogdians are founded on oversimplistic readings of isolated incidents and are contradicted by evidence that the number of Sogdian guardsmen in the Tang imperial guards increased after the An Lushan Rebellion.[6] A number of satirical poems by Yuan Zhen (779–831) and Bai Juyi (or Bo Juyi; 772–846) are often cited as reflections of a xenophobic turn against Central Asian (Hu) music and fashions, but several of the poems actually indicate that, regardless of their authors' own sentiments, the Tang elite's famous appetite for all things Hu had only grown since the An Lushan Rebellion ended.[7] Further belying the image of a society obsessed with purging itself of alien elements, there is evidence of large and flourishing foreign communities in the imperial capital (Chang'an) and other major Chinese cities throughout the ninth century—including even Yangzhou, the site of a massacre in 760 of several thousand Arab and Iranian merchants that originated in a Tang military commander's opportunistic rapacity but has frequently been misinterpreted as a sign of the new xenophobic mood.[8]

Some historians have pointed to the Tang emperor Wuzong's (r. 840–46) persecution of Buddhism and other "foreign" religions (including Manichaeism, Zoroastrianism, and Christianity) in 842–46 as a prime example of late Tang anti-foreign hostility. The motivations behind the persecution remain a subject of investigation and debate.[9] It seems clear, however, that the Daoist alchemists who turned Wuzong against the Buddhists were driven by sectarian and personal agendas that cannot be simply ascribed to xenophobia and that the persecution—which was swiftly abandoned after Wuzong's death—was not typical of elite attitudes toward Buddhism.[10] Furthermore, many prominent Guwen writers of the late Tang were avid practitioners of Buddhism who took no issue with its foreign origins. Although some historians (notably the renowned Chen Yinke) have argued that Han Yu differed from them in seeing Buddhism as a "barbarian" menace like An Lushan's rebellion, Han's extant writings indicate his agenda was much broader than attacking Buddhism as a foreign religion.[11] He consistently denounced both Buddhism *and* Daoism as heterodox enemies of Classicism and, at the end of his essay "Tracing the Way to Its Source" (Yuandao; hereafter abbreviated as "Tracing the Way"), infamously called on the government to laicize the clergies of both religions, burn their scriptures, and close down their temples.[12] Moreover, he believed that Chinese civilization had been in moral decline for a thousand years and that Buddhism was only the latest system of thought or belief to contribute to the decline. Comparatively, the closest analogues to Han Yu's ideological agenda are not modern nationalist or nativist movements but instead Renaissance humanism and the Protestant Reformation, both of which were founded on a reinterpretation of most of Western Christendom's prior history as a long age of degeneration—a decline from the glories of Greco-Roman civilization in the humanists' case and from Christian orthodoxy in the case of the Protestants.[13]

THE CHINESE-BARBARIAN DICHOTOMY AND THE TROUBLE WITH "CULTURALISM"

The image of ninth-century Tang society in general, and of Han Yu in particular, as xenophobic and nativist remains common in Chinese historiography, but has become less prevalent in Western historical scholarship as more historians have come to recognize its flaws. In some cases, it appears to have been replaced by an interpretation of Han Yu as a "culturalist" or "universalist" in a tradition going back to Confucius himself. According to the earliest such reading, Han Yu's objections to Buddhism were "cultural, not racial," and cannot be called xenophobic because he did not conceive of the Chinese-barbarian dichotomy "in the familiar modern terms of ethnicity, race, or nationality." A more recent iteration argues that for Han Yu "the distinction between Self and Other is not a question of ethnicity or origins per se but rather is dependent on abstract cultural values based on timeless norms."[14] Indeed, historian Charles Holcombe has proposed, in place of the cosmopolitanism-to-xenophobia narrative, an alternative cosmopolitanism-to-culturalism narrative in which Han Yu represents a late Tang transition from cultural and intellectual pluralism to the "Confucian universalism" of the more culturally homogeneous Northern Song, in which "civilization was a matter of adherence to universal Confucian truths, and was theoretically open to anyone."[15]

Such assessments of Han Yu are based not on "Memorial on the Buddha Relic" but on a well-known passage from "Tracing the Way":

> When Confucius wrote the *Annals*, if [any of] the lords used barbarian rites (*Yili*), then [Confucius] regarded him as a barbarian, and if barbarians were promoted to the level of the Central Lands, then he regarded them as [people of the] Central Lands.[16] The Classic [of the *Analects*] says, "The barbarians have rulers but are still not equal to Chinese states that do not."[17]

The *Odes* (Shi) [Classic] says, "He smote the Rong and Di; he punished Jing and Shu."[18] Now we are elevating a law of the barbarians (*Yi-Di zhi fa*) above the teachings of the former [sage-]kings—how much longer [can this go on] before we all become barbarians?[19]

In this argument, Han Yu draws on commentarial traditions surrounding the *Annals* to make Chinese rites (and, by extension, Classicist orthodoxy) integral to Chinese identity. Han's argument, with its forceful simplicity and claim to Confucius's sagely authority, eventually attained a kind of canonical status in discussions of the Chinese-barbarian dichotomy and has thus exerted considerable influence on modern understandings of the nature of Chinese identity in the period during which the *Annals* was composed.

The available textual evidence suggests that by Confucius's day, the political elites of various North China Plain states that recognized the Eastern Zhou king's authority had begun interpreting themselves as a single Xia or Hua people divided into "many Xia" (*zhu Xia*) or "many Hua" (*zhu Hua*) states, as distinct from neighboring peoples who were labeled as Yi, Man, Rong, and Di.[20] These Xia or Hua states were also known collectively as "the Central States" (Zhongguo, the same term translated today as "China"), while the Yi, Man, Rong, and Di peoples came to be identified with the east, south, west, and north, respectively. Later, under the Western Han dynasty, the original Yi, Rong, and Di peoples of north China came to identify and be identified as Xia or Hua, but the processes by which this happened are poorly documented and thus difficult to reconstruct. Han officials also began applying labels like Yi and Man to other peoples who had had little or no contact with the Xia or Hua prior to the territorial expansion of the Qin and Han empires: the ancient forebears of the Koreans and Vietnamese, for example.[21] Meanwhile, they continued referring to the original Xia or Hua ethnocultural heartland in north China by the classical term Zhongguo, but also began applying it to the expanded ethnocultural zone dominated by the Xia or Hua, or even to the empire as a whole, via a principle of synecdoche—a figure of speech that uses a part or parts to represent the whole. The latter two usages of Zhongguo outlasted the term's identification with north China alone and persisted for some two millennia of imperial Chinese history.[22]

In this book, the ethnonyms Xia and Hua are translated as "Chinese," the toponyms Zhongguo and Zhonghua (the latter of much later date) as "the Central Lands" and "the Central Lands of the Chinese," respectively, and the topo-ethnonym Zhongguoren as "person/people of the Central Lands."

By translating Zhongguo as "the Central Lands," rather than either "Central State/Country" or "Central States," I retain some of the term's original plural character while acknowledging that the area thus designated had become part of a unified empire.[23] In the Tang and Song periods, other ethnonyms like Hanren ("Han person") and Tangren ("Tang person") also existed and may even have been used more commonly than Xia or Hua in frontier regions. But they typically did not connote superiority over other peoples by invoking the classical Chinese-barbarian dichotomy, and therefore do not appear in the discourses analyzed here.[24]

Two clarifying points on classical Chinese names for ethnocultural others are relevant here. The first is this: although some modern scholars have denied that the ancient Chinese ever had a "blanket term for all foreign peoples" equivalent to the Greco-Roman *barbaros/barbarus*,[25] numerous classical Chinese texts do refer collectively to the Yi, Man, Rong, and Di via synecdochic combinations including Yi-Di, Man-Yi, Rong-Yi, Rong-Di, and occasionally Yi-Mo and Man-Mo, Mo being a label associated with foreign peoples of the northeast. The Chinese began using such "ethnonym compounds," as well as Yi alone and the numerical expression *siyi* ("four kinds of Yi" or "Yi of the four quarters"), as generic labels for all foreign peoples during the Warring States period, corresponding to the last two centuries of the Eastern Zhou, and continued doing so for over two millennia.[26]

The second point relates to translation of the generic Yi and the equivalent synecdochic combinations as "barbarian." As will be evident from the sources studied in this book, these labels eventually acquired strong pejorative associations due to an emerging Classicist discourse associating them with a lack of "ritual propriety and moral duty" (*liyi*), as well as classical passages such as *Analects* 3.5 (quoted in "Tracing the Way"), in which Confucius asserts that Yi-Di are inferior to the "many Xia" even when the former have rulers and the latter are living in anarchy. These associations mean that translating Yi and its synecdochic equivalents as "barbarian" is—contrary to some recent arguments—more appropriate than using neutral terms like "foreigner."[27] Although the Chinese language later acquired other generic or semi-generic labels for foreign peoples, notably Fan and Hu, the absence of pejorative statements containing these labels in classical texts meant that in Tang and Song times, at least, they were rarely used in elite discourse to make claims about the inferiority of foreign peoples.[28]

Numerous modern historians have claimed that a shared "culture," perceived as superior to all others, served as the primary yardstick for defining who belonged in the Chinese multistate community of the Eastern Zhou. Ancestry was, supposedly, irrelevant: non-Xia or non-Hua people could become Xia or Hua, and vice versa, through cultural change alone. Among historians who believe that Confucius and his peers subscribed to this "cultural" interpretation of Chineseness, many also assume this interpretation persisted and predominated throughout Chinese history until modern times.[29] The foundations for this assumption were laid in the 1940s and 1950s by a number of eminent Sinologists. Writing in 1942, John K. Fairbank argued that until modern times the Chinese "stood always ready to judge a man by cultural rather than by racial or national standards," and he termed this mentality as "culturism." In 1953, Joseph R. Levenson termed it as "culturalism," which (unlike "culturism") has stuck, in part because Fairbank himself had adopted it by 1958.[30] Levenson further theorized that the Chinese saw themselves as members of a universal culture or civilization, rather than a nation, until the early twentieth century. According to this original version of "culturalism-to-nationalism" thesis, Chinese nationalism was born only when the Western powers' technological advances and global dominance made it impossible for the Chinese to claim to have a superior civilization, let alone the only true civilization in the world, and thereby also made it possible for them to prioritize preserving their independence over maintaining their traditions.[31]

While Levenson's thesis popularized the concept of Chinese "culturalism" in Western scholarship, contemporaneous developments in China produced a similarly influential "culturalism, not racism" interpretation of premodern Chinese identity. Earlier in the twentieth century, Chinese nationalist ideologues and historians had reinterpreted history to redefine China's ethnocultural majority, now known as the Han, as a biological race with a common ancestry going back to the ancient Xia or Hua.[32] By the 1940s, however, global reaction against the extremes of Nazi racialism seems to have shifted the balance in favor of "culturalist" thinking among Chinese scholars. During that decade, for example, the historians Qian Mu and Chen Yinke—both of whose influence in the Chinese-speaking world matches that of Fairbank and Levenson in the United States—asserted in their works that "culture" (*wenhua*), not "bloodline" (*xuetong*), was the sole standard by which the Chinese distinguished themselves from other peoples in ancient and medieval times, such that a "barbarian" who adopted enough Chinese culture would thereafter be regarded as Chinese. Qian quoted a famous line from "Tracing the Way" in support of his claim: "As they say, 'If [any of] the lords used barbarian rites, then [Confucius] regarded him as a barbarian, and if barbarians were promoted to the level of the Central Lands, then he regarded them as [people of the] Central Lands.' This is clear evidence that [the ancient Chinese] used culture to differentiate Chinese from barbarians."[33]

As a result of the combined influence of the "culturalism-to-nationalism" and "culturalism, not racism" theses, many early twenty-first century historians, especially in the Chinese-speaking world, have continued to assert that participation in a shared culture (*wenhua*) was central to premodern or "traditional" Chinese identity and that over the course of history this emphasis on culture over birth repeatedly facilitated the assimilation and absorption of "barbarian" groups into the Xia or Hua (or, more anachronistically, "Han") people via acculturation (or "Sinicization").[34] This "culturalist" reading of Chinese identity is potentially misleading, however, because it imposes a modern conceptual category, "culture," on a premodern discursive context in which no equivalent existed. The absence of an exact equivalent does not preclude the possibility, even the necessity, of translating concepts across languages. Such an absence calls, however, for a level of caution in interpreting primary sources that has not generally been the norm when applying the "culturalist" model. What is needed here is the sort of nuanced position that Robert Ford Campany, in a seminal article, took on applying the category "religion" to premodern China: "That premodern Chinese 'lacked a word for religion(s)' . . . does not, prima facie, constitute a reason for modern scholars not to use the term. . . . But use of this category without regard to whether Chinese usages work differently constitutes a sort of category blindness to aspects of the historical evidence and can enable the illusion that the category is universal and natural."[35]

Whereas Campany was able to identify a few categories or usages in early medieval Chinese discourse that were analogous (but not identical) to the Western term "religions," I have found no premodern Chinese concept analogous to "culture" as it is usually understood today—that is, "culture" in the broad anthropological sense of the shared values, beliefs, and practices of people living in a given community. Instead of having a single category encompassing all aspects of society that we would term as "culture," the premodern Chinese distinguished social customs or folkways, termed *feng* or *su* (or collectively *fengsu*), from ritual practices, termed *li*.[36] The same term, *li*, was used for the normative ethical virtue of "ritual propriety" both in interactions between human beings and in human interactions with ancestral spirits and gods.

From the Han period onward, Chinese imperial governments tended to judge the *feng* and *su* of various geographical regions as compatible or incompatible with "ritual propriety," based on how closely they conformed to the ritual practices identified with the ancient Zhou elite in the Confucian classics. Classically educated government officials were credited almost exclusively with the ability to make such judgments. For most of the imperial period, local officials were expected to suppress or reform customs that they deemed contrary to *li* and thus damaging to public morality, and the local population was expected to defer to their superior knowledge of *li*. This imperative of "regulating *su* with *li*" became increasingly strong from the Song period onward.[37] The distinction between *li*, on one hand, and *feng* or *su*, on the other, is therefore akin to one that sociologists draw between mores (which are ascribed with positive moral or ethical significance) and folkways (which are not), based on the work of William Graham Sumner (1840–1910). As Sumner himself observed, ritual is the "process by which mores are developed and established" but, in secularized Western societies, "is so foreign to our mores that we do not recognize its power" even though modern mores are effectively "social ritual in which we all participate unconsciously."[38] The same modern tendency to ignore the power of ritual arguably lies behind historians' tendency to elide its premodern moral significance by subsuming it into "culture," a conceptual category more relevant not only to the modern West but also to East Asian societies heavily influenced by Western concepts.

Further contributing to the problem with identifying "culture" as the basis for the premodern Chinese-barbarian dichotomy, modern Sinological scholarship frequently uses "culture" to translate another concept, *wen*. The word *wen* originally meant "decorative patterns," but in the Warring States period, its association with beauty caused it also to be increasingly employed as a term for "moral refinement" and "civility"—a metaphorical usage both narrower and more closely related to *li* than the word "culture" as typically used today.[39] Due to another semantic shift that began around the first century CE, *wen* had, by Tang times, a close connection to writing, literary composition, and a textual tradition extending back to antiquity.[40] But the Chinese of the Han and Tang periods apparently did not identify *wen* as the basis of their supposed superiority to the barbarians, whether in terms of possessing a literary culture or in terms of well-known conceptual dichotomies like *wen* (civil) versus *wu* (martial) and *wen* (sophistication or refinement) versus *zhi* (simplicity).

Although one first-century Classicist text does claim that "the barbarians are simple (*zhi*) and not as sophisticated (*wen*) as the Central Lands," other Han discussions of the distinction between *zhi* and *wen* show that they were more often seen as equal and complementary attributes—the *locus classicus* being *Analects* 6.18, in which Confucius argues that a preponderance of *zhi* over *wen* makes one a mere peasant (a man "of the fields," *ye*), a preponderance of *wen* over *zhi* makes one a mere scribe (*shi*), and a perfect balance of the two makes one a noble man (*junzi*).[41] Indeed, Tang discourses on the conceptual binary of *zhi* and *wen* often praised the Han dynasty for valuing *zhi* over *wen*, while faulting subsequent periods for an excess of *wen*.[42] Even among the literati of the Northern Song period, known for identifying strongly with *wen* and seeing it as indispensable to transmitting the Classicist norms that they termed collectively as the Way (*Dao*), one does not find statements identifying *wen* as the quality that set the Central Lands apart from the barbarians.[43] The correct relationship between *wen* and *Dao* was the subject of much discussion under the Song, especially among literati of the Guwen and Daoxue persuasions, but the Chinese-barbarian dichotomy played no part in these discussions.[44]

The terms *wenming* ("illumination by *wen*") and *wenhua* ("transformation by *wen*") are not significantly more relevant than *wen* in this regard. These terms have classical origins but were in premodern times only rarely, if ever, used in a manner similar to the modern Western concepts "civilization" and "culture," before being redefined (by way of Japanese influence) to translate these concepts in the late nineteenth century.[45] I have seen no instance of *wenhua* being used in discussions of the Chinese-barbarian dichotomy before the twentieth century, even though the term is ubiquitous in such discussions in modern Chinese historical writing.[46] As for *wenming*, only two relevant Tang and Song instances are known to me. One of these is a fragment from a lost *Documents* (Shangshu) commentary by Zeng Min (fl. 1073–99), which reads: "The Central Lands are the land of illumination by *wen* (*wenming zhi di*), so they are called Hua-Xia." Unfortunately, the context for Zeng's statement is no longer known. But Cai Shen (1167–1230), when quoting it, apparently understood it to hinge on an etymological interpretation of Xia as meaning "bright" (*ming*), rather than on the concept of *wen*.[47] The other instance is in a ninth-century essay, "Chinese at Heart" (Huaxin). Its author speaks of the entire world's peoples coming to the Tang empire to receive "the transforming influence of illumination by *wen*" (*wenming zhi hua*), but he also identifies "ritual propriety and moral duty" (*liyi*), not *wen*, as the only valid standard for distinguishing between Chineseness and barbarism.⁴⁸

As the language of "Chinese at Heart" indicates, the premodern Chinese elite came to define barbarians not only in terms of foreign customs and folkways (i.e., as peoples with non-Chinese *feng* and *su*), but more fundamentally as peoples without "ritual propriety" (*li*; i.e., mores) and therefore also without morality—even when they did have ritual practices or rites (also *li*) of their own.⁴⁹ This is evidently an ethnocentric view, according to the conventional understanding of ethnocentrism as a subjective belief that one's own people and their ways are superior to all others. Incidentally, the inventor of the term *ethnocentrism* to describe a "view of things in which one's own group is the center of everything, and all others are scaled and rated with reference to it" was also William Graham Sumner, who made this insightful observation on ethnocentrism's prevalence in all ethnic communities: "Each group thinks its folkways the only right ones, and if it observes that other groups have other folkways, these excite its scorn."⁵⁰ This is even truer of how a group thinks about its mores compared to the mores of other groups, such that it is very prone to equating having different mores with having none at all.

In an early example of the ethnocentric definition of the barbarian, an *Analects* commentary by Bao Xian (7 BCE–65 CE) speaks of "the lands of the barbarians, which do not have ritual propriety and moral duty," when interpreting Confucius's statement in *Analects* 13.19 that one should not forsake the essentials of humaneness (*ren*) even when "going to the barbarians."⁵¹ The practice of elevating *li* to the same level of importance as *yi* (moral duty, not to be confused with Yi, "barbarians") by pairing the two as a compound (*liyi*) probably originates from the Warring States Classicist philosophers Mencius (ca. 372–ca. 289 BCE) and Xunzi (ca. 315–ca. 215 BCE), and became increasingly common from the Han dynasty on.⁵² In Classicist thought, *yi* denotes the morally correct response to a given situation, especially one in which no obvious rule of *li* applies.⁵³ A noble man (*junzi*)—that is, a man of superior moral character—will choose moral duty even when it conflicts with his self-interest or desires, whereas an inferior man (*xiaoren*) will most likely do the opposite and show himself to be unscrupulously self-seeking.⁵⁴

To a large extent, Chinese discourse on the moral inferiority of barbarians projected the Classicist *junzi-xiaoren* moral dichotomy onto an ethnic dichotomy by assuming that under normal circumstances, all barbarians—being devoid of *liyi*—were inferior men, whereas the Chinese were governed by noble men whose commitment to *liyi* would inspire their compatriots to be moral as well. For that reason, the Chinese did not see changes in *feng* or *su* alone as sufficient or even essential for barbarians to overcome their inferiority. It was more important for barbarians to learn *liyi*, provided they were capable of doing so in the first place. Unlike *wen*, *wenming*, and *wenhua*, the term *liyi* is ubiquitous in late Tang and Song arguments about the Chinese-barbarian dichotomy. But it has virtually vanished from the Chinese language in modern times, leading Chinese people to confuse it frequently with the near-homophonous but semantically much narrower phrase *liyi* ("ceremonial and etiquette").[55] The disappearance of *liyi* as a central concept in Chinese identity discourse is probably one of the main reasons why modern Chinese historians feel compelled to use problematic equivalents like *wenhua* or *wenming* in its place, mirroring their Western counterparts' reliance on the concept of "culture."

THE CONCEPT OF ETHNICIZED ORTHODOXY

Having surveyed the vocabulary of Chinese discourse on the meanings of Chineseness and barbarism, let us return to the significance of Han Yu's contribution to the discourse. Although the term "culturalism" has recently been used to describe rhetoric like Han Yu's contention in "Tracing the Way" that Chinese Buddhists were on the verge of turning into barbarians because they were "elevating a law of the barbarians above the teachings of the former [sage-]kings," there are several problems with this usage. One of these is the broad and imprecise nature of the category "culture" itself. Another is that, as explained earlier, many historians assume "culturalism" was the standard mode of Chinese identity discourse from the Eastern Zhou onward. Calling Han Yu a "culturalist" thus implies, misleadingly, that he was only summarizing long-standing conventional wisdom about Chineseness in "Tracing the Way." A third and related problem is that the term "culturalism" suggests Han Yu was primarily concerned with policing the boundary between Chinese and foreign ritual or cultural practices, rather than the boundary between orthodox Classicism (which he called the "Way of the Sages," Shengren zhi Dao) and all alternative philosophies or value systems. In fact, it would be more accurate to say that he sought to render the latter boundary more absolute by conflating it with the former rhetorically. In other words, he *ethnicized* what he believed to be the boundaries of Classicist orthodoxy by claiming their maintenance to be integral to Chinese ethnocultural identity.

This book, therefore, refers to Han Yu's radically *new* rhetorical strategy of conflating Chineseness with a revived and redefined concept of Confucian/Classicist ideological orthodoxy, while representing alternative philosophical or religious traditions as un-Chinese and barbaric, as "ethnicized orthodoxy." According to such rhetoric, there was fundamentally no such thing as a Chinese Buddhist or even a Chinese Daoist: Classicist (Ru) identity and Chinese identity were one and the same thing, and one could not compromise the former without also losing the latter. This conflation of ethnocultural and ideological boundaries cannot be described as "ethnicized orthopraxy" because, despite claiming that Confucius used ritual practices as a standard for distinguishing Chinese from barbarians, Han Yu's reinterpretation of Chineseness went beyond ritual propriety (*li*) to encompass "the teachings of the former [sage-]kings" as a whole: that is, the entire set of ideals, beliefs, values, and practices associated with Classicism or "Confucianism." It was not enough to eschew Buddhist or Daoist rituals; more importantly, one had to recognize that Buddhist and Daoist beliefs and values were fallacious and morally corrupting. It is also important to note that part of ethnicized orthodoxy's logic remained inchoate in "Tracing the Way," since Han Yu did not explicitly associate Daoism with barbarism. As we shall see, it was certain Northern Song Guwen writers, figures in a "Guwen revival," who finally took ethnicized orthodoxy to its logical conclusion by merging the orthodox-heterodox and Chinese-barbarian dichotomies completely in their polemics against Buddhism and Daoism.

SONG CHINESE IDENTITY AND THE TROUBLE WITH "NATIONALISM" AND "RACISM"

In the 1970s, Rolf Trauzettel and Hoyt Tillman interpreted certain Southern Song responses to the Jurchen invasion as the earliest forms of Chinese nationalism, while contrasting them to the "cultural universalism" or "culturalism" of the Daoxue philosophers.[56] Two newer versions of the Song nationalism/proto-nationalism theory trace the beginnings of Chinese nationalism to the Northern Song instead. Ge Zhaoguang has argued that in the eleventh century, the Northern Song literati elite began to see "the Central Lands" as a nation rather than a universal civilization or culture. Ge claims that the threat posed by the Kitan Liao empire stimulated greater anxiety about the political and cultural boundaries of Chineseness; the Jurchen invasion only intensified this nationalist anxiety, manifested in irredentist and xenophobic statements among the Southern Song elite.⁵⁷ Building on Ge's arguments, Nicolas Tackett argues that the eleventh-century Northern Song elite developed a kind of premodern nationalism, a view of the Song "not as a universal empire, but rather as a culturally and ethnically Han state," due to several interrelated factors: the establishment of an interstate system regulating relations between the Song and Kitan Liao states on the basis of diplomatic parity; a growing sense of irredentist solidarity with Chinese populations under foreign rule, especially the Chinese of the Yan region (northern Hebei), which had been ceded to the Kitan Liao in 938; and an emerging conception of the Central Lands as "a homogeneous cultural and ecological zone" whose boundaries should (but currently did not) coincide with the Song state's borders.⁵⁸

The theories described above have developed in response to Levenson's claim that Chinese identity was typically "culturalistic," not nationalistic, from ancient times to the early twentieth century—Ge Zhaoguang, for example, has openly objected to the idea that China developed a concept of the nation so late in its long history and only under the influence of the Western world.⁵⁹ However, these various theories have yet to stimulate a wider debate about the applicability of the concepts of nationalism and the nation-state to a premodern Chinese context.⁶⁰ Such a debate would have to include a consideration of the relationship and differences (if any) between national identity, cultural identity, and *ethnic identity*. The last of these concepts was still very new to the social sciences lexicon in the 1970s and therefore made no appearance in the arguments by Trauzettel and Tillman, but is now widely used in Western analyses of premodern Chinese identities, including Tackett's. The concept of "ethnicity" has been subject to multiple definitions, but in referring to Tang-Song Chinese identity as ethnic or ethnocultural (e.g., in the term "ethnicized orthodoxy"), this book will follow the broad definition of an ethnic group—that is, a group of people sharing the same ethnicity or ethnic identity—proposed by John Hutchinson and Anthony D. Smith: "a named human population with myths of common ancestry, shared historical memories, one or more elements of common culture, a link with a homeland and a sense of solidarity among at least some of its members."⁶¹

The Song sociopolitical elite was ethnically and culturally homogeneous to a distinctly greater degree than that of the Tang, despite being more diverse in socioeconomic origin. In part, this homogeneity was due to geopolitical circumstances: the Kitan Liao empire to the northeast and the Tangut-ruled Xi Xia state to the northwest effectively cut the Song state off from Inner Asia (or Central Eurasia), the main source of the peoples, commodities, and tastes in fashion, food, art, and music that had given the Tang and its predecessors, the Northern Dynasties and Sui, their multiethnic and multicultural character. But there were other reasons, including the ethnocultural assimilation of Inner Asian immigrant families during the tenth century and the Northern Song state's lack of interest in integrating Tibetan and Tangut allies from the northwestern frontier into its civil and military elites.[62] Numerous texts and arguments produced by the Song literati elite reflect a shared ethnocultural identity as Zhongguo, Hua, or Xia people.[63] Whether it can also be called a *national* identity that could form the basis for a kind of nationalism is ultimately a question of definitions that is not of central importance here.[64] There is also insufficient evidence to ascertain the degree to which this ethnocultural identity was shared between elites and commoners in the Song, although newer and more regionally distinctive forms of ethnic self-identification—for example, Tangren along the southern coast—likely were more common at non-elite levels.[65]

When Song elite irredentists advocated excluding or expelling barbarians from a geographical space that they understood as "the Central Lands," this need not have been predicated on a concept of national sovereignty or independence, or the ideal of an ethnically homogenous nation-state as opposed to what Tackett terms "a universal empire." As recent research has shown, Northern Song irredentists who spoke of recovering "the former frontiers of the Han and Tang" (*Han Tang jiujiang*) were effectively arguing for the restoration of direct Song rule over parts of the Tang empire's "Central Lands" core that had been absorbed into the "barbarian" periphery during the late Tang and Five Dynasties periods.[66] This did not imply, however, that the Song had renounced its claim to authority over other parts of the periphery. The key difference here was that Northern Song subjects in the "Central Lands" core demonstrated their submission to the emperor's authority by paying taxes of various kinds, while "barbarian" vassals in the periphery were meant to do so via the presentation of tribute.[67]

There is good evidence that Northern Song officials, like their Tang predecessors, took for granted the validity of their emperor's claim to suzerainty over "barbarian" lands, despite the Song state's ineffectiveness at enforcing this claim via military power.[68] For example, Zhu Yu (fl. ca. 1102–48) expresses a notion of universal rulership when he argues, circa 1119, that the barbarians should not refer to things associated with "the Central Lands" by the dynastic name Song, as this implies that only the Chinese people are under the Song emperor's authority: "Why not have them change to [using] the word 'Chinese' (Hua)? From here out to the remote lands, all are subjects (*chenqie*) [of the Song emperor], and there is only a difference between Chinese and barbarians (Yi)."[69] If the An Lushan Rebellion "was . . . an intellectual divide between the glories of empire and the search for something else," a search that ultimately produced both Guwen and Daoxue, and if "political universalism—the rhetoric of a greater empire—was problematic" in the face of Northern Song geopolitical realities, nonetheless the glories and rhetoric of empire had yet to lose their attraction and give way to an idea of "treating the state as the national community of an ethnic group."[70] I am inclined to agree with Hilde De Weerdt's recent argument that even Southern Song literati continued to believe in the ideals of universal rulership and an expansive "normative empire" with a Chinese core and ethnically diverse frontiers, rather than a Chinese nation-state defined by a shared ethnocultural identity in "a de facto multinational world."[71] It is worth noting, too, that Ge Zhaoguang's most recent work has shifted from emphasizing the Song elite's emerging "national" identity to highlighting their continued attachment to imperial or universalist understandings of the Song state.[72]

Nationalism is not the only concept that has been employed as the opposite of "culturalism" in recent historical scholarship on premodern China. Partly in response to the Chinese "culturalism, not racism" thesis, some historians—starting with Frank Dikötter in the early 1990s—have used the concept of racism or racialism to interpret classical and imperial Chinese discourses that denied the barbarians' moral or cultural transformability and asserted that their innate natures were inherently immoral and inferior, often through theories of environmental determinism based on the cosmological concept of *qi* ("material force"). Dikötter claims such discourses were a "defensive reaction" when the Chinese sense of cultural superiority was threatened by foreign invasion, but they "remained in the minority" and never overcame the "dominant rhetoric of cultural universalism" before modern times.[73] Peter C. Perdue also argues that opposing "culturalist" and "racialist" perspectives on foreign peoples coexisted throughout imperial Chinese history and that "broadly speaking, dynasties ruled by Han-dominant elites, especially in periods of division, were most likely to embrace racialist perspectives."[74] Similarly, Emma Jinhua Teng has drawn a distinction between "racialist discourse," which "focuses on physical differences and innate differences in human nature," and "ethnical discourse," which "focuses on cultural differences and constructs difference as a matter of degree within certain human universals." Teng's "ethnical discourse" is essentially the same as the idea of "culturalism," and she has occasionally used the two terms interchangeably.[75] In mainland China, too, the late Liu Pujiang posited a general "law" of history that when the Chinese (or "Han") were politically dominant over other peoples, they were more inclined to use "culture" (*wenhua*) to define Chineseness, but when that dominance was threatened or lost, they would tend to favor a definition based on "race" (*zhongzu*).[76]

In Song-period texts, including those of Daoxue thinkers, we do indeed see arguments claiming that non-Chinese peoples' turbid or imbalanced endowment of *qi* makes them innately inferior, less than human, and incapable of improvement. Such claims have prominent precedents in anti-expansionist rhetoric from the Han and Tang periods.[77] However, if we interpret them uniformly as evidence for a view of "barbarians" as a biologically separate and inferior race, we miss an important aspect found in Daoxue uses of *qi*-determinist discourse: many of its users did not believe that the purported superiority of Chinese *qi* made the Chinese permanently superior and immune to barbarism. Instead, it was supposedly all too possible for Chinese people to turn into barbarians and then into animals, albeit in moral rather than either ethnic or physical terms.[78] In the 1970s, John Fincher noted this paradox in the case of the early Ming Daoxue scholar and official Fang Xiaoru (1357–1402), whose dehumanizing rhetoric about the Mongols appeared to be "racist" in nature: "Yet if racism in a Chinese context means that the border between Chinese and barbarians is impermeable and based on the biological fact of an individual's parentage, Fang was still only half a racist. . . . Despite his conviction of the impossibility of *entering* the Chinese pale, he still argued that it was possible to *leave* it. Emperors who were born Chinese could, by the manner they attained or used the throne, literally become barbarians, Fang allowed."[79]

Fincher argued that Fang Xiaoru's notion of barbarization "accords with the culturalist views of most traditional Chinese historians and moralists" and suggested that although "the historian's vocabulary has as yet no very satisfactory definition of the strong sense of political community in 'traditional' China," the term that comes closest is "'culture' as the anthropologists define it"—in his view, "trying to stretch 'nationalism' back to the fourteenth century" would be anachronistic, while "'racism' appears to be even less than half the explanation."[80]

THE CONCEPT OF ETHNOCENTRIC MORALISM

Both nationalism and racism/racialism are unsatisfactory concepts for interpreting the Song-period sources used in this study. At the same time, "culturalism" is (*pace* Fincher) not a satisfactory alternative, for reasons like those requiring a new name for Han Yu's rhetoric of barbarization. The most interesting feature of most of the Song sources used in this study is that they *reject* the convention of interpreting the Chinese-barbarian dichotomy merely in terms of differences in practices and customs that originated from differences in ancestry, history, or homeland. They do not, for example, claim that Chinese people will turn into barbarians if they change their *wen*, *feng*, or *su*: that is, if they start writing, dressing, making music, or eating differently. Although an anthropological definition of culture would encompass all of these activities, it would obscure the fact that to these sources' authors, *li* (ritual propriety) and *yi* (moral duty) were the only qualities separating the Chinese from barbarism or, worse, animality. In other words, we are dealing with a discourse that holds the *moral* significance of the Chinese-barbarian dichotomy to be higher than, and effectively independent of, its more outwardly visible ethnocultural dimensions. Just as importantly, we should be wary of taking Song-period claims about this discourse's antiquity at face value, as some historians have tended to do when characterizing "culturalism" as "traditional" or "Confucian."

This book therefore reinterprets numerous Song-period arguments about barbarization via immorality or ritual impropriety neither as the "traditional" antithesis of a newly emerging (and by implication more "modern") sense of nationalism nor as representing an age-old "culturalist" view of the barbarians that competed with an equally old "racialist" view over the centuries. Rather, I read these arguments as expressions of a *new* interpretation of the Chinese-barbarian dichotomy that I term "ethnocentric moralism." Whereas ethnicized orthodoxy conflated Chineseness with the exclusive Guwen version of Classicist identity, ethnocentric moralism conflated Chineseness with certain moral values (especially "ritual propriety and moral duty") and represented deviation from these values as a descent into barbarism. This conflation effectively created a false dichotomy between Chineseness and immorality in which a person's subjective ethnic identity was all but irrelevant. There was, of course, some potential for overlap between the two discourses, since ethnocentric moralism tended to identify correct moral values exclusively with Classicist teachings. The difference tended to be one of emphasis and rhetorical intent: ethnicized orthodoxy was used as a rhetorical weapon against the kind of ideological pluralism that saw Classicism, Buddhism, and Daoism as compatible and complementary, whereas ethnocentric moralism was used to condemn immoral behavior, usually without reference to the offending party's ideological affiliations. More succinctly, ethnicized orthodoxy made Han Yu's "Way of the Sages" synonymous with Chineseness, while ethnocentric moralism equated any form of immorality with "the way of the barbarians" (*Yi-Di zhi dao, Yidao,* or *Didao*).

Although ethnocentric moralist discourse represented barbarism as a moral problem that had universal relevance, it continued to regard other ethnocultural groups as inferior barbarians and thus contained both an ethnocentric interpretation of morality ("the Chinese are moral and the barbarians are immoral") and a moralistic interpretation of ethnicity ("to be immoral is to become a barbarian"). The moralistic interpretation of ethnicity served to elevate moral self-cultivation to the place of supreme importance that Daoxue thinkers believed it deserved, and to curb the kind of moral laziness or complacency that an ethnocentric interpretation of morality might otherwise produce. But it also implicitly posed the question of whether foreign peoples could ever rise out of their barbarism and become as moral as the Chinese—which might, in ethnocentric moralist terms, amount to *becoming Chinese.* To put the question more boldly: Can, and should, the Way of the Chinese sages transform the way of the barbarians and eventually produce a fully moral and civilized world, in which all human beings can be "regarded as people of the Central Lands"?

Contrary to most accounts of premodern Chinese "culturalism," few of the writers and thinkers covered in this book engaged seriously with the possibility of barbarians transforming into civilized and moral beings. This lack of interest in the idea of "Sinicization," relative to the idea of barbarization, brings up a bizarre but telling point: During the Tang-Song transition, the discourses of ethnicized orthodoxy and ethnocentric moralism were mostly concerned with persuading a Chinese audience to change its behavior, rather than exhorting "barbarians" to change theirs. Indeed, rather than a dialogue between the Chinese and their "barbarian" neighbors or adversaries, our sources give us little more than an extended monologue in which the "barbarians" are usually rhetorical props, not even bit players. The leading prose writers, ideologues, and philosophers of the age, all of them self-identifying as "Chinese," occupy center stage, addressing a similarly Chinese audience, while the "barbarians" of whose barbarism they speak seem to never get a chance to join in the conversation. However, this does not mean that the "barbarians" remained silent or passive, for there is good evidence that the Kitan empire—apparently without the knowledge of the Song—appropriated the identity of "the Central Lands" and used it to assert its own superiority over other non-Chinese peoples.

Having to recognize the Kitan Liao as an equal was undoubtedly galling to the Song court. But a far bigger psychological blow came within just five years of the Liao's destruction at the hands of the Jurchens, when Jurchen armies overran the Chinese heartland, the original "Central Lands," and forced the Song to retreat to south China. The 1141 peace agreement that formalized the Jurchen empire's rule over north China and suzerainty over the Southern Song was a defining event, after which hopes of an immediate Song reconquest of the north—most famously represented by general Yue Fei's (1103–1142) military campaigns—gave way to the new reality of the Chinese world's humiliating submission to "barbarian" political and military dominance. That dominance did not, ultimately, lead to a debate or dialogue between Chinese and Jurchens over whether the Chinese had a permanent monopoly on civilized morality. But it did finally force Chinese thinkers, including the leading Daoxue thinkers of the late twelfth century, to grapple with the question of whether "barbarian" peoples like the Jurchens were indeed morally inferior and, if so, whether such inferiority was a perpetual condition. The results of that questioning are properly the subject of a different study, one for which this book will, hopefully, have laid a strong foundation.

CHAPTER 1

Han Yu, the *Annals*, and the Origins of Ethnicized Orthodoxy

HAN YU's significance in the intellectual history of the Tang-Song transition is well known: historians have long recognized that his literary and intellectual predilections, while eccentric in his own time, became an inspiration and eventually a norm for leading writers and thinkers of the Song period and beyond. Without Han Yu, some have argued, there would have been no Guwen in the Song and no Daoxue.[1] Nonetheless, one aspect of Han Yu's influence has gone largely unacknowledged: a way of talking about Chinese identity that is frequently labeled as "culturalism" or "Confucian universalism" but can more aptly be described as two distinct discourses, "ethnicized orthodoxy" and "ethnocentric moralism." Of the two, Han Yu was directly responsible for the former's origins and supplied the inspiration for the latter.

Ethnicized orthodoxy interpreted Chinese identity as synonymous with an exclusive form of Classicist ("Confucian") identity and associated non-Classicist intellectual or religious traditions with barbarism. Han Yu sought to endow this interpretation of Chineseness with prestige by attributing it to Confucius, but it gained little support in the highly pluralistic intellectual culture of late Tang times. Nonetheless, his rising stature after the Tang eventually led so many Chinese scholars to accept his claim of Confucian authority that his interpretation's radical originality has frequently been overlooked or underestimated. Han Yu's innovations relating to the Chinese-barbarian dichotomy involved utilizing the *Annals* commentaries' idea of "barbarizing" demotion as a rhetorical strategy in the separate (and previously

Daoist-dominated) genre of anti-Buddhist polemic; claiming unambiguously that the "barbarization" seen in the *Annals* was an objective consequence (i.e., becoming a barbarian) rather than just a subjective judgment (i.e., being deemed morally barbaric by Confucius); implying that any descent into barbarism would be permanent rather than brief and reversible; and linking barbarization not only to standards of ritual orthopraxy but also to a concept of ideological orthodoxy. In other words, Han Yu appears to have given the idea of barbarization a literal, ideology-centered interpretation with new implications for the identity of those being "regarded as barbarians."

HAN YU'S REINTERPRETATION OF CHINESE CIVILIZATION

Han Yu's unconventional views on writing, Classicism, the history of civilization, and his place in that history had already taken shape by 798 when, aged thirty, he held an administrative post in Bianzhou (Kaifeng) while teaching literary composition to the civil service examination candidates Li Ao (ca. 772–836) and Zhang Ji (ca. 766–ca. 830). In a letter written that year to Feng Su (767–836), Han remarks that by choosing him as a teacher, Li and Zhang are "abandoning conventional fashions to follow a lonely Way and use it in vying for fame in our time."[2] This "lonely Way," a prose style modeled on the "ancient" texts of the Eastern Zhou and Han periods rather than the florid parallel prose literature of the Northern and Southern Dynasties, had emerged among a handful of Tang writers soon after the An Lushan Rebellion and had come to be known as Guwen, but was still favored by only a tiny literary fringe.

Complaining to Feng Su that his peers applaud his embarrassingly conventional and clichéd pieces while being baffled and bemused by the Guwen works of which he is most proud, Han Yu takes some comfort in comparing himself to the Eastern Han Classicist thinker and writer Yang Xiong (53 BCE–18 CE), whose peers ridiculed his *Classic of Supreme Mystery* (Taixuan jing) for being abstruse. According to Han Yu, Yang confidently predicted that a second Yang Xiong would appreciate his work in a future age. Han then laments that this second Yang Xiong has yet to appear, hinting none too subtly that *he* is that man.[3]

A letter from Zhang Ji to Han Yu, also dated to 798, reveals that Han's sense of affinity with Yang Xiong went beyond his perception of Yang as a misunderstood and underappreciated writer.[4] In past conversations, Zhang notes, Han Yu credited Yang Xiong as the last person who understood the "Way of the Sages," the moral essence of civilization. This Way, Han claimed, had previously gone through two cycles of decline and revival: one from Confucius's death and the rise of the philosophies of Mozi (ca. 470–391 BCE) and Yang Zhu (ca. 440–360 BCE) to the Classicist thinker Mencius's (Mengzi; ca. 372–ca. 289 BCE) successful attack on these philosophies; and one from the Qin "burning of books" and the rise of the syncretic Huang-Lao philosophy (most likely based on *Laozi's Classic of the Way and Its Power* [Laozi daodejing] and texts or teachings attributed to the legendary sage-king Huangdi)[5] in early Western Han to Yang Xiong's promotion of Classicism some two centuries later.

Han Yu placed himself in the third cycle's exceptionally long decline phase, in which Buddhism and the Daoist religion (which he conflates with Huang-Lao) had defined the moral values of the Central Lands for six centuries since the end of Eastern Han. This cyclical model was probably based on *Mencius* 3B.9, in which Mencius posits that history from the age of the sage-kings Yao and Shun to his own day has been divided into three cycles of "order followed by disorder" and that he is living in the third cycle's nadir as the "Way of Confucius" has been eclipsed by Mozi and Yang Zhu.[6] Past scholarship on Han Yu's narrative of the Way of the Sages has tended to focus on the final section of the *Mencius*, 7B.38, as an inspiration for that narrative, while neglecting 3B.9.[7] This is partly because Han Yu's narrative did eventually shift toward the linear model of 7B.38, in which the Way of the Sages was transmitted continuously from Yao and Shun to Confucius, only to be forgotten in Mencius's day.

According to Zhang Ji, Han Yu explained that Buddhism and Daoism had been especially damaging to "the customs of this age" because the Chinese were still using the material aspects of the civilization that the ancient sages created, but had forgotten its moral essence and turned to "heterodox learning" (*yixue*): "Now in this world, every tool or implement used for sustaining life was invented by the sages. But when it comes to human relationships, we are immersed in heterodox learning and do not follow the Way of the Sages. This has caused the moral duties between rulers and ministers, fathers and sons, husbands and wives, and friends to be obscured in this age, and our country repeatedly suffers disorder. This is certainly painful to any humane man."[8] The repeated "disorder" mentioned here is probably a reference to the frequent armed clashes between the Tang court and independent-minded provincial governors since the end of the An Lushan Rebellion. But

Han Yu was tracing this disorder not to the rebellion alone, but to what he saw as a fundamental problem of ideological impurity that had corrupted and weakened Chinese civilization since the fall of the Han.

The main section of Han Yu's farewell or valedictory preface (*songxu*) for the Buddhist monk Wenchang, composed in the spring of 803, presents a second version of his narrative of the history of civilization:

> When our people first appeared, they were like animals or barbarians. The sages arose, and only then did they know how to live in houses and eat grains, to love their kin and respect their superiors, to nurture the living and bury the dead. That is why there is no greater Way than humaneness and moral duty, and no teaching more correct than that of rites and music, laws and government. . . . Yao passed them on to Shun, Shun passed them on to Yu, Yu passed them on to Tang, Tang passed them on to Kings Wen and Wu, and Kings Wen and Wu passed them on to the Duke of Zhou. Confucius wrote them into books,[9] and the people of the Central Lands have followed them generation after generation.[10]

This passage is noteworthy for containing the first known iteration of a theory that the Way of the Sages was transmitted or passed on from one sage to the next, often across a span of centuries. In this theory, the narrative of the Way's history is essentially linear, unlike the cyclical model found in Zhang Ji's letter, and is therefore a continuation of the narrative presented in *Mencius* 7B.38. There has long been speculation that Han Yu borrowed this idea of linear transmission from Chan Buddhism and not directly from Mencius. This hypothesis has had prominent supporters, including Chen Yinke and Qian Mu, but its most significant weakness is the fact that Chan lineages do not allow for transmission between patriarchs separated by long gaps of time.[11]

An equally striking feature of the preface is that it contradicts the most crucial and controversial aspect of the narrative in Zhang Ji's 798 letter: the idea of civilizational decline. Instead of blaming Buddhism for bringing disorder to the Central Lands by obscuring the Way of the Sages, Han Yu claims that the Chinese have been practicing the Way of humaneness and moral duty and the teaching of rites and music continuously since Confucius compiled the Classics. He merely faults Buddhist monks like Wenchang for teaching an inferior "Way" and not acknowledging their debt to the sages who created the civilization whose comforts they enjoy.[12] This somewhat incomplete version of Han Yu's narrative of the Way of the Sages suggests that as of 803, he remained reluctant to promote the full narrative beyond a small circle of friends. In the 798 letter, Zhang Ji had already faulted him for his unwillingness to publish it in writing for a wider audience. Han's reply to Zhang at the time revealed that he feared a reputation for opposing Buddhism and Daoism would jeopardize his already difficult prospects for career advancement by offending patrons of both religions at the imperial court.[13]

The third and last version of Han Yu's narrative is found in the essay "Tracing the Way," conventionally dated to 804 but more likely (for reasons explained in the next chapter) written in or after 812. Like the preface for Wenchang, "Tracing the Way" includes an account of how the sages created civilization, although its intent is to rebut the primitivist philosophy of Laozi's *Classic of the Way and Its Power*, not to fault the Buddhists for taking civilization for granted. Moreover, the essay's larger narrative of civilization's history differs from both the picture of continuity presented in the preface for Wenchang[14] and the cyclical version told to Zhang Ji in one significant respect: it claims that the Way of the Sages has been lost for a single thousand-year period from Mencius's death to the present, thus denying that there was a revival of the Way in Han times. Early in the essay, Han Yu introduces this theme of continuous decline, claiming, "The Way of the Zhou dynasty declined, Confucius died, and [the Way was destroyed] by fire in the Qin, by Huang-Lao in the Han, and by Buddhism in the Jin, [Northern] Wei, Liang, and Sui. Of those who spoke of the Way's moral power (*de*), humaneness, and moral duty, anyone who did not go for Yang Zhu's [philosophy] went for Mozi's; anyone who did not go for Laozi's [teaching] went for the Buddha's."[15]

There are clear echoes of Zhang Ji's letter here, but both Mencius and Yang Xiong are conspicuously absent, along with the revivals of the Way that they supposedly achieved. Near the essay's end, Han Yu does restore Mencius to the narrative, in a way that greatly diminishes Yang Xiong's stature and implies that Han Yu now sees himself as Mencius's direct successor:

> You may ask, "This Way [that you speak of], which Way is it?" I say, "This is what *I* call the Way, not what others have called the Way of Laozi and the Way of the Buddha." Yao passed it on to Shun, Shun passed it on to Yu, Yu passed it on to Tang, Tang passed it on to Kings Wen and Wu and the Duke of Zhou, Kings Wen and Wu and the Duke of Zhou passed it on to Confucius, and Confucius passed it on to Mencius. When Mencius died, it was not passed on. Xunzi and Yang Xiong chose parts of it, but not the finest parts; they spoke of it but not in detail.[16]

As is well known, this theory of a linear transmission of the Way of the Sages that was broken after Mencius's death eventually became a central concept and founding myth of Daoxue philosophy, in which it came to be called the Daotong (Transmission/Succession of the Way).[17]

Han Yu's main polemical strategy in "Tracing the Way" involves caricaturing Daoism and Buddhism as self-centered, socially irresponsible creeds undeserving of the exalted title "the Way." In this he is relatively unsuccessful, as his ham-fisted assaults ignore the philosophical complexity and diversity of practice in both religious traditions. Nonetheless, the essay's true power, as well as the basis of its fame and influence, lies in its narrative of the transmission *and loss* of the Way of the Sages. This narrative is both original and outrageously radical in that it simultaneously negates the value of all Classicist teaching since Mencius, implies that no imperial dynasty has ever been truly civilized and moral, and accuses the Tang elite of having no real understanding of moral values like humaneness and moral duty. Han Yu was also effectively rejecting a pillar of Tang political culture: the state's concurrent use of legitimating ideological and ritual resources from Classicism, Daoism, and Buddhism. Indeed, at the end of "Tracing the Way," he issued a militant appeal for the dynasty to proscribe Daoism and Buddhism and burn their scriptures, implying that anything short of such drastic action would leave civilization mired in moral confusion and turpitude.

But "Tracing the Way" contains another argument that is arguably even more provocative: namely, that permitting Buddhism's continued presence in the Central Lands would lead to the extinction of Chineseness as an identity and hand the world over to civilization's inferior enemies, the barbarians. In this famous passage, already quoted in the introduction, Han Yu briefly shifts from reinterpreting the essence of civilization and morality to redefining the meaning of being (and not being) Chinese. This redefinition is seldom acknowledged as such, since Han Yu used an idea from the field of *Annals* exegesis to represent it as Confucius's own definition. Nonetheless, Han Yu's rhetorical use of that idea was creative and provocative for his time, in relation to what *Annals* commentators had and had not previously used it to do.

THE DISCOURSE OF "BARBARIZING" DEMOTION IN THE *ANNALS*

By the Han period, Classicists generally believed that the *Annals* was much more than a historical chronicle, for the identification of Confucius as its editor or author implied that it communicated a sage's interpretation of history and politics along moral lines. The text's terse language was thought to follow certain conventions, subtle inconsistencies or variations in the observance of which were understood as Confucius's coded or hidden messages of moral judgment on specific rulers, ministers, and states.[18] Han exegetical scholarship on the *Annals* thus came to be concerned primarily with identifying such editorial inconsistencies and using them to decipher Confucius's moral judgments, which "were understood to serve not only as assessments of past events but also as universal models for present and future actions, deterring wrongdoing and encouraging upright conduct."[19]

Two of the three major commentarial traditions on the *Annals*, the *Gongyang* and *Guliang* commentaries, were compiled into written form between the late Warring States and the early Han, purportedly from older oral traditions, and acquired additional layers of subcommentary in later centuries.[20] Both commentaries held that several of the coded messages in the *Annals* involved Chinese states, particularly their rulers, being editorially demoted to the level of barbarians and thus "regarded as barbarians" (*Yi-Di zhi* / *Yi zhi*), an unusual phrase that used a noun as a verb and literally meant "barbarian-ed." The reasons for such demotions often involved states engaging in immoral or unprincipled behavior in the sphere of foreign relations. For example, the *Gongyang* and *Guliang* agreed that Confucius demoted the state of Qin to the level of barbarians in 627 BCE because its ruler launched a sneak attack on the state of Zheng against the advice of his wisest ministers. This expedition ended in an ambush and major defeat by the state of Jin and its Rong barbarian allies at Xiao (also pronounced Yao). According to the *Guliang Commentary*, "The Qin became barbarians, beginning with the Battle of Xiao."[21]

The Battle of Xiao is a relatively rare case of total agreement between the *Gongyang* and *Guliang*. In most cases, the two commentaries identified different passages of the *Annals* as instances of "barbarizing" demotion. In one extreme example of disagreement, the *Gongyang* interpreted the *Annals* record of the Battle of Jifu in 519 BCE, in which the southern barbarian state of Wu defeated Chu (another supposedly barbarian southern state) and its Chinese vassal states, as conveying the message that Chu's vassal states were "new barbarians" (*xin Yi-Di*).[22] This was occasioned by language that seemed to demote the Chu vassals to the same level as Wu. He Xiu's (129–182) subcommentary to the *Gongyang* offers the following explanation: "The Central Lands are different from the barbarians because of their ability to respect those deserving of respect. The royal dynasty was in disorder, yet none [of the lords] was willing to save it; relations between rulers above and ministers below were in a state of ruin. Thus they, too, had newly begun behaving like barbarians. That is why [Confucius] did not allow [Chu's Chinese vassals] to have superiority over [Wu]." In contrast, the *Guliang Commentary* assumed that on this occasion, Chu's Chinese vassals still represented the Central Lands as opposed to Wu. Their editorial demotion was merely an unintended consequence of the need to record that two vassal rulers were killed in the battle. Fan Ning's (ca. 339–401) *Guliang* subcommentary even argues that Confucius's intent in noting these rulers' deaths was to commend their sacrifice in defense of their states![23]

As the examples above reflect, both the *Gongyang* and the *Guliang* occasionally produce a sense of ambiguity as to whether they are speaking of barbarization in literal/ethnic or figurative/moral terms—in other words, whether being "regarded as barbarians" reflected an ethnocultural shift taking place in real historical time ("becoming barbarians"), or only a mode of retrospective rhetorical condemnation ("behaving like barbarians") that Confucius directed at immoral rulers and states as he compiled the *Annals* record.[24] To some extent, commentators mitigated this ambiguity by assuming that while peripheral states like Chu, Wu, and even Qin were indeed ethnoculturally barbarian, the Central Lands states only lapsed into temporary bouts of metaphorical and moral barbarism that Confucius, with his exceptional sagely insight, was able to discern and record in coded form.

The clearest expression of this exegetical strategy is found in a text from the *Gongyang* commentarial school, *Luxuriant Gems of the Annals* (Chunqiu fanlu), traditionally but problematically attributed to Dong Zhongshu (179–104 BCE).[25] An imaginary questioner asks why, when "the normal language of the *Annals* credits the Central Lands, not the barbarians, with behaving in accordance with ritual propriety," the opposite was the case with the entry on the Battle of Bi (597 BCE), in which Jin, a Chinese state, suffered an editorial demotion that placed it beneath its barbarian opponent Chu. The author responds by claiming, "The *Annals* does not employ consistent terminology; it shifts according to changes [in the circumstances]. Now [the lord of] Jin had changed and become a barbarian, and [the lord of] Chu had changed to become a morally superior man, so [Confucius] shifted his language to accord with the circumstances."[26] The author explains that at Bi the Jin army showed excessive belligerence by attacking the Chu army even though the Chu ruler had demonstrated restraint by ceasing his assault on

Jin's ally, Zheng.[27] No suggestion is made, however, that either the Jin ruler's descent into barbarism or Chu's attainment of moral superiority was a permanent or lasting change. The *Annals* record for the later Battle of Yanling (575 BCE) gives no indication of demoting Jin editorially vis-à-vis Chu.[28] Likewise, *Luxuriant Gems* interprets the Jin attack on the Di barbarian state of Xianyu in 530 BCE as a brand-new case of "barbarizing" demotion for Jin that arose from recent Jin aggression toward the state of Lu, rather than the Jin army's behavior at Bi.[29]

The *Zuo Tradition* (Zuozhuan), a narrative history that was probably completed by the end of the fourth century BCE but incorporates many earlier sources and oral traditions, was regarded as a third *Annals* commentary from Eastern Han on. It contains numerous detailed narratives that supply background and context to events recorded in the *Annals*, interspersed with commentarial passages that present interpretations of selected *Annals* passages.[30] The *Zuo Tradition*, unlike the *Gongyang* and *Guliang*, never employs the phrase "regarded as barbarians." But it does implicitly identify "barbarizing" demotions in two instances, both relating to the rulers of Qǐ (a minor state in Shandong).[31] In the first instance, the *Zuo Tradition* explains the posthumous editorial demotion of Lord Cheng of Qǐ (r. 654–637 BCE) with the cryptic statement, "[The lord of] Qǐ was a Yi," even though the Qǐ ruling house was believed to be descended from the Chinese kings of the ancient (and possibly mythical) Xia dynasty. Du Yu's (222–285) commentary to the *Zuo Tradition* interpreted this line as Confucius demoting Lord Cheng to the level of a barbarian because he had begun using "Yi rites" (*Yili*) and had continued doing so until his death. The basis for this interpretation is a subsequent passage that attributes the editorial demotion of Lord Cheng's successor Lord Huan (r. 637–567 BCE) to his use of "Yi rites" when visiting the court of Lu (Confucius's home state) in 633 BCE; this is our second case of implicit "barbarizing" demotion in the *Zuo Tradition*.[32]

The Yi referenced in these *Zuo Tradition* passages were indigenous peoples of Shandong, most of whom Lu and other Chinese states in the region had subjugated or reduced to vassalage. Du Yu attempted to explain the Qǐ rulers' use of "Yi rites" by arguing that because the people of Qǐ lived in close proximity to the Yi, "their *feng* and *su* had become mixed and corrupted, and their language and clothing were sometimes those of the Yi." But geopolitical conflict between Lu and Qǐ, not ethnocultural differences, best explains why the *Zuo Tradition* (which, like the *Annals*, takes a Lu-centered perspective) sometimes represents Qǐ as barbaric or inferior: it reflects Lu propaganda meant to assert superiority over Qǐ. Indeed, in 633 BCE Lu used the Qǐ ruler's "disrespectful" and "ritually improper" use of Yi rites in diplomatic ritual as a pretext to invade Qǐ.[33]

The demotions of Lords Cheng and Huan of Qǐ involved their noble title being stated as "master" (*zi*) instead of the higher-ranking "prince" (*hou*) or "liege" (*bo*).[34] When a later Qǐ ruler, Lord Wen (r. 550–536 BCE), received an identical demotion in 544 BCE, the *Zuo Tradition* explained it as a gesture "to show his inferiority" without making any reference to his ethnicity or use of Yi rites. Du Yu's commentary attempted to harmonize the discrepancy by stating that Lord Wen's inferiority was due to his reversion to Yi rites. According to Du, Lord Huan had "given up using Yi rites" by 615 BCE, as seen from his reversion to the title "liege" in the *Annals* record. One century after Du Yu, however, Fan Ning's *Guliang* subcommentary implicitly rejected the *Zuo Tradition* interpretation of the Qǐ rulers' demotions by arguing that these were not editorial demotions imposed retroactively by Confucius at all. Instead, they were actual (but unexplained) demotions received from the reigning Zhou king. According to Fan Ning, Lord Huan's reversion to his original title in 615 BCE was likewise an actual promotion by the king.[35]

The *Zuo Tradition* contains no instances of barbarian rulers being editorially "promoted" (*jin*) to the level of the Central Lands in the manner claimed by "Tracing the Way," but the *Gongyang* and *Guliang* commentaries do contain several such instances. However, the phrases "promoted to the level of the Central Lands" (*jinyu Zhongguo*) and "regarded as [people of] the Central Lands" (*Zhongguo zhi*) are original to "Tracing the Way" and do not occur in any of the *Annals* commentaries. Also, even though the word *jin* normally means "to enter," both "Tracing the Way" and the *Annals* commentaries use it in a specialized context that bears no relation to barbarians physically immigrating to the Central Lands.[36]

The *Gongyang* and *Guliang* commentaries' differences of interpretation when it came to cases of promotion were less serious than those over demotion. Later subcommentators even attempted to reconcile some of them.[37] The *Gongyang* and *Guliang* also assumed that such promotions could be very short-lived and were not necessarily based on permanent changes in a barbarian ruler's behavior. Both commentaries agreed, for example, that in the *Annals* record of the decisive Wu victory over Chu in the Battle of Boju (506 BCE), Confucius promoted the Wu ruler by referring to him by his noble title, "Master of Wu," rather than as "Wu," because he had saved his Chinese ally, the state of Cai, from an attack by Chu—thus demonstrating that he "felt concerned for the Central Lands" and helped them to "repel the barbarians" despite being a barbarian himself.[38] Yet the very next line of the *Annals*, which records the Wu army's capture of the Chu capital, refers to the Wu ruler as "Wu." The *Gongyang* and *Guliang* commentaries rationalized this inconsistency by concluding that Confucius was revoking the Wu ruler's promotion because he had "returned to barbarism" (*fan Yi-Di*) or "returned to his barbarian way" (*fan qi Didao*) by forcibly taking the Chu ruler's consort or mother as a concubine.[39]

The Wu ruler's case illustrates an interesting distinction between "barbarizing" demotion and the promotion of barbarians in the *Gongyang* and *Guliang* traditions: one could be demoted for generally immoral behavior, even if it was directed toward barbarians, but only behavior that demonstrated concern for the interests of the Central Lands and respect for its ritual norms could merit a promotion for a barbarian ruler. It is also important to note that Cai, the "Central Lands" state that the Wu ruler was supposedly promoted for saving, was previously a vassal of Chu and was one of the states the *Gongyang* commentator believed Confucius had subtly denigrated as "new barbarians" when recording the earlier Battle of Jifu. This is another example of how temporary "barbarizing" demotions could be in the *Gongyang* and *Guliang* traditions, due to the frequency with which the commentators believed the language of the *Annals* could shift "to accord with the circumstances."

HAN YU'S INNOVATIVE INTERPRETATION OF BARBARIZATION

Historians of early China have long argued that the idea of "transforming" or civilizing barbarians is prevalent in classical "Confucian" texts like the *Annals* commentaries, the *Analects*, and the *Mencius*.[40] Apart from the occasional promotion of barbarian rulers in the *Gongyang* and *Guliang* commentaries, the *Analects* and the *Mencius* do appear to complicate the oft-cited notion of immutable barbarian inferiority in *Analects* 3.5 by claiming that barbarians can, through the influence of a noble or morally superior man (*junzi*), cease to be "benighted" (*lou*; *Analects* 9.14),[41] that "using Chinese [ways] to change the barbarians" (*yong Xia bian Yi*) is possible and perhaps even desirable (*Mencius* 3A.4), and that two of the ancient sage-kings were barbarians (Yi; *Mencius* 4B.1). However, none of these classical texts asserts the possibility of barbarians *transforming into Chinese*.[42] No Chinese text even hints at this possibility before Han Yu's "Tracing the Way," which effectively uses the *Annals* concept of editorial promotion to credit Confucius with the ability to recognize certain barbarians as having become Chinese. Past scholarship has thus given too much credence to Han Yu's claims to be following or reviving classical precedents, rather than reinterpreting the Confucian classics for new rhetorical or intellectual ends.

It is also important to note that Han Yu's emphasis in "Tracing the Way" was not on the possibility of "Sinicization" but rather on the danger of barbarization, for his argument aims to shock the reader by using the *Annals* to argue that the Chinese are turning themselves into barbarians by adopting the foreign religion of Buddhism. This was not an ancient or "traditional" idea Han Yu simply picked up from studying the Classics, even though his citing of the *Annals* conveys that impression. Prior to "Tracing the Way," no Chinese text had ever used the *Annals* commentaries' language of barbarization and promotion to support a political or philosophical argument, as distinct from a commentarial interpretation. Many pre-Tang texts have been lost, of course, but I find it significant that even surviving quotations or fragments from lost pre-Tang texts do not use the *Annals* in this way. This suggests that the notion of being barbarized by immorality (in the *Gongyang-Guliang* version) or by ritual orthopraxy (in the *Zuo Tradition* version) was generally regarded as an idiosyncrasy unique to the *Annals*, rather than a principle that should be applied to the Chinese-barbarian dichotomy in general. The *Annals* commentarial tradition thus provided some good material for at least two different philosophical reinterpretations of the meanings of Chineseness and barbarism: modifying the framework outlined in the introduction, we might call these "ethnocentric moralism" and "ethnicized orthopraxy." But the potential for these interpretations remained unexplored before Han Yu wrote "Tracing the Way."

Nor do other Classics unambiguously express the idea of Chinese turning into barbarians. In *Analects* 14.17, Confucius affirms that the statesman Guan Zhong (ca. 720–645 BCE)—toward whom he was usually quite critical—deserves credit for building a multistate coalition to ward off barbarian incursions, thus saving the Chinese states from the fate of "leaving our hair untied and folding our robes to the left." The implication is that the Chinese, if conquered by barbarians, would have been forced to give up their distinctive attire: tying their hair in a topknot (for men) or chignon (for women) and folding the lapels of their robes to the right. But this remark is ambiguous: one cannot assume that to Confucius's mind, dressing like a barbarian was equivalent to becoming a barbarian, especially if such dress had been forcibly imposed by barbarian conquerors. Likewise, Mencius (in *Mencius* 3A.4) famously criticized a Chinese follower of a philosopher from Chu for "being changed by a barbarian" (*bian yu Yi*) rather than "using Chinese [ways] to change the barbarians," but did not accuse him of having *changed into* a barbarian.⁴³

Texts written under the pre-Tang imperial dynasties do not employ the idea of barbarization for polemical purposes either. The third-century scholar Fu Xuan (217–278) did argue, in his philosophical treatise *Fuzi*, that if the Central Lands should lose the "teachings of ritual propriety and moral duty" (*liyi zhi jiao*), then the Chinese would "be like the barbarians" (*tonghu Yi-Di*). But even this is a warning about *becoming as bad as* barbarians, not about becoming barbarians.⁴⁴ The distinction between the two warnings may be subtle, but we can nonetheless recognize that Han Yu makes a claim about the boundaries of Chinese *identity*, whereas Fu Xuan does not.

Pre-Tang and Tang Daoist polemicists, motivated by competition with Buddhism for influence and patronage, often criticized the Chinese Buddhist clergy for serving a barbarian god, adopting barbarian dress, and adopting barbarian habits like sitting cross-legged.⁴⁵ But again, they claimed not that the Buddhists had thereby become barbarians, only that they were acting *like* barbarians. In fact, the only aspect of Daoist polemics that involved a Chinese person turning into a barbarian was the rhetorical use of a myth, already current in late Eastern Han times, that the Daoist sage-deity Laozi adopted a new identity as the Buddha after leaving China and vanishing into the far west.⁴⁶ The Daoist *Scripture on Laozi Transforming the Westerners* (Laozi huahu jing) of circa 300 CE and later derivatives reinterpreted this myth along anti-Buddhist lines by alleging that Laozi created Buddhism as a way of "transforming" or civilizing the "Westerners" (Hu, i.e., Central Asians and Indians), whose inhumane and immoral natures made them incapable of practicing Daoism's superior teachings.⁴⁷ According to this ethnocentric version of the myth, Buddhist teachings originated in a magnanimous act of self-barbarization. But they were not inherently barbarizing: they were designed to transform barbarians into moral beings, not to transform the Chinese into barbarians.

On the surface, the only basis for Han Yu's claim, "If [any of] the lords used barbarian rites, then [Confucius] regarded him as a barbarian," would seem to be the *Zuo Tradition* interpretations of the Qí rulers' demotions, especially as harmonized by Du Yu. The more numerous "barbarizing" demotions in the *Gongyang* and *Guliang* commentaries operate on a completely different morality-based logic in which ritual is irrelevant. In that case, Han Yu's argument would involve a rather strained overstatement of the role of ritual in Confucius's understanding of Chineseness and barbarism. There is a strong likelihood, however, that Han Yu was not entirely unusual or original with this heightened emphasis on ritual and was instead drawing upon a new trend in *Annals* exegesis that had begun in the late eighth century.

THE INTERPRETATION OF BARBARIZATION IN LATE TANG *ANNALS* EXEGESIS

In the 760s and 770s, Dan Zhu (724–770) and Zhao Kuang (fl. 770–75) developed the first new major tradition of *Annals* exegesis since the Han period.[48] Dan and Zhao still assumed the existence of coded messages from Confucius in the *Annals*, but unlike nearly all earlier exegetes, who began by accepting every interpretation in just one of the three received commentaries as correct, they found many interpretations in all three commentaries to be implausible. They therefore denied that any of these commentaries was authoritative and wrote new commentaries to present their own interpretations, explaining in each case why earlier interpretations could not be true to Confucius's intended message. The works of Dan Zhu and Zhao Kuang have been lost, but many quotations from them are preserved in the extant works of Dan Zhu's disciple Lu Chun (d. 805), which essentially collate, synthesize, and systematize interpretations made by Dan and Zhao.[49]

In an example of the new commentaries' independent-minded approach that is directly relevant to "Tracing the Way," Zhao Kuang rejected the *Zuo Tradition* author's "barbarian rites" explanation for the Qǐ rulers' demotions and preferred Fan Ning's interpretation of the demotions as literal, not editorial. This was due not to a general preference for the *Guliang Commentary*, but rather to the application of standards of logic and consistency. Zhao argued:

> Promotions and demotions in noble title were a prerogative of the king. If the Lu annalist could demote lords on his own initiative, this would be tantamount to the *Annals* itself creating political disorder. Besides, if the messages of the *Annals* were really conveyed through demotions in title, then the immoral deeds of the [other] lords were many—why did [the

Annals] not demote their titles? Moreover, [the rulers of] Qǐ were later referred to as lieges, upon which [Du Yu] claims that they had given up using barbarian rites; and then again referred to as masters, upon which [Du Yu] claims that they were using barbarian rites again. They were descendants of the Xia kings and frequently made covenants with major states, so how is it possible that they were [behaving like] children, constantly switching between giving up and using [barbarian rites]?

At the same time, Zhao did not accept Fan Ning's interpretation unreservedly. Instead, he modified it by attributing the Qǐ rulers' demotions not to the Zhou kings but to the hegemons (*ba*)—powerful lords who acted in the king's stead, regulating interstate relations and leading multistate military alliances against foreign enemies or wayward lords.[50]

So far, Zhao Kuang's work seems unpromising material for constructing a theory of barbarization via ritual. But Zhao did not completely reject the idea that the use of "barbarian rites" could be grounds for a "barbarizing" demotion. Instead, he transferred this explanation to the editorial demotion of the rulers of Zhu, Mou, and Ge to "a man of Zhu, a man of Mou, and a man of Ge" (Zhuren, Mouren, and Geren) when they visited the court of Lord Huan of Lu (r. 711–694 BCE) in 697 BCE. Since this demotion involved not a change in titles but rather an omission of these rulers' titles from the historical record, crediting it to Confucius would not make him guilty of usurping the king's prerogatives. In this case, Zhao Kuang chose to follow the *Gongyang Commentary*, which identified the case of Zhu, Mou, and Ge as a "barbarizing" demotion without providing a reason for it. But he also implicitly rejected the *Luxuriant Gems of the Annals* explanation that the three rulers were demoted for choosing not to attend the Zhou king's funeral, as well as He Xiu's alternative argument that the rulers were demoted for demonstrating submission to Lord Huan despite his having seized power by assassinating his elder brother Lord Yin (r. 722–712 BCE).[51]

Also of particular interest is a passage by Lu Chun that, perhaps for the first time in any work of *Annals* exegesis, systematically outlines the principles for "barbarizing" demotion in the *Annals*. The passage begins with the general principle, "When lords behave like barbarians (*you Yi-Di zhi xing*), then they are written of as barbarians (*yi Di shu zhi*)." The accompanying annotation explains: "The same language is used for rulers and their ministers; they are referred to only by the name [of their state]." Lu Chun then supplies examples indicating that barbaric behavior by a Chinese ruler could include acting perfidiously or opportunistically against other states, as well as allying with a barbarian state against a Chinese state. This reflects the approach of the *Gongyang* and *Guliang* commentarial traditions, albeit with a stronger emphasis on perfidy.[52]

However, Lu Chun also incorporates and expands the *Zuo Tradition* interpretation of "barbarizing" demotion by reading its emphasis on differences in ritual as a general principle of the *Annals* and a method for distinguishing between Chinese states, barbarian states, and semi-barbarian states: "When lords use purely barbarian rites, they are referred to only by the name of their state, examples of this being Jing (i.e., Chu), Wu, Xú, and Yue.[53] . . . Those who mix barbarian rites [with Chinese rites] are referred to as 'a man'—for example, 'a man of Zhu, a man of Mou, and a man of Ge came to [the Lu] court.'"[54] Lu Chun thus accepted Zhao Kuang's interpretation of the Zhu, Mou, and Ge case as a demotion for using barbarian rites, although he believed these rulers were not using "purely barbarian rites" and therefore did not receive a full demotion to the level of barbarian states.[55]

Whereas Zhao Kuang confidently asserted that the Qĭ rulers' demotions originated from the hegemons and had nothing to do with barbarian rites or with Confucius, Lu Chun implicitly accepted the *Zuo Tradition* interpretation by stating that "subtle messages" (*weizhi*)—presumably from Confucius—were to be found in such changes in title: "The meanings of these [changes] contain subtle messages. They were originally not barbarians (*benfei Yi-Di*), nor were they vassals [of Lu], so they are not referred to as 'a man.' This means that they were originally lords of the Central Lands, not barbarians; hence [Confucius] passed judgment on them."[56] Lu Chun seems to be suggesting that the rulers of Qĭ belonged to a special category of lords who used a mix of barbarian and Chinese rites but were not vassals of Lu, unlike the rulers of Zhu, Mou, and Ge. But there is some ambiguity in Lu's use of the phrase "originally not barbarians." Does it mean that the Qĭ rulers literally became barbarians at some point?

Lu Chun's interpretation of the states of Chu, Wu, and Yue may well provide an answer to this question. The notion that the Chu, Wu, and Yue rulers had Chinese origins was not new in Tang times. During Confucius's lifetime, the rulers of Wu were already claiming kinship with the Zhou royal house through Taibo, an uncle of King Wen (r. 1099–1050 BCE) who, according to legend, had gone south and founded his own state.[57] Sima Qian's (ca. 145–ca. 86 BCE) *Record of the Historian* (Shiji) gave the Taibo legend its final form and also ascribed sage-king ancestors to the Chu and Yue rulers.[58] These myths of Chinese ancestry entered the sphere of *Annals* exegesis through Fan Ning's *Guliang* subcommentary, which followed the *Record of the Historian* in claiming that the first Chu rulers were descended from Zhurong, a minister under the sage-king Ku. According to Fan Ning, because "their state was close to the southern Man and gradually adopted their customs (*su*)," the people of Chu were finally "abandoned and regarded as barbarians" (*qi er Yi zhi*), but Confucius promoted them back to the level of Chinese states once they "knew how to submit to the Central Lands and also became great and powerful."[59] Building on Fan Ning's position, Lu Chun writes:

> Barbarian rulers and ministers are referred to only by the name of their state, examples being the Di, Jing (i.e., Chu), Wu, Xú, and Yue. . . . Jing, Wu, and Yue all adopted barbarian customs, so they are referred to according to the conventions for barbarians. The labels Rong and Di are not added [to the names of these states] in order to clarify that they were originally not barbarians (*benfei Yi-Di*). The Chu people initially followed barbarian customs (Yisu), so they were referred to as "Jing" to label them with the name of a province, as if saying that they were the barbarians of Jing [province]. Later, they voluntarily established diplomatic relations [with the Central Lands] and were no longer like barbarians, so they were [labeled] using the same conventions as the Central Lands.[60]

By stating that Chu, Wu, and Yue had "barbarian rulers and ministers" but were "originally not barbarians," Lu Chun indicates they were Chinese states that actually became barbarian after adopting "barbarian customs" and "purely barbarian rites." This goes further than Fan Ning's claim that the Chu people were "regarded as barbarians." We may infer that Lu Chun had the same understanding of Qǐ as an "originally not barbarian" state, but read its rulers' changing noble titles as a sign that Confucius regarded them as only semi-barbarized in their customs and rites, not so barbaric as to necessitate being "referred to only by the name of their state."

Han Yu's "Tracing the Way" applied a similarly sweeping, literal, ritual-based, and acculturative interpretation of barbarization in the *Annals* to the contemporary context of Buddhism's influence on the Chinese. The similarity is unlikely to be coincidental, and the reading of the *Annals* in "Tracing the Way" is likely to be Lu Chun's, not that of the *Zuo Tradition* alone. Does this indicate that Lu Chun's *Annals* exegesis had a strong influence on Han Yu's ideas, as some historians have claimed?

Apart from "Tracing the Way," a number of Han Yu's other writings support their arguments with quotes or principles from *Annals* commentaries, but these are limited to the *Gongyang, Guliang,* and *Zuo Tradition.*[61] Indeed, it seems clear from Han Yu's writings that he was, at best, uninterested in Lu Chun's scholarship, probably because he saw it as tainted by Lu's association with the disgraced Wang Shuwen (d. 806) faction, which held power during the brief reign of Shunzong (r. 805). The extent to which Lu Chun's ideas influenced the reforms attempted by the Wang Shuwen faction remains disputed. But one member of the faction, Lü Wen (772–811), became a student of Lu Chun's *Annals* scholarship as early as 792.[62] Another faction member, the prominent Guwen writer Liu Zongyuan (773–819), formally became Lu Chun's disciple in 804, and one of Liu's letters shows that at least three other members of the faction were familiar with Lu's works of *Annals* scholarship by that time.[63] Han Yu's animosity toward the Wang Shuwen faction predated its political downfall and was not dictated by mere political expediency. Indeed, he suspected that the faction's leaders had played at least an indirect role in his demotion to the magistracy of Yangshan in early 804.[64] It may be significant that in the Veritable Records (Shilu) for Shunzong's reign, which Han Yu compiled for the imperial court in 813–15, Lu Chun's name appears at the head of a list of "famous men of the time who opportunistically sought rapid advancement" by aligning themselves with Wang Shuwen.[65] Saiki Tetsurō's claim that Han Yu held Lu Chun in high regard is based on a misreading of one of Shunzong's edicts, quoted in the Veritable Records, as reflecting Han's own assessment of Lu.[66]

In 811, Han Yu wrote a poem of apology to the reclusive Luoyang poet and scholar Lu Tong (d. 835), after Lu protested that Han (then magistrate of Luoyang) was being too harsh in applying the death penalty to a group of ruffians against whom Lu had lodged a complaint. Two lines of the poem suggest that Lu Tong's style of *Annals* exegesis was very similar to Lu Chun's: "The [scrolls for the] three commentaries to the *Annals* are left tied up on the shelf / While you cradle the ancient classic alone, investigating it from beginning to end."[67] Nonetheless, Han Yu describes Lu Tong's exegetical style not to endorse it, but as part of a flattering depiction of Lu as a high-minded eccentric who disregards societal norms.[68] As historian E. G. Pulleyblank has observed, Han Yu "is mainly interested in [Lu Tong] as a recluse and a poet, and his comments on his scholarship, although appreciative, are made from the outside and show nothing of Liu Zongyuan's fervor [for Lu Chun's scholarship]." That said, there is no evidence for Pulleyblank's description of Lu Tong as "a follower of the Dan Zhu school of criticism of the *Spring and Autumn Annals*." Although Lu Tong's poems have survived, his works of *Annals* exegesis have not, and nothing is known of their connections (if any) with Dan Zhu, Zhao Kuang, or Lu Chun. The similarity in approach may well be coincidental.[69]

If Han Yu was decidedly unenthusiastic about Lu Chun's approach to the *Annals*, it is surely also instructive to compare this with Han's warm praise, in a letter from 818, for Yin You's (767–838) new *Gongyang* subcommentary—the first since He Xiu's from the late Eastern Han. Yin You's commitment to the *Gongyang* commentarial tradition was such that he memorialized the throne in 822 to request that a new examination on the three traditional *Annals* commentaries be instituted in order to reverse declining interest in studying them.[70] When Yin You gave Han Yu a copy of the subcommentary and explained its general arguments to him, Han Yu claims that "in my heart I rejoiced at my good fortune, regretted meeting you so late in life, and wished that you would transmit all your learning to me." Although he laments that official duties and laziness have kept him from following up on his initial enthusiasm, he also affirms that rescuing the *Gongyang* tradition from near extinction and reviving people's interest in this "worthy commentary on a sagely Classic" remains "a most urgent matter to my humble heart."[71]

Given that Yin You had just honored Han Yu by asking him to compose a preface for the subcommentary, some of the language in this letter may be polite hyperbole. But it does seem to reflect the fact that Han Yu sympathized with the old Han-era commentarial traditions, perceiving them as the unfashionable underdogs of his day (Yin You, he claims, "savors a flavor that the majority have no taste for"), and associated them and not the new commentarial school with the outsider status that he ascribed to Guwen.[72] If Han Yu did derive the concept of literal barbarization from Lu Chun's commentarial works, his interest in those works was likely limited to interpretations that he might use to turn Lu's admirers against Buddhism. He may, however, have been responding to an argument that Liu Zongyuan made in or around 811, a possibility that suggests his use of the *Annals* in "Tracing the Way" was part of a prolonged debate between these two men over whether Buddhism was compatible with a Classicist identity.

CHAPTER 2

Han Yu, Liu Zongyuan, and the Debate over Buddhism and Barbarism

Han Yu and Liu Zongyuan, the two most celebrated Guwen writers of the late Tang, apparently had a tense and competitive relationship despite their mutual efforts at maintaining a semblance of amity or cordiality. Han seems eventually to have discarded any letters and essays that reflect his literary and intellectual competition with Liu, preserving only an eloquent funeral oration and a laudatory epitaph that he composed after Liu's death.¹ But that competition can still be discerned from Liu's collected works, which contain letters and essays criticizing Han's positions on various subjects, including his reluctance to complete the politically risky assignment of compiling the Veritable Records for Shunzong's controversial reign, as well as his conceited (to Liu's eyes, at least) readiness to assume the role of a teacher of literary style.²

The biggest source of disagreement between Han Yu and Liu Zongyuan was clearly the issue of Buddhism. The Tang elite mainstream favored a fluid, eclectic relationship of complementarity, balance, accommodation, and interconnectedness between the "three teachings" of Classicism, Buddhism, and Daoism, without insisting on complete agreement or compatibility in beliefs and values.³ Han Yu believed that this pluralistic relationship had to end because it was detrimental to Classicism and thus to civilization itself. Liu Zongyuan, whose lifelong interest in Buddhism is well known, openly and firmly disagreed with such ideological exclusivity, seeing it as ill-informed and unreasonable.[4] The widespread notion that Han Yu and Liu Zongyuan were at the forefront of a "Confucian revival" (*Ruxue fuxing*) thus overlooks the fact that they differed fundamentally over what a good "Confucian" or Classicist would look like.[5] The "Confucian revival" paradigm also assumes that late Tang literati shared a common notion of Classicist or "Confucian" orthodoxy, as well as a notion that this orthodoxy had declined due to competition from Buddhism and Daoism. In reality, Han Yu practically invented those notions, albeit with inspiration from Mencius and Yang Xiong. What he represented as a struggle to defend, revive, or preserve Classicist orthodoxy actually consisted of largely futile efforts to convince other people—including Liu Zongyuan—that such an orthodoxy existed at all, in part by redefining the concepts of Ru and the Way of the Sages. Since the majority of Han Yu's peers did not accept his premise that Classicism was in decline, the idea of a "Confucian revival" is too rooted in Han's partisan perspective to be useful as an objective historical explanation of his motives.

HAN YU'S FIRST SALVO: THE PREFACE FOR WENCHANG

Han Yu seems to have begun publicizing his ideological differences with Liu Zongyuan in 803 through his valedictory preface for the monk Wenchang, already mentioned and quoted in the previous chapter. The choice of a valedictory preface for this purpose is not surprising, since Han Yu and Liu Zongyuan had adapted this previously minor genre of social prose into one of their favorite vehicles for polemic and self-expression. This particular preface originated from a visit that Wenchang paid to Han Yu at the College of the Four Gates (Simen Xue) in Chang'an, where Han held the low-ranking position of academician (*boshi*). Wenchang was an avid traveler who made considerable efforts at soliciting valedictory poems and prefaces from the Chang'an literati elite whenever he was about to depart on a trip, perhaps as a way of both widening his social network and increasing his prestige within the Buddhist community. This time, he was preparing to leave for his home region in the southeast and had come to request a poem or preface from Han Yu. He had come armed with an introductory letter from Liu Zongyuan, as well as his entire collection of more than a hundred poems and prefaces.[6]

Han Yu browsed through the collection and found it devoid of statements about the Way of the Sages—in other words, the poems and prefaces did not use ideas drawn from the Classics, as their authors had chosen to praise and exhort Wenchang in purely Buddhist terms.[7] This apparently provoked Han

Yu into writing a preface based on the unlikely premise that Wenchang did not want Buddhist-themed poems and prefaces and was instead seeking to be educated in the Way of the Sages. The preface begins by implying that Wenchang is more of a Classicist in spirit than Liu and the other literati who have written Buddhist-themed prefaces and poems for him: "Some men are Classicists in name but Mohists in deed. When you ask them for their name, it sounds correct, but when you look at their deeds, they are wrong. Can one associate with such men? If a man is a Mohist in name but a Classicist in deed, when you ask him for his name, it sounds wrong, but when you look at his deeds, they are correct. Can one associate with such a man, then?"[8] Here, "Mohist" is clearly serving as code for "Buddhist."

Han Yu's exaggerated praise of Wenchang as a Classicist in all but name, solely on the basis of his passion for collecting poems and prefaces, is meant as oblique criticism of Liu Zongyuan and other mainstream literati as Classicists in name only and Buddhists "in deed." Han Yu then makes this point more overtly, citing Yang Xiong's philosophical treatise *Exemplary Figures* (Fayan): "Yang Xiong said, 'If he were at our doors and walls, I would drive him away, but if he dwelt among the barbarians (Yi-Di), then I would let him in.' I take this as my model."[9] To understand the import of this allusion, we must turn to the original *Exemplary Figures* passage. It reads: "Someone asked me, 'Suppose there was a person leaning on Confucius's wall while strumming the music of Zheng and Wei or reciting the books of Han Fei (ca. 280–233 BCE) and Zhuangzi (fourth century BCE?).[10] Would you bring such a man into the house through the main door?' I replied, 'If he dwelt among the barbarians (Yi-Mo), then I would bring him in, but if he were leaning on [Confucius's] doors and walls, I would drive him away. A pity that before he finishes weaving an upper garment, he has turned his attention to weaving a lower garment.'"[11] Yang Xiong's point is not that the Chinese should try converting barbarians to Confucius's teachings.[12] Rather, it is that barbarians, being outside the Central Lands, can be expected to get their values wrong, but Chinese people with full access to the Classics (the "upper garment") have no excuse to turn away and follow inferior traditions (the "lower garment") like Han Fei's amoral "Legalism" and the anarchistic naturalism of the *Zhuangzi*. In other words, Yang is saying that there is more hope for a heathen than for a heretic.

It is unclear whether Han Yu quoted Yang Xiong with the intention of insinuating that Wenchang and other Chinese Buddhist monks had been barbarized by following a barbarian religion. As we have seen, the preface claims that the Chinese lived like "animals or barbarians" before the sages created civilization. Han Yu goes on to say that he and Wenchang have the sages to thank for not having to live like animals, but does not suggest that Wenchang has reverted to barbarism—only that the monk is unaware of civilization's origins. If we read the preface for Wenchang in the light of "Tracing the Way," it may seem reasonable that Han Yu would see Wenchang as having been barbarized by Buddhism, but we cannot assume that Han had already formulated this idea in 803.[13] The most we can say with certainty is that Han Yu had Buddhism's "barbarian" origins in mind when he decided to quote Yang Xiong's statement and that he meant to imply that Liu Zongyuan and the other authors of the poems and prefaces in Wenchang's collection were *worse than barbarians* for knowing the Classics (i.e., "leaning on Confucius's wall") yet still "speaking thoughtlessly to [Wenchang] with Buddhist teachings" (i.e., "reciting the books of Han Fei and Zhuangzi").[14] From this, Han Yu would not have had to go far rhetorically to get to his "Tracing the Way" argument that all Chinese people who practiced Buddhism were becoming barbarians.

Although Han Yu evidently found it easy to associate Buddhism with barbarism in the abstract, he seems to have refrained from labeling individual Buddhists as barbarians. The reality is that he found many of them anything but barbaric. It has long been noted that his opposition to Buddhism did not prevent him from interacting extensively with monks and recognizing some of them as admirable or at least interesting individuals. One notable example is a monk named Lingzong, who, like Wenchang, loved traveling and cultivating ties with the literati. In an undated valedictory preface for Lingzong, Han Yu praises his literary talent, calls him "a Buddhist of excellent qualities," and claims that he behaves so much like a literatus that "I forget that Lingzong is a son of the Buddha." Echoing the opening lines of the preface for Wenchang, Han begins his preface for Lingzong by asserting, "If a man's deeds are different [from ours] but his sentiments are similar, then a noble man may approve of him coming in."[15] The deeds-sentiments dichotomy used here is similar to but more generous than the name-deeds dichotomy in the preface for Wenchang, as it implies that a man's character (sentiments) matters more than his religious practice or formal ideological affiliation (deeds or name). But if Han Yu was sometimes able to display such open-mindedness toward monks like Lingzong, he evidently found it harder to focus on Liu Zongyuan's character and "forget" Liu's refusal to join him in criticizing Buddhism.

HAN YU'S LETTER OF REBUKE AND LIU ZONGYUAN'S SELF-DEFENSE

Liu Zongyuan's valedictory preface for the Buddhist monk Haochu reveals that Han Yu's criticisms of Liu's positive attitude toward Buddhism continued after Liu was demoted and effectively exiled to the southern prefecture of Yongzhou in 806, as punishment for his membership in the Wang Shuwen faction. The preface mentions, quotes, and rebuts an anti-Buddhist letter that Han Yu had recently sent to Liu Zongyuan via a mutual acquaintance, Li Chu. This letter is no longer extant but can be dated to 810 or 811 based on a valedictory preface that Han Yu wrote for Li Chu in the autumn of 810, on the occasion of Li's departure from Luoyang.[16] From the letter's date, we can infer that the preface for Haochu was also written around 811.

Han Yu's letter to Liu Zongyuan was itself a response to an earlier valedictory preface that Liu had written for a Daoist traveler known by the nickname Yuan the Eighteenth.[17] Liu begins that preface by claiming that the philosophy of Laozi is merely "a distributary of [the teaching of] Confucius" and implicitly attributing the rivalry between Classicists and Daoists to narrow-mindedness. He goes on to assert that even the other competing traditions of classical philosophy, including those of Yang Zhu, Mozi, and the Legalists, all contain ideas that could "assist in [governing] the age." Buddhism is the latest addition to the mix, "and so it has faced the most shock, fear, and misguided resistance from men of learning." Liu draws an explicit contrast between such partisan tendencies and Yuan the Eighteenth's eclectic approach to learning, which "adopts all things that have hitherto been different and joins them together, making them the same," "invites them to be in the same Way as Confucius," and "does not seek to make the age conform to his Way."[18]

Han Yu seems to have read a copy of the preface for Yuan the Eighteenth at some point and to have interpreted (probably correctly) the comment on anti-Buddhist sentiment as a sardonic swipe at him. Indeed, Liu Zongyuan's laudatory description of Yuan's integrative method was also an indirect expression of his own intellectual eclecticism and an implicit criticism of Han Yu's exclusive brand of Classicism. The letter that Han Yu had Li Chu bring to Liu Zongyuan in 810–11 was ostensibly a personal rebuke to Liu, but also effectively a defense of Han's reasons for opposing Buddhism. Liu Zongyuan in turn decided to use his preface for Haochu as a platform for defending both himself and Buddhism because Haochu was based in

Changsha and a friend of Li Chu and could therefore pass a copy of the preface to Han through Li.[19]

The preface for Haochu begins with background to the history of disputation between Han Yu and Liu Zongyuan over Buddhism: "The Classicist Han Tuizhi (i.e., Han Yu) is on good terms with me and has previously worried about my fondness for Buddhist teachings, berating me for associating with Buddhist monks. Recently, Mister Li Chu of Longxi came from the eastern capital (Luoyang), and Tuizhi again entrusted him with a letter censuring me.[20] He says, 'I have seen the Valedictory Preface for Mister Yuan, and it does not denounce Buddhism.'" Liu Zongyuan proceeds to explain his reasons for not rejecting Buddhism. His main argument is that there is no fundamental incompatibility between the ways of Confucius and the Buddha: "The truth is that there are teachings in Buddhism that cannot be denounced because they are often in accord with the *Changes* (Yijing) and the *Analects*. I find pleasure in them, that is true, because they calm my temper and do not belong to a different Way from that of Confucius." In fact, later in the preface Liu reveals that Haochu, too, "reads his books and is familiar with the *Changes* and the *Analects*."[21] Such classical learning was not unusual for a Buddhist monk during the Tang period: an inscription that Liu Zongyuan composed for the Confucius temple in Daozhou (adjacent to Yongzhou) in 815 names a monk as its *Changes* lecturer.[22]

Perhaps remembering that Han Yu had once used Yang Xiong's *Exemplary Figures* to criticize him in the preface for Wenchang, Liu Zongyuan argues that even Yang Xiong would have disagreed with Han Yu's narrow-mindedness toward Buddhism: "Tuizhi's love of Classicism cannot be greater than that of Yang Xiong, yet Yang Xiong's book [*Exemplary Figures*] adopts ideas from Zhuangzi, Mozi, [and the Legalists] Shen Buhai (ca. 400–337 BCE) and Han Fei. Can Buddhism be more outlandish than Zhuangzi and Mozi and more treacherous than Shen Buhai and Han Fei?"[23] Liu next addresses Han Yu's justifications for denouncing Buddhism. Unfortunately, he does not quote these justifications at length and merely summarizes or paraphrases them, but the first paraphrase clearly shows that Han invoked the Chinese-barbarian dichotomy in his letter: "He says, 'Because it is barbaric (Yi).' If he really doesn't believe in the [Buddhist] Way and denounces it as barbaric, then is he going to be friends with Elai and Bandit Zhi, and despise Jizha and You Yu? This is not what they call doing away with names and focusing on essences. What I adopt [from Buddhism] is in accord with the *Changes* and the *Analects*, and even if the sages were reborn [in this age], they would find nothing in it to denounce."²⁴ Liu seeks to render the Chinese-barbarian dichotomy irrelevant to the question of Buddhism's worth by arguing that the dichotomy only concerns names or labels (*ming*), not moral essences (*shi*). As evidence that Chinese people can be just as immoral as barbarians, he cites the evil Shang-dynasty minister Elai and the ferociously amoral namesake and protagonist of the "Dao Zhi" (Bandit Zhi) chapter in the *Zhuangzi*, while the wise barbarians Jizha and You Yu serve as evidence that barbarians need not be inferior to the Chinese.²⁵

Jizha, a Wu aristocrat, was best known from a *Zuo Tradition* anecdote about his insightful and prescient reading of the ritual music and politics of the Central Lands states during a diplomatic tour in 544 BCE.²⁶ Anecdotes about You Yu in a number of early Chinese texts tell of him serving as a Rong ruler's envoy to the state of Qin, only to defect to Qin after the Qin ruler corrupts the Rong ruler with a gift of female entertainers and musicians. In the *Record of the Historian* version of the anecdote, You Yu (here identified as a descendant of Chinese defectors to the Rong) surprises the Qin ruler by interpreting "rites, music, and laws" as the "cause of the Central Lands' disorder," rather than the solution to that disorder, and claiming that the Rong people's lack of the same had insulated them from civilization's corrupting influence—the earliest known instance of a "noble savage" argument in Chinese writing.²⁷ Despite this difference in their purported attitudes toward rites and music, both Jizha and You Yu later acquired a reputation for perspicacity.

In using specific counterexamples from history to challenge the idea of Chinese moral superiority, Liu Zongyuan drew on a popular and time-tested strategy in Buddhist apologetics. In *Master Mou's Discourse on Resolving Doubts* (Mouzi lihuolun), possibly the earliest extant example of the apologetic genre, an imaginary challenger quotes *Analects* 3.5 and *Mencius* 3A.4 as evidence that barbarian ways are inferior to those of the Chinese, then takes Mouzi to task for abandoning "the Way of Yao, Shun, the Duke of Zhou, and Confucius" to learn "a barbarian practice" (*Yi-Di zhi shu*). Mouzi rebuts him in part by citing examples of good barbarians and bad Chinese: "Yu came from the western Qiang and was a wise sage; the Blind Old Man (Gusou) fathered Shun and yet was foolish and devious. You Yu was born in a Di state but contributed to Qin's hegemony; the Lords of Guan and Cai were from the Yellow and Luo Rivers but spread false rumors [about the Duke of Zhou]."²⁸ Liu Zongyuan raises this rhetorical strategy to a higher philosophical level, one relating to the relative importance of names and essences. While not overtly denying the idea of Chinese superiority, Liu seems to be turning the name-deeds dichotomy from the preface for Wenchang back on Han Yu: If one cannot judge a person by his "name" without scrutinizing his deeds, how can we assume that everything and everyone with the name "barbarian" is morally inferior and to be despised?

Liu Zongyuan takes this distinction between the superficial and the essential further when he responds to Han Yu's second anti-Buddhist argument: "What Tuizhi censures [Buddhism] for are only its traces (literally, "footprints," *ji*). He says, '[The monks] shave their heads and wear black robes, ignoring the bonds between husband and wife, father and son. They do not farm or cultivate silkworms in order to sustain the people's lives.' As for this, even I take no pleasure in it. But Tuizhi, being angered by the exterior, misses the core; this is to know a rock but not know the jade that lies within it. That [core] is the reason why I am fond of the Buddha's words."[29] In other words, Liu is arguing that Buddhism and Classicism may look very different outwardly, especially if one focuses on the monastic life, but at their philosophical and ethical cores they are both morally edifying. Han Yu has been fixated on Buddhism's outward appearances, just as he has concentrated on its barbaric "name," and thereby missed the opportunity to appreciate its essence.

READING "TRACING THE WAY" AS A RESPONSE TO LIU ZONGYUAN

No direct response to Liu Zongyuan's defense of Buddhism is found in Han Yu's collected works, nor is one mentioned in Liu's subsequent writings. In the middle of the eleventh century, an impoverished young poet named Wang Ling (1032–1059), who—like several prominent literati of his day—had embraced Han Yu's ideological exclusivism, took it upon himself to write a letter in Han Yu's voice to refute Liu Zongyuan's arguments.[30]

After sharply criticizing Liu's claim that Buddhism is "often in accord with the *Changes* and the *Analects*," Wang Ling turns to Liu's arguments about Han Yu's superficial obsession with Buddhism's name and traces. He first attacks Liu Zongyuan's analogy of the rock with a jade core by taking Han Yu's allegations about Buddhist monks "ignoring the bonds between husband and wife, father and son" to an absurd extreme: "Zihou (i.e., Liu Zongyuan) says, 'What Han Yu censures [Buddhism] for are only its traces, not knowing there is jade at the rock's core.' I wonder, does Zihou's learning indeed consider the core and the traces to be different? If that is in fact the case, then would it be acceptable for him to have humaneness and moral duty in his heart while brandishing a sword and driving his father and elder brother away, claiming that the latter act is only a trace?"[31] Wang Ling next employs Han Yu's *Annals*-based argument about barbarization from "Tracing the Way" to rebut Liu Zongyuan's argument that "barbarian" is a mere name that says nothing about its bearer's moral worth or "essence":

> Zihou also dislikes it that I, Han Yu, denounce Buddhism as barbaric; he instead speaks in its defense, saying, "Is he going to be friends with Elai and Bandit Zhi, and despise Jizha and You Yu?" Alas, Zihou, again you are not thinking straight! When Confucius wrote the *Annals*, if any of the lords used barbarian rites, then [Confucius] regarded him as a barbarian—for example, he called the Prince of Qǐ a master. If I should not denounce Buddhism as barbaric, then Confucius, too, should not have denounced the Master of Qǐ because of his traces without thinking about his core. Can even one as sagely as Confucius not escape Zihou's criticism of his judgment?[32]

Although Wang Ling immediately goes on to deny the relevance of Liu Zongyuan's "good barbarian" examples, Jizha and You Yu, by arguing that these men did not "reject the bonds between ruler and minister and father and son" as the Buddhists do, it is significant that he first imagined Han Yu undermining Liu's call for "doing away with names and focusing on essences" by using a rhetorical strategy from "Tracing the Way."[33] The idea of "barbarizing" editorial demotion, as interpreted by Han Yu, was perfectly suited for this purpose, as it strongly implied that Confucius saw anyone who used "barbarian rites" as barbaric to the core, not just in his "traces." In other words, the notion that Confucius would regard a Chinese person who used barbarian rites as a barbarian implied that, to the sage, such behavior was incompatible with the very "essence" of Chineseness and therefore warranted a corresponding change of "name"—even if that change was only conveyed through the coded language of editorial demotion. According to this logic, Han Yu's view of Buddhism as barbaric was not a matter of fixating on its "name" alone, for Confucius himself would have seen it as barbaric in both name and essence. In fact, "Tracing the Way" goes so far as to suggest that any Chinese person who practices Buddhism will essentially have become a barbarian in objective terms, not just in Confucius's eyes.

As Wang Ling's imaginary letter nicely illustrates, the rhetoric of barbarization in "Tracing the Way" presents a potent challenge to Liu Zongyuan's name-essence dichotomy—so potent, in fact, that I would suggest that Han Yu wrote the essay (or, at least, its anti-Buddhist section) in response to the use of that dichotomy in the preface for Haochu, as well as Liu Zongyuan's pluralistic understanding of "the Way." It is unlikely that Liu Zongyuan knew of Han Yu's rhetoric of ethnicized orthodoxy when he wrote the preface for Haochu, for he could not then have ignored its existence when defending his pro-Buddhist sympathies.[34] There is another possibility, of course, which is that Liu Zongyuan had not had the opportunity to read "Tracing the Way" after Han Yu wrote it, while Han chose not to employ its rhetorical strategies in his letter to Liu. This is unlikely, however: given Han Yu's intent of persuading Liu Zongyuan to reject Buddhism and Liu's well-known interest in *Annals* exegesis, one would expect Han to send Liu a copy of "Tracing the Way" (if it already existed) along with his letter or at least incorporate the relevant argument into the letter. Although Liu Zongyuan's writings after 811 do not include a response to "Tracing the Way," he may by then have shifted his attention from defending Buddhism to criticizing Han Yu's timidity as a court historian, as seen from an exchange of letters between the two in 813–14.[35]

Most recent scholarship on Han Yu dates "Tracing the Way" to 804, during Han's demotion and effective exile to Yangshan county in the far south.[36] But this dating is based on flawed assumptions surrounding two of Han Yu's other writings. Various scholars have proposed that Han referred to "Tracing the Way" and its four companion essays (whose titles all begin with *yuan*) in a poem addressed to the prefect of Chenzhou. The poem ends with the line, "Minister Yu is presently writing a book"—an allusion with which Han compares himself to the Warring States figure Minister Yu (fl. 262–260 BCE), who turned to writing a treatise after his political career failed.[37] This poem can indeed be dated to late 804, during Han's Yangshan exile, but the hypothesis that the "book" that he claimed to be writing contained "Tracing the Way" rests purely on an inference that he refers to the same work in a letter dated January 2, 806. The relevant line of the letter reads, "I have respectfully enclosed one scroll (*juan*) of my past writings; these are edifying and will clarify my views (*fushu jiaodao, yousuo mingbai*)."[38] Starting with Fang Songqing (1135–1194) and Zhu Xi (1130–1200) in the twelfth century, commentators on Han Yu's writings have argued that of all his works, only "Tracing the Way" and its companion essays fit this description. This wrongly assumes, however, that Han Yu never wrote other edifying texts that, for some reason, did not make it into his collected works. Since there is clear evidence that not all of Han's writings have been preserved, we cannot discount the possibility that he wrote "Tracing the Way" later than 804 and that the "book" of 804 and the "past writings" of 806 have nothing to do with "Tracing the Way." Arguments that the Yangshan exile provided Han with conditions conducive to writing "Tracing the Way" also ultimately fail to convince, since similar conditions existed at other points in his life.[39]

If the preface for Haochu indeed compelled Han Yu to develop the discourse of ethnicized orthodoxy, it would partly explain why Han Yu never explicitly applied that discourse to Daoism by arguing that Daoist ideas and practices were as uncivilized and barbaric as the Buddha's. Although some modern scholars have claimed to see Han Yu imputing a barbaric essence to Daoism in "Tracing the Way,"[40] the text is ambiguous regarding whether the contrast that it sets up between "a law of the barbarians" and "the teachings of the sage-kings" places both Buddhism and Daoism in the former category or leaves Daoism in an undefined gray area between Buddhism and Classicism. Although the term *fa* (law) was most often used to refer to the Buddhist *dharma*, it could also be applied to Daoism.[41] Han Yu's original readers would probably have assumed that "law of the barbarians" refers only to Buddhism, given Daoism's Chinese origins, but Han's ambiguity as to whether the phrase *Yi-Di zhi fa* is singular or plural—unlike "Memorial on the Buddha Relic," which calls Buddhism "a (literally, "one") law of the barbarians" (*Yi-Di zhi yi fa*)[42]—leaves open the possibility of an alternative reading, "laws of the barbarians," that encompasses Daoism too.

Certainly, the utopian view of pre-civilized humanity in *Laozi's Classic of the Way and Its Power* would have made it an easy target for an argument that Daoism *was* essentially barbaric, given Han Yu's assertion in the preface for Wenchang that human beings without civilization would live like "animals or barbarians." In fact, there was a recent precedent for such a strategy in Du You's (735–812) encyclopedia of institutional history, the *Comprehensive Institutions* (Tongdian; ca. 801), which sought to discredit Laozi's primitivism by associating it with various barbarian customs that were now distasteful to the Chinese but, Du argued, had also been common to the ancient Chinese before the sages civilized them.[43] Yet none of Han Yu's polemical works takes the idea of ethnicized orthodoxy to its logical conclusion by dismissing Daoism's ethnocultural origins as irrelevant to its essential barbarism. A letter that Han Yu wrote in late 820 to the pro-Buddhist official

Meng Jian (d. 823), to refute rumors of his conversion to Buddhism, comes close to this by effectively equating all non-Classicist ideologies with barbarian customs and languages and, by extension, a barbarian identity. Han Yu claims that although "the correct Way declined" after Mencius, Mencius nonetheless deserves credit for civilization's partial survival: "If there were no Mencius, we would all be folding our robes to the left and babbling in a foreign tongue!"[44] The allusion to the folding of robes invokes the career of Guan Zhong, whom Confucius credited with saving the Chinese from a fate of "leaving our hair untied and folding our robes to the left" under barbarian rule. Whereas Guan Zhong protected the Chinese states from barbarian invaders by military means, Han Yu seems to be claiming that Mencius protected the Chinese from barbarization by defending the Way of the Sages with his polemics against Yang Zhu and Mozi.

In *Mencius* 3B.9, Mencius first argues that Yang Zhu's philosophy of self-centeredness and self-preservation amounts to "not recognizing one's ruler," while Mozi's philosophy of completely impartial love amounts to "not recognizing one's father," and then successively identifies an attitude of "not recognizing one's father and ruler" as animalistic and barbaric:

> To not recognize one's father and ruler is to be an animal. . . . If the ways of Yang Zhu and Mozi do not cease and the Way of Confucius is not made evident, then perverse doctrines will deceive the people and obstruct humaneness and moral duty. If humaneness and moral duty are obstructed, that leads wild animals to devour people, and people will even begin to devour one another [like wild animals]! . . .
>
> The Duke of Zhou conquered the barbarians and drove away fierce wild animals, and the people were then at peace. . . . The ode says, "He smote the Rong and Di; he punished Jing and Shu; and none dared to resist us." The Duke of Zhou thus smote those who did not recognize their fathers and rulers.[45]

Such rhetoric allows Mencius to liken the followers of Yang Zhu and Mozi to both wild animals and barbarians and paint them as existential threats to civilization. Han Yu could easily have used the same logic to argue that both Buddhism (arguably an anti-familial creed) and Daoism (arguably anarchistic in its philosophical form) would have a morally barbarizing effect on the Chinese, but he does not proceed to do so in the letter to Meng Jian. Instead, he merely declares that although "the harmfulness of Buddhism and

Daoism exceeds that of Yang Zhu and Mozi," he is determined to preserve and restore the Way of the Sages even if it costs him his life.[46] Likewise, right before invoking the "barbarizing" demotions in the *Annals*, "Tracing the Way" appears to criticize both Buddhism and Daoism for teaching "sons not to treat their fathers as fathers, ministers not to treat their rulers as rulers, and commoners not to perform their rightful duties."[47] But Han Yu does not use the obvious Mencian precedent to unequivocally characterize both Buddhism and Daoism as "laws of the barbarians" on account of their moral perversity.

Han Yu's intolerance for intellectual pluralism, his bellicose, oppositional brand of Classicist identity, his sense of living in an age of moral decline, and his self-image as civilization's last hope all seem to be modeled on Mencius's polemics in passages such as *Mencius* 3B.9.[48] Had Han Yu desired to explore or elucidate the philosophical ramifications of his ideology-centered redefinition of the Chinese-barbarian dichotomy, he certainly had, in the *Mencius*, the rhetorical and intellectual resources for arguing that Daoism was as barbaric as Buddhism. But there is no indication that he ever did so. It is thus likely that his redefinition was a rhetorical means to a specific polemical end, rather than an intellectual end in itself. He was focused on rebutting Liu Zongyuan's argument that Buddhism was barbaric in name only, not on thinking through his argument's implications to arrive at a conclusion on whether Daoism, too, was barbaric in essence.

Han Yu's lack of interest in arriving at a philosophically coherent theory of barbarism reflects his personality as a man who never developed a "consistent and systematic philosophy" and was indeed "temperamentally unsympathetic" to such a goal.[49] He was at heart a prose stylist and polemicist, not a thinker; a master of words, not a man of ideas. A comprehensive view of the full corpus of his work shows that whereas his literary inventiveness was almost limitless, his sporadic attempts at developing a concept of Classicist orthodoxy never advanced far beyond the radical but simple idea, inspired by the *Mencius*, that the Way of the Sages had been lost for many centuries and now had to be revived through the forceful suppression of Buddhism and Daoism. To borrow an analogy that Isaiah Berlin first applied to Tolstoy, Han Yu was a literary fox (who knows many things) trying on occasion to be a philosophical hedgehog (who knows one big thing).[50]

Although Han Yu's "big thing," his new narrative of the Way of the Sages, later became one of Daoxue philosophy's foundational claims, the first Daoxue thinkers themselves believed that he only attained a limited understanding of the Way he claimed to be reviving.[51] In conversations with his students, the Daoxue philosopher Cheng Yi (1033–1107) expressed approbation for two of Han Yu's ideas that he regarded as rare flashes of philosophical insight. One of these was the idea that the Way of the Sages ceased to be passed on after Mencius because of flaws in the ideas of Xunzi and Yang Xiong (although Cheng also felt that Han was not hard enough on the latter two thinkers); the other was Han's interpretation of "barbarizing" demotion in the *Annals* as a reflection of how Chinese people could become barbarians if they lost their ritual propriety.[52] We have little reason to believe, however, that Han Yu took the second idea as seriously as he did the first. He *was* serious about advancing a new definition of what it meant to be a Classicist, a Ru, and it happened to suit his rhetorical purposes to claim that only true Classicists were truly Chinese. It would be a mistake to assume that such claims had any significant bearing on Han Yu's sense of ethnic identity. It was the Classicist identity that really mattered to him. But the fact that he assumed these claims would be effective rhetorically tells us something indirectly: being Chinese mattered enough to his audience—that is, elite literati like Liu Zongyuan—that denying their Chineseness was about as bad as denying their morality. It was certainly much worse than merely denying their identity as Classicists (i.e., their Ru-ness), since that identity meant very little in an intellectual culture of pluralism.

CHAPTER 3

Ethnocentric Moralism in Two Late Tang Essays

THE discourse of ethnocentric moralism, like that of ethnicized orthodoxy, first appeared during the ninth century, and its origins can be traced both to Han Yu's literary influence and to specific rhetorical agendas that were unrelated to Han Yu's ideology of Classicist orthodoxy. There is good reason for seeing Han Yu's rhetoric of barbarization as a radical innovation distinct from—albeit inspired by—the language of "barbarizing" demotion in *Annals* commentaries. By the same token, we should recognize the rhetorical conflation of Chineseness and morality in Chinese texts from the Song period and later not as a direct descendant of *Annals* commentarial practices from the Han and earlier periods, but rather as a product of rhetorical strategies pioneered by two late Tang essays, Chen An's (ca. 805–871) "Chinese at Heart" (Huaxin) and Cheng Yan's (fl. 895–904) "A Call to Arms against the Inner Barbarian" (Neiyi xi).[1]

These essays are the earliest extant fully developed examples of ethnocentric moralism, but that does not necessarily mean they exerted significant influence on subsequent expressions of the same discourse.[2] Neither essay appears to have been quoted or imitated in Song writings. Both essays' authors were virtually forgotten after the Song, most of their literary output lost forever through neglect. Since the essays' rediscovery by twentieth-century historians, however, numerous studies have cited them as classic examples of a "culturalist" interpretation of Chineseness.[3] Unfortunately, most existing studies that cite these essays have done little to assess the specific context that produced them and have assumed them to be transparent statements of their authors' views on the Chinese-barbarian dichotomy and, by extension, to be reflective of widely shared attitudes during the Tang. Zhang Weiran, for example, describes them as "excellent explications of Tang-period people's views on the Chinese-barbarian dichotomy" and suggests that they reflect recognition of foreign peoples' equality with the Chinese. Fan Wenli has used both essays to argue that the theory of late Tang xenophobia is only valid for the highest stratum of the Tang elite, including emperors and chief ministers, whereas "ordinary people," including "Classicist literati" like Chen An and Cheng Yan, were becoming even less concerned with the Chinese-barbarian dichotomy than before.[4]

Such arguments fail to take the essays' highly rhetorical and polemical nature into account and thus also neglect to address the question of what the authors' motivations and audiences would have been. Marc Abramson has convincingly argued that these two essays reflect a new understanding of Chineseness that differed from that seen in the early Tang: "By arguing for a non-ethnic definition of Self and Other but using the vehicle of ethnicized discourse to do so, the two works establish a new benchmark for conceptualizing the notion of China itself. . . . The belief that non-Han [i.e., foreigners], acknowledged as the ethnic Other even while living in China, could possess a Chinese ethos superior to some or even many Han [i.e., Chinese] was a new development in the late Tang."[5] However, Abramson underestimates these essays' functions as displays of rhetorical skill and creativity and overstates their authors' intellectual ambition when he argues that they "probably represented the views of growing numbers of literate elites of the late Tang" who wished to "highlight ethnic oppositions in order to solidify a Chinese self-identity that went beyond ethnic boundaries to embody 'universal' values."[6] Both Chen An and Cheng Yan were more likely using an innovative ethnocentric moralist interpretation of the Chinese-barbarian dichotomy for the limited purpose of directing flattery or criticism at certain powerful Chinese individuals.

It may be useful to begin contextualizing the essays by reviewing what little information we have about their authors' lives and works. Our main source for biographical information on Chen An is a preface to his collected works, written by his nephew Huang Tao (ca. 840–911). This is supplemented by short biographical notes in the *New History of the Tang* (Xin Tangshu) "Treatise on Literature" and the *Complete Prose Literature of the Tang* (Quan Tangwen). From these we know that Chen An was born and raised in the port city of Quanzhou. Although he demonstrated talent as a poet from a young age, the responsibility of caring for his widowed mother delayed him from sitting for the *jinshi* ("presented scholar") civil service examination until he was in his early forties. After failing the examination about eighteen times between 845 and 864, he gave up and spent his last years as a recluse. Many of his prose writings were later lost or scattered in the "flames of war," probably when the warlord Wang Chao's (846–898) army besieged and captured Quanzhou in 885–86. Huang Tao began compiling Chen's surviving works in 895, shortly after passing the *jinshi* examination, and finally published a collection of thirty-one prose pieces and an unspecified number of poems in late 902.[7] Three *juan* of Chen's works were still extant in the eleventh century, but only nine essays and one valedictory preface have survived to the present via inclusion in Song-period anthologies.

Cheng Yan passed the *jinshi* examination in the same 895 cohort to which Huang Tao belonged. This was Huang's twelfth attempt since 872 and probably not Cheng's first. The *Tang Gleanings* (Tang zhiyan), a collection of anecdotes about the civil service examinations, states that both Cheng and Huang were of humble birth—a severe disadvantage in the Tang examinations, due to the crucial importance of patronage and connections—and that they were the only truly outstanding graduates in their cohort.[8] Many of the other graduates were of unusually poor quality, causing a scandal that led Emperor Zhaozong (r. 888–904) to order a retest for all twenty-five graduates. Ten of these, including the first-placed scholar, failed the retest, presumably having passed the original examination via family connections alone; Zhaozong thereupon sent the original examiner into exile. Cheng Yan placed second in the retest.[9] Nothing is now known about his subsequent career, although one could surmise that the Tang empire's steady descent into collapse and fragmentation made it perilous and unhappy. The *New History of the Tang* "Treatise on Literature" indicates that a seven-*juan* edition of his collected works circulated in the eleventh century, but only seven of his prose pieces are now extant, again due to their inclusion in Song anthologies.[10]

CHEN AN'S "CHINESE AT HEART"

The full text of "Chinese at Heart" reads:

> In the first year of the Dazhong era (847) the Duke of Fanyang, who was the governor of Daliang, came to know Li Yansheng, a man from the country of the Arabs (Dashi), and recommended him to the throne. The emperor

issued an edict ordering the Department of Rites to examine his abilities. In the second year (848), he made his name by passing the *jinshi* examination. Among the ordinary recommended guest candidates, none was his equal.[11] Someone might argue, "Daliang is a large city, and the governor is a very worthy man. He was appointed by a Chinese ruler, and his salary comes from taxes paid by Chinese people. Yet when he recommends men, he seeks them from the barbarians. How can there be no worthy candidate among the Chinese? Are barbarians the only ones suitable for employment? I remain perplexed by the governor even now." I would reply, "The governor truly recommends men based on their talent, without any favoritism toward his own people. If we speak in terms of land [of origin], then there is a distinction between the Chinese and the barbarians. But in terms of [moral] teaching, is there also a distinction between Chinese and barbarians? Now, the distinction between Chinese and barbarians lies in their hearts, and to distinguish a [Chinese heart from a barbarian] heart, one must examine [the heart's] inclinations. One who is born in the Central Lands, but whose deeds go against ritual propriety and moral duty, is Chinese in physical form but a barbarian at heart. One who is born in the lands of the barbarians, but whose deeds accord with ritual propriety and moral duty, is a barbarian in physical form but a Chinese at heart. Take the cases of Lu Wan (256–194 BCE) and Li Ling (d. 74 BCE), who rebelled and defected [to the 'barbarian' Xiongnu empire]—were they barbarians? Consider [the Xiongnu captive] Jin Midi's (134–86 BCE) steadfast loyalty [to Han Wudi (r. 141–87 BCE)]—was he Chinese?[12] From this we can see that it all depends on a person's inclinations. Now, Li Yansheng came from across the sea, and he came to the attention of the governor because he is able to analyze things using the Way. The governor therefore recognized him as an exceptional talent and recommended him in order to encourage the barbarians, so that all peoples who receive the light of the sun and moon will turn to the transforming influence of illumination by *wen*. He perceived Li Yansheng to be Chinese at heart, and therefore did not consider him a barbarian based on his land of origin." Hence I wrote [this essay,] "Chinese at Heart."[13]

Apart from what little is said of him in "Chinese at Heart," we know nothing about this Arab man who went by the Chinese name Li Yansheng in Tang polite society. He is the only Arab known to have passed the *jinshi* examinations under the Tang, but we do not know whether he was an immigrant or only descended from immigrants.[14] The *jinshi* examiner in 848, Feng Ao, had a preference for "literary men" (*wenshi*) or "men who could write [good] rhapsodies" (*nengfu ren*), which indicates that he did not pass candidates who performed well only in the examination's Classics and policy essay sections.[15] We may infer from this that Li Yansheng's proficiency in composing Chinese poetry was exceptional for a foreigner. That said, most past analyses of "Chinese at Heart" have overestimated the degree to which Li Yansheng's *jinshi* candidacy itself was unusual or unprecedented. This is mainly a result of misunderstanding or ignoring the phrase *chang suo bingong zhe*, which I translate as "ordinary recommended guest candidates."

Beginning with Yan Gengwang in the 1950s, various scholars have established that from around 821, the *jinshi* examinations included a special category for foreign candidates, known as *bingong* ("recommended guests"). Whereas the earliest studies assumed that *bingong* candidates sat for a separate test that was easier than the regular *jinshi* examination, more recent work suggests that they were examined at the same time as Chinese candidates, answering the same questions and writing poetry on the same set topics. They may, however, have benefited from a fixed pass quota for foreign candidates that effectively increased their chances, given their much smaller numbers.[16] Fifty-eight *bingong* candidates earned the *jinshi* degree by the time the Tang dynasty ended. Most were scholars from the Korean state of Silla, the main source of foreign students in the Tang capital. But a chief minister of the Manchurian Bohai (Kor: Parhae) kingdom and his son also passed as *bingong* candidates, as did Li Xun (ca. 855–ca. 930), a descendant of Iranian immigrants who spent most of his life in Sichuan and became a noted lyricist.[17] Chen An's claim that Li Yansheng was superior in accomplishment to "ordinary" *bingong* candidates implies that Li was a *bingong* candidate himself, albeit an exceptionally talented one.[18]

The Duke of Fanyang referenced in "Chinese at Heart" is Lu Jun (776–862), who was appointed governor of the Xuanwu Army and prefect of Bianzhou (i.e., Daliang or Kaifeng) in 847.[19] Since Lu was conferred the title "Duke of Fanyang" in 850, when he returned to Chang'an from Bianzhou to take up the post of junior tutor to the heir apparent, Chen An must have written "Chinese at Heart" at least two years after Li Yansheng passed the *jinshi* examinations.[20] This temporal gap makes it highly unlikely that Chen was responding to a real controversy surrounding Lu Jun's decision to recommend a "barbarian" for the *jinshi* examinations.[21] For such a controversy to rage for two years or more, there would have had to be something truly unprecedented about opening up the examinations to foreign candidates. The existence of the *bingong* category demonstrates, on the contrary, that foreign *jinshi* candidacies had been sanctioned for nearly thirty years by the time Li Yansheng gained his *jinshi* degree. Moreover, it is difficult to believe that Chen An, a serially unsuccessful *jinshi* candidate with no official post, was in any position to defend a high-ranking statesman like Lu Jun from his critics. The "someone might argue" (*huoyue*) construction is typical of hypothetical debates used to present an argument, and the debate over Li Yansheng in "Chinese at Heart" is almost certainly hypothetical as well, although Lu Jun's imaginary critic may also be subtly expressing Chen An's own private chagrin at having failed the examinations of 848 whereas a foreigner passed.

Considering Chen An's situation at the time of the essay's writing, "Chinese at Heart" may well have originated as part of his *xingjuan*, a literary portfolio presented to influential officials and literati in Chang'an in the hope that they would endorse his candidacy to the *jinshi* examiner and thus greatly improve his chances of passing.[22] If so, the essay's intended audience was probably none other than Lu Jun. Lu's recommendation had been crucial in Li Yansheng's success at the examinations; Chen An was probably trying to secure a similar advantage for himself. His eloquent but redundant defense of Lu Jun against a "straw man" ethnocentric complaint was carefully designed to achieve two effects at once: flattering Lu with praise for his perspicacity and impartiality, while impressing him with a creative reinterpretation of the Chinese-barbarian dichotomy. Chen An may also have hoped that Lu Jun's patronage would translate into an opportunity for employment after passing the examinations: we know that Lu appointed another graduate from the *jinshi* cohort of 848 to his staff during another stint as a provincial governor in 852–55.[23] Nonetheless, "Chinese at Heart" evidently did not open any doors for Chen An, whose dreams of an official career remained unfulfilled.

The imaginary critic in "Chinese at Heart" asks, "How can there be no worthy candidate among the Chinese? Are barbarians the only ones suitable for employment?" The somewhat nativist assumption underlying these rhetorical questions is that a Chinese-ruled state, sustained by taxes paid by Chinese people, should give priority to Chinese aspirants to the *jinshi* degree. Even the most outstanding foreigner should be admitted to the examinations only after all qualified or "worthy" Chinese candidates have been identified and registered. Lu Jun is being faulted for flouting this principle of preferential treatment, but so, implicitly, is the emperor who accepted his recommendation of Li Yansheng.

Chen An responds to the imaginary critic in two ways. First, he dismisses the idea of preferential treatment for the Chinese as "favoritism toward [one's] own people" and credits Lu Jun with practicing a fully meritocratic policy of recommending the most talented man, regardless of ethnicity. Second, he subverts the conceptual categories framing the critic's questions, for they carry the long-standing assumption that barbarians are not only outsiders to the Central Lands but also morally inferior to the Chinese. Rather than adopt Liu Zongyuan's Buddhist apologetics strategy of dismissing "Chinese" and "barbarian" as mere names that do not determine an individual's moral worth or "essence," Chen An takes an approach similar to that of an undated essay, titled "Discourse on the Legitimacy of the Eastern Jin Emperors and the Illegitimacy of the Northern Wei Emperors" (Dongjin Yuan-Wei di zhengrun lun), by Han Yu's close friend and fellow Guwen writer Huangfu Shi (ca. 777–ca. 835).

Huangfu Shi's essay deals with a subject that had occasioned some vacillation and controversy earlier in the Tang: namely, which of the contending post-Han dynasties the imperial court should identify as legitimate bearers of the Mandate of Heaven. Normally, the Tang court recognized the Northern Zhou and Sui as the two legitimate dynasties immediately preceding it. But Tang rulers left the question of the Northern Wei's legitimacy open for over a century, before recognizing it as legitimate in 748–50 and again after 753.[24] In 491, the Northern Wei emperor Xiaowendi (r. 471–99) had decided to trace his dynasty's legitimacy directly from the Western Jin even though Wei rulers only began using the imperial title in 399, over eighty years after the Western Jin's fall in 316.[25] This claim—bolstered in 493 by the Northern Wei court's move to the former Western Jin capital, Luoyang—implied that the Eastern Jin in south China was not a legitimate continuation of the Western Jin and thus also negated any claim to legitimacy by the Eastern Jin's successors, Liu-Song and Southern Qi. The Tang court tacitly accepted the Northern Wei claim as valid, but Huangfu Shi argued instead that the Eastern Jin, Liu-Song, Southern Qi, and Liang were legitimate, with the Mandate of Heaven moving to north China only in 557 upon the founding of the dynasties of Northern Zhou in the north and Chen in the south.

During the Three Kingdoms and Northern and Southern Dynasties periods, it was common for both northern and southern regimes to use "the Central Lands" in its pre-imperial sense as a synonym for the geographical region of the North China Plain, although southern regimes occasionally appropriated the name because of its prestigious associations.[26] In the Tang, this interpretation of "the Central Lands" as a synonym for north China coexisted with a view of the Tang empire as a whole as "the Central Lands"—a case of multiple definitions also seen in Tang uses of the term Han.[27] Huangfu Shi therefore anticipates an argument that the Central Lands are equivalent to north China, such that whichever dynasty holds all of north China is ipso facto legitimate. He asserts instead that north China can cease to be the Central Lands when it is ruled by "barbarians" like the ethnically Xianbi (or Xianbei, *Särbi) emperors of Northern Wei, who hailed from present-day Inner Mongolia:

> The Central Lands are what they are because of ritual propriety and moral duty; the barbarians are called such because they do not have ritual propriety and moral duty. How could [this distinction] be tied to the land? When Qǐ used barbarian rites, then the people of Qǐ were barbarians. If Confucius went to live among the nine kinds of Yi, the Yi would no longer be benighted. Immersed in the [corrupting] influence of [the last Shang king,] Zhou, the people of the Shang dynasty became rebellious subjects. Because of the resettlement of the Rong, the Yi River became the land of Luhun. [Chineseness and barbarism] are not tied to the land. When the Jin retreated to the south, all men of talent went over to it, and its rites and music remained intact. There is historical evidence of the legacy of good customs and good governance that it inherited.[28]

In other words, Chineseness is not dependent on geographical location. Rather, it is contingent on the observance of civilized, "Chinese" ritual and moral standards, and the Eastern Jin's observance of these standards ("rites and music," "good customs and good governance") meant that the Central Lands had effectively shifted to the south.[29]

Huangfu Shi supports this argument with the case of the Qǐ rulers' "barbarizing" demotion and the resettlement of the Rong of Luhun to the Yi River, both drawn from the *Zuo Tradition*. The *Zuo Tradition* records the resettlement of the Rong people of Luhun to an area adjacent to the Eastern Zhou capital in 638 BCE and interprets this event as the fulfillment of a prophecy made at some time after 770 BCE (probably around 738 BCE), when the Zhou minister Xin You saw "someone making a sacrifice in the fields with his hair untied" near the new Eastern Zhou capital at Luoyang and exclaimed: "Will this not be [a land of] the Rong in less than a hundred years? We have already lost our ritual propriety (*li*) [to them]." Although Xin You objected not to the sacrificer's choice of location but to his hairstyle, which resembled that of the Rong instead of the traditional Chinese man's topknot, this is a case in which a change in *su* came together with a violation of *li*, since one's attire was especially important in the context of ritual sacrifice. The Zuo Tradition goes on to state that Xin You's fears were realized in a way when "in the autumn [of 638 BCE], [the states of] Qin and Jin resettled the Rong of Luhun on the banks of the Yi River," where Xin You had encountered the sacrificer with untied hair.[30]

There appear to be two models of barbarization in Huangfu Shi's argument: the literal barbarization of individuals (the people of Qĭ) and the demographic barbarization of a place via migration (the Yi River). Since the *Zuo Tradition* interpreted the Luhun resettlement as a consequence of Chinese people making sacrifices with their hair untied in the Rong style, however, both models hinge on the barbarizing effect of adopting barbarian ways. Huangfu's use of *Analects* 9.14, in which Confucius contemplates living among the "benighted" Yi and civilizing them, also implies that his argument cuts both ways: if the Chinese and their lands can be barbarized, barbarians too can theoretically cease to be barbaric if they adopt Chinese "rites and music." Indeed, Huangfu implies that if Xiaowendi's effort to "use Chinese [ways] to change the barbarians (*yong Xia bian Yi*) by changing surnames and reforming laws" had come earlier in the dynasty's history, then the Northern Wei *could* have become a legitimate Chinese dynasty instead of committing various acts of barbarism that disqualified it.[31] It should be noted that since Huangfu Shi accepted the legitimacy of the Northern Zhou emperors, who were also Xianbi, the common perception of his argument as motivated by xenophobia is probably as oversimplistic as a view of Chen An as a champion of "culturalism."[32] Unfortunately, it is no longer possible to reconstruct the reasons for Huangfu's bias against the Northern Wei, since there is no other piece concerning the Northern and Southern Dynasties in his extant works.[33]

Like "Chinese at Heart," Huangfu Shi's argument rejects geographical location ("land") as the primary means of defining the boundaries of Chineseness and argues for a more fluid boundary marked by "ritual propriety and moral duty." Whoever has ritual propriety and moral duty is Chinese; whoever does not is a barbarian. But there are also significant differences between the two arguments.[34] Huangfu Shi's boundary shifts with the movement of peoples (e.g., the Rong of Luhun) or due to the influence of sages (e.g., Confucius) or foreign rites on entire peoples or states (e.g., the nine kinds of Yi or the state of Qĭ). It also shifts across geographical areas, in keeping with his larger argument that the Central Lands are not invariably located in north China. Chen An's boundary, in contrast, is made up of individual human hearts and therefore impossible to map spatially; the geographical locations of "the Central Lands" and "the lands of the barbarians" remain static, but the actual distribution of Chinese hearts and barbarian hearts has nothing to do with location and everything to do with inborn moral "inclinations." These inclinations are distributed randomly across humanity, as reflected in the differing moral choices that individuals make and the fact that they do not correspond neatly to ethnocultural differences: "Take the cases of Lu Wan and Li Ling, who rebelled and defected—were they barbarians? Consider Jin Midi's steadfast loyalty—was he Chinese?" The implicit answer to these rhetorical questions is "no, but also yes": Lu Wan and Li Ling were not barbarians ethnoculturally, but they had barbarian hearts; Jin Midi was not Chinese ethnoculturally, but he had a Chinese heart.

This is an argument for moral universalism that is, paradoxically, couched in the language of ethnocentrism or (in Abramson's terms) "ethnicized discourse." Rather than using the existence of moral barbarians and immoral Chinese to deny the notion of Chinese moral superiority altogether, as Liu Zongyuan did, it redefines Chineseness so that moral barbarians are *essentially* Chinese and immoral Chinese are *essentially* barbarians. One can perhaps identify a precedent for this in the *Gongyang* and *Guliang* commentaries' emphasis on immoral behavior as a cause of "barbarizing" demotions in the *Annals*. But the *Gongyang* and *Guliang* focused on the demotion of state rulers and saw such demotions as temporary, rather than fundamental changes in an individual's moral essence or "heart." Moreover, the commentators interpreted Confucius as editorially promoting certain barbarian rulers for "good deeds" or for aiding the Central Lands states, but did not claim that these promoted rulers had become essentially Chinese. Even if the "Chinese at Heart" discourse of ethnocentric moralism was partly inspired by the *Gongyang* and *Guliang* interpretation of barbarism, it was not identical to that interpretation.

Although "Chinese at Heart" claims that any moral human being is essentially Chinese, it also carries an implicit assumption that the Jin Midis and Li Yanshengs of the world will always be in the minority, since the majority of barbarians still have to be "encouraged" to "turn to the transforming influence of illumination by *wen*"—an influence that emanates from a specific geographical location, the Central Lands, rather than the small number of Chinese hearts scattered among the lands of the barbarians. A tension between nature ("inclinations" and "heart") and nurture ("teaching" and "transforming influence"), or between universalism ("anyone can learn to be moral") and ethnocentrism ("morality originates from the Central Lands"), thus remains unresolved in Chen An's redefinition of Chineseness. The very same tension is present in Cheng Yan's "Call to Arms" and is, in fact, a characteristic of nearly all ethnocentric moralist discourse.

CHENG YAN'S "A CALL TO ARMS AGAINST THE INNER BARBARIAN"

Marc Abramson argues that the title "Neiyi xi" is "open to at least two readings": one in which *nei* is a verb meaning "to draw in" and one in which it is an adjective meaning "inside" or "inner." Abramson prefers the first reading and translates the essay's title as "Announcement on Drawing the Barbarians Inward," presumably because the essay contains the phrase, "Those among the barbarians of the four quarters who turn inward" (*siyi neixiang*).[35] However, *nei* actually has three possible meanings as a verb in Classical Chinese: "to enter," "to take in," or "to regard as an insider." The last of these meanings occurs in a well-known line in the *Gongyang Commentary*: "The Annals regards [the people] of [Confucius's] own state (i.e., Lu) as compatriots (literally, "insiders") and the [other] Chinese states as foreigners [in the context of relations between Chinese states], but also regards the Chinese states as compatriots (literally, "insiders") and the barbarians as foreigners [in the context of relations between Chinese states and barbarians]."[36] If the essay's title alludes to this line, then it would mean "Declaration on Regarding Barbarians as Compatriots."

But the meaning of the word *xi*, which has hitherto received insufficient attention in analyses of "Call to Arms," makes it even more likely that *nei* should be read as an adjective. The *xi* was a prose genre most often used to issue formal declarations of war or calls to arms against an enemy; as such, the contents of a *xi* usually asserted the justice of the author's cause by describing and denouncing the enemy's crimes.[37] Since the most important element in the title of a *xi* was the enemy's identity, it stands to reason that the title of Cheng Yan's essay indicates a declaration of war or a call to arms against "inner barbarians." The essay itself reads:

> There have long been people from the barbarians of the four quarters who came here, their speech passing through several translations before it could

be understood, out of admiration for the humaneness, moral duty, loyalty, and trustworthiness of the Central Lands of the Chinese. Although their bodies originate from foreign lands, they are able to direct their hearts toward the Chinese as swiftly as a galloping horse. Therefore, I do not call them barbarians. There have long been people in the Central Lands who stubbornly resist the emperor's transforming influence, forgetting and abandoning the virtues of humaneness, moral duty, loyalty, and trustworthiness. Although their bodies have a Chinese origin, they have instead banished their hearts into exile among the barbarians. Therefore, I do not call them Chinese. When I say that they have banished their hearts into exile among the barbarians, it is not that the empire banished them. Rather, they have banished their own hearts into iniquity. How could it be just a matter of calling people Chinese because they have the name "Chinese," or calling people barbarians because they have the name "barbarian"? Some people who are Chinese in name are barbarians at heart. Some people who are barbarians in name are Chinese at heart. From this we know that people who live in the Central Lands but abandon humaneness, moral duty, loyalty, and trustworthiness are barbarians of the Central Lands, and there is no need for the barbarians of the four quarters to invade us [from outside]. Since they rebel against the Central Lands, arrogantly usurp and reject the emperor's authority, and abandon humaneness, moral duty, loyalty, and trustworthiness, they cannot even be counted as human beings. Are they not then barbarians of the Central Lands? People from the barbarians of the four quarters who turn inward [to the Central Lands] and delight in our humaneness, moral duty, loyalty, and trustworthiness, desiring to be counted as human beings—are they not Chinese from the barbarians of the four quarters? Remember these words of mine! Those who are barbarians in name are, nonetheless, not barbarians, and those who are Chinese in name are instead not equal to those who are barbarians in name.[38]

The similarity between this text's rhetorical strategies and those of "Chinese at Heart" is striking. Both essays assume that the names "Chinese" and "barbarian" do matter, but assert that these names are sometimes applied incorrectly because the quality of one's heart is more important than the land of one's birth when it comes to determining Chineseness. Like Chen An, Cheng Yan assumes that Chineseness is concentrated (but not confined) in a specific space: any "Chinese from the barbarians of the four quarters" will demonstrate the Chineseness of his heart by "turn[ing] inward" from foreign lands and traveling a long distance to learn about humaneness, moral duty, loyalty, and trustworthiness from the original "Chinese of the Central Lands." The commonality between the two essays' arguments is too pronounced to be coincidental. It is likely that Cheng Yan's essay was inspired by Chen An's; if so, it is also likely that Cheng read "Chinese at Heart" only after Huang Tao published Chen's collected works in late 902, given Chen's prior obscurity.[39]

"Call to Arms" does go a little further than "Chinese at Heart" in equating morality with both being truly Chinese and being truly human. It describes moral states using metaphors of movement that are absent from "Chinese at Heart": barbarians "direct their hearts toward the Chinese as swiftly as a galloping horse," and Chinese people "banish their hearts into exile among the barbarians." And it speaks of a discrepancy between names and hearts, whereas "Chinese at Heart" speaks of a form-heart discrepancy. Besides these minor differences, there is also a more significant and intriguing aspect in which "Call to Arms" departs from the model of "Chinese at Heart." Whereas "Chinese at Heart" uses a hypothetical debate over Lu Jun and Li Yansheng as a device for framing its argument, "Call to Arms" conspicuously refuses to reveal its agenda by naming names more specific than "Chinese" and "barbarian." Cheng Yan subverts conventional understandings of Chineseness and barbarism, but makes no attempt to substantiate that subversion by revealing the identities of its objects of condemnation and praise, the "barbarians of the Central Lands" and the "Chinese from the barbarians of the four quarters." This suggests that "Call to Arms" was written as a satirical essay and not as a genuine call to arms and that its reader was expected to recognize the target of its political satire based on the events of the time. If the essay was written after late 902, that target was almost certainly the warlord Zhu Wen (or Zhu Quanzhong; 852–912).

Abramson, too, has argued that "it was probably Zhu whom Cheng Yan had in mind as the archetypal 'barbarian of the Central Kingdom.'" However, his inference that the essay "probably dates to the late 890s" overlooks the fact that Zhu Wen's expanding sphere of influence on the North China Plain was not perceived as a significant threat to the imperial court at that time.[40] Instead, in 895–901 the warlords who posed the greatest threat to the court were Han Jian (855–912) of Huazhou and Li Maozhen (856–924) of Fengxiang, due to their geographical proximity to the capital. This changed only in 901–3, when Zhu Wen played a crucial role in the success of a bid by Zhaozong and Chief Minister Cui Yin (854–904) to end the eunuchs' well-entrenched power over the imperial court. In response to a summons from Cui, Zhu marched west from his home base at Bianzhou, secured Han Jian's surrender, and gained effective military control over Chang'an. He then besieged Fengxiang, where the leading eunuchs had taken refuge with Li Maozhen as their protector and Zhaozong as a hostage. In early 903, a desperate Li Maozhen chose to kill his eunuch allies and make peace with Zhu Wen. Zhu escorted Zhaozong back to Chang'an and massacred the remaining eunuchs before returning to Bianzhou.[41]

The alliance between Cui Yin and Zhu Wen broke down in early 904 when Cui realized that Zhu had designs on the throne. Cui and his closest supporters plotted to raise an army against Zhu, only to be discovered and killed by troops loyal to Zhu. Zhu Wen then moved Zhaozong and his court east to Luoyang on the pretext of preempting an attack by Li Maozhen. Zhaozong, aware that Zhu intended to reduce him to a puppet, secretly sent pleas for help to Zhu Wen's rival warlords. These warlords began issuing calls to arms (i.e., *xi*) to one another, hoping to form an alliance to defeat Zhu Wen and, at least ostensibly, restore power to the emperor, but their conflicting interests and fear of Zhu's military strength meant that no alliance materialized. Zhu was soon able to have Zhaozong assassinated and replaced with a young imperial prince. In 905, he arranged the murder of Zhaozong's older sons. Finally, in 907, he forced the puppet emperor to abdicate the throne and replaced the Tang with his own dynasty, the Later Liang.[42]

We have no information on Cheng Yan's response to Zhu Wen's actions, but his use of the *xi* genre suggests that "Call to Arms" was written as a response to the political situation in 904. Abramson has argued that Cheng Yan's primary intention was "almost certainly" to defend the Shatuo Türk Li Keyong (856–908), one of Zhu's warlord rivals, from suspicions of disloyalty that reflected ethnic prejudice: "[Li's] autonomy, combined with his often-boorish behavior and unconcealed disdain for the educated Chinese civilian elite, as well [as] his non-Han ethnicity, made him the object of suspicion and occasional attacks by court officials. In one memorial, Li complained to the throne of poor treatment, particularly the constant labeling of him and his family as 'barbarians.' . . . ['Call to Arms'] thus was not only a general statement on the nature of Chineseness, . . . but also specifically served as a defense of Li and a criticism of the knee-jerk cultural chauvinism still practiced by some, if not many, literati." Although this interpretation is plausible, it suffers from weaknesses of chronology and contextualization, particularly if we also take into account Abramson's suggestion that Cheng Yan was setting up a contrast between the loyal Li Keyong, the Tang court's "principal military support," and the "rebellious Han general" Zhu Wen.⁴³ Even if such a contrast was intended, Abramson's belief that the emphasis of the contrast was on defending Li Keyong does not cohere with the rhetorical function of a *xi*, which is offensive and not defensive. A more critical problem with the "pro-Li" interpretation is that there was never a moment when Li Keyong was simultaneously the Tang court's military protector and a target of ethnic denigration at court.

Both Li Keyong and Zhu Wen played key roles in defeating the Huang Chao Rebellion of 875–84, but a feud subsequently arose between the two men.⁴⁴ The Tang court did not take sides in the dispute until 890, when Zhu Wen and two other warlords persuaded Zhaozong's chief minister Zhang Jun (d. 904) to lead a military expedition against Li Keyong. Zhang Jun was motivated by a personal grudge against Li Keyong and an ambition to gain political advantage over the eunuch Yang Fugong (d. 894) by achieving a prestigious military victory. Li Keyong's foreign origins thus played no part in his becoming the target of Zhang Jun's expedition; he did, however, submit a memorial complaining of the court's hypocrisy in now disparaging him as a "Rong and Jie" or "foreign barbarian" (Fanyi) when it had previously praised his martial prowess in glowing terms when it needed his aid against Huang Chao.⁴⁵ Apparently, then, the Tang court was making rhetorical use of the Chinese-barbarian dichotomy to justify its sudden and unprovoked hostility toward Li Keyong. Since this rhetoric arose from the unique circumstance of Zhang Jun's expedition, there is no evidence for Abramson's claim that it reflects a "constant labeling" by the court. In any case, the expedition's defeat at Li Keyong's hands quickly forced Zhaozong to mend fences with Li and send Zhang Jun into exile.

If "Call to Arms" was written as a defense of Li Keyong, the most appropriate time to do so would have been during the period in 890 when Zhu Wen and Zhang Jun were aligned against him. It is very unlikely, however, that Cheng Yan was aware of the existence of "Chinese at Heart" in 890, and Zhu Wen showed no sign of "arrogantly usurp[ing] and reject[ing] the emperor's authority" until 903–4. In 890, Zhu's reputation was still that of a meritorious military commander who, like Li Keyong, had saved the Tang dynasty from Huang Chao. Moreover, Li Keyong did not act as the Tang court's main protector until 895, when Li Maozhen, Han Jian, and their ally Wang Xingyu (d. 895) seized control of Chang'an and attempted to depose Zhaozong. Li Keyong's intervention on Zhaozong's behalf resulted in the Li-Han-Wang alliance's defeat and Wang Xingyu's assassination, but Zhaozong's advisers persuaded him to restrain Keyong from attacking Fengxiang, on the grounds that a balance of power between Li Maozhen and Li Keyong was preferable to a situation in which the latter's Shatuo Türks enjoyed military superiority.[46] There is no indication that Zhaozong's advisers cited the Chinese-barbarian dichotomy as a reason to be wary of Li Keyong—his status as a powerful autonomous warlord was reason enough. This was a strategic calculation based on pragmatism, rather than "knee-jerk cultural chauvinism" or distrust of foreigners.

By the time Zhu Wen was able to pose a threat to the Tang dynasty itself, Li Keyong had lost his stomach for warfare with Zhu after narrowly surviving two assaults on his home base by Zhu's troops.[47] Cheng Yan thus probably wrote "Call to Arms" in 903–7 to condemn Zhu Wen's usurpation of imperial power, not to defend a politically irrelevant Li Keyong from ethnocentric accusers who probably never existed. Cheng did not have a specific "Chinese-hearted" barbarian in mind and merely used this idea as a vehicle to direct a veiled attack at a particular "barbarian-hearted" Chinese. The essay's cryptic lack of specificity is a deliberate tactic to shield its author from persecution with a thick layer of plausible deniability: Zhu Wen could not react negatively to the piece without showing that he recognized himself as the immoral usurper that it attacks.

INFLUENCES ON "CHINESE AT HEART" AND "CALL TO ARMS"

If "Call to Arms," with its name-heart discrepancy, was directly inspired by "Chinese at Heart," what inspired the rhetoric of "Chinese at Heart"? These essays have previously been compared to "Tracing the Way" because of their emphasis on a fluid interpretation of the Chinese-barbarian dichotomy. Scholars have argued that "Tracing the Way" and "Chinese at Heart" express the "exact same sentiment" on the Chinese-barbarian dichotomy, only "illustrated and elaborated" in the latter piece, that Chen An and Cheng Yan are "likely intellectual inheritors of Han Yu" because of their use of the Guwen style, and that both "Chinese at Heart" and "Call to Arms" are modeled on "Tracing the Way" in particular.[48] Yet neither "Chinese at Heart" nor "Call to Arms" mentions the "barbarizing" editorial demotions in the *Annals* and uses them to identify typically Classicist moral values like humaneness, moral duty, and ritual propriety as the essence of Chineseness.

Han Yu's preface for Wenchang and a satirical piece now known as the Third Miscellaneous Discourse (Zashuo san) are the more likely rhetorical models for Chen An's use of a form-heart discrepancy and his argument about judging individuals' hearts by their deeds. As we have seen, the preface for Wenchang begins with a name-deed discrepancy linked to a Classicist-Mohist dichotomy. The Third Miscellaneous Discourse uses myths that the ancient sages had animal-like physical features to argue that it is better to look like an animal than to have an animal's heart:

> A sage of the past had a head like that of a bull, another had a body like that of a snake, another had a beak like a bird's, and another had a face as ugly as an exorcist's mask.[49] They resembled [these things] in outward appearance but not in their hearts. Can one say that they were not human? Some people have excellent physiques and complexions, with faces as ruddy as cinnabar; they are handsome but vicious. Such people have the appearance of human beings but the hearts of animals; how can they be called human? In that case, judging people by the rightness or wrongness of their appearance is not as reliable as judging them by their hearts and deeds.[50]

This argument could be reframed easily in ethnocentric moralist terms, if one substitutes barbarism for animality and ethnic origin for appearance. That is exactly what "Chinese at Heart" does.

"Chinese at Heart" can be read as evidence that the rhetoric of ethnocentric moralism originated in the middle of the ninth century and that it was inspired by the rhetoric of discrepant names (or appearances) and deeds (or hearts) found in a couple of Han Yu's essays—not, as one might assume, by the innovative conflation of the Chinese-barbarian and orthodox-heterodox dichotomies in the more famous "Tracing the Way." In short, both ethnicized orthodoxy and the earliest form of ethnocentric moralism can be traced either directly or indirectly to Han Yu's rhetoric, but they may not both have sprung from "Tracing the Way." "Tracing the Way" did eventually serve as a source of inspiration for a Daoxue version of ethnocentric moralism in the late eleventh and early twelfth centuries, but that development must be understood in the context of preceding Northern Song developments in the discourses of ethnicized orthodoxy and ethnocentric moralism.

CHAPTER 4

Ethnicized Orthodoxy in the Northern Song Guwen Revival

THE essays "Chinese at Heart" and "A Call to Arms against the Inner Barbarian" employ a rhetorical strategy of drawing a false dichotomy between immorality and Chineseness—a dichotomy founded on a kind of ethnic essentialism that regards immorality as the defining characteristic of barbarians. Ethnocentric stereotyping of this sort had a long history by late Tang times, but Chen An and Cheng Yan were the first to push it to its logical limits by claiming that immoral Chinese are Chinese in name only, while moral barbarians are barbarians in name only.

The kind of essentialism that represents any immoral Chinese as no longer truly Chinese is not so different from the deliberately provocative attempts by Han Yu to insinuate that his literati peers were Classicist "in name" but Buddhist "in deed," in part by contrasting them to monks whom he identified as Buddhist "in name" but Classicist "in deed." The very idea that every individual's deeds had to be either fully Classicist or fully Buddhist not only essentialized the features of both traditions, but also constructed an oppositional, exclusive dichotomy between self-identifying Classicists and self-identifying Buddhists that would have been alien to most literati of the time, including Liu Zongyuan. Han Yu's ethnicized orthodoxy took this false Classicist-Buddhist dichotomy one step further, turning it into one between Classicism and barbarism: one who turned away from the Way of the Sages was effectively becoming a barbarian. This was another example of ethnic essentialism, identifying a certain interpretation of Classicism as the defining characteristic of being Chinese.

Han Yu never took this rhetorical move to its logical conclusion by using the idea of barbarization to criticize Daoism. In his polemics, barbarism did not fully shed its ethnocultural associations and transform into an abstract concept with universal applications. When literati of the early Northern Song rediscovered Han Yu as a writer and thinker, however, leading to his "ideological appropriation and redefinition" and "elevation . . . to the status of Confucian culture hero," the rhetoric of ethnicized orthodoxy finally expanded beyond its ninth-century limits and came to be used against Buddhism and Daoism alike.[1] One could say that the Guwen definition of Classicist orthodoxy became fully ethnicized.

THE GUWEN REVIVAL

The eleventh century was a pivotal period in Chinese literary and intellectual history, during which the literary and ideological positions associated with Han Yu came to occupy the mainstream of literati culture. Although Han Yu's writing seems to have been widely admired and imitated during his lifetime, the parallel prose that he so despised remained the standard style of literati writing throughout the ninth and tenth centuries. From 1009 to the 1030s, moreover, the most celebrated prose works in the Northern Song literary scene were in an ornate, allusive parallel style that Yang Yi (974–1020) and other editors of the *Outstanding Models from the Storehouse of Literature* (Cefu yuangui) had originally developed for use in poetry. Nonetheless, a small but vocal minority of contrarians favored the Guwen style: these included Liu Kai (947–1000), Wang Yucheng (954–1001), and Sun He (961–1004) in the late tenth century and Yao Xuan (967–1020) and Mu Xiu (979–1032) in the first two decades of the eleventh.[2] Han Yu's works therefore continued to circulate and began to gain a strong following in the early 1030s, among the generation of Song literati born between 990 and 1010.

Guwen prose surpassed parallel prose in prestige by the middle of the 1040s, due in large part to the literary brilliance of Ouyang Xiu (1007–1072). Around 1061, Ouyang looked back on this transformation in the literary scene and remarked that whereas no one spoke of Han Yu's writings when he was a *jinshi* candidate in 1030, now "men learning [how to write] refuse to learn from anyone but Han Yu."[3] Ouyang Xiu's genius lay in his ability to transcend Han Yu's influence in highly original ways, rather than imitating Han slavishly, but very few Song literati who sought to write Guwen prose were anywhere near as creative.[4] As early as 1047 another Guwen writer, Li Gou

(1009–1059), complained about the tendency for lesser writers to ride the Guwen wave by "imitating Mencius and plundering [phrases] from Han Yu."[5]

Modern historians usually refer to this literary shift as either the second "Guwen movement" (*Guwen yundong*) or the Guwen movement's second phase, based on the assumption that the first movement or phase took place during the ninth century. The idea of a historical "Guwen movement" originated in 1928 with Hu Shi, then leading his own literary movement to replace Classical Chinese with the spoken vernacular. However, Higashi Hidetoshi—building on an argument by Luo Liantian—has cautioned that the modern concept of literary movements may convey the misleading impression that the Guwen writers were a cohesive, organized group united by a single cause. This was true neither in the ninth century nor in the eleventh. The eleventh-century "rediscovery" of Han Yu is thus better described as a Guwen revival (*Guwen fuxing*).[6] The Northern Song Guwen writers themselves usually referred to it as a revival of "this literary culture of ours" (*siwen*). In *Analects* 9.5, Confucius used *siwen* to refer to the Zhou dynasty's ritual practices or "morally refined tradition of values and institutions," but Song Guwen rhetoric reinterpreted the phrase to mean writing that combined a Guwen style with Han Yu's notion of Classicist orthodoxy, thus emulating both the language of the Classics and the values of their sage authors.[7] By the early 1030s, for example, the influential Guwen writer Shi Jie (1005–1045) was using "this literary culture of ours," "the Way" (*Dao*), "this Way of ours" (*si Dao*), and "the Way of the Sages" (*Shengren zhi Dao*) as interchangeable concepts.[8]

With the notable exception of Liu Kai, no Song Guwen writer prior to the 1030s was strongly anti-Buddhist. Wang Yucheng is known to have submitted an anti-Buddhist memorial partly modeled on Han Yu's polemics; Shi Jie later cited both him and Han as prominent critics of Buddhism.[9] But Wang also had positive interactions with the Buddhist community, including friendship with the monk-literatus Zanning (919–1001) and authorship of several commemorative inscriptions for Buddhist monasteries.[10] Mu Xiu's extant works also reflect an evenhanded and tolerant attitude toward Buddhism.[11] In contrast, the Guwen revival of the 1030s and 1040s had a pronounced anti-Buddhist ideological aspect that occasionally expanded to include anti-Daoist sentiment, as influential Guwen writers embraced Han Yu's exclusivist redefinition of Classicist identity and blamed intellectual and religious pluralism for the decline of the Way of the Sages.

Despite their shared affinity for Han Yu and opposition to Buddhism, the Guwen revivalists were intellectually diverse when it came to the question of how Guwen writing could be used to change society for the better. Shi Jie and Sun Fu (992–1057), who may be considered "Guwen radicals," believed in reviving and defending the Way of the Sages by using Han Yu's rhetoric of ethnicized orthodoxy against not only Buddhism but also Daoism and even various defunct philosophical traditions (e.g., Legalism and Mohism) commonly seen as Chinese in origin. In this, they were following the lead of the first Song-period Guwen radical, Liu Kai. By contrast, Ouyang Xiu and Li Gou—the "Guwen moderates" of their generation—discreetly rejected ethnicized orthodoxy's flawed logic and redeployed its rhetoric of barbarization toward pragmatic arguments for sociopolitical reform, not ideological exclusivism.[12]

THE FIRST GUWEN RADICAL: LIU KAI

Scholarly interest in Liu Kai has generally focused on the fact that, around 970, he became the first Song literatus to move beyond championing Guwen writing and embrace Han Yu's ideologically exclusive narrative of the lost Way of the Sages. Liu affirmed that Han Yu had rediscovered the Way and claimed to be carrying on Han's mission, although he differed in the final form of Han's narrative by crediting Yang Xiong and the Sui Classicist philosopher Wang Tong (ca. 584–ca. 617) with being legitimate inheritors of the Way of the Sages.[13] Thus, in a letter probably written during the early 970s, Liu explains that Yang Xiong's success in combating "Huang-Lao" philosophy—which Liu, like Han Yu, probably equated with Daoism—was undone by Buddhism's meteoric rise in popularity during the Wei-Jin period. As a result, "the people were like barbarians and the Way of the Sages collapsed as if dead." Liu Kai goes on to claim that Heaven was angered by this collapse and sent Wang Tong to re-illuminate the Way of the Sages; unfortunately, he never gained recognition as a sage and therefore failed to reverse the Way's decline. Heaven next sent Han Yu into the world, and "the Way of the Sages was restored to greatness under the Tang." Liu Kai claimed that Heaven had now created him to carry on Han Yu's work: "The Way of the Sages undoubtedly does reside in me!" The letter's recipient, Zang Bing (940–992), was apparently convinced by Liu Kai's claim to sagehood and hailed him as "the Song Confucius" (*Song zhi Fuzi*).[14]

Liu Kai is now recognized as an important precursor to the Guwen revival despite the fact that few literati of his generation followed Zang Bing in accepting his bold and somewhat arrogant claims to sagehood. In recent years, historians have also become interested in interpreting the sociopolitical context for his violent, impetuous personality, his alleged cannibalistic taste for human livers, his strong interest in irredentist warfare against the Kitan Liao empire, and his decision to switch from civil officialdom to a military career at the age of forty.[15] One aspect of Liu Kai's career that has hitherto escaped notice is his attempt at using Han Yu's rhetoric of barbarism against both Buddhism and Daoism, although the lack of dates for many of Liu's writings makes it impossible to determine when this innovation occurred.

In the letter to Zang Bing, Liu Kai appears to be sticking to Han Yu's "Tracing the Way" strategy of associating Buddhism, but not Daoism, with barbarization. In an undated letter addressed to one Chen Zhaohua, however, he claims that both Buddhism and Daoism are barbarian teachings:

> The followers of Laozi and the Buddha arose from among the barbarians (*qiyu Yi*), and the barbarians say that theirs are the highest of teachings. But when they come to the Central Lands, they cannot equal the Way of father-son and ruler-subject relations. The barbarians do not know the Classics; if they knew the Classics, then how could the teachings of Laozi and the Buddha have come into being among the barbarians?

Curiously, the very mention of barbarian teachings contradicts a claim that Liu made earlier in the letter: that barbarians do not engage in learning and are thus not truly human.

> One might ask, "What is a human being?" I would say, "To learn is to be human. One who does not learn may have the appearance, the robe, and the cap of a human being, but he cannot be called human. The barbarians live beyond the four quarters of the world, and their heaven and earth, sun and moon, stars, mountains and rivers, vegetation, and climate are no different from ours. But they do not know how to learn, and that is what makes them barbarians."[16]

This argument may have been inspired by the rhetoric of Han Yu's Third Miscellaneous Discourse, but it differs from Han in identifying learning, rather than moral character, as the criterion for humanity, and in contrasting human beings with barbarians rather than animals. Indeed, Liu's argument bears a closer resemblance to Cheng Yan's "Call to Arms," which also conflated Chineseness with humanity—if only briefly for rhetorical effect.

If barbarians "do not know how to learn," does that imply that following "the teachings of Laozi and the Buddha" involves no real learning? It is doubtful that Liu Kai himself could answer that question. In no other extant piece of writing does he repeat either his claim of Daoism's origin "from among the barbarians" or his theory about learning as the basis of humanity and Chineseness, let alone attempt to connect or reconcile the two in a coherent manner. Instead, a valedictory preface (also undated) that Liu composed for Chen Zhaohua employs a polemical strategy of analogizing Classicist orthodoxy to the Central Lands and other traditions to barbarian invaders:

> When a true king does not appear [in the world], the laws and government go into decline; the barbarians then grow powerful and invade the Central Lands from every side. When a sage passes away, rites and music decline; the teachings of Yang Zhu, Mozi, Laozi, and the Buddha then grow powerful and bring confusion to the Great Way from every side.... Our state is well-governed, but the Great Way has still not been illuminated, and the teachings of Yang Zhu, Mozi, Laozi, and the Buddha continue to invade and confuse it. Who can say that we lack the means [to change this]?[17]

Later in the same text, Liu Kai represents himself as a fearless warrior on an ideological battlefield: "I am like one engaged in battle, I have the courage to fight, and I am going to first muster all my strength and slay Yang Zhu, Mozi, Laozi, and the Buddha."[18]

Considering these martial metaphors, it is significant that, in the 980s, the new irredentist cause of reclaiming the Youzhou (i.e., Yan) region from the Kitan Liao empire after some fifty years of Kitan occupation seems to have awoken an ambition for military glory in Liu Kai. Putting his literary and ideological pursuits aside, he requested a military command on the northern frontier in the winter of 986–87, shortly after the second Song attempt at capturing Youzhou failed as disastrously as the first.[19] His request was denied, probably because he lacked military experience. But in the summer, Liu was one of five court officials who responded to an edict calling for civil officials with knowledge of military affairs to volunteer for positions in the army. The court assigned him to command a newly established military prefecture on the northern frontier, where he soon initiated a plan to seize Youzhou from the Kitans with the aid of a defecting general. This plan was aborted a year later, upon Liu's reassignment to a prefecture in the far south.[20] He did not return to the northern frontier until 998, but seemed poised for prominence in the escalating Song-Liao conflict at the time of his sudden death from a tumor in 1000. One historian claims that Liu Kai's choice of a military career doomed him to obscurity because of the Song state's growing aversion to warfare; another disagrees and lays the blame for his lack of advancement on his impetuous and indecorous conduct, cannibalism, and brazen fame-seeking.[21] Both arguments ignore the evidence that Liu's career on the northern frontier revived in 998–1000, only to be cut short by his untimely death, although the Chanyuan peace covenant of 1005 (which ended Song-Liao hostilities for over a century) would have limited his career's further advancement in any case.

THE SECOND GENERATION OF GUWEN RADICALS: SHI JIE AND SUN FU

Upon reading Han Yu's prose for the first time around 1032, Shi Jie was won over by the power of both Han's Guwen style and his narrative of the Way of the Sages. By 1034, Shi Jie had also discovered Liu Kai's works, leading him to accept Liu's expanded list of legitimate followers of the Way of the Sages after Mencius (i.e., Yang Xiong, Wang Tong, and Han Yu) while adding Xunzi and Liu Kai himself to that list.[22]

The first hint of ethnicized orthodoxy's influence on Shi Jie's polemics appears in a letter from Shi to the renowned classical scholar Sun Shi (962–1033) in 1033. Sun had just retired from office at the imperial court and moved to the prefecture where Shi Jie held a post. Shi concluded that Sun Shi was destined to be Han Yu's next ideological successor, perhaps because Sun had written a commentary on the *Mencius* and was known to have criticized emperor Zhenzong's (r. 997–1022) patronage of Daoism on a few occasions. Shi therefore wrote to Sun, explaining the latter's historic mission and begging to be accepted as his disciple.[23] Shi Jie employs the Chinese-barbarian dichotomy in a metaphor that likens the decline of the Way of the Sages to a burglary and imputes barbarian origins to all other ideologies, including those of Yang Zhu and Mozi: "Alas! Confucius died, and his seventy-two disciples later died too. The Way of the Sages had no bolts or locks to protect it, so at midnight someone tore down the walls and removed the doors, taking them with him when he left. Then anyone could come and go through the entrances. Unfortunately, there next came a burglar who stole it and took it out of the Central Lands, leaving it among the barbarians of the four quarters. Thus were the teachings of Yang Zhu, Mozi, the Buddha, and Laozi invented."[24] Whereas Liu Kai likened "the teachings of Yang Zhu, Mozi, Laozi, and the Buddha" to invading barbarians, Shi Jie's letter effectively claims that these teachings originated as barbarian distortions of Confucius's Way after it was stolen from the lands of the Chinese.

To Shi Jie's disappointment, Sun Shi fell ill and died two months later. In 1034, Shi was reassigned to the Southern Capital (Yingtian prefecture, modern Shangqiu) as the principal of the prefectural school. Soon afterward, his commitment to Han Yu's exclusivist ideology led him to mount an audacious challenge to the authority of the Southern Capital's new prefect, Liu Sui (971–1035). During an inspection of the prefectural school's library, Liu came across a set of portraits of the Buddha, Laozi, and Confucius and remarked that the teachings of all three men were worthy of respect. The next day, Liu also remarked to Shi Jie that the ancient Chinese sage-kings and the Buddha were all sages. Shi found this eclecticism intolerable and decided to write Liu Sui—who was senior to him by thirty-four years—a protest letter modeled on Han Yu's Buddha relic memorial. In it, he accused Liu of "[wishing] to bring in a man of the barbarians (*Yi-Di zhi ren*) and elevate him to the level of the sage-kings; to bring in a way of the barbarians (*Yi-Di zhi dao*) and cause it to be practiced within the Central Lands."[25]

Shi Jie then ordered the library staff to destroy the portraits of the Buddha and Laozi, citing Liu Sui's prior instructions to remove all books that were not "the books of the sages" from the library and arguing that the same was applicable to unsagely images. He also wrote an official explanation of his actions and had the text inscribed in stone. In it, he argued that grouping portraits of the Buddha and Laozi with that of Confucius amounted to considering them as equals to the sages. How could this not mislead the Chinese into "changing our robes and caps, abandoning our Master [Confucius], discarding our honored parents, ceasing our sacrificial rites, and all going together to follow barbarism (Yi)?"[26] Such rhetoric came close to repeating Liu Kai's assertion, in the letter to Chen Zhaohua, that Laozi's teachings were as foreign to the Central Lands as Buddhism. Indeed, that very assertion lies at the center of Shi's essay "The Central Lands" (Zhongguo lun). Chen Zhi'e believed that Shi Jie wrote this essay in 1034, but there is no direct evidence for this.[27] Chen's date seems to be based on the direction in which Shi Jie's disagreement with Liu Sui was taking him: namely, a rhetorical effort at linking both Buddhism and Daoism with barbarism in the clearest and most literal way possible.

In "The Central Lands," Shi Jie attempts to construct a historical narrative that equates all heterodoxy with barbarism, but he can only do so by committing some glaring errors of fact and logic. The first part of the essay explains the Chinese-barbarian dichotomy in terms of geography and customs. Adopting the conventional definition of the Central Lands as "that which lies at the center of heaven and earth" and the barbarians as "those who dwell on the fringes of heaven and earth," Shi Jie repeats the long-obsolete descriptions of barbarian diet and dress in "Kingly Institutions" (Wangzhi), a chapter of the *Record of Rites* (Liji), which contains a well-known passage purporting to describe foreign peoples in the time of the early Western Zhou.[28] He also argues that these geographical and cultural distinctions correspond to astrological and ethical boundaries. Cosmic order requires that barbarians not "infringe on" (*gan*) or "enter" (*ru*) the Chinese lands and that the Chinese differ from barbarians in valuing proper relationships "between rulers and subjects, fathers and sons, husbands and wives, elder brothers and younger brothers, [hosts and] guests, or friends." Should the barbarians invade, or the Chinese cease to value these relationships, "then our land (*guo*) would no longer be the Central Lands."[29]

Shi Jie goes on to claim that the Song state is indeed in danger of ceasing to be the Central Lands, but he identifies the barbarians who have invaded the Central Lands as the Buddha and Laozi, not—as one might expect—the Kitans:

> I have heard that there was a giant called the Buddha who came from the west and entered our Central Lands, and an old man named [Lao] Dan (i.e., Laozi) who came from among the Westerners (Hu) and entered our Central Lands. Each [sought to] change the people of the Central Lands with his people, the Way of the Central Lands with his way, the customs of the Central Lands with his customs, the books of the Central Lands with his books, the teachings of the Central Lands with his teachings, the houses of the Central Lands with his houses, the rites and music of the Central Lands with his rites and music, the literary arts of the Central Lands with his literary arts, the clothing of the Central Lands with his clothing, the diet of the Central Lands with his diet, and the sacrificial rites of the Central Lands with his sacrificial rites.[30]

Shi Jie's claim that the Buddha himself came to the Central Lands can be read as hyperbole.[31] His claim that Laozi was a barbarian like the Buddha, however, is obviously not just exaggerated but false. Shi may have been attempting to reverse the Daoist myth that Laozi became the Buddha after going west, but he was probably also imitating Liu Kai's letter to Chen Zhaohua.[32] In any case, the argument that Daoism is alien to the Central Lands is simply untenable: Daoist rites, ritual music, temple architecture, religious dress, and dietary practices all had essentially Chinese origins, even if they did not conform to Classicist norms.[33]

"The Central Lands" ends with a prescription that alludes to the infamously radical ending of "Tracing the Way," in which Han Yu calls for government action to "turn these people (i.e., the Buddhist and Daoist clergy) into commoners, burn their books, and turn their dwellings (i.e., monasteries) into houses." Whereas Han Yu most likely meant *min qiren* ("turn these people into commoners") but had to write *ren qiren* (literally, "turn these people into human beings") because of the Tang official taboo on the character *min*, which was part of Tang Taizong's (r. 626–49) given name,[34] Shi Jie adapts the phrase *ren qiren* into *ge ren qiren* ("let each people be a distinct people") and thereby constructs an argument for strict ethnic and cultural segregation: "One may ask, 'What then can be done about it?' I would answer, 'Let each people be a distinct people and have distinct customs, distinct teachings, distinct rituals, distinct clothing, and distinct dwellings. Let the barbarians of the four quarters live in their own lands, and the [people of the] Central Lands live in the Central Lands. That is all there is to it. Then the Central Lands would be the Central Lands, and the barbarians of the four quarters would be the barbarians of the four quarters.'"[35] Shi Jie's recommendation is thus that the Chinese stop practicing Buddhism and Daoism so that they can be truly Chinese again.

Unlike "Tracing the Way," this recommendation does not include any specific measures to be taken by the government. But in another essay titled "Clarifying the Prohibitions" (Mingjin), Shi Jie includes "heterodox doctrines bringing disorder to our customs" (*zuofa luansu*) in a long list of social ills that he wants the state to prohibit, arguing that they cause "the Chinese of the Central Lands to become barbarians" (*Zhonghua, Yi ye*). The essay "Clarifying the Four Capital Offenses" (Ming sizhu) apparently seeks to surpass Han Yu in radicalism by arguing that the government should put all Buddhist and Daoist clergy to death: "The Buddha and Laozi were men of the barbarians (*Yi-Di zhi ren*), yet the Buddhists and Daoists bring disorder to the teachings and doctrines of the Central Lands with the barbarians' teachings and doctrines (*jiaofa*), bring disorder to the clothing of the Central Lands with the barbarians' clothing, and bring disorder to the language of the Central Lands with the barbarians' language. There is no crime greater than that, yet they are not put to death for it."[36] Shi Jie does not reserve this harsh punishment for Buddhist and Daoist clergy only—he also calls for it to be applied to proponents of other heterodox philosophies and to writers of florid, frivolous prose (i.e., anything other than Guwen).

In recent years, some historians have interpreted "The Central Lands" as evidence for the existence of nationalism or proto-nationalism in the Northern Song.[37] This interpretation does not explain why Shi Jie focuses his polemic on religions or systems of thought that he considers to be ideological enemies of the Way of the Sages (which he equates with the "Way of the Central Lands"), rather than on the Song state's geopolitical rivals. The same is essentially true of essays like "Clarifying the Prohibitions" and "Clarifying the Four Capital Offenses," although they cast their net wider in terms of ideas or practices that they call on the state to suppress. Chen Zhi'e has argued that ideological warfare against Buddhism and Daoism was a way for Shi Jie and other Northern Song literati to vent their anxiety about a "deepening national crisis" of foreign threats: "Defeats on the battlefield further forced them to vent the accumulated national sentiment in their hearts in an intense manner by making great efforts to revive traditional Classicist learning and reject Buddhism and Daoism, so as to conquer and destroy 'barbarians' in the cultural sphere."[38] But even this reading is not supported by a close analysis of those of Shi Jie's works that deal with geopolitical conflict—all of which, interestingly, are poems, not essays.

A poem that Shi Jie composed in 1035, titled "The West and the North" (Xibei), does express concern that the Kitan Liao and Xi Xia will eventually pose an insurmountable threat to the Song if their power continues to grow unchecked. The poem complains that Kitan control of Youzhou has left the Song without defensible frontiers in the north, accuses Song political and military leaders of complacency, and ends by lamenting that the imminent danger is "enough to make one weep."[39] However, most of Shi Jie's other poetic rhetoric on foreign relations is aggressively irredentist or expansionist in nature, not driven by fear of foreign threats. Shi evidently admired Liu Kai's militant stance toward the Kitans and his plans for the reconquest of Youzhou. A poem that he wrote after a visit to Liu Kai's grave implies that Liu's death not only deprived the Guwen cause of its leader but also robbed the Song state of a chance to put the Kitans and Tanguts in their place:

> The world is without heroes,
> And this literary culture has lost its leading light.
> Whippersnappers dare to cavort wildly,

And crafty Rong dare to be arrogant and insulting.
I think of Mister Liu,
And tears stream down my face like rain.[40]

Another poem, which is not dated, builds on the irredentist theme by emphasizing Youzhou's strategic importance and lamenting two lost opportunities to regain it from the Kitans: the Later Zhou emperor Shizong's (r. 954–59) untimely death, which came on the eve of his planned military expedition to retake Youzhou, and Liu Kai's transfer away from the northern frontier, which derailed his plan to do the same. Shi Jie claims yet again to be moved to tears by these unfortunate twists of fate.[41]

Historian Fang Cheng-hua recently interpreted Shi Jie's poems about Liu Kai as reflecting "romantic literati longings for personal military glory on the frontier in an age of peace."[42] Indeed, Shi Jie's laments over Youzhou suggest that his preferred foreign policy was not to strengthen frontier defenses against threatening barbarians, but rather to invade neighboring states and reclaim territory that he believed rightfully belonged to the Song. We see this tendency again in a poem from the late 1030s or early 1040s, in which a game of chess leads Shi to fantasize about playing general and embarking on an expansionist/irredentist spree that includes campaigns against Xi Xia, the Kitans, north Vietnam (independent from Chinese rule since 938), and even the Korean state of Koryŏ:

Where can I get a million cavalrymen
With their steel armor plates all rattling?
To the west, we'd take [the Xi Xia ruler] Yuanhao's (r. 1038–48) head
And present it to the emperor in his palace.
To the north, we'd enter the lands of the Xiongnu (i.e., the Kitans)
And return south with the Rong king a bound captive.
To the east, we'd cross to the other side of the cerulean sea
And shoot Koryŏ's cities to pieces.
To the south, we'd charge into the kingdom of Jiaozhi (i.e., north Vietnam)
And the Man ruler would come to surrender with an empty coffin.[43]
We'd turn the barbarians of the four quarters into the emperor's subjects
And return to proclaim that an age of great peace has begun![44]

This martial fantasy suggests that we should read Shi Jie's poetic weeping as tears of frustrated irredentist ambition, not defensive-minded patriotic anxiety. If the argument of "The Central Lands" is ostensibly about keeping foreign religions and customs out of the Central Lands, most of Shi Jie's poems on foreign affairs are about the need for offensive warfare to recapture lost territory and assert suzerainty over foreign peoples.

Given this key distinction between exclusionist and expansionist messages, we have little basis for interpreting Shi Jie's militant rhetoric of ethnicized orthodoxy as a xenophobic or "nationalistic" reaction to the Song state's foreign policy challenges. It would be more accurate to say that Shi Jie's Guwen radicalism, like Liu Kai's, was driven by the same burning ambition for greatness and militancy of personality that made him an aggressive irredentist. Shi Jie's small physical stature made it impossible for him to aspire to a military career: in a letter to his friend and mentor Sun Fu, he hyperbolically describes himself as "not even three *chi* in height" (i.e., less than three feet tall). He may have tried to compensate for this by constructing a self-image as a fearless soldier on an ideological battlefield; the same letter to Sun Fu claims that "when it comes to [defending] this Way, I feel like I have a body eight or nine *chi* tall, with glaring eyes and a broad forehead, dressed in rhinoceros-hide armor, a steel helmet on my head, riding in an army of a hundred thousand cavalry, as valorous as a great hero, fearing nothing at all."[45]

Shi Jie had met Sun Fu through a mutual friend in 1034, during his period of service in the Southern Capital. Impressed by Sun's devotion to classical scholarship, Shi invited him to establish a private academy of classical learning on Mount Tai, near Shi's hometown. Sun Fu, who had finally tired of pursuing an official career after failing to pass the *jinshi* examinations on his fourth try, eventually accepted the invitation. In the winter of 1035, he moved into an academy compound on Mount Tai that had been built with Shi Jie's sponsorship, and Shi Jie and two friends formally entered into discipleship under him. Shi Jie also taught *Annals* and *Changes* exegesis at the Mount Tai Academy while observing the three-year mourning period for his mother in 1038–41. It was probably during this period at Mount Tai that Shi Jie converted two Daoist priests to Classicism and accepted them as students after giving them new, Classicist-themed names. In a letter explaining his decision to rename one of the former Daoists Guilu (Returning to Lu), he analogized the pursuit of the Way of the Sages to a physical journey that had as its destination the region of Lu (which included Mount Tai), since it was the Duke of Zhou's fief and Confucius's birthplace.[46]

Like some of Shi Jie's other writings, the letter to Zhang Guilu reflects a sense of local pride at being a native of the Lu region, as well as a belief that the revival of the Way of the Sages will begin in Lu.[47] Indeed, Shi Jie equates the Way itself with Lu and analogizes heterodox ideologies to other parts of the world:

> The Way of the Sages is all in Lu. One can only get to see the Way of the Sages after arriving at Lu. But now people do not go to Lu and instead go to Qin, Chu, Wu, or Yue. Is that not going further from the Way of the Sages? Alas! There is worse, for there are also some who go to the barbarians, and that is even further from Lu. If one wants to return to Lu from Qin, Chu, Wu, and Yue, it is no more than a month's travel. That is how easy it is, but I have not seen anyone manage to do it. If one wants to return to Lu from the barbarians, he may travel for a season or even an entire year and still not arrive there. That is how hard it is, yet I have now seen one who could do it. The meaning of the *Annals* is that when the barbarians are barbarians, one regards them as barbarians, but when they are promoted to the level of the Central Lands, one regards them as [people of] the Central Lands. How much more so for [a barbarian] who can get to Lu by his own strength? I would like to give you, Mister Zhang, the name Guilu. Returning to Lu is how one honors the Way of the Sages. May you take encouragement from this [name]![48]

In this passage, Shi Jie quotes (or rather, misquotes) Han Yu's *Annals* formula from "Tracing the Way," but shifts its emphasis from warning about the danger of barbarization to asserting the possibility of barbarians becoming followers of the Way of the Sages. That assertion has nothing to do with literal barbarians, however: Zhang Guilu, the former Daoist, was Chinese and had almost certainly never traveled to foreign lands. One might read this as an expression of ethnicized orthodoxy: Laozi was a barbarian, so Daoism is barbaric and all Daoists are barbarians. But Shi Jie's point here seems to be more metaphorical: it emphasizes how rare and difficult it is for a Daoist priest to turn to Classicism by claiming that Daoism is as far from orthodoxy as the lands of the barbarians are from Lu.

There is a universalist implication in this message: just as Chinese people can lose their way and wind up among the barbarians, barbarians can also come to the Central Lands and become like the Chinese. But Shi Jie uses it for a very "safe" rhetorical purpose. Indeed, Shi Jie simultaneously raises the possibility of barbarians becoming civilized *and* represents geographical distance as a nearly insurmountable barrier to it. Nonetheless, the letter to

Zhang Guilu does give us cause to doubt the extent of Shi Jie's commitment to the central rhetorical assertion of "The Central Lands"—namely, that the Chinese-barbarian dichotomy has to be founded on immutable differences and physical separation, failing which the universe would descend into chaos and the Chinese would cease to be Chinese.

Perhaps the most surprising thing about the letter to Zhang Guilu is not that Shi Jie associated Daoism with barbarism for rhetorical purposes—we have already seen him doing so in "The Central Lands" and "Clarifying the Four Capital Offenses"—but rather that he seems to have been unwilling to stick to a single way of equating heterodoxy with barbarization. His letter to Sun Shi analogized the rise of the various heterodoxies to a burglar stealing the Way of the Sages and leaving it in the lands of the barbarians. The Zhang Guilu letter uses the metaphor of people trying to get to Lu (which symbolizes orthodoxy) but traveling a long way in the wrong direction and ending up among the barbarians (who symbolize heterodoxy). These metaphors are both inconsistent with "The Central Lands," which claims that two barbarians, the Buddha and Laozi, literally brought their teachings *into* the Central Lands. My sense of this inconsistency is that Shi Jie's pursuit of literary creativity—a quality that he generally lacked, especially compared to peers like Ouyang Xiu—made him averse to using a metaphor more than once, even if this weakened the coherence of his ideological message. Nonetheless, all three metaphors clearly share the same rhetorical objective of representing Classicism as the only legitimate ideology by making it synonymous with Chinese identity and equating all other ideologies with barbarism. The expanded rhetoric of ethnicized orthodoxy that Liu Kai had experimented with briefly thus became a recurring strategy in Shi Jie's polemics.

By the beginning of Shi Jie's teaching stint at Mount Tai, Sun Fu seems to have adopted his tendency of attacking all non-Classicist ideologies with the rhetoric of barbarism. Unlike Liu Kai and Shi Jie, however, Sun is not known to have claimed that Daoism came from the barbarians; Sun also differed from them in employing the rhetoric of barbarization and the rhetoric of bestialization in tandem. In 1038, Sun Fu wrote an inscription for a temple to Mencius that the prefect Kong Daofu (ca. 985–ca. 1039), a descendant of Confucius, had built in Zou county (Mencius's birthplace). Whereas Mencius (in *Mencius* 3B.9) accused Yang Zhu and Mozi and their followers of descending to the level of animals by denying their rulers and fathers, Sun Fu represents their pernicious influence using the metaphor of a mass migration of Chinese to the lands of the barbarians:

[The teachings of Yang Zhu and Mozi were] driving all the people of the realm to abandon the Central Lands and go to the barbarians; there could be no calamity greater than this, and Mencius was the only one who could save them from it. Thus Mencius rose up in a passionate rage and loudly explained the doctrines of Yao, Shun, Yu, Tang, King Wen, King Wu, the Duke of Zhou, and Confucius. He drove out and exterminated [the teachings of Yang Zhu and Mozi] and left them with no descendants. He picked up all the people of the realm from among the barbarians and put them back in the Central Lands, so that our Way of the Sages would shine brightly and not fall into ruin.[49]

A few lines down, Sun Fu switches to a metaphor of bestialization, claiming: "If [the teachings of] Yang Zhu and Mozi had continued running rampant and Mencius had not arisen, then all the people of the realm would have become animals."[50]

On another occasion, Shi Jie wrote to Sun Fu informing him that Kong Daofu had recently added portraits of Mencius, Xunzi, Yang Xiong, Wang Tong, and Han Yu to the Confucius temple in Qufu. Since Sun had come to accept Shi Jie's argument that all five of the men thus honored were true followers of the Way of Confucius, he was elated and wrote a letter to commend Kong.[51] Sun Fu explained in his letter that these five worthies were born in different times because Heaven knew that there would be "empty, absurd, weird, seductive, and strange teachings bringing disorder to the Way of our Confucius" in every age. Here, Sun again conflates barbarization and bestialization as consequences of heterodoxy, this time in the very same sentence: "If a new worthy did not arise as soon as the previous worthy died and shield [the Way of Confucius] with his wings, [the Way] would have been obscured and fallen into ruin. Once it was obscured and fell into ruin, then everyone in the world would have become barbarians and the people would have become animals. In that case, the contributions of these five worthies were great indeed!"[52]

Sun Fu's most famous polemical essay, the undated "The Humiliation of the Classicists" (Ruru), argues that it is an unparalleled humiliation for Classicists that they have allowed Daoism and Buddhism to "bring disorder to the teachings of our sages with the doctrines (*fa*) of the barbarians (Yi-Di) and the philosophers (*zhuzi*)."[53] I do not think we can assume that Sun Fu intends the pairing of Yi-Di and *zhuzi* to mean "barbarian philosophers." More likely, Yi-Di refers to the Buddha and *zhuzi* to Laozi, since the category *zhuzi* was typically applied to Chinese thinkers of the Eastern Zhou period.[54] But Sun does go on to claim that if not for Mencius's attacks on Yang Zhu and Mozi, Yang Xiong's resistance to the Legalists, and Han Yu's rejection of Buddhism and Daoism, "then all the people of the realm would have become barbarians."[55] This sweeping statement, self-consciously echoing the famous rhetorical question in "Tracing the Way," again fits squarely with Guwen radicalism's tendency to represent all non-Classicist teachings as barbarizing.

GUWEN MODERATES: OUYANG XIU AND LI GOU

In a famously testy exchange of letters in 1035, Ouyang Xiu chided Shi Jie for using a deliberately eccentric style of calligraphy and identified this as a symptom of a larger problem: Shi was "fond of being different in order to claim superiority" and "haughtily making [himself] different for the sake of shocking the people of this age." To Ouyang's mind, such a pursuit of novelty and nonconformity for its own sake was contrary to Confucius's preference for moderation over extremes. He also found Shi Jie's essays to contain "excessively high self-praise, excessively harsh criticism of the present age, and arguments that seem not to look into the sources of things deeply enough"—the last of these perhaps partly a reference to Shi's attribution of foreign origins to Daoism in "The Central Lands."[56]

Shi Jie's reply to Ouyang Xiu claimed that his strange calligraphy was simply a result of poor technique, not a desire to be different. But Shi also effectively confirmed Ouyang's diagnoses of egotism and rhetorical excess by asserting that his true claims to difference lay in following the Way of the Sages in an age when everyone else was a Buddhist or a Daoist, in writing in the language of the Classics in an age when everyone else was writing like Yang Yi, and in attacking Buddhism, Daoism, and parallel prose with all his might when no one else even tried. Shi Jie claimed that while Ouyang Xiu was fixated on superficial matters of calligraphic style, *he* was devoting himself to the far weightier matter of teaching the Way of the Sages.[57]

Ouyang Xiu could not let Shi Jie's stubborn self-importance go unchallenged. His second letter took Shi Jie to task for claiming to be the world's only true Classicist: "Buddhism and Daoism are practiced by deluded people, while overly embellished literary composition is practiced by shallow people. How do you know that in this age there are no other enlightened, sincere, honest, and upright noble men who do not practice these? By thinking you are different from everyone else, you assume that there are no noble men like yourself in the realm."[58] Ouyang was expressing indignation at Shi's refusal to recognize him and other Guwen writers as champions of the Way of the Sages and the Guwen style.[59]

Ouyang Xiu's literary talent and capacity for original thinking exceeded Shi Jie's by far, but none of Shi's extant works indicates that he ever gave Ouyang the respect that the latter felt he deserved. Instead, he simply chose to ignore Ouyang's second letter. In contrast, Ouyang Xiu's respect for Shi Jie's fearless outspokenness seems to have grown over time, particularly after both men ended up on the losing end in imperial court politics. On the occasion of the moving of Shi Jie's tomb to his ancestral home in 1065, Ouyang Xiu even wrote a highly generous epitaph that interpreted the most eccentric and controversial aspects of his personality as his greatest strengths.[60] Nonetheless, Ouyang Xiu consistently differed markedly from Shi Jie in literary taste. When teaching at the Imperial University in 1042–44, Shi Jie popularized a gratuitously eccentric, ostentatious, abstruse, and long-winded form of prose writing that came to be known as the Imperial University style (*Taixue ti*). This style dominated the Guwen revival until the famous *jinshi* examinations of 1057, in which Ouyang Xiu, as chief examiner, rejected all candidates who wrote in it and passed candidates who shared his preference for a restrained, dignified style—most notably Zeng Gong (1019–1083) and the brothers Su Shi (1037–1101) and Su Zhe (1039–1112). Ouyang Xiu thus erased Shi Jie's literary legacy and replaced it with his own, to the point where only a handful of fragmentary examples of the Imperial University style are still extant—preserved, tellingly, in works praising Ouyang's effort at eradicating it.[61]

The differences between Ouyang and Shi went beyond prose stylistics, however. If Shi Jie (like Liu Kai) strove to be even more radical than Han Yu in his ideological rhetoric, Ouyang Xiu's attitude toward heterodoxy was significantly more moderate than Han Yu's. Ouyang Xiu's 1042 essay "On Fundamentals" (Benlun) shows that he disagreed with Shi Jie's demand for state action to prohibit and suppress Buddhism and Daoism—a demand directly inspired by the conclusion of Han Yu's "Tracing the Way."[62] Ouyang Xiu took direct aim at Han Yu's calls for the state to burn Buddhist sutras and close monasteries down, arguing that such extreme measures were hardly necessary and were likely to be counterproductive. Chinese civilization's decline after the Zhou dynasty was the fundamental cause of Buddhism's appeal to the Chinese people, rather than vice versa (as Shi Jie would have it); it therefore followed that the only way to achieve victory over Buddhism was to "restore the fundamentals" by gradually reviving classical rites and customs, beginning at the local level, and by teaching people about the benefits of ritual propriety and moral duty. In passages that read like implicit jibes at Liu Kai and Shi Jie, Ouyang pointed out that no individual spouting fiery anti-Buddhist polemics or indulging in military metaphors stood any real chance of driving out a long-entrenched religion; moreover, if the government attempted to prohibit Buddhism and impose ritual propriety and moral duty without educating the people, this would merely frighten them away.[63]

"On Fundamentals" contains two other conspicuous subversions of the kind of anti-Buddhist polemic favored by Han Yu and Shi Jie. The first of these is an argument that many people follow Buddhism, despite its unnatural denial of family bonds, because its emphasis on good works appeals to the innate goodness of human nature. Therefore, Classicism can compete with Buddhism by showing people how to do good through the practice of ritual propriety and moral duty.[64] This flatly contradicts Han Yu's depiction (in "Tracing the Way") of the Buddhist pursuit of Nirvana as inherently selfish, as well as Shi Jie's claim (in "The Central Lands") that people follow Buddhism only out of a desire for heaven and a fear of hell.[65] Whereas Han Yu and Shi Jie assumed that people practiced Buddhism for motives fundamentally different from their own motivation for following the Way of the Sages, Ouyang argues that Buddhists and Classicists are driven by similar ideals.

The same optimistic attitude toward the Buddhists enables Ouyang Xiu to make the second subversion: namely, rejecting the alarmist rhetoric of a contemporary Chinese world being barbarized by Buddhism and even Daoism. Ouyang acknowledged that "the Buddha was a barbarian (Yi-Di)" and that Buddhism had "plagued the Central Lands for more than a thousand years."[66] But whereas Shi Jie's anti-Buddhist and anti-Daoist arguments were framed rather clumsily in a rhetoric of ethnicized orthodoxy modeled on Han Yu's, Ouyang Xiu saw no point in equating heterodoxy with barbarization and chose not to make Buddhism's foreign origin the rhetorical crux of his opposition to it. Instead, he argued that Buddhism's influence was far less dangerous to Chinese civilization than the barbarian incursions of Confucius's day, and thus much easier to counteract:

> In the distant past, the barbarians lived all mixed up throughout the Nine Provinces—there were the so-called Rong of Xú, the White Di, the Man of Jing (i.e., Chu), and the Yi of the Huai River, for example. After the Three Dynasties [of Xia, Shang, and Zhou] declined, [barbarians] like these all invaded the Central Lands. Thus the Qin, as western Rong, seized and

occupied the Eastern Zhou capital, and the rulers of the Wu and Chu states illegitimately assumed the title of king.[67] The *Annals* speaks of [the men of Zhu] using the Master of Zeng [as a sacrifice],[68] the *Zuo Tradition* records the incident of a man with his hair untied at the Yi River,[69] and Confucius, too, thought himself fortunate to not be folding his robe to the left. At that time, even though Buddhism had not arrived yet, how much longer could this have gone on before the [people of the] Central Lands became barbarians?

Here, Ouyang Xiu ingeniously alludes to Han Yu's rhetorical question about barbarization, but does so to make a point exactly contrary to Han's attempt at representing Buddhism as a barbarizing religion:

> We can know from this that when the Way of the True King was obscured and humaneness and moral duty were abandoned, then the barbarians became a threat. When Confucius wrote the *Annals*, he used it to assert the superiority of the Central Lands and the inferiority of the barbarians, and the Way of the True King became clear again. Today, the people of the Nine Provinces (i.e., the Central Lands) all fold their robes to the right and wear caps and sashes. The plague that we face is nothing more than Buddhism. The way to victory over it is not some lofty or impracticable theory; the only problem is that we neglect to use it.[70]

Ouyang's observation that the Chinese of his day "all fold their robes to the right and wear caps and sashes" implicitly negates Shi Jie's far-fetched claims that the Chinese are all dressing in barbarian clothing because of Buddhism and Daoism.[71] Whereas Shi's rhetorical strategy was to represent the purportedly barbarizing effect of Buddhism as a tangible reality by applying it to such visible aspects as food, clothing, and architecture, Ouyang recognized this as a blatant misrepresentation of reality and preferred to relate the idea of barbarization to actual invasion and conquest by barbarians—a threat that he clearly believed the Song dynasty did not face.[72]

Ouyang Xiu's moderate inclinations and rejection of ethnicized orthodoxy were shared by Li Gou, a highly original thinker who, at the time of Shi Jie's death in 1045, was just beginning to achieve some renown as a teacher and writer in Jiangxi after failing the examinations twice.[73] In one of thirty essays written as a literary portfolio for the decree examination of 1042, Li criticized Han Yu's "Tracing the Way" recommendation for state persecution of heterodox ideologies as "too violent in its language and not gradual [enough] in its [approach to] driving out [Buddhism and Daoism]."[74] In a commemorative inscription composed for a local school in 1047, he argued that any edifying moral teachings in Buddhism could already be found in a few lines of the *Record of Rites* and the Ten Wings of the *Changes*. If one had to look further, one could turn to Laozi or Zhuangzi. What need was there to "hastily put on a ritual cap and grovel before a barbarian man"? The problem was simply that the literati had neglected their responsibility to educate people in Classicism, forcing the ignorant to turn to Buddhism for spiritual and moral guidance.[75] This self-critical argument—reminiscent of "On Fundamentals"—implied that although Daoism (represented by Lao-Zhuang philosophy) was inferior to Classicism, it was at least not barbaric. It also made no suggestion that whoever groveled before the Buddha, a "barbarian," would turn into a barbarian too.

Li Gou's relationship to Buddhism was complex and ambivalent, making him vulnerable to criticism for being soft on heterodoxy. In an indignant letter, his cousin Huang Hanjie criticized him for implying in the local school inscription that Buddhist doctrines had something in common with the sages' teachings. Huang was even more annoyed that Li had written commemorative inscriptions for several Buddhist monasteries, one of which again asserted that the Classicists' own failure to educate the people in classical ritual was to blame for Buddhism's appeal. In response, Li Gou insisted that he had already established his anti-Buddhist credentials in the 1030s by writing essays critical of Buddhism and had no need to prove them further.[76]

Various explanations have been proposed for Li Gou's willingness to write inscriptions for Buddhist monasteries despite being critical of Buddhism. Chang Ching-chüan argues that the inscriptions were "all a form of social courtesy in which [Li Gou] had no choice but to praise [the inscriptions' subjects]." Li Chenggui argues that Li Gou objected to Buddhist monasteries' economic and social effects but was open-minded enough to recognize Buddhism's benefits as a means of moral self-cultivation. More persuasive is Mark Halperin's argument that Li Gou accepted Buddhist monasticism's moral legitimacy and, like numerous other Song literati, "used commemorations for Buddhist establishments as forums for the critical discussion of social ills" and "to express [his] displeasure with contemporary politics and to chastise and goad [his] colleagues."[77] But Li likely was also forced to compose inscriptions and epitaphs as a source of income after failing to pass the civil service examinations for the second time in 1042. Buddhist monasteries were one of the largest markets for literati-authored inscriptions, and Li, in his impoverished state, could not afford to refuse their requests.

Apart from Li Gou's relatively moderate stance toward Buddhism, his lack of interest in equating the Chinese-barbarian dichotomy to the struggle between orthodoxy and heterodoxy may also be linked to a different and even more unconventional interpretation of barbarism that he had developed in 1043 for a short essay titled "The Enemy Threat" (Dihuan). The essay belongs to a new portfolio of Li's writings that he submitted to Fan Zhongyan (989–1052) and Fu Bi (1004–1083) in the hope of earning a recommendation to government office after failing to pass the examination of 1042.[78] Not surprisingly, Li's argument is a subtle endorsement of the reforms that Fan and Fu were then implementing with the support of Guwen figures like Ouyang Xiu and Shi Jie. But it is also a response to the first war between the Song and the Xi Xia, which had recently ended with humiliating defeats for the Song armies and thus given a sense of urgency to the reform effort.[79]

"The Enemy Threat" begins with a provocative challenge to conventional ethnocultural understandings of the Chinese-barbarian dichotomy:

> Who are the barbarians (Yi), and who are the Chinese (Xia)? I say: When we speak of barbarians, how could we be speaking only of leaving hair untied and wearing animal skins? When we speak of the Chinese, how could we be speaking only of wearing robes, caps, skirts, and shoes? The difference lies only in moral power (*de*), punishments, policies, and governance. If one cultivates moral power diligently, applies punishments justly, and has good policies and effective governance, then one may be a barbarian but could just as well be called Chinese. If the opposite is true, then can one still be called Chinese?[80]

Li Gou's argument is that moral superiority and good governance, not customs relating to dress or other aspects of material culture, define the essence of Chineseness. Theoretically, then, it is possible for barbarians to attain Chineseness without changing their way of dressing, just as it is possible for the Chinese to descend into barbarism while still dressing in Chinese style. In this, Li Gou differs from Ouyang Xiu, whose "On Fundamentals" assumed from the persistence of certain clothing styles that Chinese civilization remained essentially Chinese despite the influence of Buddhism. But Li Gou's interpretation of barbarism also has nothing in common with Shi Jie's. "The Enemy Threat" directly contradicts the beginning of "The Central Lands" by denying any relevance to the descriptions of barbarian dress in texts like "Kingly Institutions." Departing from a discursive tradition going back to classical times (recall the anecdote about Xin You), Li Gou effectively claims that how one dresses and arranges one's hair says nothing about how Chinese one is.

Li Gou next plays on the ironic fact that although the name of the Xi Xia state was derived from Xiazhou, a Tang-era prefecture in the Ordos region, Xia can also mean "Chinese" in the context of the Chinese-barbarian dichotomy:

> Some foolish Classicists boastfully claim, "*They* are barbarians and *we* are Xia (Chinese)," but they do not say, "We must reform ourselves." When we have reformed ourselves to the point of possessing superior moral power, laws, policies, and governance, then we will be justified in saying, "The Xia (Chinese) are superior to the barbarians." This is what is meant by "Know your enemy and know yourself, and in a hundred battles you will not be in peril."[81] They (i.e., the Xi Xia) want to drain our country of its wealth and reduce our people to penury [by provoking us into war], but if we respond with a frugal use of resources, then our country can instead be enriched and our people given lives of ease. If we still cannot do this, then we will have fallen for their tricks. Alas! [Today's] barbarians and Xia (Chinese) are not the barbarians and Xia (Chinese) of antiquity. It would be best if we "first make ourselves unbeatable, and then wait until they are beatable."[82] Otherwise, disasters would occur daily, and would we not then become a laughingstock to You Yu?[83]

Li's message is clear: Chinese superiority is not an immutable absolute, nor is it demonstrated through victory in war. Instead, it is founded on the ability to improve and enrich the country through political reform, failing which a Chinese state simply lays itself open to You Yu's mockery of "rites, music, and laws" as sources of moral corruption and social disorder.

Unfortunately, we know nothing about the reception that "The Enemy Threat" received, except that the essay portfolio to which it belonged failed to open a path to officialdom for Li Gou. Nor did it have any perceptible influence on later discourses on Chineseness and barbarism—unlike Ouyang Xiu, Li Gou was largely forgotten as a thinker and writer until the twentieth century. "The Enemy Threat," in particular, has only very recently received attention from intellectual historians.[84] Nonetheless, the cases of Ouyang Xiu and Li Gou show that the Guwen radicals' version of ethnicized orthodoxy did not represent the Guwen revival as a whole and that even the Guwen moderates did not display a monolithic understanding of what the essence of Chineseness was.

In fact, Guwen radicalism also failed to exert lasting influence on Song intellectual discourse relating to the Chinese-barbarian dichotomy. By the 1070s, the more creative aspects of that discourse were instead defined by the rhetoric of ethnocentric moralism, which none of the Guwen radicals had employed in their polemics. Ironically, Sun Fu may have played a pivotal role in initiating this shift by stimulating the Northern Song literati's interest in using *Annals* exegesis to frame their political and philosophical arguments as expressions of Confucius's own values. Sun's interpretations of the Chinese-barbarian dichotomy as an *Annals* commentator had strikingly little in common with his writings as a Guwen radical, as he and other eleventh-century Guwen writers identified immorality, not heterodoxy, as the root of barbarism in their interpretations of the *Annals*.

CHAPTER 5

Ideas of Barbarization in Eleventh-Century *Annals* Exegesis

B ESIDES the revival of Guwen as a literary style and an ideological position, the eleventh century saw another revival of a ninth-century trend: the writing of new commentaries on the *Annals*. This appears to have begun with Sun Fu, who is known to have written his commentary *Uncovering the Intricacies of Respecting the King in the Annals* (Chunqiu zunwang fawei) before August 1040.[1] Although some scholars have argued that *Uncovering the Intricacies* did not circulate widely before Sun Fu's death in 1057, Sun did have the opportunity to deliver lectures on *Annals* exegesis to thousands of young literati at the Imperial University in 1042–47 and again in 1054/55–57, and he almost certainly drew the contents of those lectures from his commentary.[2]

As an *Annals* interpreter, Sun Fu resembled Dan Zhu, Zhao Kuang, and Lu Chun in claiming a special insight into the language of the text that allowed—indeed required—him to dispense with the *Gongyang*, *Guliang*, and *Zuo Tradition* interpretations alike, not to mention the subcommentaries to these texts by He Xiu, Fan Ning, and Du Yu. Sun was not the only one advocating such an iconoclastic approach at the time: it appears to have been shared among the leading members of the Guwen revival. In a series of essays written in 1037, Ouyang Xiu argued forcefully that there were instances in which all three traditional commentaries contradicted the *Annals* itself; in such cases, one should reject the authority of all three commentaries and defer to the higher authority of the *Annals*.³ Shi Jie, too, dismissed all existing classical commentaries as worthless: in his 1033 letter to Sun Shi, he argued that their mutual contradictions rendered scholars in search of the Way as lost and confused as blind men in dark rooms; in another essay, he claimed that the traditional commentaries distorted the Classics like silverfish chewing holes in books.⁴ In fact, Sun Fu's lectures at the Mount Tai Academy and the Imperial University may have inspired Shi Jie to write his own commentary titled *Expounding the Annals* (Chunqiu shuo), only some eighty-four fragments of which are now extant.⁵

Whereas Dan Zhu, Zhao Kuang, and Lu Chun did not see the *Annals* as a text with a central message, Sun Fu aimed at demonstrating that Confucius wrote the *Annals* as a lament over the Zhou kings' declining authority. Sun believed this was the root of the political anarchy, moral degeneracy, and barbarian incursions that plagued the Eastern Zhou period—hence the phrase "respecting the king" in the commentary's title. A corollary to that theme was the argument that the rise of a sage-king was the only true solution to the Zhou decline: powerful lords who acted as hegemons were only usurping the king's prerogatives and making matters worse. Given this attitude toward hegemons, Sun Fu felt compelled to explain both to himself and to his readers why Confucius appears to express approval of hegemons in two cases when they formed and led military alliances against the rising power of Chu. These two occasions were the Shaoling peace covenant of 656 BCE, which followed Lord Huan of Qi's (r. 685–643 BCE) eight-state expedition against Chu, and the Battle of Chengpu in 632 BCE, at which a four-state alliance led by Lord Wen of Jin (r. 636–628 BCE) defeated Chu and its client states. In both cases, the hegemons are referred to as princes (*hou*), whereas disapproving language would have referred to them as "men" or by the names of their states.

The *Gongyang Commentary* interprets Confucius's attitude toward the Shaoling covenant as one of unqualified admiration for Lord Huan's success at intimidating Chu into proposing a truce, thus averting the further expansion of Chu influence into the Central Lands: "The southern Yi and northern Di had joined forces, and the fate of the Central Lands hung by a thread. Lord Huan saved the Central Lands and repelled the barbarians (*jiu Zhongguo rang Yi-Di*), finally bringing Jing (i.e., Chu) to submission. This was an achievement worthy of a true king."⁶ Sun Fu, on the other hand, found it difficult to accept that Confucius would approve of Lord Huan trying to play the role of a "true king." In Sun's opinion, Confucius usually demoted Lord Huan for being interested less in "saving the Central Lands" than in "exploiting the name of respecting the Zhou [dynasty] to expand his territory."[7] Yet in the *Annals* record of events leading up to the Shaoling covenant, Sun could find no sign of Lord Huan being denigrated or demoted. Citing Confucius's praise of Guan Zhong in *Analects* 14.17, he concluded that Confucius did approve of Lord Huan's actions at Shaoling, but only because the danger Chu posed to Chinese civilization was so great that the need for "repelling the barbarians and saving the Central Lands" momentarily outweighed the hegemon's political illegitimacy. Confucius thus "made a special exception and approved of Lord Huan" in this case.[8]

Sun Fu applied the same argument to Lord Wen's victory over Chu at Chengpu, stressing the magnitude of this achievement by exaggerating the severity of the barbarian threat:

> Alas! After moving the capital to the east, the Zhou dynasty was weak and the barbarians of the four quarters seized the opportunity to bring disorder to the Central Lands. They seized the territory of the former kings and cut down and killed its people, invading and harassing, raiding and destroying. The [entire land within the] four seas was in turmoil; [the civilization of] rites and music and robes and caps was at its nadir. That this came to be was not the fault of the barbarians of the four quarters; it was because the Central Lands had lost the Way. . . . If Lord Huan of Qi and Lord Wen of Jin had not arisen in succession, making a covenant with [the Chu minister] Qu Wan at Shaoling and defeating [the Chu general] Dechen at Chengpu, pursuing them, driving them out, punishing them, and cutting them down, how much longer could things have gone on before the [people of the] Central Lands all became barbarians?[9]

We have already seen Sun Fu borrowing the rhetoric of barbarization from "Tracing the Way" and expanding its targets to include all non-Classicist ideologies in his letter to Kong Daofu and "The Humiliation of the Classicists." Here, he applies it to a very different context of literal invasion and conquest by barbarians—essentially turning it into a version of the more ambiguous *Analects* 14.17, which only hints at the idea of barbarization through a metaphor of sartorial change.

As we have seen, Ouyang Xiu's slightly later "On Fundamentals" made a similar move of equating the meaning of *Analects* 14.17 with that of Han Yu's famous rhetorical question about barbarization. Another interesting similarity to "On Fundamentals" can be found in Sun Fu's assertion that Zhou political decline was to blame for the barbarian invasions, not vice versa. In other words, the very need to "save the Central Lands and repel the barbarians" was an unfortunate consequence of the Chinese "losing the Way" by failing to "respect the king." It is important to note that the phrase "respecting the king and repelling the barbarians" (*zunwang rangyi*)—commonly misidentified as a key slogan of Guwen writers and *Annals* commentators in both the late Tang and the Northern Song—never appears in Sun Fu's commentary or, for that matter, in any Chinese text produced before the seventeenth century.[10] It would have made little sense for Sun Fu to use such a phrase, since he did not perceive "respecting the king" and "repelling the barbarians" to be simultaneous and equal priorities. To his mind, a Chinese civilization that respected the king would simply have no barbarian threats to repel.[11]

Sun Fu and Ouyang Xiu differ in one significant and telling aspect when it comes to interpreting Confucius's approach to recording the deeds of Lord Huan and Lord Wen. In the original 1040 version of his essay "On Legitimate Dynasties" (Zhengtong lun), Ouyang argues that when it came to writing about Lords Huan and Wen in the *Annals*, Confucius "approved of their actions in reality but wrote in the language of disapproval because he believed that while their achievements were commendable, the Way did not permit him to approve of them."[12] Sun Fu argues the exact opposite and is thus even harder on the hegemons: Confucius used the language of approval in relation to Lord Huan's deeds at Shaoling and Lord Wen's deeds at Chengpu because they averted the barbarization of the Central Lands, but his approval was mixed with deep disappointment and sadness over the fact that these deeds were not performed by kings.[13] One can see why some eleventh-century readers of *Uncovering the Intricacies* criticized its exceptionally negative interpretations of the hegemons and lords, likening it to the "Legalist" Qin statesman Shang Yang's (390–338 BCE) use of harsh laws and severe penalties to achieve political centralization.[14]

To Sun Fu's mind, the two great hegemons' success in saving the Central Lands from barbarization was not only morally illegitimate but also merely momentary, because it failed to halt the political and moral decline that made the Chinese states vulnerable to invasion and domination by barbarian states like Chu. At the end of his commentary, Sun addresses the question of why Confucius stopped writing the *Annals* in 481 BCE, after recording the capture by hunters of a rare and auspicious beast called the *qilin* that was believed to appear only when a sage ruler was on the throne. In Sun's view, the crucial event that led Confucius to stop writing was not the capture of the *qilin* (as the *Gongyang* tradition believed) but rather the Huangchi conference of 482 BCE, at which the ruler of Wu gained hegemony over the Central Lands: "[Confucius] could still bear to speak of [events] before [the capture of the *qilin*] because [the rulers of] Jin and Lu were [at least] present at the Huangchi conference.[15] He could not bear to speak of [events] after that because the lords became passive, the authority to issue commands lay in the hands of Wu, the Central Lands no longer existed, and all the world's [people] became barbarians."[16] In other words, the Chinese-barbarian dichotomy ceased to hold any meaning after the Huangchi conference, since the lords had submitted to the leadership of Wu, an inferior barbarian state. Since, in Sun Fu's view, the *Annals* "regards the Central Lands as superior and the barbarians as inferior," the only way for Confucius to maintain this principle of Chinese superiority after Wu's rise to hegemony was to stop recording the history of the Chinese states altogether.[17] At the same time, Sun emphasized that Huangchi was merely the end of a long, slippery slope that began with lords ceasing to respect the Zhou king's authority as Son of Heaven (Tianzi):

> The Son of Heaven's loss of political authority began from the eastward move of the capital [to Luoyang], while the lords' loss of political authority began from the Juliang conference [in 557 BCE].[18] . . . From the Shen conference [in 538 BCE] to the capture of the *qilin* [in 481 BCE], the barbarians took turns to hold political authority over the realm and responsibility for the affairs of the Central Lands.[19] The sage-kings' laws and institutions, [the civilization of] rites and music and robes and caps, and the customs and methods of governance inherited from the past were all at a nadir. Having come to this point, the fall of the Central Lands was complete.[20]

Ouyang Xiu's view of the matter was significantly more optimistic: recall his claim in "On Fundamentals" that Confucius "used [the *Annals*] to assert the superiority of the Central Lands and the inferiority of the barbarians, and the Way of the True King became clear again," thus saving the Central Lands from the fate of barbarization.[21]

We have seen that by 1038, Sun Fu was following Han Yu's example by equating ideological heterodoxy with barbarism in polemical writings like "The Humiliation of the Classicists" and the inscription for Kong Daofu's Mencius temple. Yet one searches in vain for any traces of ethnicized orthodoxy in *Uncovering the Intricacies*. Sun Fu does not use his commentary to issue polemics against Buddhism and Daoism, and does not even follow Han Yu in using the *Annals* as evidence for barbarian ritual's barbarizing effects on the Chinese. As we saw in chapter 1, Lu Chun interpreted the changing titles of the Qǐ rulers in the *Annals* as a "subtle message" that they were Chinese who had become (or were becoming) barbarians as a result of using barbarian rites. Sun Fu, however, proposed another interpretation that was still related to ritual but grounded in the theme of "respecting the king," rather than barbarization: "This is probably because a sage-king had not risen and the lords acted as they saw fit, not observing consistent standards in their diplomatic visits and conferences. These three states were lacking in resources and therefore often unable to perform the full ritual. They sometimes made diplomatic visits using the ritual protocol of a prince, and at other times attended conferences using the ritual protocol of a liege or a master. Therefore Confucius recorded these [inconsistencies] so as to show their [ritual] disorder."[22] Similarly, Lu Chun and Zhao Kuang apparently agreed that the demotion of the Zhu, Mou, and Ge rulers to "men" in 697 BCE was due to their barbarization via the use of barbarian rites, but Sun Fu chose to follow He Xiu's *Gongyang* subcommentary in attributing their demotion to the unprincipled act of condoning Lord Huan's regicidal/fratricidal usurpation of power in Lu.[23] Unlike the *Gongyang Commentary* and He Xiu, moreover, Sun did not use the expression "[Confucius] regarded them as barbarians" (*Yi-Di zhi*) to characterize this demotion.

There are six instances in *Uncovering the Intricacies* where Sun Fu did use the phrase "[Confucius] regarded them as barbarians" (*Yi-Di zhi / Di zhi*) or "[Confucius] called them barbarians" (*Yi-Di cheng zhi*). These can be divided into four categories:[24]

1. Three cases of Chinese states aligning themselves with Chu while attacking other states. These include Zheng attacking Xǔ in 588 BCE, Jin attacking Xianyu while Chu was attacking Xǔ in 530 BCE, and six client states of Chu attacking Wu in 519 BCE. Sun Fu borrowed these interpretations from He Xiu's *Gongyang* subcommentary, the *Guliang Commentary*, and the *Gongyang Commentary*, respectively. But Sun is unique in characterizing the Jin ruler as following "the way of the barbarians" (*Yi-Di zhi dao*) by "attacking the Central Lands in concert with Chu."[25]

2. One case of Chu itself being demoted back to full barbarism for attacking Chinese states. Sun argues that in 666 BCE, the Chu ruler is

referred to only by the province name "Jing," stripping him of a prior editorial promotion (in 671 BCE) to "a man of Jing," in order to "again regard him as a barbarian" for reverting to aggression against Chinese states. This argument seems to be inspired by Fan Ning's *Guliang* subcommentary, which interprets this case as a demotion but does not use the expression "[Confucius] regarded him as a barbarian."[26]

3. One case of excessive aggression in war. This involves the Qin ruler being demoted (by being referred to as "Qin") for attacking Jin in 617 BCE despite the latter's war-weariness. This interpretation appears to be derived from He Xiu, but Sun Fu is again unique in calling the Qin ruler's behavior "the way of the barbarians" (*Yi-Di zhi dao*).[27]

4. One case of usurping the Zhou king's prerogatives. This involves the first mention of the Wu state in the *Annals*: Sun argues that Confucius refers to its ruler as "Wu," rather than "the Master of Wu," in order to condemn him as barbaric for adopting the title "king" in 584 BCE. This interpretation has no known precedent.[28]

The first and second of these categories relate to the geopolitical threat that Chu posed to the Central Lands and the Chinese states' lack of solidarity in resisting it. The third and fourth categories involve acts seen as barbaric due to their immorality.

Other passages in the commentary suggest that Sun Fu regarded the fourth category as particularly heinous and unforgivable, in line with his emphasis on "respecting the king." After noting that the *Annals* eventually promotes the Chu and Wu rulers "because they gradually became like the Central Lands: they participated in conferences and covenants with the lords, and learned enough ritual to send embassies to the court [of Lu]," he dismisses such "civilizing" improvements as inadequate grounds for promotion out of barbarism, because the rulers of both states illegitimately called themselves kings: "The immorality of the Wu and Chu rulers in [usurping the royal title] arrogantly and illegitimately was an unpardonable offense, for which it would have been fitting to be demoted throughout the *Annals* period. Confucius did not demote them throughout the *Annals* period because he lamented that a sage-king had not risen and that the Central Lands had lost the Way to an extreme degree."[29]

Sun's commentary on the Huangchi conference, after repeating the above passage almost verbatim, adds: "If a sage-king had risen, the institutions of government had been restored, and all things had been brought to order, then everyone in the Nine Provinces and the four seas would have come [to submit], [speaking unfamiliar languages that required] several rounds of translation and with their children strapped to their backs.[30] How could there have been this situation of [barbarians] going on the rampage, [usurping the royal title] arrogantly and illegitimately, indulging freely in warfare, and assuming leadership at covenant-making conferences without royal sanction? That is Confucius's deeper message."[31] Sun thus reads Confucius's generosity to barbarian rulers as a lament that these rulers could not be faulted for defying the Zhou king's authority, because the Central Lands states had failed to set a good moral example that would move the barbarians to submit to the king.[32] It is hard not to read this interpretation as a comment on the geopolitical situation in 1038–40, when the Song court was debating whether to go to war to punish the Xi Xia ruler's defiant adoption of the imperial title, but it remains unclear when this section of *Uncovering the Intricacies* was composed.

In summary, Sun Fu's interpretation of barbarization in the *Annals* combined a geopolitical interpretation, an interpretation based on ethics in warfare, and an interpretation that emphasized legitimate political authority and loyalty. One could be barbarized as a consequence of being conquered by barbarians, aligning militarily with barbarians against the Central Lands, accepting the hegemony of barbarians, behaving barbarically in war, or (in the case of Wu) committing the "unpardonable offense" of rebelling against one's ruler and claiming to be king. Most of these interpretations were fairly conventional, and even the last scenario was not entirely new: Chen An and Cheng Yan had already identified disloyalty and rebellion as the true essence of barbarism, and the *Guliang Commentary* claimed that Confucius regarded Chu as a barbarian state because it was the first to rebel whenever the Zhou king's authority was weak.[33] But Sun Fu was the first to argue—perhaps with a contemporary parallel to the Xi Xia in mind—that Chu and Wu did not deserve to be promoted out of barbarism no matter how much they "became like the Central Lands," since the true source of their barbarism was not ritual or custom but rather an immoral spirit of rebellion.

INTERPRETATIONS OF BARBARISM IN LIU CHANG'S *ANNALS* COMMENTARIES

A very different but no less innovative approach to the barbarism of Chu and Wu can be seen in the work of another important *Annals* commentator of the eleventh century, Liu Chang (1019–1068). Liu authored five works of *Annals* exegesis, three of which are extant, and was already an influential scholar in the Song capital in the 1040s, when he was not yet thirty.[34] Indeed, he began writing Guwen prose in 1033, at the age of fourteen, and became a good friend of Ouyang Xiu but snubbed an opportunity to study under Sun Fu and Shi Jie at the Imperial University.[35] Like Ouyang Xiu, Liu was a polymath whose curiosity about every branch of learning known to humanity probably made him unreceptive to the Guwen radicals' narrow ideological exclusivism. He was even more omnivorous in his interests than Ouyang, as seen from his familiarity with *Laozi's Classic of the Way and Its Power*, the *Zhuangzi*, and the Buddhist sutras, as well as dabbling in geography, astronomy, divination, and medicine.[36]

Liu Chang's interpretive framework relating to "barbarizing" demotions in the *Annals* draws heavily upon earlier commentaries in a highly eclectic manner. For example, he agrees with Sun Fu that Confucius regarded the Qin ruler as a barbarian for violating the rules of warfare and "acting as a barbarian" (*yi Yi-Di weizhi*) when attacking Jin in 617 BCE.[37] But Liu also differs from Sun in applying the very same interpretation to the Zheng ruler's demotion for attacking Xǔ in 588 BCE and the Jin ruler's demotion for attacking Xianyu in 530 BCE, calling these acts perfidious.[38] As we have seen, Sun Fu attributed these barbarizing demotions to the Zheng and Jin rulers' collusion with a barbarian state, Chu, rather than their perfidy. These interpretations were apparently derived from the *Gongyang*-tradition text *Luxuriant Gems* in the case of Zheng, and Dan Zhu in the case of Jin.[39]

It is possible that Liu Chang also wrote a longer comment about the Jin attack on Xianyu in a work that is now lost or that this comment was censored from his extant works under the Qing dynasty. Quoted in Ming-period editions of Qiu Jun's 1488 *Supplement to the Extended Meaning of the Great Learning* (Daxue yanyi bu) but censored from the Qing-period *Siku quanshu* edition, it reads:

> To be trustworthy and understand moral duty is the Way of the Central Lands. To seek profit and be fond of deceit is the way of the barbarians (*Yi-Di zhi dao*). Jin was one of the Central States. The people of Xianyu were barbarians. Yet Jin violated the Way of the Central Lands and instead acted as barbarians do. Hence [Confucius] referred to [its ruler] as "Jin" to regard him as a barbarian. Alas! Human beings are far [superior] to barbarians only in terms of the difference between moral duty and profit, honesty and

deceit. If the Central Lands lose this just once, they then enter a state of barbarism (Yi-Di). How can we not be prudent about this?[40]

We cannot be entirely certain that this comment's attribution to Liu Chang is correct. But if it is, this would strongly suggest that the similarly worded ethnocentric moralist warning about barbarization that has been attributed to Cheng Yi (to be discussed in chapter 6) was inspired by Liu Chang's commentarial writings on the *Annals*—even though Cheng himself linked it not to Liu but to Han Yu. It would also be likely that Liu's use of the phrase "the way of the barbarians" was borrowed from Sun Fu's commentary.

Liu Chang's understanding of barbarism was based on morality, not ritual: like Sun Fu, he implicitly rejected the idea that using barbarian rites could result in barbarization. In the three instances when he believed that the use of barbarian rites had indeed led to editorial demotions in the *Annals*, he merely used the word "demoted" (*bian*) rather than the phrase "regarded as a barbarian."[41] In one of these instances, the well-known case of the Qǐ rulers' demotions in rank, he agreed with Fan Ning that these were literal demotions decreed by the Zhou king, rather than editorial decisions by Confucius or (as Zhao Kuang had argued) demotions issued by the hegemons.[42] Another case that Zhao Kuang and Lu Chun had regarded as one of "barbarizing" demotion for the use of barbarian rites, namely that of the rulers of Zhu, Mou, and Ge, was in Liu Chang's view a case of "heavy" (but not "barbarizing") demotion due to these rulers' decision to pay court to the Lord of Lu rather than attend the newly deceased Zhou king's funeral.[43]

Liu Chang's most original interpretation of barbarization in the *Annals* is that Confucius drew a sharp distinction between two kinds of "barbarians." On one hand, there were "real barbarians" (*zhen Yi-Di*) who had always been, and would always be, morally inferior enemies of the Chinese; on the other hand, there were Chinese states that had become barbarian-like or barbaric but were still capable of returning to Chinese ways. Of Liu's four extant *Annals* commentaries, only *The Forest of Meanings in the Annals* (Chunqiu yilin), which probably dates from the 1060s, contains sustained arguments relating to this distinction between real and nominal barbarians, but these are supplemented by a shorter passage in the significantly earlier *Weighing Balance of the Annals* (Chunqiu quanheng).[44]

Early in *The Forest of Meanings*, Liu Chang argues that states like Chu and Wu were not truly barbarians but only nominally so, since their rulers were (according to Sima Qian) descendants of Chinese sage-kings or worthies.

Confucius demoted them to a step above real barbarians to censure them for usurping the royal title, while leaving the door open for them to return to Chineseness. Whereas Sun Fu believed that Confucius regarded the Chu and Wu rulers' use of the royal title as unpardonable and used their editorial promotions as expressions of lament over the decline of the Chinese states, Liu Chang argues that Confucius's magnanimity toward these rulers was founded on an awareness of their Chinese ancestry.

> People who discuss [the *Annals*] regard Wu, Chu, Xú, and Yue as barbarians, but this is wrong. Wu, Chu, Xú, and Yue were barbarians in name, but not barbarians in reality. The sage [Confucius] was careful not to cut people off. [The rulers of] Wu were descended from Taibo, [the rulers of] Chu were descended from Zhurong, [the rulers of] Xú were descendants of [Yu's minister] Boyi, and [the rulers of] Yue were descendants of the great Yu.[45] Their ancestors all had great moral power (*de*) and prominent achievements and were in contact with the Zhou dynasty. How were they any different from the capped and robed rulers of the Central Lands? Xú was the first to use the title of king. Chu later also used the title of king, and Wu and Yue followed suit. Lords should not use the royal title, so [Confucius] regarded them as barbarians. Nonetheless, he was still unwilling to cut off those of their ilk (*lei*), so he did not place them as high as the Central Lands but also did not place them as low as the barbarians. Thus he could keep them at a distance [when they became aggressive] but also invite them in [when they became submissive]. This is how the sage was careful not to cut people off.[46]

Liu reiterates and elaborates on this interpretation later in *The Forest of Meanings*, in a passage that is both highly complex and significant, and thus also worth quoting at length:

> The *Annals* is careful about [the hierarchy of] rulers and subjects above all else. [The rulers of] Wu, Chu, Xú, and Yue were all descendants of sages or worthies. They were all either paternal uncles or maternal uncles of the Zhou kings. Seeing that the Zhou [kings] were weak and the lords were acting without restraint, and knowing that they were a distance from the Central Lands and beyond the reach of the king's authority, they all usurped the [royal] title illegitimately and became no different from barbarians. Hence the Annals responded by regarding them as barbarians. The sage [Confucius] was careful in employing people and reluctant to cast

them off. Although he regarded them as barbarians, he could not bear to lower them to the same level as barbarians and therefore still stooped to making excuses for them. Thus when he spoke of their rulers and of their ministers, he did not distinguish between [rulers and ministers by mentioning] noble titles and names. In this way he merely demoted them and placed them at a distance so that they would not be equal to the Central Lands. This is what he meant by saying [in *Analects* 3.5], "The barbarians have rulers but are still inferior to Chinese states that do not." . . . As soon as they thought of doing good and repented of their error, discarding their false titles and following the practice of the Central Lands, then he would permit them to have [legitimate] rulers and ministers.[47]

As an example of Confucius's generosity, Liu Chang notes that Confucius promoted the Chu ruler to "an equal footing with the Central Lands" in response to his choice to forgo using the royal title in diplomacy with Lu as early as 618 BCE.[48] Liu then continues with a general theory about barbarism that is reminiscent of "Chinese at Heart" and "A Call to Arms against the Inner Barbarian" in its ethnocentric moralism:

> Therefore, the lords were all [held to] the same [standard], but those who could embellish themselves with rites and music were called the Central Lands, while those who could not embellish themselves with rites and music, and who behaved insolently toward their superiors and violently toward their inferiors, were called barbarians. [The difference between] the Central Lands and the barbarians is based not on geographical proximity but rather on moral worthiness and unworthiness. If one is morally worthy, though he may reside beyond the Four Seas, it is permissible to call him [a person of] the Central Lands. If one is morally unworthy, though he may dwell along the Yellow and Luo Rivers, it is permissible to call him a barbarian.[49]

Another passage in Liu Chang's commentaries indicates, however, that he believed the attainment of moral worthiness and equality with the Chinese to be possible only in Chinese states that had become barbarized, not in "real barbarians" who had no common ancestry with the Chinese. For the "real barbarians," he had nothing but contempt. In other words, he admitted to the possibility of "re-Sinicization," but not "Sinicization" per se. As Liu explains in *The Weighing Balance*:

> When barbarians defeat the Central Lands, [the *Annals*] refers to this as "defeating" (*bai*), and when the Central Lands defeat barbarians, [the *Annals*] also refers to this as "defeating." The only difference is that [the *Annals*] does not speak of real barbarians (*zhen Yi-Di*) fighting battles with the Central Lands. As for Wu and Chu, even though they were barbarians in name, they were brothers and colleagues [of the other lords] in reality. Now if we, without exception, liken the rulers of Wu and Chu to the Red Di, White Di, Rong of the Mountains, and Rong-Man, would we not be insulting [their ancestors] Taibo and Yuxiong as well?[50]

Here, Liu Chang is building on a principle found in the *Guliang Commentary*: "[The *Annals*] does not speak of the Central Lands fighting battles with barbarians; it refers to these as 'defeating [barbarians].'" According to Fan Ning's subcommentary, this was done in order "to not accord the barbarians a status of parity (*di*) with the Central Lands."[51] But the principle evidently did not apply to Chu and Wu, which the *Annals* frequently recorded as fighting battles. This led Liu Chang to conclude that it applied only to "real barbarians" like the Di and Rong.

In fact, *The Forest of Meanings* applies this principle to an *Annals* record of Jin defeating a group of Di, arguing that since these barbarians were incapable of learning the "ritual propriety and moral duty" needed for fighting battles in a civilized, honorable fashion, the Chinese were also not obliged to fight proper, civilized battles with them:

> The *Annals* regards barbarians as foreigners (literally, "outsiders") and the Central Lands of the Chinese as compatriots (literally, "insiders"). Those regarded as compatriots are to be governed with moral power (*de*); those regarded as foreigners are to be governed with force. When opposing armies meet, there is always a battle. But when it involves the Central Lands [alone], then it is recorded as a battle. Recording it as a battle means that [the parties involved] are governed with moral power. When it involves the barbarians [as well], then it is not recorded as a battle. Not recording it as a battle means that [the barbarians] are governed with force.
>
> The true king is not [intentionally] generous toward the Central Lands and mean toward the barbarians. He has no choice but to be so. The Central Lands can be taught ritual propriety and moral duty; therefore, if [a Chinese state] does not fix a date and engage in a pitched battle, then it is to be abhorred even if its cause is just. Barbarians cannot be taught ritual

propriety and moral duty; when they come and raid, all that matters is achieving victory over them. Even if [a Chinese state] does not fix a date and engage in a pitched battle [with them], it is not to be derided.[52]

In an undated essay titled "On Governing the Barbarians" (Zhirong lun), Liu Chang presents an even more elaborate analysis of the principles governing Chinese warfare with "real barbarians" in the *Annals*. In the essay's second part, Liu Chang explains why the *Annals* mentions barbarian invasions of Chinese states, but not barbarian military victories. His argument accentuates the moral inferiority of the barbarians and the moral superiority of the Central Lands, casting them as such absolute opposites that any barbarian victory over the Central Lands is too abhorrent to be acknowledged in writing. "The barbarians represent utter inferiority, utter disorder, and utter moral unworthiness. The Central Lands represent utter superiority, utter order, and utter morality. The language of the *Annals* does not permit the inferior to rise above the superior, the disorderly to rise above the orderly, and the morally unworthy to rise above the moral. . . . Therefore, when [the *Annals*] speaks of barbarians entering the Central Lands but not of them winning battles, the meaning is like that of saying, 'They can enter the Central Lands, but they can never be victorious over the Central Lands.'"[53]

It seems clear, then, that when Liu Chang interpreted the language of the *Annals*, he consistently believed that a sense of ethnic affinity made Confucius's attitude toward the "barbarized" states of Chu and Wu more favorable than his attitude toward "real barbarians" who had never been Chinese. The former had lost their Chineseness through immorality, but were capable of regaining it; the latter were irredeemably immoral and were to be met with unwavering enmity. This presents a clear contrast to Sun Fu, who assumed Chu and Wu to be the greatest barbarian threats to Chinese civilization in the period of the *Annals* and represented the Wu king's achievement of hegemony as nothing short of a total ethnocultural barbarization of the Chinese.

ETHNOCENTRIC MORALISM AND THE *ANNALS* IN THE ESSAYS OF SU SHI AND QISONG

Even Sun Fu and Liu Chang together do not fully represent the diversity of eleventh-century positions taken on the theme of barbarization in the *Annals*, in part because that theme appears not only in new commentaries but also in various essays, which apply it to creative rhetorical ends in a manner not unlike—and quite possibly inspired by—Han Yu's "Tracing the Way." Consider, for example, Su Shi's "On 'The True King Does Not Govern the Barbarians'" (Wangzhe buzhi Yi-Di lun), an essay written for the decree examination of 1061.[54] In it, Su—then a rising literary star at the age of twenty-four—takes ethnocentric moralism to a logical extreme by arguing that none of the major states in the *Annals* was fully Chinese or fully barbarian, as all were simply at different stages of moral barbarization:

> Now, when the rulers of Qi and Jin governed their states, supported and defended the Son of Heaven, and loved and nurtured the people, how can they possibly have conformed fully to ancient mores? They must have employed deception and force mixed with humaneness and moral duty. Thus they were unable to be purely of the Central Lands. Qin and Chu, too, were not merely avaricious and shameless, acting recklessly without regard for [the consequences]. They must also have had rulers who upheld the Way and did their moral duty. Thus Qin and Chu did not go to the extent of being pure barbarians.[55]

On the surface, this idea of "being pure barbarians" (*chun wei Yi-Di*) is very similar to Liu Chang's category of "real barbarians," and the idea of Qin and Chu as not purely barbaric thus seems to match Liu's category of barbarized Chinese states. On closer inspection, however, Su Shi's understanding of barbarization differs from Liu Chang's and also from Sun Fu's in important aspects. Unlike Liu Chang, who saw the barbarization of Chu and Wu as a consequence of one gravely immoral act (namely, using the royal title in defiance of the Zhou king's authority), Su Shi represents any immoral act, from reliance on deception and force to avarice, shamelessness, and recklessness, as barbarizing. And unlike Sun Fu, who credited the Qi and Jin hegemons with "repelling the barbarians" of Chu and thereby "saving the Central Lands" from being barbarized (at least for a time), Su Shi saw the difference between Qi and Jin, on one hand, and Chu, on the other, only in terms of the extent to which they had been barbarized by immorality. The ethnocentric moralism of Su Shi's essay is therefore more comprehensive than that of either Sun Fu or Liu Chang.

After a somewhat convoluted argument to show that Confucius was (again *contra* Liu Chang) particularly "inclined toward detesting Qin and Chu, in order to show that one should not turn away from the Central Lands and toward the barbarians for even one day," and that the sage was by comparison much more forgiving toward "pure barbarians" (*chun Rong-Di*) like the Rong, Su Shi concludes that "when the *Annals* expresses detestation of barbarians, it is not detestation of pure barbarians, but rather detestation of those from the Central Lands who descend into [a state of being] barbarians."[56] In other words, because the worst kind of barbarism was acquired through accumulated acts of immorality, those who were "pure barbarians" or "real barbarians" by birth were not as contemptible as Chinese people who had turned into barbarians by behaving immorally.

A similarly moralistic interpretation of barbarism in the *Annals* can be found in the work of the Chan Buddhist monk Qisong (1007–1072), who traveled to Kaifeng in 1061, the same year that Su Shi sat for the decree examination, to present his writings to the emperor and petition for them to be added to the Buddhist canon.[57] Since the 1040s, Qisong had responded to the Guwen revival by authoring a number of apologetical texts that used Classicist concepts to rebut Guwen anti-Buddhist arguments.[58] Indeed, the "ten-thousand-word memorial" that he submitted to the throne with his works also contains various refutations of common anti-Buddhist arguments. It attempts to demonstrate that Buddhism is compatible with the Classicist ideal of the Way of the True King (Wangdao), which Qisong also calls the Way of Great Centrality (Dazhong zhi Dao) and describes as a political philosophy of moderation and impartiality. As part of this argument, Qisong presents an interpretation of the *Annals* as an expression of Great Centrality:

> The doctrine of the *Annals* is to esteem the Central Lands as superior and regard the barbarians as inferior. At that time, even when a lord was of the Central Lands, if he failed to accord with moral duty, Confucius would also regard him as a barbarian. Even when [a lord] was of the barbarians, if he acted in accordance with moral duty, [Confucius] would also regard him as [part of the] Central Lands. This, too, was how Confucius used the Way of Great Centrality. Hence he said, "The noble man does not have fixed opinions for or against anything in the world, but simply aligns himself with moral duty."[59] Moral duty means *li*. The sage regards whatever accords with *li* as correct. Is that not so?[60]

This argument identifies moral duty (*yi*) as the essence of Chinese superiority and Chineseness itself, but also denies that Classicism has a monopoly on moral duty by equating it with an abstract universal moral standard, which Qisong terms *li* 理 (not to be confused with *li*, "ritual propriety").

Where did the inspiration for this apologetical strategy come from, and what exactly did Qisong mean by *li*? Qisong's extant writings do not include any clear definition or exposition of the concept, apart from an essay asserting that the mind (*xin*) is synonymous with *li*—an idea that seems to bear the marks of Huayan Buddhist philosophy rather than Qisong's own background in the Chan tradition.⁶¹ As is well known, *li* (variously translated as "principle," "pattern," "coherence," and "congruity") was also one of the foundational onto-cosmological concepts in Daoxue, which was only just emerging at the time of Qisong's death.⁶² Many scholars working on the history of Daoxue have argued that Cheng Yi and his elder brother Cheng Hao (1032–1085) appropriated the concept of *li* from Chinese Buddhist philosophy and elevated it as both a descriptive and a normative term for how all things in the world inherently operate and fit together—indeed, they considered it to be a synonym of *Dao* ("the Way"). Qisong, too, appears to have used *li* as a synonym of *Dao*: more specifically, the Way (*Dao*) of Great Centrality that he believes guided Confucius's moral judgments.

Qisong's earlier writings show that he had been developing this argument for some time before his journey to Kaifeng. We see it in "Refuting Han Yu" (Fei Han), a series of essays from 1056 criticizing Han Yu's positions on Buddhism and various other subjects.⁶³ Toward the end of the first "Refuting Han Yu" essay, Qisong invokes the concept of Great Centrality and relates it to instances of editorial demotion and promotion in the *Annals*, claiming that "goodness" (*shan*) and "moral duty" (*yi*) were Confucius's only criteria for distinguishing between the Central Lands and the barbarians:

> Confucius used the sages' Way of Great Centrality to determine the correctness of all things in the world. When he wrote the *Annals* of Lu, he praised the good and abhorred the wicked regardless of whether they were of the Central Lands or the barbarians. The *Annals* says, "Xú attacked [the state of] Ju." Xú was originally of the Central Lands, but when its actions were not good, then [Confucius] regarded it as [a] barbarian [state]. It says, "A man of Qi and a man of the Di made a covenant at [the state of] Xing." The Di people were originally a barbarian people, but when their actions were good, then [Confucius] regarded them as [part of the] Central Lands. When the sage [Confucius] esteemed the Central Lands as superior and regarded the barbarians as inferior, it was based not on territorial boundaries or peoples, but on whether they accorded with *li* 理, so to speak.

Hence he said, "The noble man does not have fixed opinions for or against anything in the world, but simply aligns himself with moral duty."[64]

The two examples in this passage adopt interpretations from He Xiu's *Gongyang* subcommentary without engaging with different, more recent interpretations by Sun Fu and Liu Chang.[65] This is hardly surprising since Qisong's interests are polemical, not exegetical. Qisong then gets to his real point, which is that the *Annals* proves Confucius himself would not have dismissed Buddhism as inferior or immoral because of its foreign origin: "As for Buddhism, its goodness in this age can be said to be a pure and great goodness. Judging according to the Way of Centrality (Zhongdao), should it be approved of, or should it be rejected? If one does not use the sage's Way of Centrality to evaluate whether it is good or bad and come to a correct opinion on whether it should be accepted or discarded, then one is just a mediocre person acting on one's subjective biases. Is that even worth discussing?"[66]

Qisong makes the same argument, with the same examples from the *Annals*, in another essay from 1056 titled "Expanding upon 'Tracing the [Buddhist] Teaching to Its Source'" (Guang yuanjiao). He then asks rhetorically: "The *Annals* surely contains the doctrines of the Classicists' sages; how then can it be that one has to judge a person by his place of origin? If a person is more than just his ethnic origin (*lei*), and the Way is more than just its traces (*ji*), then is it not absurd to seek out sages based on their ethnic origin, and is it not flippant to judge the Way of a sage by its traces?"[67] This argument about origins and traces bears some similarity to Liu Zongyuan's claim that Han Yu was criticizing Buddhism for "only its traces," as well as his use of the name-essence and exterior-core dichotomies to deflect Han's criticisms of Buddhism as barbaric and immoral. Whereas Liu Zongyuan cited the cases of the "good barbarians" Jizha and You Yu to argue that not everything from the barbarians is morally inferior, Qisong builds his argument by taking the concept of "barbarizing" demotion in *Annals* exegesis, which Han Yu had so famously used against Buddhism in "Tracing the Way," and brilliantly turning it on its head to make an argument for ethnocentric moralism in which ethnocultural differences are irrelevant. Han Yu ignored the moral dimension of barbarism in the *Annals* in order to assert that the ethnocultural dimension (as manifested in differences in ritual) is all there is. Qisong does the exact opposite. Ethnocentric moralism, it turns out, was the best counterargument against ethnicized orthodoxy.

THE WANING OF ETHNICIZED ORTHODOXY

Su Shi's essay and Qisong's apologetical arguments indicate that the 1050s and early 1060s were a transitional period during which the Guwen radicals' expanded version of ethnicized orthodoxy faded from Song discourse on the Chinese-barbarian dichotomy and was superseded by the kind of ethnocentric moralism prefigured in "Chinese at Heart," "A Call to Arms against the Inner Barbarian," and "The Enemy Threat." As I have shown elsewhere, this trend also influenced the *New History of the Tang* biographical chapters that the historian Song Qi (998–1061) composed in the 1050s, which deemed the autonomous provinces of late Tang Hebei as barbarized because of their disloyalty to the throne and not because of either ethnocultural or ideological change.[68] The only works dating to the 1050s that reflect influence from the expanded version of ethnicized orthodoxy are the writings of the short-lived Wang Ling. Wang was born in 1032, the year of Shi Jie's conversion to the Guwen cause, and was thirteen years old when Shi died. The two almost certainly never met, but one of Wang's essays shows that he did read some of Shi's polemical works, including "Clarifying the Prohibitions," and was greatly impressed by their ideological fervor. Wang Ling evidently also found Shi Jie's version of ethnicized orthodoxy compelling as rhetoric, since two of his pieces—a valedictory preface for a Daoist and an essay comparing Daoism and Buddhism to the teachings of Yang Zhu and Mozi—denigrate Daoism and Buddhism as "the two barbarians" (*er Yi*).[69]

Wang Ling's death in 1059, just two years after Sun Fu's, effectively marked the end of such rhetorical efforts at equating all non-Classicist ideologies with barbarism. As we have seen, Guwen moderates like Ouyang Xiu and Li Gou had never been persuaded of this rhetorical strategy's effectiveness. Moreover, the priorities of leading Guwen writers had long shifted from anti-Buddhist and anti-Daoist polemics to questions of political and socioeconomic reform. The uncritical adulation and imitation of Han Yu that animated the ideological fervor of men like Liu Kai and Shi Jie had also passed from the scene, replaced by Ouyang Xiu's more objective and rational attitude toward the late Tang prose master's achievements. By the 1060s, younger Guwen writers like Liu Chang and Su Shi were even ready to dismiss Han Yu as a moral and philosophical lightweight who did not really understand the Way of the Sages.[70] Indeed, correcting and transcending Han Yu, rather than just emulating and exalting him, became the new fashion for literati who came of age during the

1040s and 1050s—men like Liu Chang, Sima Guang (1019–1086), Wang Anshi (1021–1086), Su Shi, and the Cheng brothers.[71]

Surprisingly, this trend did not lead to attempts at surpassing Han Yu in militant opposition to Buddhism and Daoism. On the contrary, both Su Shi and Wang Anshi were deeply interested in Buddhism, while Sima Guang (like Ouyang Xiu and Li Gou) found Han Yu's call for state persecution of Buddhism too extreme. Wang and Sima, whose political differences over reform are legendary, are both known to have written commentaries on *Laozi's Classic of the Way and Its Power*.[72] We have already seen that Liu Chang was as familiar with the Buddhist sutras and the classics of Daoist philosophy as he was with the *Annals*. Cheng Yi was significantly more critical of Daoist and Buddhist philosophy than most contemporaries, an attitude that became characteristic of Daoxue thought, but even he dismissed Daoism's influence as marginal and asserted that Wang Anshi's interpretations of the Classics were more dangerous than Buddhism.[73] The all-out war on Buddhism and Daoism that Liu Kai and Shi Jie dreamed of launching never truly became a major theme of the Guwen revival. Instead, the revival's literary success was not matched on the ideological front. Most Northern Song literati, on both sides of an increasingly polarized and factional political landscape, remained highly tolerant of the "heterodox" beliefs and practices that Han Yu and the Guwen radicals had deplored as a mortal threat to Chinese civilization.[74]

Guo Tian credits Qisong's "Refuting Han Yu" essays with initiating the shift in attitudes toward Han Yu.[75] While this may be an overstatement, it is likely that Qisong was at least partly responsible for neutralizing the rhetorical trope of ethnicized orthodoxy by demonstrating its incompatibility with the ethnocentric moralist understanding of Chineseness that Song literati now assumed could be found in the *Annals*. If Buddhism was morally good, then it was essentially not barbaric but Chinese. One could still dispute whether Buddhism was indeed morally good, but that dispute would take one into questions of moral philosophy for which Daoxue was far better equipped than the comparatively crude polemics of ethnicized orthodoxy.

Qisong should not get all the credit for ethnicized orthodoxy's decline. The Guwen moderates, especially Ouyang Xiu, probably also played a role in marginalizing it, simply by choosing not to employ it in their writing. But the biggest factor in the decline was the fact that no *Annals* commentator of the eleventh century took an interest in using ethnicized orthodoxy as the guiding principle of *Annals* exegesis that Han Yu's "Tracing the Way" claimed it was. Instead, there is an ethnocentric moralist core to Sun Fu's approach to barbarization in the *Annals* that contrasts with the ethnicized orthodoxy in his polemical writings. Given the complete absence from his commentary of rhetoric linking barbarization to Buddhism, to any other non-Classicist ideology, or even to "barbarian rites," one must conclude that Sun kept his craft as a classical exegete separate from his ideological stance as a Guwen radical. Nor was Shi Jie any different, judging from what has survived of his *Expounding the Annals*.[76]

The untapped potential for synergy or complementarity between the Guwen radicals' anti-heterodox polemics and their classical exegesis can be glimpsed in an undated essay by Zheng Xie (1022–1072), who was not an *Annals* commentator and is best known as a poet rather than a Guwen writer. The essay, titled "On Ritual Standards" (Lifa lun), is obviously imitating "Tracing the Way" and "The Central Lands" but attacks only Buddhism, not Daoism. I quote selectively from its arguments:

> When Confucius wrote the *Annals*, he did not record ordinary events but did record changes in ritual, to make it clear that the sages' institutions and rites have been guarded by the Central Lands for generations and cannot be changed. Yet how extreme is the change that the Buddhists have brought to the Central Lands! Buddhism is a barbarian rite. . . . So the sages' institutions and rites from antiquity have all collapsed; how much longer can this go on before everything becomes barbaric (Yi)? If Confucius were here to record today's changes in ritual, he would be writing about them without pause, feverishly taking up bamboo slips and wetting his brush with ink. Yet the world takes them calmly and does not find them strange; the imperial court has never issued a prohibition against them. So they attack, undermine, and destroy [our civilization].[77]

No eleventh-century *Annals* commentary employed such anti-Buddhist rhetoric, effectively leaving the field of *Annals* interpretation open to a vision of Chineseness that viewed morality, not ideological or intellectual orthodoxy, as its essence. This is the vision that we saw, in varying forms, in Liu Chang, Su Shi, and Qisong. Interest in *Annals* interpretation continued to grow throughout the late eleventh and twelfth centuries, and so did the prevalence of ethnocentric moralism. By this time, the Guwen revival had run its course, and the rhetoric of ethnocentric moralism came instead to be closely identified with the new moral philosophy of Daoxue.

CHAPTER 6

Chineseness and Barbarism in Early Daoxue Philosophy

IN the 1070s, Cheng Hao and his younger brother Cheng Yi began developing a philosophical system in which human morality was both integrally linked to cosmic order and the key to understanding that order. Soon after Cheng Hao's death in 1085, Cheng Yi claimed him, not Han Yu, to have been the first man since Mencius who understood the Way of the Sages, and he began calling their teachings Daoxue, "the learning of the Way."[1] Cheng Yi outlived Cheng Hao by twenty-two years and clearly had greater influence on the Daoxue system's central concepts. But it is now quite difficult to distinguish between the two men's ideas, because their disciples tended not to do so when recording their oral teachings.

One of four chapters of statements securely attributed to Cheng Hao in *The Surviving Writings of the Cheng Brothers* (Chengshi yishu) contains a theory about the innate differences between animals and barbarians, on one hand, and "human beings," on the other: "The *li* of equilibrium (*zhong*) is perfect. Nothing that is purely *yin* can come into existence; nor can anything that is purely *yang* come into existence. When [*yin* and *yang*] are out of balance, then one is [born] an animal or a barbarian (Yi-Di); when they are in equilibrium, then one is [born] a human being. That which is in equilibrium does not go out of balance; that which is constant does not change. However, 'equilibrium' (*zhong*) by itself is inadequate for expressing this idea, so we call it 'equilibrium and normality' (*zhongyong*)."[2] In at least one version of *The Surviving Writings*, one finds a similar statement elsewhere, attributed more generally to the Cheng brothers: "Human beings and animals differ only in the balance of their *qi*. Nothing that is purely *yin* can come into being; nor can anything that is purely *yang* come into existence. Those that receive an imbalance of *yin* and *yang* are animals, plants, and barbarians; those that receive the correct balance of *qi* are human beings."[3]

This *qi*-based theory of a human-barbarian-animal-plant taxonomy both builds on and departs from previous discourses on barbarians. The idea that *qi* imbalance was the reason for the barbarians' inferiority to the Chinese goes back to Han-period and Tang-period arguments against imperial expansion.[4] Unlike those arguments, Cheng Hao takes Chinese identity out of the picture, elides the existence of ethnic differences among human beings, and effectively dehumanizes foreign peoples by using the category "human being" in place of "Chinese" or "the Central Lands." This is thus not a conventional ethnocentric discourse on barbarian inferiority, but rather an anthropocentric understanding of cosmology that includes an ethnocentric redefinition of humanity. Even this redefinition was not unprecedented: Han Yu's essay "Tracing Humanity to Its Source" (Yuanren) had divided living beings into humans, barbarians, and animals, while arguing that the three categories could collectively be termed "humanity" because barbarians and animals, despite not being truly human, were nonetheless dependent on the proper functioning of the "Way of humanity" (*rendao*) just as plants, mountains, and rivers were dependent on the "Way of earth."[5]

A similar denial of full humanity to the barbarians is implied in a statement attributed to Cheng Yi in *The Surviving Writings*: "In later generations, human beings' ritual propriety was completely destroyed. When it was lost to a small degree, then [human beings] entered a state of barbarism (Yi-Di); when it was lost to a great degree, then they entered a state of animality."[6] Some editions of the text have *li* 理 instead of the homophonous "ritual propriety" (*li* 禮), so that what is destroyed is "the *li* of humanity." Given the importance of the first *li* as a concept in Cheng Yi's philosophy, one might be tempted to accept that reading, and some scholars have previously done so.[7] However, the "ritual propriety" reading is supported by a longer quotation, dated to 1079 and most likely from Cheng Yi:

> If one loses ritual propriety just once, one becomes a barbarian; if one loses it again, then one becomes an animal. The sage [Confucius] was afraid that human beings would turn into animals, so his method of writing the *Annals* was extremely careful and strict. If the Central Lands [rulers] used barbarian rites, then [Confucius] regarded them as barbarians. When Han Yu said

that the *Annals* was careful and strict, he deeply understood [Confucius's] intent. One cannot do without knowing Han Yu's way. His words, "[the language of] the *Changes* is unconventional yet exemplary; that of the *Odes* is correct yet flowery; that of the *Annals* is careful and strict (*jinyan*); that of the *Zuo Tradition* is given to hyperbole," are both linguistically and philosophically sound.⁸

Select Sayings of the Cheng Brothers (Chengshi cuiyan), compiled by the Cheng brothers' disciple Yang Shi (1053–1135), contains an abbreviated version that replaces rites with the generic "way" (*dao*):

> The method of the *Annals* is that if the Central Lands [rulers] used the way of the barbarians (*Yidao*), then [Confucius] regarded them as barbarians. When Master Han said that the *Annals* was careful and strict, he deeply understood [Confucius's] intent.⁹

In these versions of the passage, Cheng Yi openly attributes his theory of barbarization to Han Yu's understanding of the *Annals* and thereby traces it to Confucius himself, further elevating the *Annals* as a key text for understanding how Confucius interpreted the meanings of Chineseness and barbarism. Rather strangely, however, Cheng Yi avoids mentioning "Tracing the Way" and instead quotes another of Han Yu's essays, "An Explication of Advancement in Learning" (Jinxue jie), which uses the phrase "careful and strict" to describe the general literary characteristics of *Annals* prose.¹⁰ Cheng Yi's somewhat circuitous way of crediting Han Yu by reinterpreting "careful and strict" as a statement about "barbarizing" demotions may be due to Cheng's ambivalent attitude toward "Tracing the Way," which he believed to have "many flaws" (*duobing*) philosophically but also the occasional flash of insight—for example, the claim that the Way of the Sages was lost after Mencius.¹¹

Han Yu's "Tracing the Way" equated the "barbarian rites" of the *Annals* with the Buddhism of his day; the Northern Song Guwen radicals attempted, without lasting success, to expand that reinterpretation of "barbarian rites" to include Daoism. Cheng Yi is much more ambiguous as to what he means by a loss of "ritual propriety" or (in the *Select Sayings* version) by using "the way of the barbarians," but the fact that he does not explicitly associate it with Buddhism, Daoism, or any other non-Classicist tradition suggests that he has moral decline, not ideological heterodoxy, in mind—in other words, that he reinterpreted Han Yu's rhetoric of ethnicized orthodoxy as an ethnocentric moralist argument. This is particularly likely if Cheng Yi's "lose it just once" formulation for barbarization was borrowed from the passage attributed to Liu Chang in *Supplement to the Extended Meaning of the Great Learning*, which claimed that "the way of the barbarians" was to "seek profit and be fond of deceit."[12]

Daoxue moral philosophy held that although a universal *li* gave all living beings some innate understanding of morality, humans had the purest *qi* among living beings, making them uniquely able to comprehend that *li* and thus cultivate their moral natures.[13] Because of this, all human beings—regardless of their individual *qi* endowment—innately possessed the capacity to purify and refine their *qi* through moral self-cultivation until they overcame all selfish desires, achieved complete alignment with cosmic order or "Heaven-ordained *li*" (*tianli*), and became sages. But this optimistic vision of humanity apparently came with a corollary warning: a human being's potential for advancing to sagehood was mirrored by the danger of descending to the level of barbarians and animals if he neglected ritual propriety.

Moreover, Cheng Yi's optimism seems not to have extended to the foreign peoples whom he regarded as less than fully human. His recorded teachings do not contain any statement on whether the process of moral change could move in the opposite direction: that is, whether barbarians had the capacity to become fully human by learning ritual propriety from the Chinese. The question was apparently unimportant or irrelevant to his philosophical concerns. Instead, he was interested in warning his audience that Chinese moral superiority, whether based on *qi* balance or otherwise, was not permanent and unshakable and therefore had to be maintained and strengthened with vigilant effort. A conviction that the only truly worthy endeavor for human beings was the pursuit of moral perfection (i.e., sagehood) through rigorous self-cultivation gave Daoxue thinkers a distinctly and uncompromisingly moralistic approach to all aspects of politics and society. Understanding that perspective is essential for making sense of Cheng Yi's radical reinterpretation of the most unequivocal statement of Chinese superiority attributed to Confucius: namely, *Analects* 3.5.

CHENG YI'S ETHNOCENTRIC MORALIST READING OF *ANALECTS* 3.5

Departing from long-standing exegetical tradition, Cheng Yi reinterpreted *Analects* 3.5 as a lament over the Chinese states' moral decline into an age of rampant "usurpation and disorder," while even the barbarians remained loyal to their rulers:

> This is Confucius saying that his was an age of great disorder, when insubordination toward rulers (*wujun*; literally, "not having rulers") was at an extreme. It is like saying, "The barbarians still have rulers, unlike the Chinese states that do not."

> Even the barbarians had rulers, unlike the usurpation and disorder in the Chinese states, which no longer observed the proper distinctions between those above and those below.[14]

Cheng Yi's interpretation is predicated on reading the phrase *buru*, literally, "unlike," to mean "not as bad as" instead of its usual meaning "inferior to," and on reading the Chinese states' not having rulers in the figurative sense of *behaving as if they have no rulers*.[15] This reinterpretation was not completely unprecedented, but it nonetheless effectively rejected some eight centuries of Classicist commentary and was highly atypical even for the Northern Song, although it has become so widely accepted in modern times—mainly due to Zhu Xi's endorsement in commentaries regarded as authoritative for centuries—that some scholars assume it to be the only possible meaning of 3.5.[16]

The only *Analects* commentator to make a similar interpretation of 3.5 before Cheng Yi was the eminent Eastern Han Classicist Zheng Xuan (127–200). Zheng's commentary, written in 184–200, presents the following interpretation: "Because these were times of decline and disorder, [Confucius said this] in order to rectify people's hearts."[17] This seems to have gone against the prevailing interpretation of *Analects* 3.5 even in Han times, since Wang Chong (27–ca. 100 CE) did not anticipate any conflicting interpretation when he used 3.5 to argue that *Analects* 9.14 made no sense: How could Confucius have thought that he had any chance of improving the "benighted" Yi people morally, when he had failed to do so with the inherently superior Chinese?[18] Zheng Xuan's contemporary and rival He Xiu also clearly assumed *Analects* 3.5 to be a statement on the barbarians' permanent inferiority, since his *Gongyang* subcommentary uses 3.5 to explain why the *Annals* regards Chu as inferior to the Chinese states even when the latter have failed to act with integrity.[19]

John Makeham has suggested that Zheng Xuan's interpretation of *Analects* 3.5 and numerous other *Analects* passages reflects his pessimism about the political situation toward the end of his life (i.e., in 190–200), when the Han empire was collapsing into a multitude of regional regimes and the emperor was a puppet in the hands of one warlord or another.[20] He Xiu, who died in 182, was fortunately spared such anguish. Nonetheless, their contrasting interpretations of *Analects* 3.5—one conventional and ethnocentric, the other unconventional and self-critical—probably coexisted and competed for at least a century after Zheng Xuan's death. That competition is now visible in only one extant text: *Master Mou's Discourse on Resolving Doubts*, which dates from a period between 190 and 370. In it, Mouzi appears to use Zheng Xuan's interpretation to rebut his imaginary opponent's citing of *Analects* 3.5 as evidence of Buddhism's inferiority, arguing that his opponent has misunderstood the sage's words: "What Confucius said was a method for rectifying the age."[21]

The ethnocentric reading clearly held dominance in the Eastern Jin and Southern Dynasties, as seen from interpretations by Sun Chuo (314–371), Huilin (fl. fifth century), and Huang Kan (488–545).[22] Unlike Mouzi's imaginary opponent, none of these commentators had an anti-Buddhist agenda: Sun Chuo composed an essay of Buddhist apologetics, Huilin was a Buddhist monk, and Huang Kan composed his *Analects* subcommentary under the strongly pro-Buddhist Liang dynasty.[23] Yet all three of them understood *Analects* 3.5 as a statement about barbarian inferiority. According to Sun Chuo, Confucius was saying that barbarians chose their leaders according to a principle of "might makes right" and that this could never be equal to the Chinese way of governance: "The Chinese states at times do not have rulers, but the Way is not completely lost, whereas among barbarians the strongest man is king, their principles being the same as those of animals." In Huilin's reading, Confucius was delivering veiled criticism of the Ji (or Jisun) ministerial family that dominated politics in the state of Lu, by insinuating that its members were as immoral as barbarians in usurping the Lu ruler's authority and ritual prerogatives: "Having a ruler but not having ritual propriety is worse than (*buru*; literally, "inferior to") having ritual propriety but not having a ruler." Huang Kan quoted both interpretations, declining to choose one over the other, but added the comment, "This makes it clear that Confucius favored the Central Lands and saw the barbarians as inferior."[24]

In an influential modern commentary on the *Analects*, historian Qian Mu argued that commentators from the Eastern Jin and Southern Dynasties preferred the ethnocentric reading of *Analects* 3.5 because they felt threatened by the "barbarians" in the north; being "without rulers" was less of a problem to them because they were members of great clans accustomed to challenging the emperor's authority.[25] But this argument ignores the fact that the ethnocentric reading was just as common in the "barbarian"-ruled Northern Dynasties. The Northern Wei emperor Xiaowendi used it to denigrate the Qiang ruler of Dangchang, who had "behaved in a highly unseemly (*wu fengli*) fashion" during a visit to the Wei court.[26] Wei Shou (ca. 506–572), author of the Northern Wei dynastic history, also used the ethnocentric reading to criticize the tendency for Eastern Jin emperors to be dominated by powerful ministers. According to Wei, the "barbarians" of the south had rulers but were still worse off than Chinese (i.e., northern) states that had none.[27] The application of this argument to the Eastern Jin may strike the reader as bizarre, since it is that regime's northern rivals that we usually regard as "barbarian" states. But precisely because the Southern Dynasties regularly used the Chinese-barbarian dichotomy for propaganda purposes against the Northern Dynasties, Wei Shou—as a northern court historian—made a point of asserting the north's claim to political legitimacy by denigrating southern rulers as "island barbarians" (*daoyi*) and associating their subjects with the ancient states of Chu, Wu, and Yue.[28]

Han Yu's use of the ethnocentric interpretation of *Analects* 3.5 in "Tracing the Way," more than four centuries after *Master Mou's Discourse*, shows that it was consistently seen as a useful polemical device for denigrating foreign peoples, or their beliefs and practices, as barbaric and thus morally inferior.[29] But such rhetorical utility alone cannot account for Zheng Xuan's self-critical interpretation's lack of success. Students of the *Analects* must have found it less persuasive, most likely because the standard meaning of *buru* in Classical Chinese was indeed "inferior to" and not "not as bad as." Grammatical logic, and not just ethnocentric bias, made the self-critical interpretation unattractive for about seven centuries, until its revival by Cheng Yi.

It is unlikely that Cheng Yi ever read Zheng Xuan's commentary, since that text seems to have been lost by the eleventh century, and no extant *Analects* commentary written between the third and eleventh centuries quotes Zheng's self-critical interpretation or even acknowledges its existence.[30] Cheng's reinterpretation of *Analects* 3.5 was therefore effectively original to him. Qian Mu claimed that most Song-period commentators on the *Analects* adopted the self-critical interpretation because of their focus on the message of "respecting the king," and numerous later scholars have taken Qian's word on this.[31] In fact, Qian was incorrect as far as the Northern Song is concerned. Consider the first major *Analects* commentary from the Song period: Xing

Bing's (932–1010) *Commentaries and Subcommentaries to the Analects* (Lunyu zhushu), completed around 999. On *Analects* 3.5, Xing Bing writes:

> This passage tells us that the barbarians have none of the abundant ritual propriety and moral duty that the Central Lands have. . . . [Confucius] says that even though the barbarians have rulers and leaders, they do not have ritual propriety and moral duty; on the other hand, even though the Central Lands occasionally go without a ruler, such as during the joint regency of the Dukes of Zhou and Shao, ritual propriety and moral duty are not destroyed [as a result]. That is why [Confucius] said, "The barbarians have rulers but are still inferior to Chinese states that do not."[32]

Xing Bing essentially endorses Sun Chuo's argument that even on the rare occasions when the Chinese are without a ruler, they remain morally superior to the barbarians. His example of a period when the Chinese had no ruler is the so-called Gonghe regency (841–828 BCE), which began after Western Zhou subjects drove the highly unpopular King Li (d. 828 BCE) out of the capital and ended upon the king's death in exile. Xing follows the *Records of the Historian* interpretation of "Gonghe" as a joint regency by the Dukes of Zhou and Shao, but most historians now accept the alternative *Bamboo Annals* (Zhushu jinian) interpretation of this period as a sole regency by He, the Liege (*bo*) of Gong.[33]

Although we know nothing about Xing Bing's life before 976, the fact that his family resided in Caozhou (in southwestern Shandong) makes it almost certain that as a fifteen-year-old, he experienced the brief Kitan occupation of the North China Plain in 947, which was accompanied by rampant pillaging and massacres of Chinese civilians.[34] Yet we have little or no reason to see Xing's adherence to the ethnocentric interpretation of *Analects* 3.5 as driven by strong anti-Kitan sentiment. His commentary does not contain any other denigration of barbarians. Instead, his interpretation of *Analects* 9.14 assumes Confucius was correct in believing that the presence of a noble man (*junzi*) among barbarians would "transform" them and "cause them to have ritual propriety and moral duty."[35] This implies that barbarians are not incapable of learning ritual propriety and moral duty; it is just that they need a *junzi*, not just a *jun* (ruler), to teach them.

The more likely explanation for Xing Bing's interpretation is that he was following the conventional reading of *Analects* 3.5 in his day and that Qian Mu overstated the typicality of Cheng Yi's interpretation. Quotations preserved in *Essential Meanings of the Analects* (Lunyu jingyi), Zhu Xi's anthology of ten late Northern Song *Analects* commentaries, suggest that Cheng's interpretation did not gain unanimous acceptance during his lifetime. Even Lü Dalin (ca. 1040–ca.1092), one of Cheng's senior disciples, hewed close to Xing Bing's interpretation in his own *Analects* commentary, writing: "The superiority of the Chinese states lies in their continuing to have ritual propriety and moral duty. 'When they establish an infant as ruler and hold court audiences with only the deceased ruler's clothes placed on the throne, the realm does not fall into disorder';³⁶ this is because it has ritual propriety and moral duty to sustain it. This is why the barbarians cannot [be allowed to] usurp(?) [the Chinese states]."³⁷ Similarly, the historian Fan Zuyu (1041–1098), who was close to the Cheng brothers and adopted many of Cheng Yi's views on Tang history,³⁸ proposed a reading that essentially followed Xing Bing's interpretation but abandoned the long-standing practice of glossing the character 亡 (usually read *wang*) as a classical variant of *wu* ("to be without"), instead reading it more literally as denoting the fall of a state:

> Heaven and earth have determined people's positions [in society], such that there are rulers and subjects. [A society's] superiority lies in there being a hierarchy of rulers and subjects, so that ritual propriety and moral duty can be put into practice. Even though the barbarians have rulers, they have neither ritual propriety nor moral duty;³⁹ therefore, they are inferior to (*buru*) even Chinese states that have fallen (*wang*). A state cannot remain a state without ritual propriety, so if there is a state that does not have ritual propriety, it is better for it to fall (*wang*). If the Chinese states do not have ritual propriety, then they are inferior to (*buru*) barbarians.⁴⁰

We see here that Fan attempted to accommodate Cheng Yi's interpretation at the end of this passage. But that attempt had the result of weakening his argument's overall coherence, especially since he persisted in reading *buru* as "inferior to." Fan's scenario of the Chinese becoming worse than barbarians is highly compatible with Cheng Yi's argument that the loss of ritual propriety leads to barbarization followed by bestialization, but he presented it as a hypothetical scenario, rather than the historical situation that Cheng Yi believed Confucius was commenting on.

Although Lü Dalin did not follow Cheng Yi's reading of *Analects* 3.5, at least three of Cheng's other leading disciples adopted and built on it—albeit in disparate ways—when writing their own commentaries to the *Analects*.

Xie Liangzuo's (ca. 1050–ca. 1120) commentary, written between 1086 and 1093,[41] tries to embrace the essence of Cheng Yi's interpretation while reverting to a more conventional reading of *buru* as "inferior to":

> In this world, how can there be a state without a ruler? It is the same for barbarians as for the Central Lands. As to the matter of rites, music, and laws "where the five means of [moral] government are applied and the seven crops cultivated," these are only customs (*su*) [of the Central Lands], nothing more.[42] In the Central Lands during the time of Lords Ding (r. 509–495 BCE) and Ai (494–468 BCE) [of Lu], the affairs of the states fell into the hands of the stewards of the ministers, and political power was in the hands of the ministers.[43] "Who was in charge" of the rites, music, and laws, then?[44] Where, then, was the moral duty between rulers and their subjects? Consider the barbarians who have rulers: they obey [their ruler's] every command and go wherever [their ruler] directs them. Were [the Central Lands] anything like this? By that measure, [the Central Lands] were inferior to (*buru*) the barbarians who have rulers.[45]

The most unexpected feature of this passage is its strategy of emphasizing the importance of respect for legitimate political authority by dismissing rites (*li*) as mere "custom" (*su*), making ritual propriety an inadequate basis for Chinese superiority over barbarians in the absence of moral duty. We see a similar strategy and the same subtle adherence to the conventional meaning of *buru* in Yang Shi's commentary, which argues:

> When the ministers' stewards can use the Son of Heaven's rites and music, their insubordination to their ruler (*wujun*; literally, "not having a ruler") is at an extreme.[46] That is why [Confucius] said that [they are] inferior to (*buru*) the barbarians. He [said so] as a lament.[47]

Yin Tun's (1071–1142) commentary, on the other hand, follows Cheng Yi's reading of *buru* but seems to redirect Confucius's criticism from the ministers to the ruler:

> Confucius lamented over the disorder of his times, saying, "The barbarians still have rulers, unlike (*buru*) the Chinese states that do not." The word *wu* does not really mean not having [rulers], but rather having rulers who are unable to live up to the way [of rulership].[48]

In the 1190s, when one of Zhu Xi's students asked him why Yin Tun's interpretation has Confucius blaming the rulers for disorder in the Chinese states whereas Cheng Yi's interpretation has Confucius blaming the ministers, Zhu deftly reconciled the two by arguing that they were two sides of the same coin: "They mean the same thing: they both are saying that there was usurpation and disorder between those above and those below, and that they could not live up to the way of [proper] relations between rulers and subjects, as if there was no ruler at all."[49]

Zhu Xi is also the only Song-period Daoxue philosopher known to have explained his disagreement with the ethnocentric interpretation of *Analects* 3.5. Zhu's own *Analects* commentary, *Queries on the Analects* (Lunyu huowen), explains his support for Cheng Yi's reading of 3.5 in the following terms:

> The meaning of this passage is clear, but Fan [Zuyu] and Lü [Dalin] read it differently. Nonetheless, a subject cannot be without a ruler, just like a body cannot be without a head. Establishing an infant as ruler and holding court audiences with only the deceased ruler's clothes placed on the throne are temporary measures taken when there is no choice. But ever since the Central Lands came into being, it has been very rare for such a state of affairs not to descend into disorder. How could the sage [Confucius] possibly have thought that this could be the normal state of affairs?[50]

Zhu Xi also once told his disciples that he found the ethnocentric interpretation "meaningless" (*wu yiyi*). When a student mentioned the interpretations by Fan Zuyu and Lü Dalin and commented that he found them unconvincing, Zhu Xi answered: "I don't know how they could say that. Even if the sage [Confucius] did say that, how could it have done any good? Wouldn't that mean it's just as well that the Central Lands not have a ruler?" Zhu then agreed with the same student's suggestion that the word *wu* ("to not have") really meant having a mind that did not recognize the ruler's authority (literally, "a mind without a ruler," *wujun zhi xin*).[51]

Zhu Xi's discomfort with the interpretations by Fan Zuyu and Lü Dalin illuminates a key difference between the ethnocentric and self-critical understandings of *Analects* 3.5 and gives us some sense of Cheng Yi's reasons for breaking with exegetical tradition. Whereas the ethnocentric reading interprets "not having a ruler" literally as a rare and temporary political situation for the Central Lands, such as a regency, the self-critical reading interprets "not having a ruler" metaphorically as a rebellious state of mind. It is impossible for any society to possess such a state of mind only temporarily, and also impossible for a Chinese state pervaded by this state of mind to still have the ritual propriety and moral duty that make it superior to the barbarians. In contrast to the ethnocentric reading's confidence that Chinese civilization's moral superiority would survive the brief lack of a ruler, Cheng Yi's version of the self-critical reading is haunted by the specter of civilizational decline. In other words, it is a reading informed by ethnocentric moralism, not just ethnocentrism.

CHENG YI ON MORAL BARBARIZATION IN CHINESE HISTORY

Cheng Yi's reading of *Analects* 3.5 is not, strictly speaking, a statement about moral barbarization, only a statement about descending to a level worse than barbarism. But Cheng did claim elsewhere that moral barbarization had taken place in another period of Chinese history, the Cao-Wei and Western Jin dynasties. When a disciple asked Cheng Yi to explain Confucius's claim (in *Analects* 2.23) that one could predict the history of the next hundred generations based on how the Shang and Zhou dynasties had each altered the preceding dynasty's ritual institutions, Cheng replied with a theory that each imperial dynasty's ethos was simply a reaction to that of its predecessor, making it possible to extrapolate historical patterns.[52] The Qin was oppressive and suppressed classical scholarship; the Western Han therefore ruled with a light touch and esteemed Classicists. The promotion of Classicist values, including loyalty, resulted in an abundance of Han loyalists under Wang Mang's short-lived Xin dynasty (9–23 CE); the early Eastern Han naturally commended these loyalists' moral integrity, resulting in a grim, puritanical political culture obsessed with martyrdom. In reaction, the Wei-Jin literati turned toward free-spirited, unrestrained behavior and philosophical escapism, losing all regard for "ritual standards" (*lifa*). The literati then became "no different from barbarians," causing the loss of north China to Xiongnu rebels in the early fourth century. Whereas conventional accounts of this event tended to blame the Cao-Wei and Western Jin for allowing large numbers of Xiongnu and other "barbarian" peoples to settle permanently in north China during the third century, Cheng Yi argued that the Chinese elite's barbaric behavior was the catastrophe's root cause.

"When the disorder caused by barbarians has reached its height, there will surely be a hero who emerges to pacify it," Cheng Yi claims. Hence the

Sui-Tang reunification of the Chinese world, which "cleared away" (*quchu*) the barbarian rule of the Northern Dynasties. Cheng went on to claim, however, that even the Tang dynasty at its height under Taizong and Xuanzong (r. 713–56) also displayed lingering "barbarian customs" (*Yi-Di zhi feng*) in its disregard for the ethics of father-son, ruler-subject, and husband-wife relationships.[53] This barbarism began with Taizong's behavior during and after the Xuanwu Gate coup of 626, which consisted of killing two of his brothers (fratricide); forcing his father, Gaozu (r. 618–26) to abdicate (an unfilial and disloyal act); and taking the wife of one of the slain brothers as a concubine (incest). As a result, Tang political history was plagued by princes rebelling against their fathers, provinces rebelling against the court, and ministers usurping authority from emperors. This moral decline finally led to the collapse of the Tang and decades of political chaos and division under the Five Dynasties.[54] Interestingly, Cheng Yi sees in the faults of the Tang not an overcorrection to the preceding period's excesses, as had been the case with the Han and Wei-Jin, but rather the residual effects of barbarian rule and moral barbarization.

Cheng Yi's interpretation of Tang history reflects a growing tendency for Northern Song literati to criticize the Tang empire in general, and Tang Taizong in particular, on moral grounds.[55] But he seems to have been the first person to accuse the Tang of barbarism, and his interpretation of the Western Jin collapse also broke new ground by interpreting the Wei-Jin elite's famous flouting of ritual propriety as a state of barbarization that served as an invitation for real barbarian invaders. Liu Kai and Shi Jie analogized the fight against ideological heterodoxy to defending the Central Lands from barbarians; Ouyang Xiu and Sun Fu saw the Central Lands of Confucius's day as teetering on the edge of ethnocultural barbarization through barbarian conquest or domination. Cheng Yi differed from them all by drawing a connection between the security of the Central Lands and ethnocentric moralism by identifying barbarian invasion as a *consequence* of moral barbarization among the Chinese.

BARBARIANS AND BARBARISM IN THE *ANNALS* SCHOLARSHIP OF CHENG YI AND HU ANGUO

The Song dynasty's traumatic and unexpected loss of north China to the Jurchens twenty years after Cheng Yi's death gave a new sense of contemporary relevance and urgency to his interpretation of history. In a memorial submitted to the first Southern Song emperor, Gaozong (r. 1127–62), around early 1135, the young Daoxue philosopher Hu Hong (1105–1161) argued: "All things in the world respond to their own kind: those who live in the Central Lands but behave like barbarians (*Yi-Di xing*) will surely suffer disaster from the barbarians."[56] Then, modifying Cheng Yi's narrative slightly, Hu Hong claimed that the Western Jin lost north China and the Eastern Jin and Southern Dynasties failed to reconquer it because these regimes were all founded through immoral acts of usurpation. Likewise, the An Lushan Rebellion and the Tang dynasty's troubles with foreign enemies like the Tibetans resulted from the unfilial and incestuous behavior of Tang Taizong and his successors, which was "close to barbarism" (*jinsi Yi-Di*). Hu Hong follows by arguing that the Jurchen invasion was the direct result of a moral decline in the Song government that Wang Anshi's controversial reforms had precipitated.[57] Hu Hong comes close to claiming that Wang Anshi's reformist faction behaved like barbarians—as close as would be possible without committing lèse-majesté, since Gaozong's grandfather Shenzong (r. 1067–85) and father, Huizong (r. 1100–26), had supported Wang's reforms.

When Hu Hong's father, Hu Anguo (1074–1138)—himself a noted Daoxue philosopher—presented his commentary on the *Annals* to Gaozong in late 1136 or early 1137, the preface and memorial that accompanied it blamed Wang Anshi and his followers for causing a moral decline that "led barbarians to bring disorder to the Chinese" (*shi/zhi Yi-Di luan Hua*), but also stopped short of accusing them of having caused a moral barbarization of the Chinese.[58] After Hu Anguo's death in 1138, however, his adopted son Hu Yin (1098–1156) wrote an obituary for him that claimed the elder Hu, in the years before the Jurchen invasion, often lamented that the marginalization of *Annals* scholarship under Wang Anshi and his reformist faction had made it possible for the reformists to "bring disorder to human relations and destroy the *li*, using barbarian [ways] to change the Chinese."[59]

Many modern studies of Song-period *Annals* exegesis represent Hu Anguo as the leading proponent of a militantly revanchist and barbarophobic approach to the *Annals* that supposedly characterized the Southern Song, in contrast to a Northern Song approach that was supposedly more focused on the idea of "respecting the king" (*zunwang*) than that of "repelling the barbarians" (*rangyi*).[60] More recently, Wang Leisong has argued that Hu Anguo differed from most *Annals* scholars in combining a strong emphasis on "respecting the king and repelling the barbarians" (a phrase that Hu, in fact, never used) with a belief, drawn from Han Yu, that the boundary between

Chineseness and barbarism was fluid and based on moral standards.[61] A closer reading of Hu Anguo's *Annals* commentary reveals, however, that it has much more in common with Northern Song *Annals* exegesis than has generally been assumed. Hu was heavily influenced by Cheng Yi's interpretations of the *Annals* and of *Analects* 3.5, and both the revanchist and ethnocentric moralist rhetoric in Hu's commentary had precedents in Cheng's own unfinished commentary. This suggests that Hu Anguo's understanding of the *Annals* influenced his position on Song-Jurchen relations, rather than vice versa.

Cheng Yi is said to have decided to write a commentary to the *Annals* after being disappointed by a commentary that his disciple Liu Xun (1045–1087) had produced. But he did not begin this project until around 1101, by which time Liu Xun had been dead for fourteen years and Cheng himself was nearly seventy years old.[62] His preface to the commentary is dated 1103, and he had only finished commenting on the first twenty years of the *Annals* when he died in 1107. The rest of his commentary comprises oral teachings recorded by his students and added to the text posthumously.[63] Hu Anguo began studying Cheng Yi's *Annals* commentary in 1116 and was a devoted follower of Cheng's philosophy by the time he made the final revision to his own commentary in 1135–37; indeed, he also collaborated with Yang Shi on the compilation of the Cheng brothers' recorded sayings in 1132–35.[64]

The first passage relating to barbarians in Cheng Yi's commentary is on Lord Yin of Lu's conference with a Rong leader at Qian in the spring of 721 BCE. Whereas both Sun Fu and Liu Chang had interpreted Confucius's attitude toward the Qian conference as one of disapproval,[65] Cheng Yi seems to have been the first commentator to tie that disapproval to an idea that the conference violated a principle against appeasing barbarian invaders:

> The Zhou dynasty was in decline, and barbarians were bringing disorder to the Chinese, with groups of them living scattered throughout the Central Lands. If the hegemons and larger states clearly understood their highest moral duty (*dayi*) and repelled [these barbarians], that would have been morally correct (*yi*). As for the other states, it would have been acceptable for them to "be prudent in strengthening their defenses."[66] But if they made peace with [the barbarians] in order to be spared from invasion and violence, this would not be "smiting the Rong and Di";[67] rather, it would be permitting them to bring disorder to the Chinese. That is why the *Annals* is especially careful with the difference between Chinese and barbarians (*Hua-Yi zhi bian*). If [the barbarians] stayed in their own lands and were

friendly to the Central Lands, then [Confucius] would have approved of having covenants and conferences with them. Lord [Yin's] act of holding a conference with the Rong was immoral (*feiyi*).[68]

Cheng reiterates this point more concisely regarding the covenant that Lord Yin made with the same Rong at Tang later that year: "The Rong brought disorder to the Chinese, yet [Lord Yin] made a covenant with them; this was immoral."[69]

The most striking aspect of Cheng Yi's interpretation of the Qian conference is his view of the Rong involved as aggressors and unwelcome intruders in Lu territory—a view contrary to the *Zuo Tradition* account, which speaks of a previous history of friendship with the Rong under earlier Lu rulers.[70] Less noticeable but just as significant is Cheng Yi's use of the phrase *Hua-Yi zhi bian*, "the difference between Chinese and barbarians." Modern Chinese scholarship generally refers to premodern discourses of Chinese ethnic identity using this and a similar phrase, *Yi-Xia zhi bian* ("the difference between barbarians and Chinese"). It is widely assumed that these terms have a classical or at least an early imperial origin. On the contrary, the concept of a Chinese-barbarian dichotomy seems to have existed for more than a thousand years without a name unambiguously designating it as an ethnic dichotomy. The phrase *Hua-Yi zhi bian* does not occur in any text earlier than Cheng Yi's commentary to the *Annals*, while the first occurrence of *Yi-Xia zhi bian* that I know of is in Shao Bo's (d. 1158) *Sequel to the Record of Things Heard and Seen by Mister Shao* (Shaoshi wenjian houlu), composed in 1157.[71]

It is quite possible that Cheng Yi himself invented the phrase *Hua-Yi zhi bian*. But there is also a possibility that the originator was Cheng Hao, whose influence on Cheng Yi's reading of the *Annals* was apparently considerable. Li Mingfu's (1174–1234) *Collected Meanings of the Annals* (Chunqiu jiyi) has this to say about Cheng Hao's interpretations of the *Annals*: "Cheng Hao, too, did not write any books about the *Annals*, but he argued that the *Annals* was careful about the difference between Chinese and barbarians (*Hua-Yi zhi bian*) above all else; discoursed brilliantly on the difference between kings and hegemons; and deeply understood the difference between Heaven-ordained *li* (*tianli*) and human desires. . . . His younger brother Cheng Yi also used many of his interpretations when writing a commentary to the *Annals*."[72] This implies that Cheng Yi's interpretation of the Qian conference and Tang covenant followed that of Cheng Hao.[73] But we cannot be certain that the phrase

Hua-Yi zhi bian was already present in Cheng Hao's oral interpretation and that Li Mingfu did not apply it anachronistically.

When in 1079 Cheng Yi endorsed Han Yu's opinion that the language of the *Annals* was "careful and strict," he was referring to what he believed to be Confucius's fears about the barbarizing and ultimately bestializing effect of losing ritual propriety. Over twenty years later, however, Cheng's observation that "the *Annals* is especially careful with the difference between Chinese and barbarians" was based on the danger of invading barbarians "bringing disorder to the Chinese."[74] We do not know whether Cheng Yi's perception of Confucius's message shifted over time; it is equally plausible that he simply deferred to Cheng Hao's position when writing his *Annals* commentary. In any case, neither of the Cheng brothers could have foreseen the Jurchen invasion or seen the Song as facing any other imminent foreign threat. Instead, the key foreign policy issue that divided their generation was the aggressive (and expensive) irredentist warfare against Xi Xia that Shenzong, Huizong, and their pro-reform ministers seemed intent on waging.

The geopolitical situation had changed dramatically by the time Hu Anguo completed his commentary, which includes an original attempt at explicating a philosophical basis for Confucius's supposed prejudice against barbarians. Hu's commentary on the Qian conference begins with a question: "[The *Annals*] refers to barbarians only by the names of their states because it regards them as foreigners. Heaven shelters all things and earth bears all things, and the Son of Heaven is equivalent to heaven and earth. The *Annals* speaks for the Son of Heaven, so why does it regard the barbarians as foreigners?"[75] The *Gongyang Commentary* had posed a similar question and resolved it by claiming that Confucius's regarding the barbarians as "foreigners" was only a temporary attitude that a "True King" had to adopt in the initial stages of unifying the world: "He begins [the unification] from the places closer to him."[76] Hu Anguo's solution eschews such universalist ambitions and links the Chinese-barbarian dichotomy to two other binary oppositions: that of noble men (*junzi*) to inferior men (*xiaoren*) and that of the hexagram *tai* (representing flow and flourishing) to the hexagram *pi* (representing obstruction and decline). In this, Hu follows Cheng Yi's interpretation of the *Changes*, in which *tai* symbolizes the political dominance of noble men and *pi* symbolizes the dominance of inferior men.[77] Hu writes: "The Central Lands are to the barbarians just as noble men are to inferior men. When noble men are brought in and inferior men kept out, that is 'flourishing' (*tai*), but when inferior men are brought in and noble men kept out, that is 'decline' (*pi*). The *Annals* is the sage [Confucius's] book for reversing 'decline,' so it regards the [people of the] Central Lands as compatriots (literally, "insiders") and the barbarians of the four quarters as foreigners, causing each to be content in its place."[78]

Hu Anguo then brings in a third binary opposition frequently used in Chinese philosophical argumentation: that between a thing's essence or substance (*ti*) and its application, function, or manifestation (*yong*).[79] "To shelter all and bear all is the essence (*ti*) of the True King's moral power (*de*), but to regard the [people of the] Central Lands as compatriots and the barbarians of the four quarters as foreigners is the function (*yong*) of the True King's way."[80] In more mundane terms, one could say that universalism is theory or ideal; drawing ethnic distinctions and acting based on ethnic identity is what really happens in practice.

This effort at justifying the limits of Confucius's universalism evades the question of *why* all barbarians would be as morally inferior as the inferior men of the Central Lands. Instead, Hu Anguo shifts from philosophical theorizing to laying out what he sees as the practical policy implications of regarding barbarians as inferior "foreigners." The Chinese should not pay tribute to barbarians, since this contravenes the principle of Chinese superiority.[81] When barbarians pay homage at the imperial court, they should not be accorded a ritual protocol higher than that of Chinese nobles.[82] Barbarians should not be allowed to migrate into the Chinese lands because of the likelihood of them rebelling later; here, Hu invokes the much-abused *Zuo Tradition* quotation, "They are not our kin and kind (*zulei*), so their hearts are sure to be different."[83] By the end of a commentarial passage ostensibly attempting to reconcile universalism with ethnocentrism, Hu Anguo seems to have abandoned the notion that a Son of Heaven should be above ethnic distinctions, and for reasons that seem to have had much to do with the Jurchen invasion.

Hu Anguo's interpretation of the Tang covenant of 721 BCE continues in this vein:

> The "Bishi" [chapter of the *Documents*] speaks of the Yi of the Huai River and the Rong of Xú.[84] These [Rong who made the covenant with Lu] were probably Rong of Xú province who had long lived in the Central Lands and were in the eastern outskirts of Lu. Han Yu said, "The *Annals* is careful and strict," and a noble man (*junzi*; i.e., Cheng Yi) believed that [Han Yu] deeply understood its intent. What is being "careful and strict" being careful

about? It is careful about the difference between Chinese and barbarians (*Hua-Yi zhi bian*) above all else. When the Central Lands are like the barbarians, one regards them as barbarians; when the barbarians bring disorder to the Chinese, one smites them. That is the intent of the *Annals*. As for swearing a covenant with the Rong by smearing blood on one's mouth, that was immoral (*feiyi*).[85]

"Smearing blood on one's mouth" was the conventional Chinese rite for sealing an interstate covenant in Zhou times; Hu Anguo is criticizing the inclusion of barbarians in this rite, not the rite itself, as immoral. Despite having claimed, on the basis of the *Documents*, that the Rong of Xú had been living on the edges of Lu territory since the days of the first Lu ruler, Hu persists in viewing any covenant with them as immoral appeasement of barbarian invaders.

Hu Anguo went on to liken the Tang covenant to Western Han marriage diplomacy with the Xiongnu, the Tang dynasty's reliance on the Uighurs as military allies during and after the An Lushan Rebellion, and emperor Dezong's (r. 779–805) attempts at reaching a truce with the Tibetan empire—all cases in which diplomatic appeasement of barbarians was seen to have failed to prevent further humiliation at their hands.[86] Of course, the unspoken contemporary parallel on Hu Anguo's mind was the ongoing debate at Gaozong's court over whether to negotiate peace with the Jurchens. It may be easy for us to assume that Hu Anguo was simply using his commentary as a vehicle for hawkish arguments against appeasement. But the similarity between his interpretation of the Tang covenant and Cheng Yi's raises the strong possibility that a serious interest in applying Cheng's interpretation to current geopolitics drove his opposition to peace negotiations, rather than vice versa.

Thus far, we appear to have good reason to characterize both Cheng Yi and Hu Anguo as ethnic exclusionists whose primary concern with regard to barbarians was keeping them out of the Chinese world. But that view becomes problematic when we come to their treatment of the Lu state's next covenant with the Rong, in 710 BCE. The oath ceremony was held at Tang as it had been eleven years before, but two things were different this time: first, the Lu ruler was now Lord Huan, who had seized power by murdering his brother Lord Yin; second, the *Annals* records Lord Huan's return from Tang, whereas it had not done so for Lord Yin. Cheng Yi notes a likely reason for this: The *Annals* records a ruler's return if his travels have extended from one season to the next, which was the case for Lord Huan's trip to Tang but not Lord Yin's. Yet Cheng Yi prefers a different reason: that Confucius wanted to show that Lord Huan had been in danger of not returning from Tang. Rather than attribute the danger to the Rong people's perfidy, however, Cheng Yi suggests that the danger lay in the chance that the Rong would seek to bring Lord Huan to justice for his fratricide, unlike various Chinese rulers who had condoned his crime:

> Lord Huan became ruler through assassination and had previously gone to a conference with the rulers of Zheng, Qi, and Chen, but [these rulers] were all as immoral as him. When he traveled afar and made a covenant with the Rong, [Confucius] knew the danger he had been in and thus recorded, "he returned." If the Rong were not as (*buru*) evil as the rulers of those three states (Zheng, Qi, and Chen), then they would attack him.[87] This is what [Confucius] meant when he said he wanted to live among the Yi and sail out to sea; since the Central Lands did not understand moral duty, perhaps the barbarians might be able to understand it.[88]

Here, Cheng Yi alludes to *Analects* 9.14 and also 5.7, in which Confucius expresses a desire to go to sea on a raft, out of despair that "the Way does not prevail" in his society. Beginning in the first century CE, these two passages were frequently conflated, due to a mistaken assumption that the Yi to whom Confucius referred in 9.14 were the people of Korea.[89] Cheng Yi seems to be recognizing that, to Confucius, "barbarians bringing disorder to the Chinese" was not the worst thing that could happen to "the difference between Chinese and barbarians." The worst that could happen was for the Chinese to behave so barbarically toward each other that life among the barbarians appeared preferable.

Hu Anguo adopts Cheng Yi's interpretation of this second covenant at Tang, paraphrasing it and then linking it to Cheng's interpretation of *Analects* 3.5: "Master Cheng was right to say, 'This is what [Confucius] meant when he said he wanted to live among the Yi and sail out to sea.' Does the *Analects* not say, 'The barbarians still have rulers, unlike the Chinese states that do not'?"[90] Hu's interpretations of both the Tang covenants therefore reflect a belief that the *Annals* is as much about condemning Chinese moral barbarism as about repelling barbarians: recall that his commentary on the first covenant did include the line, "When the Central Lands are like the barbarians, one regards them as barbarians (*Zhongguo er Yi-Di ze Di zhi*); when the barbarians bring disorder to the Chinese, one smites them."[91]

This balanced emphasis can also be demonstrated statistically. Twenty-eight commentarial sections in Hu Anguo's commentary assert the importance of repelling barbarians, the need for keeping barbarians out of the Central Lands, or the moral illegitimacy of covenants or any other form of alliance between Chinese states and barbarians, sometimes using the phrase *Hua-Yi zhi bian* or the similar *bian Hua-Yi zhi fen* ("telling the difference between Chinese and barbarians").[92] One of these sections (on the first Tang covenant) also speaks of barbarization. Twenty-six other sections in the commentary criticize the moral decline of Chinese states using either the concept of barbarization—sometimes together with the concept of bestialization—or Cheng Yi's reading of *Analects* 3.5.[93] The discourse of moral barbarism therefore occurs in nearly as many sections (twenty-seven) as the discourse of repelling barbarians (twenty-eight). One of the sections concerned with moral barbarization quotes Cheng Yi's commentary directly; another three correspond closely to oral teachings appended to Cheng's commentary.[94] Out of these three, one section relating to the "barbarizing" demotions of the Qǐ rulers interprets the phrase *Hua-Yi zhi bian* in terms of Cheng Yi's theory of barbarization, warning: "The Central Lands are the Central Lands because of ritual propriety and moral duty; lose them once and we become barbarians, lose them again and we become animals, bringing humankind to extinction!"[95] The evidence of Hu Anguo's commentary therefore does not support the conventional view that Hu, responding to the geopolitics of his time, began a distinct shift toward anti-"barbarian" militancy in Song-period *Annals* exegesis. Instead, two of the commentary's major themes, the discourse of "repelling barbarians" and the discourse of moral barbarism, are both already present in Cheng Yi's commentary and other works, and neither theme predominates over the other.[96]

In studies on the Southern Song statecraft thinker Chen Liang (1143–1194), Hoyt Tillman argued that Chen's use of the phrase "the way of the barbarians" (Didao) to describe Jurchen customs contradicted the Daoxue belief in a universal Way (Dao) applicable to all humanity, marking his thought as a kind of "proto-nationalism" opposed to the "culturalistic" thinking or "cultural universalism" of Daoxue thinkers.[97] But five of the twenty-seven sections in Hu Anguo's commentary that speak of barbarization or *Analects* 3.5 also refer to immoral behavior by the term *Didao*.[98] In fact, this term already appears in the *Guliang Commentary*; moreover, it is semantically equivalent to the term *Yidao* that appears in *Select Sayings of the Cheng Brothers*, and also to *Yi-Di zhi dao*, which occurs twice in the oral teachings appended to Cheng Yi's *Annals* commentary: once with reference to the pursuit of revenge without regard for right and wrong and once with regard to "forgetting moral duty at the sight of potential profit."[99] Moreover, since the phrase *Yi-Di zhi dao* also appears in the *Annals* exegesis of Sun Fu and possibly Liu Chang, it seems likely that both Hu Anguo and Chen Liang continued a common Northern Song practice of using the word *dao* both to refer to a transcendent, universal set of moral norms ("the Way") and to describe narrower sets of nonnormative values or behaviors.

Departing from earlier scholarship that associated Daoxue thinkers with a moral universalism that transcended ethnic differences, some recent studies have argued that Daoxue thought reflected a growing tendency in Song elite society to reject foreign peoples and cultures simply because they were not Chinese.[100] On the contrary, the earliest Daoxue thinkers seem to have been most interested in using the idea of "the way of the barbarians" to condemn any kind of immorality as un-Chinese. Both Cheng Yi and Hu Anguo had a complex understanding of "the difference between Chinese and barbarians" that was not determined solely by foreign geopolitical threats; instead, they alternated between the language of "repelling the barbarians" and that of ethnocentric moralism to warn their audience about the danger of appeasement and the specter of moral decline at the same time. When it came to explicating the Chinese-barbarian dichotomy in the *Annals*, therefore, ethnic identity and moral philosophy sometimes pulled both men in opposite directions, even as they tried to fuse the two rhetorically. The tension that arose from harnessing ethnocentric habits of thought to the Daoxue cause of moral reform, rather than resisting or rejecting those habits altogether, would only increase as Southern Song thinkers responded to the new cause of revanchist war against the Jurchens.

Conclusion

> . . . Night has fallen and the barbarians have not come.
> And some who have just returned from the border say
> there are no barbarians any longer.
> And now, what's going to happen to us without barbarians?
> They were, those people, a kind of solution.
> —C. P. CAVAFY, "Waiting for the Barbarians"

THIS book began by analyzing the ninth-century origins of two new interpretations of Chinese identity and its presumed opposite, barbarism: "ethnicized orthodoxy" and "ethnocentric moralism." These discourses arose in specific rhetorical or polemical contexts previously obscured by historians' tendency to classify some Tang discourses as "cosmopolitan" or "universalistic" and others as "xenophobic." Ethnicized orthodoxy (often mischaracterized as xenophobia or proto-nationalism) reached a peak in the Northern Song Guwen revival and then faded away as the more radical side of that revival lost influence, whereas ethnocentric moralism (often mischaracterized as "culturalism") gained strength during the late eleventh and early twelfth centuries, in part due to its use by the emerging Daoxue philosophical tradition.

Using Cavafy's famous poem as a framing device, one could say that the expanded and more abstract definition of barbarism created by ethnicized orthodoxy and ethnocentric moralism served rhetorically as "a kind of solution" for Guwen writers and Daoxue thinkers. It was a way to show pluralist or pragmatist detractors how much orthodoxy or morality mattered by casting the Way of the Sages as the "Way of the Central Lands," the essential core of Chineseness, apart from which there was only the way of the barbarians.

But in the Song period, this conflation of ideology or values with ethnocultural identity also inadvertently produced "a kind of problem" when it came to thinking about the peoples whom the Chinese saw as barbarians in ethnocultural terms: Since it was possible for the Chinese to be barbarized ideologically or morally, would it not also be possible for the barbarians to be "Sinicized" by embracing orthodoxy and morality? In that case, was barbarian moral inferiority merely a temporary condition that prolonged contact with Chinese civilization would bring to an end?

Universalism of this kind was a relatively easy position to take when the Chinese state was a powerful empire that could claim to be civilizing barbarians by bringing them to submission—indeed, Han and Tang officials who insisted that barbarian moral inferiority was permanent usually did so because they opposed imperial expansion on practical grounds.[1] Even in the mid-ninth century, when Tang imperial expansion had long ceased to be possible, Chinese confidence in their inherent superiority over their neighbors remained undiminished and perhaps even received a boost from the collapse of the once-mighty Uighur and Tibetan empires in the 840s. This sense of confidence is well reflected in Chen An's praise of Li Yansheng as a barbarian with a Chinese heart, whose success would encourage other barbarians to follow his example and embrace the Tang empire's "transforming influence." Consider also the Guwen writer Sun Qiao's (fl. 838–84) "Preface on the Southwestern Barbarians" (Xu xinanyi), which boasts that the Tang, by providing a classical education to elite young students from Silla and the Yunnan kingdom of Nanzhao, has succeeded in transforming the "bestial hearts" of the people in these states, such that they now "understand ritual etiquette" and "put Classicist teachings first, resembling the Chinese (zhu Xia) in their level of refinement (binbin)."[2]

In Song times, however, the idea of barbarians becoming like the Chinese seems to have been a source of anxiety, not pride, as certain Inner Asian "barbarian" peoples now used it as a basis to assert equality or even superiority to the Song state. The first of these were the Kitans, who, despite controlling only the northern edge of the North China Plain from their Manchurian homeland, came to see their powerful empire as a new civilization with a claim to centrality to rival that of the Chinese "Central Lands." The full name of the Kitan empire found in numerous Kitan-script epitaphs from the eleventh century, as well as the covering stone inscription for the Liao emperor Daozong's (r. 1055–1101) epitaph, translates as "the Great Central Liao Kitan State." A Chinese-language memorial from circa 1094 by a Liao Chinese literatus refers to all of Daozong's subjects as "the people of the Central Lands," while referring to Chinese subjects only as "Chinese (Han) households." Moreover, the Chinese epitaph of an eminent Liao Buddhist monk, dated 1118, refers to "the Central Lands of the Great Liao" (Da Liao Zhongguo). It would thus seem that by the time of Daozong's reign, the Kitan empire referred to itself as "central" in both the Kitan and Chinese languages.[3]

The Kitan claim to centrality is strikingly reflected in a story that the Song envoy Hong Hao (1088–1155) heard while a prisoner of the Jurchen Jin in 1129–43: "During the reign of Daozong of the Great Liao, a Chinese man (Hanren) was giving a lecture on the *Analects* [in the imperial palace] and got to the line, '[He who rules by moral power (*de*) is like] the polestar, which remains unmoving in its place while all the other stars revolve respectfully around it.'[4] Daozong remarked, 'I've heard that [the lands] below the polestar are the Central Lands (Zhongguo). Wouldn't that be this land we're in?'"[5] Daozong's claim about the polestar seems to have been derived from the Chinese Buddhist apologetic text *Master Mou's Discourse on Resolving Doubts*.[6] The author of *Master Mou's Discourse* spuriously attributed the claim to a classical commentary (possibly the *Zuo Tradition*) and used it to challenge the Chinese world's traditional claim to geopolitical centrality, which had served to justify ethnocentric claims that Buddhism, being from the "barbarians," must be inferior to "the Way of Yao, Shun, the Duke of Zhou, and Confucius." Liao Daozong, on the other hand, uses it to assert the centrality of his own, more northern polity and implicitly reject the Song dynasty's claim to the same.

But Daozong does more than this in the anecdote that Hong Hao heard from his Jurchen captors, who in turn had probably heard it from the Kitans. The Liao emperor next notices his Chinese classics lecturer's awkward attempt at avoiding the ethnocentric implications of *Analects* 3.5 (in its traditional, pre–Cheng Yi interpretation) and uses it as an opportunity to reject the Chinese-barbarian dichotomy as an outmoded way of viewing the world: "When [the Chinese scholar] got to the line, 'The barbarians have rulers [but are still not equal to Chinese states that do not],' he recited it hurriedly and dared not lecture on it. [Daozong] then remarked, 'In ancient times, the Xunyu and Xianyun were utterly devoid of ritual standards (*lifa*), so they were called barbarians (Yi). We, however, have developed ritual institutions (*wenwu*) and are no different from the Central Lands of the Chinese (Zhonghua) in refinement (*binbin*). Why should I take offense?' He then ordered [the Chinese scholar] to lecture on this passage."[7] Since the Xunyu and

Xianyun peoples were believed to have lived on the steppe some two to three millennia before this,[8] Daozong was effectively saying that the nomadic peoples of the north had long ceased to be barbarians; if *Analects* 3.5 was relevant in Confucius's day, it certainly was not applicable to the Kitans now. Instead, there were now two great civilizations in the world: the "Central Lands of the Chinese," ruled by the Song dynasty, and the Central Lands of the Kitans.

The Song official Chao Yuezhi (1059–1129), after returning from an embassy to the Liao capital around 1100, claimed that the Liao empire's exceptional longevity by the standards of "barbarian" states was largely due to Daozong's embrace of the "civilized" norms of governance associated with the Chinese: "Although the enemy (*lu*) ruler was born in a land of sheep and dogs, he is humane and gentle, avoids talking about war, and dislikes capital punishment.[9] He admires [the late Song emperor] Renzong's (r. 1022–63) moral power (*de*) and emulates it; whenever he mentions Renzong, he touches a hand to his forehead to show his respect."[10] As further evidence of Daozong's sentiments, Chao Yuezhi claimed that he had commissioned two large gold statues of the Buddha bearing this inscription on their backs: "May I be born in the Central Lands in my next life." Chao, assuming that Daozong was referring to the Song dynasty, understood his wish as an expression of admiration for Chinese civilization and longing to be Chinese. Historians Zhang Qifan and Xiong Mingqin have recently argued persuasively, however, that Daozong was referring to the Buddhist holy land of central India, which was (somewhat confusingly) also known as "the Central Lands" (Sanskrit: Madhyadeśa) in Buddhist cosmology.[11] Three different "Central Lands" thus existed in the Liao spatial consciousness, and the Song Chinese recognized only one of them.

In fact, Daozong appropriated not just "the Central Lands" but also Hua as names for the Liao empire, redefining both terms as supra-ethnic markers of civilization.[12] A poem that Daozong composed as a gift for his mother in 1057, two years into his reign, bears the title "Ruler and Subjects Share the Same Aspirations; Hua and Yi Share the Same Customs" (Junchen tongzhi, Hua-Yi tongfeng).[13] This poem is no longer extant, but a companion poem written by Daozong's young empress has been preserved and indicates that the theme "Hua and Yi share the same customs" celebrates the Liao empire's success in spreading civilization as far as the steppe and the Korean peninsula.[14] In that case, the Hua in the title almost certainly refers to both the Kitans and their Chinese subjects, while Yi, "the barbarians," refers to peoples like the Tatars and Koreans who had accepted Liao suzerainty. There are other examples of such usage. An epitaph for a Liao aristocrat, composed in 1112, mentions his grandfather commanding a military expedition against the recalcitrant "eastern barbarians of the Han [River]" (*dong Han Yi*) during the reign of Shengzong (r. 982–1031)—clearly a reference to the three Kitan invasions of Koryŏ between 993 and 1019. The epitaph also speaks of Daozong "ruling over all of *zhu Xia*"—another case of appropriating one of the names that Chinese empires routinely used.[15]

Chao Yuezhi's misreading of Daozong's inscription and his interpretation of Daozong as a Renzong wannabe suggest that Northern Song literati never understood the extent of the Kitans' facility at appropriating Chinese claims to centrality and civilization.[16] But perhaps there was willful misunderstanding as well. The Chanyuan covenant of 1005, by compelling the Song to recognize the Liao ruler as an emperor of equal standing to their own, was a serious blow to the idea of Chinese superiority that may have made the Song elite prone to shoring up their ethnocentric pride with patronizing readings of the Kitans as slavish imitators of Chinese political culture. Consider Zhu Yu's description of the Liao (around 1119) as "addicted to learning from the Central Lands," to the extent of copying every institutional or ritual move that the Song court made, when in reality the Kitans had selectively blended elements of Tang political and ritual culture with their own Inner Asian traditions.[17]

The Tangut Xi Xia's brazen bid for Song recognition as another imperial state in 1038–44, while ultimately unsuccessful, may have precipitated an even deeper crisis of confidence at the Song court. This context evidently informs Li Gou's lament-cum-warning in 1043, "[Today's] barbarians and Chinese are not the barbarians and Chinese of antiquity," and his damning criticism of "foolish Classicists" who persisted in boasting of Chinese superiority without thinking about the reforms necessary for preventing its permanent disappearance. In 1044, Fu Bi, one of the intended readers of Li Gou's "The Enemy Threat," delivered a similar warning to Renzong:

> [The Kitans and Tanguts] have acquired territory from the Central Lands, drafted people of the Central Lands [as laborers and soldiers], used the imperial title of the Central Lands, imitated the bureaucracy of the Central Lands, employed men of worth and talent from the Central Lands, read the books of the Central Lands, used the official carriages and court dress of the Central Lands, and implemented the laws and statutes of the Central

Lands. Thus, whatever these two enemy (*lu*) [peoples] have done is equal to the Central Lands, whereas their crack troops and brave generals are better than those of the Central Lands. Whatever the Central Lands have, they too have it; what they excel in, the Central Lands cannot match. We must treat them as formidable enemies of the Central Lands, and perhaps then we may be able to resist them. How can we treat these two enemy [peoples] like the barbarians of antiquity?[18]

The point of Fu Bi's memorial was that the Song would have to adopt new, more sophisticated military strategies to defeat the Liao and Xi Xia, not that it should recognize these "formidable enemies" as civilized equals. Likewise, Li Gou's contention that "one may be a barbarian but could just as well be called Chinese" if one achieves just, moral governance was meant at spurring his Chinese audience to maintain its superiority through reform, not encouraging the Tanguts to attain parity with the Song. In both cases, it was not Chinese ethnocentrism per se that was being rejected, only the dangerous complacency it might encourage.

The same geopolitical context of imperiled superiority may explain Liu Chang's choice to draw a seemingly hairsplitting distinction, in the field of *Annals* interpretation, between barbarized Chinese states that could return to Chineseness and "real barbarians" who would always be barbaric. It should be noted that Liu, like Chao Yuezhi and numerous other Song officials, witnessed the size and power of the Kitan empire firsthand during an assignment as ambassador to the Liao court.[19] Su Shi, while differing with Liu Chang's view that Confucius was more magnanimous toward barbarized Chinese than toward "real" or "pure" barbarians, himself felt no attraction to the idea of transforming barbarians in the Chinese image. Hence, he faulted Han Yu's essay "Tracing Humanity to Its Source" for claiming that a sage would relate to human beings (i.e., Chinese people), barbarians, and animals with an attitude of "seeing them as one and with the same humaneness" (*yishi er tongren*).[20] To Su's mind, a different expression of humaneness was appropriate to each category of being: "To give them skills by teaching them, and to give them understanding by transforming them—that is how to treat human beings humanely. To reciprocate their [friendly] sentiments without despising the [inadequate] ritual [by which those sentiments are expressed], and to commend them when they come [to submit] without rebuking them when they depart [after submitting]—that is how to treat barbarians humanely. To slaughter them in the right season and use them in moderation—that is the way to treat animals humanely. That being so, how can we treat them as one?"[21] In other words, the barbarians' proper place was as boorish bearers of tribute who interacted intermittently with the Chinese (or, in Su's terms, "human") world. Attempting to teach them civilized Chinese ways would be as inappropriate as using them as food or beasts of burden.

Somewhat surprisingly, when it came to assessing historical—as opposed to contemporary—dynasties ruled by "barbarians," Northern Song literati chose not to let ethnocentrism and wounded pride dictate their conclusions.[22] Both the 1040 version and the heavily revised 1071–72 version of Ouyang Xiu's essay "On Legitimate Dynasties" classified the Northern Dynasties and the Southern Dynasties alike as illegitimate on the grounds of their failure to achieve reunification, without regard to the ethnicity of their rulers. Likewise, when Ouyang reversed an earlier position he had taken on the Five Dynasties and rejected them all as illegitimate, he did so on grounds of their rulers' immorality, rather than singling out the Shatuo Türk dynasties of Later Tang, Later Jin, and Later Han.[23]

Ouyang Xiu even anticipated an argument that the Northern Wei's longevity and accomplishments meant that it should not be "dismissed as [a] barbarian [state]" simply because it had not conquered the south.[24] This is the position taken, for example, by Zhang Fangping's (1007–1091) essay "On the Legitimacy of the North and the Illegitimacy of the South" (Nanbei zhengrun lun), which argues that the Northern Wei, despite being of "Hu stock" (*Huzhong*), was the legitimate successor to the Western Jin because it ruled the North China Plain, adopted Chinese laws and customs, and was more successful than the Southern Dynasties in establishing lasting, stable governance. Zhang uses a variation on *Mencius* 4B.1 to argue that barbarians, too, can occasionally merit receiving the Mandate of Heaven: "It is the same as the Xia dynasty's [founder] Yu emerging from the eastern Yi, and King Wen receiving Heaven's favor among the western Qiang.[25] Both gained the great Mandate to bring relief to the lands of the Chinese. This is recorded in the *Odes* and the *Documents*, so what do you say to that?"[26] Also worth mentioning in this regard is an essay by Chen Shidao (ca. 1053–ca. 1101) that bears the same title as Ouyang Xiu's. Chen's essay endorses the early seventh-century philosopher Wang Tong's argument that the Northern Wei became legitimate upon the end of the Liu-Song dynasty in 479, due to Xiaowendi's merits as a ruler, and that the Southern Qi, Liang, and Chen dynasties in the south should therefore be "rejected as barbarians of the four quarters."[27] Chen, a protégé of Su Shi, also affirms the Northern Wei's legitimacy using the approach to *Annals* exegesis taken in Su's "On 'The True King Does Not Govern the Barbarians'":

> King Wen was a man of the western Yi, and [the rulers of] Qin, Wu, and Chu were Rong and Man barbarians, but a noble man (*junzi*; i.e., Confucius) promoted them and regarded them as people of the Central Lands. [The rulers of] Qĭ were descendants of the Xia dynasty, but a noble man rejected them and regarded them as barbarians. ... Someone might ask: "To regard the [Northern] Wei as Chinese and reject the [Southern] Qi, Liang, and Chen as Man barbarians—is that not perverse?" I would reply: "When barbarians transformed, a noble man promoted them even if they had not become purely Chinese. When the Chinese transformed, a noble man rejected them even if they had not become purely barbarian. How much more so when they have become purely [Chinese or barbarian]?"[28]

Unlike Su Shi, however, Chen Shidao takes for granted the notion that barbarians *can* transform into Chinese via adopting Chinese mores and customs, just as the Chinese can become barbarians via immorality.

Ouyang Xiu's "On Legitimate Dynasties" preempted arguments like Zhang Fangping's and Chen Shidao's by implying that a dynasty's success in other areas could not outweigh its failure to achieve reunification. The idea of a barbarian dynasty unifying—in effect, conquering—the entire Chinese world was merely a hypothetical historical scenario to Northern Song literati like Ouyang, Zhang, and Chen, despite the military challenges posed by the Kitans and Tanguts. This made it possible for them to adopt an even-handed attitude toward the Xianbi rulers of the Northern Wei. But a Southern Song editor of Ouyang Xiu's works evidently objected to even his ethnicity-blind explanation for the Northern Wei's illegitimacy and appended this comment to the 1040 version:

> The Central Lands are superior [to the barbarians] because they have ritual propriety and moral duty. That is why the superior ruling over the inferior accords with [what is right], while the inferior infringing on (*gan*) the superior goes against it. The sage's (i.e., Confucius's) sincerity in extending his approval to the good was such that when barbarians admired the Central Lands, he would promote (*jin*) them. For barbarians to be promoted to the level of the Central Lands is a fortunate thing, but

how can it be acceptable for them to then infringe on the legitimate succession of emperors and kings?[29]

As this comment shows, the Jurchen invasion made it significantly more difficult for Southern Song literati to espouse a fluid or relativistic view of the Chinese-barbarian dichotomy, since such a notion threatened to legitimize the Jurchen Jin's efforts at asserting suzerainty over the Song.

A story told by Zhang Di, a north Chinese man who defected to the Southern Song around 1192,[30] concerns a conversation that the Jin emperor Wanyan Liang (r. 1150–61; posthumously demoted as Prince of Hailing) had with two of his ministers in the 1150s: "On another day, he was conversing with Hanlin Academician and Recipient of Edicts Wanyan Zongxiu (1116–1157) and Left Vice Grand Councilor Cai Songnian (1107–1159), and said: 'Whenever I read the *Analects* and come to the line "Although the barbarians have rulers, they are still not equal to Chinese states that do not," I secretly detest it. Wasn't [Confucius] calling his [people] superior and ours inferior simply because of the difference between north and south and his affinity for his own kind?' The two ministers both said, 'Yes, yes,' and [tactfully] made no other response."[31] Even though the story may be apocryphal, its existence in north China suggests that the Jurchens remained unaware of the self-critical interpretation of *Analects* 3.5 that had by then become standard among Daoxue thinkers in the south. It also suggests that their typical response to the ethnocentric interpretation of 3.5 was to resent it as an offensive expression of Chinese ethnic prejudice, rather than calmly dismiss it as a relic of ancient history as Liao Daozong had purportedly done. Indeed, the story's subtext is that such resentment contributed to Wanyan Liang's decision to break the Song-Jin peace agreement of 1141—which had already subordinated the Southern Song to the Jin as a tributary state—and lead an ambitious (and ill-fated) invasion of the south in 1161.[32]

Due to Southern Song perceptions of Jurchen rulers like Wanyan Liang as determined to assert supremacy over the Chinese, one's commitment to the notion of Chinese superiority and barbarian inferiority came to be seen as a litmus test for distinguishing revanchist or irredentist Southern Song literati from their pro-appeasement opponents. This made affirmations of that notion a common feature of revanchist rhetoric both before and after 1141.[33] But we should not overestimate the unanimity or completeness with which Southern Song thinkers who favored revanchism shifted to speaking of barbarism as a condition of moral inferiority found only in foreign peoples. We have already seen that revanchism and ethnocentric moralism hold equal weight in the *Annals* commentary by Hu Anguo, who lived through the Jurchen invasion. Indeed, Hu Anguo's son Hu Hong argued that the two were closely connected, not only in his 1135 memorial to Gaozong but also in his only full-length philosophical treatise, *Understanding Words* (Zhiyan), which contains the following argument: "When the Central Plains (Zhongyuan; i.e., north China) have lost the Way of the Central Plains, only then do the barbarians enter the Central Plains. When the Central Plains return to practicing the Way of the Central Plains, then the barbarians will return to their own lands."[34] In other words, inner barbarism among the Chinese was the root cause of the Jurchen invasion, and only a restoration of Chinese moral superiority would lay the necessary foundations for retaking the north. Earlier in the text, Hu Hong warned that human beings could "descend to the nature of barbarians and animals" by behaving inhumanely and that even "capped and sashed rulers of the Central Lands" sometimes became barbarians from not understanding the Way.[35]

In a work of historical commentary completed in 1155, Hu Hong's fervently revanchist brother Hu Yin made a similar argument when condemning a Southern Dynasties ruler who violated a classical ethical norm of warfare by taking advantage of his Northern Wei counterpart's death to launch an invasion of the north. Hu Yin claims that the southern ruler's decision to follow the "way of the barbarians" (*Didao*) for the sake of strategic expediency made this nothing more than a case of "barbarians attacking barbarians": "The Central Lands are the Central Lands only because they have humaneness and moral duty; when they lose these, then they become barbarians. One who resides in the Central Lands but behaves like a barbarian is in no way worthier than the barbarians. If one is no worthier than them, how can one expect to bring them to submission?"[36] If even a Chinese ruler residing in the "Central Lands" of north China could forfeit his superiority to the barbarians by behaving immorally, surely this was even truer of a Chinese ruler whose domain was now limited to the south.

Hu Yin's commentary, *Limited Views from Reading History* (Dushi guanjian), adopts a polemically didactic approach to historical interpretation throughout. It occasionally engages in veiled criticism of the Song court's peace policy, especially via condemnation of the Later Jin founding emperor Shi Jingtang's (r. 936–42) submission to Kitan suzerainty in exchange for military aid in overthrowing the Later Tang dynasty. This act of expediency led directly to the Yan region's cession to Kitan rule, and Hu Yin perceived it as an ignominious precedent for the Song-Jin peace agreement of 1141. The sections of *Limited Views* pertaining to the Later Jin dynasty's rise and fall contain some of the text's most strident rhetoric about the inferiority, otherness, greed, and perfidy of barbarians and the necessity of "being careful about the difference between Chinese and barbarians" (*jin Hua-Yi zhi bian*), all meant as indirect denunciation of the Song-Jin peace agreement's moral illegitimacy.[37]

In a particularly intriguing passage of *Limited Views*, Hu Yin builds on his father's discussion of the Qian conference and unknowingly preempts the anecdote about Wanyan Liang, arguing that Confucius was not acting "contrary to Heaven" when he viewed barbarians as inferior to the Chinese. Although Heaven, being impartial, did not draw ethnic distinctions when it created human beings and gave them an innately moral nature, the fact was that barbarians were endowed with highly impure and imbalanced *qi* that clouded their moral nature, making them "inhumane and immoral, avaricious and murderous, contrary to the *li* of humanity."[38] In later sections of the text, however, we find Hu Yin contradicting this *qi*-determinist interpretation of barbarism by acknowledging historical examples of individual "barbarians" who displayed exemplary moral behavior.[39] Hu Yin seems to have been caught between two conflicting rhetorical objectives: arousing revanchist sentiments in his readers by appealing to their ethnocentric prejudices against the Jurchens and exhorting them toward higher moral standards by arguing that there were barbarians whose moral virtues made the Chinese look barbaric by comparison. The choice between these two seems to have been made more difficult by the fact that Hu Yin sincerely admired certain "barbarians" of the past, including Xiaowendi of the Northern Wei.

The resulting rhetorical and intellectual tension is particularly evident in sections of *Limited Views* that deal with the question of the Northern Wei dynasty's political legitimacy. In one such section, Hu Yin argues that Xiaowendi's moral worthiness—as reflected by his enthusiasm for Chinese institutions and cultural practices—was such that he would have reunified north and south China if he had not died in the prime of life. He anticipates his reader objecting to the idea of a barbarian dynasty ruling the entire Chinese world: "One might say, 'Although the five [southern] dynasties were confined to a peripheral region, they still successively inherited political legitimacy (*zhengshuo*). Although the [Northern] Wei encompassed the Central Lands of the Chinese, it was essentially a barbarian [dynasty]. Heaven would surely not cause barbarians to hold political legitimacy; even if

Xiaowendi had lived on, how could he have reunified north and south?'" But Hu Yin merely responds to this argument with a cryptically skeptical expression: "Alas! But is that really so?" (Wuhu! Qiran, qi qiran hu?).[40] The expression "Qiran, qi qiran hu?" is an allusion to *Analects* 14.13, where Confucius uses it to suggest that what he has just heard sounds too good to be true. Hu Yin's language thus implies that while he would *like* to believe that the Chinese people's innate superiority is sufficient to shield the Southern Song from the prospect of losing the Mandate of Heaven to a "barbarian" dynasty, something is keeping him from embracing that reassuring assumption.

That "something" was not just the reality of Jurchen military power, but also the effect of a century of ethnocentric moralist discourse in inoculating Daoxue thinkers from moral complacency. For these thinkers, the problem was not that there were no longer barbarians in the world. Rather, the problem with arguing that anyone could become a barbarian, and that one's ethnicity was entirely contingent on one's morality, was that the force of the rhetoric could make ethnic identity seem altogether irrelevant to how one should respond when faced with invasion by "real" barbarians. Yet Hu Yin and later Daoxue thinkers persisted in believing that the normative world order was one in which the Chinese reigned supreme over all other peoples and that when this supremacy was properly rooted in superior morality, the barbarians could not but recognize and defer to it. Because this supremacist myth provided a reassuring basis for believing that the Chinese, regardless of momentary setbacks and moral failings, would finally prevail against their external enemies, Daoxue's rise to intellectual hegemony and orthodoxy in the Southern Song during the thirteenth century did not encourage the development of a truly universal Classicist identity that placed the fundamental moral unity of human beings above ethnic differences. Instead, the myth of Chinese superiority received a boost from the Jurchen empire's destruction at the hands of the Mongols in 1211–34, giving rise to a complementary myth that although Heaven might occasionally permit "barbarian" empires to dominate the Chinese, they would never do so for more than a hundred years at a time.[41] Even the Southern Song's own fall to the Mongol empire some forty years later did not discredit these myths for long, since they resurfaced during the Mongol Yuan dynasty's mid-fourteenth-century collapse (which seemingly confirmed their validity) and remained pervasive under the Ming.[42]

It took the combined effects of the Manchu conquest in the seventeenth century, the Qing empire's apogee in the eighteenth, and its decline in the new European-dominated world of the nineteenth to shake the Chinese people's entrenched assumptions about their natural moral superiority and consequent right to supremacy over other peoples. By the mid-eighteenth century, Qing imperial propaganda and censorship had tempered the ethnocentrism embedded in the Chinese-barbarian dichotomy and replaced it with a universalist view of "the distinction between center and periphery" as an arbitrary man-made construct, a mere "line drawn on the earth." The Yongzheng emperor (r. 1722–35) argued that from Heaven's perspective, high above petty ethnic and geographical distinctions, the Manchus' homeland in the far northeast was in no way different from or inferior to any "ancestral home" (*jiguan*) in the "Central Lands" of the Chinese. It certainly had no bearing on their morality, which was why the Qing emperors' "moral power" (*de*) had earned them Heaven's mandate to rule over the Chinese and a multitude of other peoples, making them "one family."[43]

Unfortunately for the Manchus, the onset of imperial decline in the nineteenth century exposed their universalist ideology to disrepute and to the mockery of a Western world newly steeped in its own versions of supremacism and exceptionalism. The nationalism that emerged to take Qing universalism's place in the early twentieth century was fueled by Chinese anger and anxiety over the empire's humiliating loss of power and prestige. It successfully used Chinese ethnocultural identity (now identified as "Han") as a rallying call against Manchu rule, promising to reverse China's decline via revolutionary means that included overthrowing the Qing, doing away with emperors altogether, and creating a new "modern" culture. For pragmatic reasons, however, both the Republic of China and its Communist successor, the People's Republic, have repudiated the idea of a Han nation-state and sought to redefine all inhabitants of the former empire's expansive territories as a new multiethnic "family," the "Zhonghua nation."[44] The resulting tension between ethnocultural and territorial versions of Chineseness remains unresolved today even as the Han Chinese, divested of their belief in barbarians yet reluctant to abandon their millennia-old sense of superiority and centrality, pursue "the Chinese Dream": a position of restored preeminence and prestige for their civilization, founded on wealth and military might rather than "moral power."

Glossary

Note: The bibliography gives Chinese characters for additional personal names and titles of works.

An Lushan 安祿山

ba 霸
bai 敗
Bai/Bo Juyi 白居易
Bandit (Dao) Zhi 盜跖
Bao Xian 包咸
benfei Yi-Di 本非夷狄
"Benlun" 本論
Bi 邶
bian 貶
bian Hua-Yi zhi fen 辨華夷之分
bian yu Yi 變於夷
bian('er) wei Yi 變(而)爲夷
Bianzhou 汴州
"Bigong" 閟宮
"Biming" 畢命
binbin 彬彬
bingong 賓貢
"Bishi" 費誓
bo 伯 (liege)
Bohai 渤海 (Parhae)
Boju 柏舉
boshi 博士
Boyi 伯益/柏翳
buru 不如

Cai 蔡 (state)
Cai Songnian 蔡松年
caifu 財賦

"Caiping" 采萍
Caozhou 曹州
Cefu yuangui 冊府元龜
Chan 禪
chang suo bingong zhe 常所賓貢者
Chang'an 長安
Chanyuan 澶淵
Chao Yuezhi 晁說之
Chaozhou 潮州
Chen 陳 (state)
Chen An 陳黯
Chen Liang 陳亮
Chen Shidao 陳師道
Chen Zhaohua 陳昭華
Cheng Hao 程顥
Cheng Yan 程晏
Cheng Yi 程頤
Chengpu 城濮
Chengshi cuiyan 程氏粹言
Chengshi waishu 程氏外書
Chengshi yishu 程氏遺書
chenqie 臣妾
Chenzhou 郴州
Chu 楚 (state)
chun Rong-Di 純戎狄
chun wei Yi-Di 純爲夷狄
Chunqiu 春秋
Chunqiu fanlu 春秋繁露
Chunqiu jijie 春秋集解
Chunqiu quanheng 春秋權衡

Chunqiu shuo 春秋說
Chunqiu yilin 春秋意林
Chunqiu zunwang fawei 春秋尊王發微
Cijian Zhongni wu Yi-Di zhi shen yi 此見仲尼惡夷狄之甚矣
Cui Yin 崔胤

Da Liao Zhongguo 大遼中國
Dadai liji 大戴禮記
Daliang 大梁
Dan Zhu 啖助
Dangchang 宕昌
Dao 道
Daotong 道統
Daoxue 道學
daoyi 島夷
Daozhou 道州
Daozong 道宗
Dashi 大食
Daxue yanyi bu 大學衍義補
dayi 大義
Dazhong 大中 (era)
Dazhong zhi Dao 大中之道
de 德
Dechen 得臣
Dezong 德宗
Di 狄 ("barbarian")
di 敵 (parity)
Didao 狄道
"Dihuan" 敵患
dong Han Yi 東韓夷
"Dongjin Yuan-Wei di zhengrun lun" 東晉元魏帝正閏論
Du You 杜佑
Dushi guanjian 讀史管見

Elai 惡來
er Yi 二夷

fa 法
Fan 番
fan qi Didao 反其狄道
Fan Rugui 范如圭
fan Yi-Di 反夷狄

Fan Zhongyan 范仲淹
Fan Zuyu 范祖禹
Fang Songqing 方崧卿
Fang Xiaoru 方孝孺
Fanyang, Duke of 范陽公
Fanyi 蕃夷
Fayan 法言
"Fei Han" 非韓
feiyi 非義
feng 風
Feng Ao 封敖
Feng Su 馮宿
fengsu 風俗 (customs/folkways)
Fengxiang 鳳翔
Fu Bi 富弼
Fu Xuan 傅玄
fushu jiaodao, yousuo mingbai 扶樹教道，有所明白
Fuxi 伏羲

gan 干
Gao Hou 高厚
Gaoyao 皋陶
Gaozong 高宗
Gaozu 高祖
Ge 葛 (state)
Ge (Palace) edition 閣本
ge ren qiren 各人其人
Gonghe 共和 (regency)
Gongyang 公羊 (commentary)
Guan 管 (state)
Guan Zhong 管仲
"Guang yuanjiao" 廣原教
Guangzhou 廣州
Guliang 穀梁 (commentary)
guo 國
Gusou 瞽叟
Guwen 古文
Guwen fuxing 古文復興
Guwen yundong 古文運動

Han 漢 (dynasty/ethnicity)
Han Fei 韓非
Han Jian 韓建

Han Tang jiujiang 漢唐舊疆
Han Wudi 漢武帝
Han Yu 韓愈
Hangzhou edition 杭本
Hanren 漢人
Haochu 浩初
He, the Liege of Gong 共伯和
hou 侯 (prince)
Hu 胡
Hu Anguo 胡安國
Hu Hong 胡宏
Hu Shi 胡適
Hu Yin 胡寅
Hua 華
Huai River 淮水
Huang Chao 黃巢
Huang Hanjie 黃漢傑
Huang Kan 皇侃
Huang Yigang 黃義剛
Huang Zhen 黃震
Huangchi 黃池
Huangdi 黃帝
Huang-Lao 黃老
Huaren 華人
Hua-Xia 華夏
"Huaxin" 華心
Huayan 華嚴
Hua-Yi zhi bian 華夷之辨
Huazhou 華州
Huilin 惠琳
Huizong 徽宗
huoyue 或曰
Huzhong 胡種

ji 跡/迹 (traces)
jian 僭
jiaofa 教法
Jiaozhi 交趾
Jie 羯
Jifu 雞父/雞甫
jiguan 籍貫
Ji/Jisun 季/季孫 (family)
Jilin 雞林
jin 進 (promoted)

Jin 晉 (state)
Jin, Lord Wen of 晉文公
jin Hua-Yi zhi bian 謹華夷之辨
Jin Midi 金日磾
jing 經 (classics)
Jing 荊 (state = Chu)
jinshi 進士
jinsi Yi-Di 近似夷狄
"Jinxue jie" 進學解
jinyan 謹嚴
jinyu Zhongguo 進於中國
jiu Zhongguo rang Yi-Di 救中國攘夷狄
Jizha 季札
Ju 莒 (state)
ju qidi 居其地
juan 卷
Juliang 湨梁
jun 君
"Junchen tongzhi, Hua-Yi tongfeng" 君臣同志, 華夷同風
junzi 君子

Kaifeng 開封
Kong Daofu 孔道輔
Kongzi 孔子 (Confucius)
Ku 嚳 (sage-king)

Lao Dan 老聃
Laozi daodejing 老子道德經
Laozi huahu jing 老子化胡經
lei 類 (ilk / ethnic origin)
li 理 (principle/pattern/coherence/congruity)
li 禮 (ritual practices / ritual propriety)
Li, King 厲王
Li Ao 李翱
Li Chu 李礎
Li Gou 李覯
Li Han 李漢
Li Keyong 李克用
Li Ling 李陵
Li Maozhen 李茂貞
Li Xun 李珣

Li Yansheng 李彥升
Liang Wudi 梁武帝
Liezi 列子
lifa 禮法
"Lifa lun" 禮法論
Liji 禮記
Lingzong 令縱
Liu, Lord Ding of 劉定公
Liu Chang 劉敞
Liu Kai 柳開
Liu Sui 劉隨
Liu Xun 劉絢
Liu Yuxi 劉禹錫
Liu Zongyuan 柳宗元
liyí 禮儀 (ceremonial and etiquette)
liyi 禮義 (ritual propriety and moral duty)
liyi zhi jiao 禮義之教
Longxi 隴西
lou 陋
lu 虜 ("caitiff," enemy)
Lu 魯 (state)
Lu, Lord Ai of 魯哀公
Lu, Lord Ding of 魯定公
Lu, Lord Huan of 魯桓公
Lu, Lord Min of 魯閔公
Lu, Lord Xi of 魯僖公
Lu, Lord Yin of 魯隱公
Lu, Lord Zhuang of 魯莊公
Lü Benzhong 呂本中
Lu Chun 陸淳
Lü Dalin 呂大臨
Lu Guimeng 陸龜蒙
Lu Jun 盧鈞
Lu Tong 盧仝
Lu Wan 盧綰
Lü Wen 呂溫
Lu Zhi 陸質
Lü Zuqian 呂祖謙
Luhun 陸渾
Luli 鹿蠡
"Lun fogu biao" 論佛骨表
Lunyu bijie 論語筆解
Lunyu huowen 論語或問

Lunyu jingyi 論語精義
Lunyu zhushu 論語注疏
Luo River 洛水
Luoyang 洛陽

Man 蠻
Meng Jian 孟簡
Mengzi (Mencius) 孟子
min qiren 民其人
ming 明 (bright)
ming 名 (name)
"Ming sizhu" 明四誅
"Mingjin" 明禁
Mo 貊
Mou 牟 (state)
"Mougong" 謀攻
Mouzi lihuolun 牟子理惑論
Mozi 墨子
Mu Xiu 穆修

"Nanbei zhengrun lun" 南北正閏論
Nanzhao 南詔
"Neiyi xi" 內夷檄
nengfu ren 能賦人
Nüwa 女媧

Ouyang Xiu 歐陽修

pi 否
pian 篇

qi 棄 (abandon)
qi 氣 (cosmological concept)
Qi 齊 (state)
Qǐ 杞 (state)
Qǐ, Lord Cheng of 杞成公
Qǐ, Lord Huan of 杞桓公
Qi, Lord Huan (or Lord Wei) of 齊桓公 (威公)
Qǐ, Lord Wen of 杞文公
qi er Yi zhi 棄而夷之
Qian 潛
Qiang 羌
qifu 七賦

qilin 麒麟
Qin 秦 (state/dynasty)
Qinzong 欽宗
Qisong 契嵩
Qiu Jun 邱濬
qiyu Yi 起於夷
Qu Wan 屈完
Quanzhou 泉州
quchu 驅除

rang Yi-Di, zun tianwang 攘夷狄，尊天王
Red Di 赤狄
ren 仁
ren qiren 人其人
rendao 人道
renqing 人情
Renzong 仁宗
Rong 戎
Rong of the Mountains 山戎
Rong-Man 戎蠻
Ru 儒 (Classicist/"Confucian")
ru 入 (enter)
"Ruru" 儒辱
Ruxue fuxing 儒學復興

shan 善
Shang Yang 商鞅
Shangqiu 商丘
Shangshu 尚書
Shao, Duke of 召公
Shaoling 召陵
Shatuo 沙陀
Shen 申
Shen Buhai 申不害
Shen Qinhan 沈欽韓
Shengren zhi Dao 聖人之道
Shengzong 聖宗
Shennong 神農
Shenzong 神宗
shi 實 (essence)
shi 士 (literatus/literati)
shi 史 (scribe)
Shi Jie 石介
Shi Jingtang 石敬瑭

Shiji 史記
Shilu 實錄
Shi/Shijing 詩/詩經 (*Odes*)
shi/zhi Yi-Di luan Hua 使/致夷狄亂華
Shizong 世宗
Shu 舒 ("barbarian" statelets)
Shu (Sichuan) edition 蜀本
shui qi shizhi 誰其尸之
Shun 舜 (sage-king)
Shunzong 順宗
si Dao 斯道
Siku quanshu 四庫全書
Sima Guang 司馬光
Simen Xue 四門學
siwen 斯文
siyi 四夷
siyi neixiang 四夷內向
Song Qi 宋祁
Song zhi Fuzi 宋之夫子
songxu 送序
su 俗
Su Shi 蘇軾
Su Zhe 蘇轍
Sun Chuo 孫綽
Sun Fu 孫復
Sun He 孫何
Sun Shi 孫奭
Sunzi bingfa 孫子兵法

tai 泰
Tai, Mount 泰山
Taibo 泰/太伯
Taixuan jing 太玄經
Taixue 太學
Taixue ti 太學體
Tang 唐 (conference)
Tang 湯 (sage-king / first Shang king)
Tang Taizong 唐太宗
Tangren 唐人
ti 體
tianli 天理
Tianzi 天子
tonghu Yi-Di 同乎夷狄
Tuizhi 退之 (Han Yu's courtesy name)

GLOSSARY 159

wai 外
wang (or *wu*) 亡
Wang Anshi 王安石
Wang Chao 王潮
Wang Chong 王充
Wang Ling 王令
Wang Mang 王莽
Wang Shuwen 王叔文
Wang Tong 王通
Wang Yucheng 王禹偁
Wangdao 王道
"Wangzhe buzhi Yi-Di lun" 王者不治夷狄論
"Wangzhi" 王制
Wanyan Liang (Prince of Hailing) 完顏亮（海陵王）
Wanyan Zongxiu 完顏宗秀
Wei 衛 (state)
weizhi 微旨
wen 文
Wen, King 文王
Wenchang 文暢
wenhua 文化
Wenlan'ge 文瀾閣
wenming 文明
wenming zhi di 文明之地
wenming zhi hua 文明之化
wenshi 文士
wenwu 文物
Wenyuan'ge 文淵閣
White Di 白狄
wu 武 (martial)
Wu 吳 (state)
wu 無 (to be without)
Wu, King 武王
wu fengli 無風禮
wu yiyi 無意義
wuchang 五常
Wuding 武丁
Wuhu! Qiran, qi qiran hu? 嗚呼!其然，豈其然乎？
wujun 無君
wujun zhi xin 無君之心

wuzheng 五政
Wuzong 武宗

xi 檄
Xia 夏 (ethnonym)
Xianbi 鮮卑
Xianyu 鮮虞 (state)
Xianyun 獫狁
Xiao (or Yao) 殽
xiaoren 小人
Xiaowendi 孝文帝
Xiazhou 夏州
"Xibei" 西北
xie 偕
Xie Liangzuo 謝良佐
xin 心 (heart/mind)
xin 信 (trustworthiness)
xin Yi-Di 新夷狄
Xin You 辛有
"Xing" 形 (chapter of *Master Sun's Art of War*)
Xing 邢 (state)
Xing Bing 邢昺
xingjuan 行卷
xingzheng 刑政
Xiongnu 匈奴
Xǔ 許 (state)
Xú 徐 (state/province)
"Xu xinanyi" 序西南夷
Xuanwu Army 宣武軍
Xuanwu Gate 玄武門
Xuanzong 玄宗
xuetong 血統
Xun Yue 荀悅
Xunyu 獯鬻
Xunzi 荀子

Yan 燕 (region)
yang 陽
Yang Fugong 楊復恭
Yang Huizhi 楊晦之
Yang Shi 楊時
Yang Xiong 揚雄

Yang Yao 楊幺
Yang Yi 楊億
Yang Zhu 楊朱
Yangshan 陽山
Yangzhou 揚州
Yanling 鄢陵
Yao 堯 (sage-king)
Yao Xuan 姚鉉
ye 野
Ye Mengde 葉夢得
Yi 夷 ("barbarian")
yi 義 (moral duty)
yi Di shu zhi 以狄書之
Yi er 夷而
Yi River 伊水
yi Yi-Di weizhi 以夷狄爲之
Yidao 夷道
Yi-Di cheng zhi 夷狄稱之
Yi-Di xing 夷狄行
Yi(-Di) zhi 夷(狄)之
Yi-Di zhi dao 夷狄之道
Yi-Di zhi feng 夷狄之風
Yi-Di zhi ren 夷狄之人
Yi-Di zhi shu 夷狄之術
Yi-Di zhi suowei 夷狄之所爲
Yi-Di zhi (yi) fa 夷狄之(一)法
Yi-Di zhu Zhongguo 夷狄主中國
Yijing 易經
Yili 夷禮
yin 陰
Yin Tun 尹焞
Yin You 殷侑
Yingtian prefecture 應天府
yishi er tongren 一視而同仁
Yisu 夷俗
Yi-Xia zhi bian 夷夏之辨
yixue 異學
yong 用
yong Xia bian Yi 用夏變夷
yong Yi bian Xia 用夷變夏
Yongzheng 雍正
Yongzhou 永州
you Yi-Di zhi xing 有夷狄之行

You Yu 由余
Youzhou 幽州
Yu 禹 (sage-king)
Yu, Minister 虞卿
Yuan Jixu 元集虛
Yuan the Eighteenth 元十八
Yuan Zhen 元稹
"Yuandao" 原道
Yuanhao 元昊
"Yuanren" 原人
Yue 越 (state)
Yue Fei 岳飛
Yuxiong 鬻熊

Zang Bing 臧丙
Zashuo san 雜說三
Zeng 鄫 (state)
Zeng Gong 曾鞏
Zeng Min 曾旼
Zhang Di 張棣
Zhang Guilu 張歸魯
Zhang Ji 張籍
Zhang Jun 張濬
Zhao Kuang 趙匡
Zhaozong 昭宗
zhen Yi-Di 真夷狄
Zheng 鄭 (state)
Zheng Xie 鄭獬
Zheng Xuan 鄭玄
zhengshuo 正朔
"Zhengtong lun" 正統論
Zhenzong 真宗
zhi 質
"Zhirong lun" 治戎論
Zhiyan 知言
zhong 中 (center, centrality, equilibrium)
Zhongdao 中道
Zhongguo 中國
Zhongguo er Yi-Di ze Di zhi 中國而夷狄則狄之
"Zhongguo lun" 中國論
Zhongguo zhi 中國之

Zhongguoren 中國人
Zhonghua 中華
Zhonghua, Yi ye 中華，夷也
Zhongxia 中夏
zhongyong 中庸
Zhongyuan 中原
zhongzu 種族
Zhou 紂 (last Shang king)
Zhou, Duke of 周公
Zhou Bida 周必大
Zhou Wudi 周武帝
Zhu 邾 (state)
zhu Hua 諸華
Zhu Wen (Quanzhong) 朱溫(全忠)
Zhu Xi 朱熹
zhu Xia 諸夏

Zhuangzi 莊子
Zhuren, Mouren, Geren
　　鄀人、牟人、葛人
Zhurong 祝融
Zhushu jinian 竹書紀年
zhuzi 諸子
zi 子 (master)
Zihou 子厚 (Liu Zongyuan's courtesy name)
Zou county 鄒縣
zu 族 (lineage)
zulei 族類
zunwang rangyi (Japanese: sonnō jōi)
　　尊王攘夷
zuofa luansu 左法亂俗
Zuozhuan 左傳

Notes

INTRODUCTION

1 For a concise but comprehensive survey of modern scholarship on these changes, see Tackett, "A Tang-Song Turning Point."
2 Detailed maps of the An Lushan Rebellion and the Jurchen invasion can be found on the author's website at https://denison.academia.edu/ShaoyunYang.
3 Historians have questioned whether the term Confucian is applicable to pre-Tang and Tang understandings of the intellectual tradition otherwise known as Ru. There have been tentative recent shifts toward affirming the term's validity for a Tang context: Loewe, "'Confucian' Values and Practices in Han China," 23–25; Shields, *One Who Knows Me*, 28–29n4. In this book, however, Ru is more commonly translated as "Classicist," and the Ru tradition's core or foundational texts (*jing*) are the Classics.
4 On the history of the attribution to Confucius, which historians have generally rejected since the early twentieth century, see Van Auken, *Commentarial Transformation of the "Spring and Autumn."*
5 Prominent early examples include Chen Yinke, *Jinmingguan conggao chubian*, 329; Fu, "Tang xing wenhua yu Song xing wenhua," 366–68; Wright, *Buddhism in Chinese History*, 83, 87–88. For "Memorial on the Buddha Relic" and its context, see *HCLW* 683–88.
6 For the increase in Sogdian guardsmen, see Bi, *Zhonggu Zhongguo de Sute Huren*, 148–61, 166–67. For the theory of an anti-Sogdian reaction, see Rong, "An-Shi zhi luan hou Sute Huren de dongxiang," 80–100. Rong's main evidence is a massacre of Uighurs and Sogdians by a Tang frontier commander in 780. But the sources indicate that while a politically motivated anti-Sogdian purge in the Uighur empire and the Tang commander's desire to weaken the Uighurs' power were among this incident's causes, anti-Sogdian sentiment in the Tang was not: *JTS* 127.3573–74, 195.5208; *XTS* 217a.6121–22; *ZZTJ* 226.7282, 226.7287–88. Étienne de La Vaissière adopts Rong's theory and cites, as further evidence, a massacre of Sogdians in Youzhou (modern Beijing) in 761. La Vaissière, *Sogdian Traders*, 220–22. But the massacre originated in a struggle for power between two factions of rebel troops, and should not be read as evidence of general sentiments among the Chinese. See *ZZTJ* 222.7110 and, for more nuanced readings of the incident, Huang Yongnian, "'Jiehu,' 'Zhejie,' 'Zazhong

Hu' kaobian," 388–89; Holcombe, "Immigrants and Strangers," 95; Abramson, *Ethnic Identity in Tang China*, 105–6. Rong and La Vaissière also interpret a number of epitaphs as evidence that Sogdians began concealing their foreign origins to avoid persecution, but a recent study argues that most of the epitaphs' subjects were not Sogdian at all: Wang Rui, *Tangdai Suteren*, 65–72.

7   Interpretations of these texts as reflecting a xenophobic turn can be found in Chen Yinke, *Yuan Bai shi jianzheng gao*, 148–50; Hu-Sterk, "Entre fascination et repulsion," 26–27, 35–38; Rong, "An-Shi zhi luan hou Sute Huren de dongxiang," 82–83; Moriyasu, *Shirukurōdo to Tō teikoku*, 222–25. Sanping Chen has reevaluated Bai Juyi's poems to argue that he, being of Central Asian descent, did not share Yuan Zhen's anti-Hu sentiments. Sanping Chen, *Multicultural China*, 172–76. I wonder if this does not still take Yuan's satire too seriously.

8   On late Tang Yangzhou, see Kim, "Tangdai houqi Yangzhou de fazhan yu waiguoren shehui." On the massacre, see Shao-yun Yang, "Letting the Troops Loose," 42–44.

9   Most recently, Shi Longdu, "Buddhism and the State in Medieval China," 173–96.

10 On the Daoists' role and motivations, see ibid., 182–85; Ge Zhaoguang, *Zhongguo sixiangshi*, vol. 2, 230–56; Luo Zhengming, "'Dongtian lingbao sanshi ji bingxu,'" 46–50. Ge seeks to trace the persecution to both Daoist agitation and anti-foreign sentiment but, in my opinion, only succeeds in proving the former. On literati attitudes, see Halperin, *Out of the Cloister*, 27–61.

11 See Chen Yinke, *Jinmingguan conggao chubian*, 329; see also two trenchant early rebuttals of Chen's interpretation: Huang Yunmei, "Du Chen Yinke xiansheng lun Han Yu"; Zhang Shizhao, *Liuwen zhiyao*, 758–61.

12 *HCLW* 20.

13 Stephen Owen has observed that the Reformation is the most obvious European analogy to the "remarkable abrogation of continuous history [by which] Han Yu declared himself and his moment a turning point in Chinese culture, a leap across more than a millennium to resume the Confucian tradition that had fallen into error and corruption after [the Confucian philosopher] Mencius." Unfortunately, Owen reverts shortly afterward to the myth of late Tang xenophobia, writing of "a China that is, for the first time, conceived in terms of excluding the foreign, as is proposed in Han Yu's famous 'Memorial on the Buddha Bone.'" Owen, *End of the Chinese "Middle Ages,"* 9, 16.

14 Hartman, *Han Yü*, 158; Abramson, *Ethnic Identity in Tang China*, 67. Earlier, when describing late Tang society and Han Yu's thought in 1972, Jacques Gernet in *A History of Chinese Civilization* (291–93) used the term "culturalism" in a different sense that was effectively synonymous with nativism, xenophobia, or cultural nationalism:

> The term "nationalism" would be an anachronism, yet it was certainly reactions analogous to nationalism that took vague shape after An Lushan's rebellion and that were to become evident again on other occasions in China's history. This attachment to an authentic tradition supposed to have been corrupted by foreign elements, this desire to return to the pure—and imaginary—sources of orthodox thought and morality are difficult to sum

up, since they do not relate to the quite recent idea of a nation, but to the idea of culture. If we wanted one word for them, we should have to invent the barbarous term "culturalism."

15   Holcombe, "Immigrants and Strangers," 104.
16   Some Song-period and most modern editions of Han Yu's works do not have the characters *Yi er* ("barbarians were"). Fan Wenli has demonstrated that these characters do appear in many premodern texts that anthologize or quote "Tracing the Way" and makes a strong case that they were in the original text: Fan, *Rujia minzu sixiang yanjiu*, 218–22. Fan is mistaken, however, in claiming that the 1009 Hangzhou edition, the mid-eleventh-century Palace (Ge) and Sichuan (Shu) editions, and Fang Songqing's (1135–1194) *Definitive Collected Works of Han Yu* (Hanji juzheng) all included these characters, whereas Zhu Xi's (1130–1200) edition followed another unspecified version in omitting them from the main text. Liu Zhenlun's study of the only extant Southern Song print edition of *Definitive Collected Works* (preserved in Japan) shows that almost the exact opposite is true: Fang Songqing followed the Hangzhou and Palace editions in omitting the characters, but noted that the Sichuan edition included them; Zhu Xi then followed Fang's lead. See *HJJZ* 195.
17   *Analects* 3.5.
18   The subject of this line from the ode "Bigong" is the reigning Lord of Lu, "descendant of the Duke of Zhou and son of Lord Zhuang," which would make him either Lord Min (r. 661–660 BCE) or, more likely, Lord Xi (r. 659–627 BCE). The ode praises his army's might and prowess in campaigns against the Rong and Di peoples, the state of Chu (also known as Jing), and the Shu—a collection of southern "barbarian" statelets between the Huai and Yangzi Rivers. Han Yu seems to be using the line as evidence of the ancient Chinese people's enmity toward barbarians.
19   *HCLW* 19. Modifications to translations are indicated by square brackets; glosses are enclosed in parentheses.
20   There have been many attempts over the centuries at explaining the etymology of these ethnonyms; none has been conclusive. For examples, see *ZZZY* 56.1587; Beckwith, "Earliest Chinese Words for 'the Chinese'"; Hu, *Neng Xia ze da yu jianmu Huafeng*, 23–45, 130–33; Bergeton, *Emergence of Civilizational Consciousness*, 172–77. For representative early instances of the terms *zhu Xia* and *zhu Hua*, see *Analects* 3.5; *GYZS* 18.400; *ZZZY* 11.303, 14.372, 29.836, 31.902, 32.911, 48.1381, 53.1517. The composite Hua-Xia is far rarer in authentic classical texts than is frequently assumed: the sole occurrence is at *ZZZY* 37.1045.
21   For a useful discussion of ethnic boundaries and categories in Han times, see Zhu Shengming, *Hua-Yi zhi jian*.
22   There is now an extensive literature on the origins and evolution of the concept of Zhongguo. The most influential recent work is Ge Zhaoguang, *Zhaizi Zhongguo*, but see also the updated views in Ge Zhaoguang, *Lishi Zhongguo de nei yu wai*. Also useful are Bol, "Geography and Culture," and the outline of five different historical definitions of Zhongguo in Yao, "Zhongguo lishi shang de liangzhong guojia jiangou moshi," 153–54.

23 Gang Zhao and Jiang Yonglin translate the premodern concept of Zhongguo as *China*, italicized to distinguish it from the eponymous modern state, but this still invites anachronistic associations while eliding the term's claim to centrality. Zhao, "Reinventing *China*," 24n1; Jiang, "Thinking about 'Ming *China*' Anew," 28–29n2.
24 On the use of Hanren and Tangren as ethnonyms or labels denoting state affiliation, see Shao-yun Yang, "Fan and Han," but also Tackett, *Origins of the Chinese Nation*, 156–66.
25 Quoting Gillett, "The Mirror of Jordanes," 397. For other examples, see Hall, *Inventing the Barbarian*, 4; Beckwith, *Empires of the Silk Road*, 357–62.
26 Bergeton, *Emergence of Civilizational Consciousness*, chap. 4.
27 Endymion Wilkinson effectively refutes a recently influential postcolonial line of argument against the translation "barbarian": Wilkinson, *Chinese History*, 360–61; see Basu, "Chinese Xenology and the Opium War"; Liu, *Clash of Empires*, 31–96. Christopher I. Beckwith has made a different argument against translating Chinese terms as "barbarian," contending that the Chinese had no "concept" of the barbarian because their discourses on the Yi-Di did not correspond exactly to certain Roman ethnic stereotypes about foreigners: Beckwith, *Empires of the Silk Road*, 357–62. This is, I would argue, too reductionist an approach to translation and does not consider scholarship (e.g., Gillett, "The Mirror of Jordanes") that demonstrates the fluidity and variability of Roman discourses on "barbarians."
28 On Fan, see Shao-yun Yang, "*Fan* and *Han*." The case of Hu is more complicated because its primary referent shifted over time from northern steppe nomads (Han period) to "Western" Central Asians, especially Sogdians (Tang), and then back to steppe nomads (Song to Qing). In some periods before the Tang, Hu may have been offensive, although the evidence for this is quite thin: see Wilkinson, *Chinese History*, 353. In Tang-Song texts, assertions about Hu inferiority are nearly nonexistent, with the notable exception of early Tang debates between Buddhists and Daoists: Abramson, *Ethnic Identity in Tang China*, 61–62.
29 For two recent examples, see Xiong, "Chaoyue 'Yi-Xia'"; Wang Rui, *Tangdai Suteren*, 48–49. For a notable exception, see Pines, "Beasts or Humans," 90–91. Pines argues that the "cultural/inclusive" approach lost ground to an "ethnic/exclusive" approach from Han times on.
30 See the works by Fairbank and Levenson cited in Bergeton, "From Pattern to 'Culture'?," 184–90; Jiang, "Thinking about 'Ming *China*' Anew," 29.
31 Levenson's thesis, being based on a broad generalization, has had its share of valid criticism over the years. For a sample of useful critiques, see Townsend, "Chinese Nationalism"; Duara, *Rescuing History from the Nation*, 56–61; Yao, "Zhongguo lishi shang de minzu guanxi yu guojia rentong"; Schneider, *Nation and Ethnicity*, 51–55.
32 Chow, "Imagining Boundaries of Blood"; Chow, "Narrating Nation, Race, and National Culture."
33 Qian Mu, *Zhongguo wenhuashi daolun*, 35; Chen Yinke, *Tangdai zhengzhishi shulun gao*, 19–20.
34 Perhaps the most influential recent version of this belief is summarized in Xu Jieshun, "Understanding the Snowball Theory of the Han Nationality."

35 Campany, "On the Very Idea of Religions," 289–90.
36 Uffe Bergeton argues that this usage of the term *su* began in the Warring States period and that in Classicist usage it also acquired the pejorative connotation "vulgar": Bergeton, *Emergence of Civilizational Consciousness*, chap. 5. On classical uses of the concepts *feng* and *su*, see also Li Chuanjun, *Han Tang fengtu ji yanjiu*, 19–40; Lewis, *Construction of Space in Early China*, 189–244.
37 Yang Zhigang, "Lisu yu Zhongguo wenhua," 77–82.
38 Sumner, *Folkways*, 60–62. See also the insightful discussion of ritual in Berkson, "Xunzi as a Theorist and Defender of Ritual."
39 This is the main argument of Bergeton, *Emergence of Civilizational Consciousness*, chap. 2. In chap. 3, Bergeton further argues that this usage of *wen* was similar to the modern concept of "civilization" but not to the current usage of the word "culture."
40 Kern, "Ritual, Text, and the Formation of the Canon"; Bol, *"This Culture of Ours,"* 84–107.
41 *BHT* 3.110–11; Loewe, "'Confucian' Values and Practices in Han China," 22–23.
42 Liao, *Tangdai de lishi jiyi*, 246–52.
43 *Pace* Hugh R. Clark, who has argued that the Chinese saw barbarians as "virtually by definition 'not-*wen*.'" Clark, *Sinitic Encounter in Southeast China*, 12–15, 76–84.
44 On Northern Song discussions of *wen* and *Dao*, see Bol, *"This Culture of Ours."*
45 See Tai, "Rethinking Culture, National Culture, and Japanese Culture," 4–5, 8–13; Huang Xingtao, "Wanqing minchu xiandai 'wenming' he 'wenhua' gainian"; Liu Wenming, "Shijiu shiji Ouzhou 'wenming' huayu yu wanqing 'wenming' guan."
46 The earliest instance of which I know is a 1907 essay by the constitutional monarchist Yang Du (1875–1931), who argued for defining Zhonghua in terms of *wenhua* in an attempt at refuting the racial-nationalist rhetoric used by anti-Manchu revolutionaries. Interestingly, Yang also sought to use the *Annals* to support his definition. Liu Qingbo, *Yang Du ji*, 374.
47 *SJZ* 1.15. On the identity of the "Mister Zeng" cited by Cai Shen, see Xu Huafeng, "Cai Shen 'Shu jizhuan' suo yinju de ziliao fenxi," 203, 208. The Ming Classicist Qiu Jun (1421–1495) mistakenly attributed this quote to Zhu Xi, probably because Cai was Zhu's student and his commentary was believed to reflect Zhu's views: Guoli gugong bowuyuan, *Siku quanshu buzheng: Zibu*, 45.
48 *QTW* 767.7986. This essay will be discussed in depth in chapter 3.
49 Cf. Bergeton, *Emergence of Civilizational Consciousness*, chap. 5.
50 Sumner, *Folkways*, 13.
51 *LYZS* 13.201.
52 On Mencius's use of the compound *liyi*, see Sato, *Confucian Quest for Order*, 205–8. On Xunzi's understanding of *yi* and *liyi*, see the differing interpretations in Sato, *Confucian Quest for Order*, 346–61; Hutton, "Ethics in the *Xunzi*," 71–73, 87; Harris, "Xunzi's Political Philosophy," 108–15. Hutton and Harris leave *yi* untranslated, while Sato translates *yi* variously as "moral duty," "morality," or "morality and justice." I have adopted the first of these translations in this book, instead of the more frequently encountered but ambiguous translations "righteousness" and "rightness." Whereas Sato translates *liyi* as "social morality," I have opted for a more literal translation.

53 On this understanding of *yi* as situational, see Sarkissian, "Ritual and Rightness in the *Analects*," 110–14.
54 On Classicist interpretations of the originally status-defined distinction between noble and inferior men, see Pines, "Confucius' Elitism."
55 On this lexical confusion, see Wang Nengxian, "'Liyi zhi bang' kaobian."
56 Trauzettel, "Sung Patriotism as a First Step toward Chinese Nationalism"; Tillman, "Proto-Nationalism in Twelfth-Century China?"
57 Ge Zhaoguang, "Songdai 'Zhongguo' yishi de tuxian"; also reprinted as chap. 1 of Ge Zhaoguang, *Zhaizi Zhongguo*.
58 Tackett, *Origins of the Chinese Nation*, esp. chaps. 4 and 6. Note that Tackett translates Zhongguo as "the Middle Kingdom," not "the Central Lands."
59 Ge Zhaoguang, *Zhaizi Zhongguo*, 23–31. Prasenjit Duara recognizes and endorses Trauzettel's theory as a challenge to Levenson's thesis, but prefers to speak of "ethnocentrism," not "nationalism," as the opposite of "culturalism." Duara, *Rescuing History from the Nation*, 56–59.
60 To illustrate the potential value of such a debate, I refer the reader to a similar one currently ongoing between two historians of the Byzantine empire: Kaldellis, "From Rome to New Rome, from Empire to Nation-State"; Kaldellis, "The Social Scope of Roman Identity in Byzantium"; Stouraitis, "Roman Identity in Byzantium"; Stouraitis, "Reinventing Roman Ethnicity in High and Late Medieval Byzantium."
61 Hutchinson and Smith, *Ethnicity*, 6, 28.
62 On the first reason, see Deng, "Shitan Wudai Songchu 'Hu/Han' yujing de xiaojie." Two recent treatments of the second reason are Skaff, *Sui-Tang China and Its Turko-Mongol Neighbors*, 299–300; Tackett, *Origins of the Chinese Nation*, 99–101, 157–59. Skaff's interpretation effectively follows the "cosmopolitanism-to-xenophobia" narrative, while Tackett's follows the "culturalism-to-nationalism" narrative. I find neither fully persuasive.
63 Whether the Song elite also thought of themselves ethnically as "Han people" (Hanren) remains a matter of debate. See Elliott, "*Hushuo*," 185; Shao-yun Yang, "*Fan* and *Han*," 26; Bol, "Geography and Culture," 92–93; Tackett, *Origins of the Chinese Nation*, 156–66.
64 I am not, however, persuaded by one argument that "the vocabulary of ethnicity" (unlike that of "cultural identity") necessarily carries an "accompanying baggage of nationalism" and an implication of "dialog with a developing national state" that makes it inapplicable to the Tang-Song transition: Standen, *Unbounded Loyalty*, 26–29.
65 On Tangren, see Shao-yun Yang, "*Fan* and *Han*," 27–29. For arguments that Song elite "national consciousness" did not spread downward (*contra* Trauzettel), see Tackett, *Origins of the Chinese Nation*, 206–7, 280–81.
66 These included areas that were now under Kitan, Tangut, Tibetan, and Viet (Vietnamese) rule. Huang Chunyan, "'Han Tang jiujiang' huayu xia de Song Shenzong kaibian"; Fang, "Cong herong dao tuobian." See also Ge Zhaoguang, *Lishi Zhongguo de nei yu wai*, 47–65.

67 Ouyang Xiu (1007–1072) alluded to this distinction when he noted that the independent southern states of the Five Dynasties period (comprising nine of the "Ten Kingdoms") behaved like barbarian polities, rather than part of the "Central Lands," because they presented tribute, not taxes, to the imperial courts in north China: *XWDS* 71.881.

68 Pace Tackett, who suggests that the Song reenvisioned the emperor's authority as "limited to the non-tribal 'civilized' center": Tackett, *Origins of the Chinese Nation*, 6. For a useful parallel, see Kaldellis, "Did the Byzantine Empire Have 'Ecumenical' or 'Universal' Aspirations?"

69 I quote here the reconstructed version of Zhu Yu's *Pingzhou ketan* found in the *Wenyuan'ge* edition of the *Siku quanshu*. The *Wenlan'ge* edition, on which modern editions of the *Pingzhou ketan* are based, has "a difference between center (*zhong*) and periphery (*wai*)" instead of "a difference between Chinese and barbarians," probably due to Qing editorial censorship of the word Yi. *PZKT(1)* 15a; cf. *PZKT(2)* 2.142. For a different reading of Zhu's argument, see Tackett, *Origins of the Chinese Nation*, 4.

70 Quoting Bol, *Neo-Confucianism in History*, 9–10, 13, 14. "Rhetoric of a greater empire" alludes to a classic essay on Northern Song foreign policy discourse: Wang Gungwu, "The Rhetoric of a Lesser Empire." Bol argues (14–15) that in the eleventh century, Tang political universalism was supplanted by cultural universalism (i.e., "culturalism") and Daoxue moral universalism, rather than ethnic nationalism. My reading of the evidence suggests that cultural universalism and moral universalism were still less influential than the rhetoric of political universalism in the Northern Song.

71 De Weerdt, *Information, Territory, and Networks*, 4, 17, 27n42, 408. A similar view of the Ming dynasty was recently proposed in Jiang, "Thinking about 'Ming *China*' Anew."

72 Ge Zhaoguang, "Xiangxiang tianxia diguo." In conversation with the author, Ge argued that the two existed in tension but were not mutually exclusive. He also clarified, however, that, unlike Tackett, he does not think that the Song elite envisioned their polity as a mono-ethnic Chinese nation-state. Instead, the Song was a truncated empire that only outwardly resembled a nation-state. Ge Zhaoguang, personal interview, June 21, 2018.

73 Dikötter, *Discourse of Race in Modern China*, 12, 20.

74 Perdue uses a conceptual dichotomy borrowed from George M. Fredrickson rather than Levenson, but Fredrickson himself observed that there is a "substantial gray area between racism and 'culturalism'" because "culture can be reified and essentialized to the point that it becomes the functional equivalent of race." Perdue, "Nature and Nurture on Imperial China's Frontiers," 252–56; Fredrickson, *Racism*, 7.

75 Teng, *Taiwan's Imagined Geography*, 13–15, 75–77, 103–16.

76 Liu's use of the culture-race dichotomy and quoting of Han Yu's "Tracing the Way" were evidently inspired by Qian Mu. But his view of the dichotomy as an alternating cycle was influenced by Duara's summation of Trauzettel's "Song nationalism" theory. Liu Pujiang, *Zhengtong yu Hua-Yi*, 57–58 (cf. 31).

77 Shao-yun Yang, "'Their Lands Are Peripheral and Their *Qi* Is Blocked Up.'"

78   None of our writers is speaking of barbarization as ethnic assimilation; nor, when they speak of humans turning into beasts, are they thinking of therianthropy, the belief in human beings who shape-shift physically into animals.
79   Fincher, "China as a Race, Culture, and Nation," 59–60 (emphasis in original); cf. Duara, *Rescuing History from the Nation*, 60. Duara summarizes Fincher but reads Fang as claiming that "Chinese who enabled barbarians to rule could themselves become barbarians."
80   I am not aware of any published response by Fincher to the Song nationalism theory, which appeared a few years later. Fincher, "China as a Race, Culture, and Nation," 67.

CHAPTER 1: HAN YU, THE *ANNALS*, AND THE ORIGINS OF ETHNICIZED ORTHODOXY

1   For a classic example, see Chen Yinke, *Jinmingguan conggao chubian*, 319–32.
2   *HCLW* 220–21.
3   Ibid. Yang Xiong wrote two essays defending the *Classic of Supreme Mystery* from its critics, neither of which contains the prediction quoted by Han Yu. See *HS* 87b.3565–78.
4   *QTW* 684.7007. This passage is translated and analyzed in Bol, "*This Culture of Ours*," 126–27. My reading of the text differs from Bol's in some places, but I agree with him that Zhang Ji is summarizing Han Yu's ideas, not expressing his own—*pace* Luo Liantian, *Tangdai wenxue lunji*, 485–89.
5   Loewe, "Huang Lao Thought and the *Huainanzi*."
6   Mencius's cycles are (1) a cycle from Yao and Shun through a decline in the "Way of the Sages," concluding with the end of the Shang dynasty; (2) a cycle from King Wu (r. ca. 1046–1043 BCE) and the Duke of Zhou (d. 1032 BCE) through a decline in the "Way," concluding with the early centuries of Eastern Zhou; and (3) a cycle from Confucius's writing of the *Annals* through an overshadowing of the "Way of Confucius" by Yang Zhu and Mozi, continuing up to Mencius's own day. On the cyclical nature of this narrative, see also Andreini, "The Yang Mo Dualism," 1119–24.
7   For notable examples, see Chen Yinke, *Jinmingguan conggao chubian*, 321; Luo Liantian, *Tangdai wenxue lunji*, 23–24; Wilson, *Genealogy of the Way*, 121–25. Wilson does quote 3B.9, but obscures its cyclical nature by omitting a passage on the roles of King Wu, the Duke of Zhou, and Confucius.
8   *QTW* 684.7007.
9   The conventional reading of this passage has "Kings Wen and Wu passed them on to the Duke of Zhou and Confucius," but this punctuation leaves "wrote them into books" without a subject. It would also make more sense chronologically for Confucius to receive the Way from the Duke of Zhou.
10 *HCLW* 282.
11 For various attempts at refining or modifying the Chan influence hypothesis, see Wilson, *Genealogy of the Way*, 111–14, 140–43; Li Junxiu, "Shilun Han Yu de daotong

shuo ji qi Mengxue sixiang," 79; Liu Chengguo, "9–12 shiji chu de daotong 'qianshi' kaoshu," 110n5.
12 *HCLW* 283.
13 *QTW* 684.7007–9; *HCLW* 147–52.
14 Pace Hartman, *Han Yü*, 147.
15 *HCLW* 15.
16 Ibid., 20; cf. the essay on 40–41, in which Han Yu states that he once rated Yang Xiong's understanding of Confucius's Way second only to Mencius but, after reading Xunzi, felt that Xunzi ranked "between Mencius and Yang Xiong." He now saw both Xunzi and Yang Xiong as "mostly pure but with small flaws" in their thought, unlike Mencius, who was "the purest of the pure." This reflects Han Yu's diminishing esteem for Yang Xiong over time.
17 On the history of the linear transmission theory and the term Daotong, see Liu Chengguo, "9–12 shiji chu de daotong 'qianshi' kaoshu"; Soffel and Tillman, *Cultural Authority and Political Culture in China*, 87–98.
18 Newell Ann Van Auken has analyzed the purported variations in *Annals* terminology and argued (*contra* most modern scholarship) that the traditional interpretation of these as messages of praise and criticism is plausible: Van Auken, "Who Is a *Rén*?"; Van Auken, *Commentarial Transformation of the "Spring and Autumn,"* esp. chap. 3.
19 Van Auken, *Commentarial Transformation of the "Spring and Autumn,"* 7.
20 The *Guliang* is evidently a slightly later work than the *Gongyang*. On dates of compilation, see Queen and Major, *Luxuriant Gems of the "Spring and Autumn,"* 10–11.
21 *GYZS* 12.270–71; *GLZS* 9.179. Neither commentary faulted the Jin ruler for allying with barbarians against Qin, but both held that Confucius gave him a milder demotion to fault him for coming out of mourning for his predecessor to lead the ambush. Note that Yuri Pines has used archaeological finds and inscriptions to argue that Qin was not a "barbarian" state to begin with and only began to be perceived as such some three centuries after the Battle of Xiao: Pines, "The Question of Interpretation," esp. 30.
22 Yuri Pines argues that the perception of Chu as a barbarian state only became common in the Warring States period and is particularly pronounced in the *Gongyang Commentary*: Pines, "Chu Identity as Seen From Its Manuscripts," 2–5.
23 *GYZS* 24.517–18; *GLZS* 18.345.
24 Zhu Shengming underestimates this ambiguity in arguing strictly for the latter interpretation: Zhu Shengming, *Hua-Yi zhi jian*, 38–39.
25 On the question of authorship, see now Loewe, *Dong Zhongshu*, 191–224; Queen and Major, *Luxuriant Gems of the "Spring and Autumn,"* 15–17, 61–66.
26 The demotion involved the battle being framed as one between the Jin commanding general and the Chu ruler, rather than between the Jin and Chu rulers. *CQFL* 2.46.
27 Ibid., 2.47; cf. *GYZS* 16.349–53.
28 The *Annals* record frames this battle as one between the Jin ruler on one side and the Chu and Zheng rulers on the other; the battle began when Jin attacked Zheng to punish it for switching its allegiance to Chu, upon which Chu intervened on Zheng's

side. Both the *Gongyang* and *Guliang* commentaries interpret the only editorial irregularity in this record as reflecting the fact that the Chu ruler was wounded by an arrow in the battle. *GYZS* 18.403; *GLZS* 14.269–70.

29 Surprisingly, of the four examples of "barbarizing" demotion cited in *Luxuriant Gems*—namely, the editorial demotions of the rulers of Zhu, Mou, and Ge on the occasion of their visit to the court of Lu in 697 BCE; of Jin at the Battle of Bi a century later; of Zheng during its attack on Xŭ (588 BCE); and of Jin again during its attack on Xianyu—the *Gongyang Commentary* only interprets the first as "barbarizing" and does not interpret the third and fourth as demotions at all. He Xiu's subcommentary, perhaps influenced by *Luxuriant Gems*, does interpret Jin's attack on Xianyu and Zheng's attack on Xŭ as "barbarizing" demotions, but for different reasons. See *CQFL* 1.5–8, 2.63–64, 4.118; *GYZS* 5.106, 16.349, 17.379, 22.495–96.

30 On the nature of these direct commentary passages, see now Van Auken, *Commentarial Transformation of the "Spring and Autumn,"* which argues that they are earlier than the *Gongyang* and *Guliang* commentaries. On the textual history of the *Zuo Tradition*, see most recently Durrant, Li, and Schaberg, *Zuo Tradition / Zuozhuan*, xxxviii–lix.

31 I have added a tone mark to Qĭ to distinguish it from the larger and better-known state of Qi, also located in Shandong.

32 *ZZZY* 15.408, 16.435. On the purported Xia ancestry of the Qĭ rulers, see *ZZZY* 39.1092, 39.1094; *SJ* 36.1583. Note, however, that the inscription on a Western Zhou bronze vessel excavated in 1988 suggests that the people of Qĭ were perceived as Yi at the time. Hu Hong reads the inscription as evidence that the Zhou dynasty felt no ethnocultural affinity to the Xia dynasty, but it is just as possible that the Qĭ rulers' identification as descendants of the Xia dynasty only emerged later. The question of whether the Xia was a historical dynasty or a Western Zhou fabrication remains hotly debated among Chinese and Western archaeologists and historians. See Hu, *Neng Xia ze da yu jianmu Huafeng*, 26–27.

33 *ZZZY* 16.435; Li Wai-yee, "Hua-Yi zhi bian yu yizu tonghun."

34 I use the new translations for these titles adopted by a recent translation of the *Zuo Tradition*, rather than the traditional translations derived from medieval European nobility: Durrant, Li, and Schaberg, *Zuo Tradition / Zuozhuan*, xxxvii.

35 *ZZZY* 19b.537, 39.1095; *GLZS* 9.166, 11.202, 16.311.

36 Some historians have read *jinyu Zhongguo* erroneously as "when they enter the Central Lands," due to unfamiliarity with the special terminology of *Annals* exegesis: e.g., Abramson, *Ethnic Identity in Tang China*, 66; Soffel and Tillman, *Cultural Authority and Political Culture in China*, 155, 198.

37 E.g., *GLZS* 6.102; *GYZS* 8.165.

38 *GYZS* 25.560; *GLZS* 19.364–66.

39 *GYZS* 25.563–64; *GLZS* 19.367.

40 E.g., Pines, "Beasts or Humans," 69–75.

41 Uses of the term in *Xunzi* suggest that the description of Yi people as *lou* in *Analects* 9.14 is primarily a comment on their ignorance regarding morality, rather than their foreign customs or supposed primitivity. My use of "benighted," rather than more

common translations like "crude," "uncouth," or "boorish," aims to convey this emphasis. Hutton, *Xunzi*, 11, 28–29.

42 In its original context, Mencius's point in 4B.1 is not about the transformability of barbarians. Rather, he is using examples of sages from the extreme eastern and western poles of the known world and born more than a thousand years apart to show that the principles for sagely governance do not vary according to time and place. The word *Yi* denotes physical distance, not ethnic difference, in this case. Crossley, *A Translucent Mirror*, 260–61; *pace* Pines, "Beasts or Humans," 73–74. A similar emphasis on distance rather than shared values is likely also intended in the references to Yi-Di and Man-Mo in *Analects* 13.19 and 15.5.

43 *Mencius* 3A.4. Some interpreters have read *bian yu Yi* as "changing into barbarians." In Classical Chinese, however, the construction verb-*yu*-object typically means verb-by-object. To mean "changed into barbarians," the phrase would have to be *bian wei Yi* or *bian'er wei Yi* (cf. *CQFL* 2.46, where the phrase *bian'er wei Yi-Di* does occur).

44 *FZ* 2.56. On Fu Xuan and the *Fuzi*, see Kong, "Fuzi"; Paper, *Fu-tzu*.

45 Li Xiaorong, *"Hongming ji" "Guang Hongming ji" shulun gao*, 265–87.

46 *HHS* 30b.1082. Han Yu did not subscribe to this myth; in his "Memorial on the Buddha Relic," he bluntly asserted that the Buddha "was originally a man of the barbarians": *HCLW* 686.

47 Raz, "'Conversion of the Barbarians' [*Huahu*] Discourse as Proto Han Nationalism"; Raz, "Buddhism Challenged, Adopted, and in Disguise." Note that I do not agree with Professor Raz's suggestion that the *Laozi huahu jing* discourse constituted a kind of ethnic nationalism.

48 There is now quite an extensive body of literature on this new exegetical tradition. Particularly useful is Ge Huanli, *Zunjing zhongyi*, 87–121.

49 Ibid., 92–94. Ge Huanli argues that Lu also authored two original commentarial works, both no longer extant: Ge Huanli, "Dan Zhu, Zhao Kuang he Lu Chun 'Chunqiu' xue zhuzuo kaobian," 23–27.

50 *JZBY* 6.1232–33. See also *JZBY* 2.1206, which traces the first demotion of a Qí ruler to Lord Huan of Qí's (r. 685–643 BCE) tenure as hegemon of the Chinese states.

51 Ibid., 6.1235; *CQFL* 4.118; *GYZS* 5.106. See also the analysis of this *Annals* passage in Van Auken, "Who Is a *Rén*?," 577–78.

52 For example, Lu Chun rejects all pre-Tang interpretations of the "barbarizing" demotion resulting from the Jin attack on Xianyu in 530 BCE. He accepts Dan Zhu's alternative interpretation, in which the Jin ruler's offense lay in lying to Xianyu and then launching a surprise attack on it—a detail reported by the *Zuo Tradition* alone and therefore not acceptable to adherents of the *Gongyang* and *Guliang* traditions. In Dan's opinion, this sort of deception was "something that [only] barbarians do" (*Yi-Di zhi suowei*), and if "a lord and hegemon of the Central Lands practiced deceit on barbarians, not the other way around," then he deserved to be spoken of as a barbarian. *JZZL* 8.1108; *CQWZ* 3.1187.

53 Little is known about the state of Xú, which fell to Wu in 512 BCE and should not be confused with the similar-sounding Xŭ. The *Guliang* commentary assumed that Xú was a "Central Lands" state: *GLZS* 17.332. However, later *Annals* exegetes tended to

see it as a barbarian state on the grounds that at least one of its rulers used the title "king," thus setting himself up as an equal of the Zhou king in the same manner as the kings of Chu, Wu, and Yue.

54 *JZZL* 8.1108.
55 Lu Chun misattributes Zhao Kuang's interpretation to the *Gongyang* commentary at *JZZL* 4.1051 and repeats it (without attribution) at *JZZL* 8.1113, but contradicts himself a few lines down by describing the rulers of Zhu, Mou, and Ge as "barbarian rulers."
56 *JZZL* 8.1108.
57 The *Zuo Tradition* account of the Huangchi conference in 482 BCE claims that the Taibo legend served as the basis for the Wu ruler's attempt to claim seniority over the Jin ruler: *ZZZY* 59.1670–71.
58 *SJ* 31.1445, 40.1689, 41.1739.
59 This promotion corresponded to the *Annals* entries for 618–617 BCE. *GLZS* 11.199–200.
60 *JZZL* 8.1109.
61 See *HCLW* 113–14, 127, 129, 137, 219.
62 On Lü Wen's engagement with Lu Chun's *Annals* exegesis, see Chen Jo-shui, *Tangdai wenshi yu Zhongguo sixiang de zhuanxing*, 400–402.
63 *LZY* 31.818–19; cf. Liu's epitaph for Lu Chun at 9.208–10. For different views on Lu Chun's influence (or lack thereof) on the 805 reforms, see McMullen, *State and Scholars in T'ang China*, 103; Pulleyblank, "Neo-Confucianism and Neo-Legalism," 99–106, 109–10, 114; Chen Jo-shui, *Liu Tsung-yüan*, 59–60, 66–77, 88; Saiki, "Eitei kakushin to shunjūgaku."
64 For various interpretations as to whether Han Yu's suspicion was correct, see Zhang Qinghua, *Han Yu nianpu huizheng*, 170–73; Luo Liantian, *Han Yu yanjiu*, 53–60; Wu Zaiqing, *Tingtao zhai zhonggu wenshi lungao*, 158–69; Hartman, *Han Yü*, 51–57.
65 *HCLW* 804; the Veritable Records refer to Lu Chun by the new name that he adopted in 804/5, Lu Zhi. On the question of whether the extant version of the Shunzong Veritable Records is Han Yu's work, Denis Twitchett essentially answers in the affirmative, but Chen Jo-shui adopts an agnostic position: Twitchett, *Writing of Official History under the T'ang*, 145–51; Chen Jo-shui, *Liu Tsung-yüan*, 66–67n1.
66 Saiki, "Kan Yu to 'Shunjū,'" 149–51 (cf. *HCLW* 787). Saiki's argument that the language of the Veritable Records reflects Lu Chun's influence on Han Yu is flawed, since its only evidence is that both the Veritable Records and Lu's exegetical writings use the phrase *renqing*, which Saiki identifies as a "key concept" in Lu's exegesis. It is evident from the examples Saiki cites that the Veritable Records do not use the phrase in the same way as Lu Chun: *renqing* means "public opinion" in the Veritable Records, whereas in Lu's writings it means "the bounds of reasonable behavior."
67 *HCLS* 7.782; Zhang Qinghua, *Han Yu nianpu huizheng*, 272–73.
68 *Pace* Chen Yinke, *Jinmingguan conggao chubian*, 321–22.
69 Pulleyblank, "Neo-Confucianism and Neo-Legalism," 112 (I have converted Pulleyblank's Wade-Giles Romanization to Hanyu Pinyin); *pace* Hartman, *Han Yü*, 174,

336n5. Hartman claims that Han "had strong sympathies and sometimes direct contact" with the new school but cites no evidence for this.
70 *THY* 76.1398.
71 *HCLW* 234–35.
72 Ibid., 234. Unfortunately, neither Yin You's subcommentary nor the preface by Han Yu is now extant.

CHAPTER 2: HAN YU, LIU ZONGYUAN, AND THE DEBATE OVER BUDDHISM AND BARBARISM

1 Some of these missing writings are mentioned in Liu Zongyuan's collected works. The Song writer Shao Bo (d. 1158) assumed their loss to be due to negligence on the part of Li Han (d. ca. 858), who edited Han Yu's collected works, but I am inclined to ascribe responsibility to Han Yu himself: *SSWJ* 14.112. For the funeral oration and epitaph, see *HCLW* 361–62, 569–73.
2 Chen Jo-shui discusses Liu Zongyuan's views on teachers but, I think, misses the sardonic tone of his comments on Han Yu's views. *LZY* 16.441–50, 31.807–9, 34.871–74; Chen Jo-shui, *Liu Tsung-yüan*, 144–47.
3 Jan De Meyer characterizes Tang "intellectual eclecticism" as "an amazing variety of attempts to shape answers to the great questions of the times by making use of elements derived from Confucianism, Daoism and Buddhism." De Meyer, *Wu Yun's Way*, 104–5.
4 On Liu Zongyuan's involvement with Buddhism, see Chen Jo-shui, *Liu Tsung-yüan*, 172–80.
5 See Bol, review of Chen Jo-shui, *Liu Tsung-yüan*, 167–68; DeBlasi, *Reform in the Balance*, 13–16.
6 Han Yu's preface states the context for Wenchang's request. Additional details about the circumstances of their meeting and Wenchang's place of origin can be found in a valedictory poem that Han later wrote for him in 806. *HCLW* 282; *HCLS* 5.584.
7 See, e.g., Liu Zongyuan's valedictory preface for Wenchang's pilgrimage to Mount Wutai ca. 801: *LZY* 25.667–70. Another example, a poem by Lü Wen, is translated and analyzed in Rouzer, "Early Buddhist Kanshi," 435–36.
8 *HCLW* 281.
9 Ibid.
10 For Confucius's criticism of the music of the states of Zheng and Wei as morally corrupting, see *Analects* 15.11 and 17.18.
11 *FYYS* 5.102–3.
12 Contra Fan, *Rujia minzu sixiang yanjiu*, 72–73.
13 Some modern scholars have suggested, based on "Tracing the Way," that Han Yu saw Wenchang and other Chinese Buddhist monks as "new barbarians": e.g., ibid., 228–31. But that term from the *Gongyang Commentary* never appears in Han's writings.
14 *HCLW* 282.

15 Ibid., 752–53. The phrase "approve of him coming in" also echoes *Analects* 7.29, in which Confucius argues that he may receive visitors without thereby condoning their past or present misdeeds.
16 Han Yu was posted to Luoyang in 807 and was appointed magistrate of the city in the winter of 810–11. Li Chu was on the staff of the governor of Hunan province (to which Yongzhou belonged) and had traveled to Luoyang to visit his father. While there, he caught up with Han Yu, whom he had not seen in thirteen years, and was asked to convey a letter to Liu Zongyuan. *HCLW* 310–11; Zhang Qinghua, *Han Yu nianpu huizheng*, 261–62, 265.
17 Scholars have long identified Yuan the Eighteenth as the Yuan Jixu mentioned in two texts that Bai Juyi wrote in 817: *QTW* 675.6895, 676.6900–901. Han Yu met Yuan the Eighteenth for the first time in 819, while en route to exile in Chaozhou. Quite surprisingly, the two men traveled together for a time and became friends. Han wrote a few poems for Yuan, in one of which he speaks of having read Liu Zongyuan's preface for Yuan long before meeting him: *HCLS* 1123–36.
18 *LZY* 25.662–63.
19 Ibid., 25.674.
20 Longxi is a reference to Li Chu's prestigious clan choronym.
21 *LZY* 25.673–74.
22 The thirteenth-century writer Zhou Mi (1232–1298), commenting on this inscription, found it "laughable" that the Tang literati would let a monk serve as a lecturer in "the temple of the former sage." Zhou's attitude reflects the degree to which Classicists reasserted a monopoly on classical exegesis in the Song period. Ibid., 5.122; *GXZS* 40 (cf. Halperin, *Out of the Cloister*, 27).
23 Liu Zongyuan is being disingenuous here: Yang Xiong only acknowledged that there were ideas worth adopting from Zhuangzi. He found nothing of merit in Mozi and the ideas of Shen Buhai and Han Fei. *LZY* 25.673; *FYYS* 6.130, 6.134, 8.177, 11.280.
24 *LZY* 25.673–74.
25 On Elai, who served the tyrannical last Shang king, see *SJ* 5.174.
26 *ZZZY* 39.1095–109. For an analysis of this anecdote, see Li Wai-yee, *The Readability of the Past in Early Chinese Historiography*, 136–47.
27 *SJ* 5.192–93. For comparison and analysis of the You Yu story's various versions, see Li Wai-yee, "Anecdotal Barbarians in Early China," 115–21.
28 *HMJ* juan 1. For the allusions to Yu, the Blind Old Man, and the Lords of Guan and Cai, see *SJ* 1.31–32, 15.686, 35.1563–65. The ethnonym Qiang has been applied to various western frontier peoples in Chinese history: Zhu, *Hua-Yi zhi jian*, 127–77.
29 *LZY* 25.674.
30 Nearly all of Wang Ling's works must have been written in the decade before his death at the age of twenty-seven, i.e., 1049–59.
31 *WLJ* 16.283.
32 Later in this piece, Wang also berates Liu Zongyuan for "sinking unrepentantly into barbarism" (*xian Yi-Di er buhui*) by supporting Buddhism. Ibid., 16.283–84.
33 Ibid., 16.284.

34   Chen Jo-shui, who accepts the conventional dating of "Tracing the Way" to 804, argues that its influence is visible in a letter that Liu Zongyuan wrote to his brother-in-law Yang Huizhi in 811. Liu had earlier written an essay that advised Yang to be less self-righteous and intolerant of others' flaws. Yang responded with a letter insinuating that Liu's preference for moderation and compromise was not in keeping with the "sagely Way." Liu insists, in his reply, that his understanding of the Way is the same as that of every sage from Yao and Shun to Confucius. As Chen recognizes in a footnote, Liu Zongyuan does not claim that the Way was transmitted from one sage to the next or that the transmission was broken after Mencius. I see these differences as indicating that the similarity between Liu's statement and the narrative of the Way of the Sages in "Tracing the Way" is merely coincidental, *pace* Chen's assumption that this statement is "directly adapted from" and "apparently identical [to]" Han Yu's narrative. Chen Jo-shui, *Liu Tsung-yüan*, 89, 168–71; *LZY* 16.461–63, 33.849–58.

35   *LZY* 31.807–9, 31.811–12.

36   For arguments dating "Tracing the Way" to 804, see Luo Liantian, *Tangdai wenxue lunji*, 443–49; Zhang Qinghua, "Han Yu de dao, daotong shuo ji 'Wuyuan' de xiezuo shijian bianxi," 4–6; Zhang Qinghua, *Han Yu nianpu huizheng*, 182–83, 185–86; Liu Zhenlun, "Wu 'yuan' de chuangzuo yu daotong de queli," 1–2.

37   For the source of the Minister Yu allusion, see *SJ* 76.2375. For the poem, see *HCLS* 213.

38   *HCLW* 162.

39   For example, Mo Qiong recently argued that Han Yu had even better conditions for writing during his term as an academician in the College of the Four Gates in 801–3. That much is true, but Mo's arguments for dating "Tracing the Way" to that period overstate its similarities to the preface for Wenchang. Mo, "Han Yu 'Yuandao' pian xiezuo shijian xinzheng," 77–86.

40   E.g., Qian Zhongshu, *Guanzhui bian*, 821; Bol, "*This Culture of Ours*," 130; De Meyer, *Wu Yun's Way*, 104; Abramson, *Ethnic Identity in Tang China*, 67.

41   Campany, "On the Very Idea of Religions," 305–6.

42   *HCLW* 684.

43   *TD* 185.4978–80.

44   *HCLW* 239–40.

45   In *Mencius* 3A.4 and 3B.9, Mencius misidentifies the subject of this ode as the Duke of Zhou, rather than a seventh-century BCE lord of Lu, and likens his own polemics against rival philosophers to the Duke's military campaigns.

46   *HCLW* 241.

47   Ibid., 19.

48   On Han Yu's lifelong fondness for the *Mencius* and his conviction that of all Confucius's followers, "Mencius alone received the orthodox transmission [of Confucius's Way]," see *HCLW* 40, 293.

49   McMullen, "Han Yü: An Alternative Picture," 606, 657.

50   Berlin, *The Hedgehog and the Fox*, 1–5.

51 *Pace* Hartman, who argues that this dismissive attitude toward Han Yu's philosophical contributions only began with "early twentieth-century Chinese intellectuals." Hartman, *Han Yü*, 173–74. For Cheng Yi's criticisms of Han Yu, see *ECJ* 182, 231–32, 252, 262; for the influence of these criticisms on later Daoxue adherents, see Guo Tian, "Songdai rushi hudong de yige anli," 120–21.
52 *ECJ* 5, 37, 43, 231–32, 262, 1201, 1195.

CHAPTER 3: ETHNOCENTRIC MORALISM IN
TWO LATE TANG ESSAYS

1   There are currently two full English translations of "Chinese at Heart" and one full translation of "Call to Arms" in print: see Hartman, *Han Yü*, 158–59; Abramson, *Ethnic Identity in Tang China*, 180–81. Unfortunately, each translation contains misinterpretations of the Chinese. The translations in this chapter are my own.
2   The rhetorical logic of ethnocentric moralism is also discernable, but only implicit, in a funerary inscription composed by Liu Yuxi (777–842) in 838. I have analyzed this text and its influence elsewhere: Shao-yun Yang, "Shi Xiaozhang's Spirit Road Stele."
3   The first Chinese historian to cite "Chinese at Heart" seems to have been Chen Yuan in 1923, but he used it as evidence for the "Sinicization" of foreigners rather than as an example of Chinese "culturalism." John Fincher was the first scholar to comment on the "unusual clarity" of the "culturalist" position in "Chinese at Heart," although he misdated the text to the early Song. Xie Haiping (in Taiwan) and Qian Zhongshu (on mainland China) appear to have been the first to notice "Call to Arms," citing it and "Chinese at Heart" as examples of "culturalism." Chen Yuan, *Yuan xiyu ren huahua kao*, 4–5; Fincher, "China as a Race, Culture, and Nation," 63–64; Xie, *Tangdai liuhua waiguoren*, 8–9; Qian Zhongshu, *Guanzhui bian*, 2311–12.
4   Zhang Weiran, "Tangren xinmuzhong de wenhua quyu ji dili yixiang," 311; Fan, *Rujia minzu sixiang yanjiu*, 231–32.
5   Abramson, *Ethnic Identity in Tang China*, 182, 187.
6   Ibid., 184.
7   *XTS* 60.1609; *QTW* 767.7983; *HYSJ* 178–82. The version of Huang Tao's preface at *QTW* 824.8684–85 contains a few errors. On Wang Chao's siege of Quanzhou, see *ZZTJ* 256.8326, 256.8339. Huang Tao's preface is vague about which war had caused the loss of Chen An's works, possibly in order to avoid offending Wang Chao and his brothers, who became the most powerful men in Fujian after 893.
8   *TZY* 7.74.
9   Xu Song and Meng Erdong, *Dengke jikao buzheng*, 1020–26.
10 *XTS* 60.1609.
11 My reading of the line "Chang suo bingong zhe bude ni" 常所賓貢者不得擬 differs significantly from that of Hartman, who translates it as "Those who had sponsored other candidates were not content with the results," as well as of Abramson, who translates it as "None of the candidates recommended in the normal fashion received an appointment": Hartman, *Han Yü*, 158; Abramson, *Ethnic Identity in Tang China*,

180. I have also followed the punctuation used in the *Quan Tangwen*: 二年以進士第名顯然,常所賓貢者不得擬. Most modern studies that quote "Chinese at Heart" punctuate this sentence as 二年以進士第名顯,然常所賓貢者不得擬, but in that case the construction *xianming* 顯名 would be more grammatically correct than *mingxian* 名顯, and the *ran* 然 would serve no useful purpose as a conjunction.

12 For Lu Wan, Li Ling, and Jin Midi, see *SJ* 93.2637–39, 109.2877–78; *HS* 34.1890–93, 54.2450–55, 68.2959–62. It would be fairer to say that Li Ling surrendered to the Xiongnu when his army was surrounded and facing certain annihilation—at least, this is the version of the story that Sima Qian favored.

13 *QTW* 767.7986.

14 Abramson argues "it is likely that he was born and raised in China and possible that his family had lived there for generations," but this seems to be based solely on Li's proficiency in literary Chinese. Abramson, *Ethnic Identity in Tang China*, 186

15 Xu Song and Meng Erdong, *Dengke jikao buzheng*, 905.

16 Yan, *Tangshi yanjiu luncong*, 432–41. Yan wrote the relevant essay in 1959 and revised it in 1968. For some important later studies that built on or revised Yan's findings, see Xie, *Tangdai liuhua waiguoren*, 124–30; Gao, "Sui Tang gongju zhidu dui Riben, Xinluo de yingxiang"; Fan, "Songdai Gaoli bingong jinshi kao"; Shi Xiulian, "Tangdai de 'bingong ke' yu bingong zhi zhi"; Dang, *Tang yu Xinluo wenhua guanxi yanjiu*, 49–60.

17 On Li Xun, see Xie, *Tangdai liuhua waiguoren*, 125–26; Cheng Yuzhui, "Wudai ciren Li Xun."

18 Fan Wenli's latest work claims that there were separate examinations for *bingong* candidates and Chinese candidates and implies that Li Yansheng sat for the Chinese candidates' examination. One of Fan's earlier articles argues, more persuasively, that separate examinations would not have made sense in the Tang context and only began under the Song. Dang Yinping has also argued that there was no separate examination for *bingong* candidates under the Tang. Nonetheless, Dang infers from the text of "Chinese at Heart" that Li Yansheng differed from other *bingong* candidates in being granted a special examination by imperial decree. Since Li was recommended in 847 but not examined until 848, it is more likely that he sat for the regular *jinshi* examination in 848. The emperor's edict merely added him to the roster of regular candidates, and he differed from ordinary *bingong* candidates in how well he performed, not how he was examined. Shi Xiulian regards this interpretation as possible, but without ruling out Dang's interpretation. Fan, *Rujia minzu sixiang yanjiu*, 235; Fan, "Songdai Gaoli bingong jinshi kao," 42–43; Dang, *Tang yu Xinluo wenhua guanxi yanjiu*, 60; Shi Xiulian, "Tangdai de 'bingong ke' yu bingong zhi zhi," 340n2.

19 *JTS* 177.4592; *XTS* 182.5368.

20 *JTS* 177.4592.

21 *Pace* Fan Wenli, who assumes Chen An was quoting and rebutting actual criticisms directed at Lu Jun. Fan, *Rujia minzu sixiang yanjiu*, 235–36.

22 On this practice, see Moore, *Rituals of Recruitment in Tang China*, 141–52.

23 Xu Song and Meng Erdong, *Dengke jikao buzheng*, 904–5.

24 Liu Pujiang, *Zhengtong yu Hua-Yi*, 2–10, 23–24.
25 Ibid., 11, 101–2.
26 For the Three Kingdoms, see Wang Mingsun, "Sanguo shidai de guojia yu Zhongguo guan." For an interesting debate between the Northern Wei emperor Xiaowendi (r. 471–99) and one of his ministers over whether south China was part of the Central Lands, see *WS* 54.1208.
27 For the broader interpretation of "the Central Lands," see Zhang Weiran, "Tangren xinmuzhong de wenhua quyu ji dili yixiang," 311–12. For the narrow and broad meanings of Han, see Shao-yun Yang, "Fan and Han," 18–21.
28 *HFCZ* 33. There is an allusion here to *Mencius* 2A.1, in which Mencius says that during King Zhou's reign, King Wuding's (r. ca. 1250–ca. 1192 BCE) "legacy of good customs and good governance still remained," thus emphasizing what a formidable challenge it was for the Zhou dynasty to overthrow the Shang.
29 Abramson reads Huangfu Shi's argument as one that "political legitimacy depended on holding Chinese cultural values rather than on possession of the Central Plain." I think "ritual and moral" would be a more precise description of Huangfu's emphasis than "cultural." Abramson, *Ethnic Identity in Tang China*, 110.
30 *ZZZY* 15.401. For the political context of the resettlement, see Li Wai-yee, "Anecdotal Barbarians in Early China," 128–29. On 738 BCE as the probable date of the Eastern Zhou court's move to Luoyang, see Yoshimoto, "Shūshitsu tōsen saikō."
31 *HFCZ* 34. Xiaowendi's reforms began soon after his capital's move to Luoyang and involved giving new Chinese-style surnames to the Xianbi aristocracy and "the massive formal restructuring of the court in the mold of a Chinese-style entity similar to those of the Chinese Southern Dynasties": Eisenberg, "Collapse of a Eurasian Hybrid," 376.
32 E.g., Liu Pujiang, *Zhengtong yu Hua-Yi*, 20 (cf. 57, which interprets Huangfu as a "culturalist" like Han Yu).
33 It is striking that Huangfu Shi, who shared Han Yu's anti-Buddhist sentiments, ignores the subject of Buddhism when assessing the legitimacy of the Northern and Southern Dynasties. Since his argument was that the Central Lands were defined by the practice of "ritual propriety and moral duty," the logic of ethnicized orthodoxy (had he chosen to apply it) could have led him to interpret the Mandate of Heaven's transfer from the Southern Dynasties to the Northern Zhou as a consequence of both the Liang dynasty's barbarization by Buddhism—Liang Wudi (r. 502–49) being known for his exceptionally fervent patronage of the religion—and Zhou Wudi's (r. 560–78) pro-Classicist decision to proscribe both Buddhism and Daoism in 574. This suggests that the essay either predates Han Yu's rhetoric of ethnicized orthodoxy or reflects Huangfu's limited interest in using it.
34 Pace Hartman, who describes Huangfu Shi's point as "the same argument [as "Chinese at Heart"], this time worked in the opposite direction," and Qian, who reads "Chinese at Heart" and "Call to Arms" as simply elaborating on Huangfu's argument. Hartman, *Han Yü*, 330n77; Qian Zhongshu, *Guanzhui bian*, 2312.
35 Abramson, *Ethnic Identity in Tang China*, 180–81.
36 *GYZS* 18.400–401.

37 For a recent study of the *xi* genre, see Goh, "The Art of Wartime Propaganda."
38 *QTW* 821.8650.
39 There is a possibility, however, that Pi Rixiu (ca. 834–883) read "Chinese at Heart" before the dispersal and partial destruction of Chen An's works in the 880s. An essay on *Annals* exegesis by Pi employs a very similar moralistic redefinition of Chineseness and barbarism: "Wu was actually Chinese (Hua) by lineage (*zu*), but its way (*dao*) was that of the barbarians (Yi). Using their strength to coerce others into a covenant—should we not call that barbaric (Yi)? The Rong were actually barbarians by lineage, but their way was that of the Chinese. Following the Way by being fond of making covenants—should we not call that Chinese?" Here, Pi is comparing the behavior of the Wu ruler at the Huangchi conference with that of a group of Rong at the Qian conference of 721 BCE, where (according to the *Zuo Tradition*) they requested a formal peace covenant with the ruler of Lu. *PZWS* 3.33.
40 Abramson, *Ethnic Identity in Tang China*, 180, 189.
41 *ZZTJ* 262.8546–47, 262.8555–66, 263.8570, 263.8573–76, 263.8580–95, 264.8602–5.
42 Ibid., 264.8623–30, 265.8634–36, 265.8640, 266.8669–70, 266.8674.
43 Abramson, *Ethnic Identity in Tang China*, 189; cf. a similar argument about Li Keyong (without mentioning "Call to Arms") in Fu, "Tangdai yixiaguan zhi yanbian," 225.
44 For the origins of the feud, see *ZZTJ* 255.8304–6, 256.8312–13; *JWDS* 1.5, 25.338–39; *XWDS* 1.5, 4.34.
45 *ZZTJ* 258.8395–400, 258.8406–9, 258.8411–12; *JTS* 179.4657–61; *XTS* 185.5412–13; *XWDS* 1.5, 4.35. On the Tang-period use of Jie (an extinct ethnonym of the third and fourth centuries) as a derogatory epithet for foreigners of Inner Asian origin, including An Lushan, see Huang Yongnian, "'Jiehu,' 'Zhejie,' 'Zazhong Hu' kaobian," 385–87.
46 *ZZTJ* 260.8469–81; *JWDS* 26.350–53.
47 *ZZTJ* 262.8551–53, 262.8569–70, 263.8599–8600.
48 Hartman, *Han Yü*, 158; Abramson, *Ethnic Identity in Tang China*, 183, 186.
49 According to various sources, Shennong had a bull-like head, Fuxi and Nüwa had snake-like bodies, Yu and Gaoyao had beaks, and Confucius had a face like an exorcist's mask: *HCLW* 38–39.
50 Ibid. Beginning with Fang Songqing in the twelfth century, scholars have noted that the argument of the Third Miscellaneous Discourse is very similar to one found in the *Liezi*, a text modeled on the *Zhuangzi*. *HJJZ* 206; *LZ* 2.83–84.

CHAPTER 4: ETHNICIZED ORTHODOXY IN THE NORTHERN SONG GUWEN REVIVAL

1 Quoting Shields, "Gossip, Anecdote, and Literary History," 110.
2 It should be noted that Yang Yi had good relations with Wang, Sun, and Yao and is not known to have been a target of criticism by Liu and Mu. He only came to be vilified by Guwen writers (mainly Shi Jie) in the 1030s, over a decade after his death. Feng, *Beisong guwen yundong de xingcheng*, 110–28.
3 *JSWJ* 23.1927.

4   Hong, "Ouyang Xiu Tiansheng xue Han."
5   *LGJ* 28.324.
6   Higashi, *Fugu yu chuangxin*, 107–11; Luo Liantian, *Tangdai wenxue lunji*, 16. But, for a defense of the term "Guwen movement" as valid and heuristically useful, see Chen Jo-shui, *Tangdai wenshi yu Zhongguo sixiang de zhuanxing*, 236–38.
7   On the use of *siwen* in the *Analects*, see Kern, "Ritual, Text, and the Formation of the Canon," 51–52; Bergeton, *Emergence of Civilizational Consciousness*, 96–97. Bol translates *siwen* as "this Culture of Ours." Adding the adjective "literary" when translating the phrase for the Northern Song context helps me avoid giving the impression that an oppositional dichotomy of "Chinese culture" and "foreign culture" is being invoked. As Bol notes, in Tang-Song times *siwen* only "belonged to that small, elite group in Chinese society known as the *shih* [i.e., *shi*, "literati"]," rather than to Chinese society as a whole. Bol, *"This Culture of Ours*," 1–4.
8   *CLWJ* 12.139, 15.180–82, 16.192.
9   Ibid., 13.154.
10 Welter, "A Buddhist Response to the Confucian Revival," 25–28; Halperin, *Out of the Cloister*, 117–18. In more recent work, Welter suggests (less persuasively) that Liu Kai and Wang Yucheng were equally hostile to Buddhism, differing only in the range of their "literary and cultural interests": Welter, "Confucian Monks and Buddhist *Junzi*," 239–40.
11 *QSW* 323.36–38, 323.40–41; Feng, *Beisong guwen yundong de xingcheng*, 125–28.
12 My basis for differentiating these two groups differs from the distinction drawn between "intolerant Guwen" and "tolerant Guwen" literati in Welter, "Confucian Monks and Buddhist *Junzi*," 244 (cf. 239–40).
13 Note that Wang Tong's rise in stature began not with Liu Kai but with the late Tang literati Pi Rixiu and Lu Guimeng (d. 881), who were also admirers of Han Yu. Wong, "Between Politics and Metaphysics," 66–72, 77–79; Feng, *Beisong guwen yundong de xingcheng*, 84–95; Skonicki, "'Guwen' Lineage Discourse in the Northern Song," 9–17.
14 *LKJ* 6.72–81. For the letter's date, see Zhu Shangshu, "Liu Kai nianpu," 123–24. On Zang Bing's relationship with Liu Kai, see Feng, *Beisong guwen yundong de xingcheng*, 83–84.
15 Ng, "Beisong chunian de beifang wenshi yu haoxia"; Wyatt, "Unsung Men of War," 196–201; Chen Feng, "Liu Kai shiji."
16 *LKJ* 6.69–71.
17 Ibid., 11.158.
18 Ibid., 11.159; *QSW* 124.343.
19 On the two failed Song attacks on Youzhou in 979 and 986, see Lorge, *Reunification of China*, 185–222.
20 Liu Kai believed his reassignment to be linked to a political scandal at the imperial court in which his patron was charged with cronyism and demoted to the provinces. It is interesting that the tales of Liu eating the livers of convicted criminals are specific to his subsequent prefectural posts (none of them on the northern frontier) in 988–94. Given his reputation for self-promoting behavior, it is possible that he adopted the liver-eating practice to salvage his military career by cultivating an image

of ferocity, although it is also possible that the tales originated in slander. Zhu Shangshu, "Liu Kai nianpu," 131–42; Wyatt, "Unsung Men of War," 198–200.

21 Chen Feng, "Liu Kai shiji," 125–28; Ng, "Beisong chunian de beifang wenshi yu haoxia," 314–39.
22 *CLWJ* 12.135–39, 15.180–81; Chen Zhi'e, *Shi Jie shiji*, 22, 26–27. See also Skonicki, "'Guwen' Lineage Discourse in the Northern Song," 8–9.
23 Chen Zhi'e, *Shi Jie shiji*, 28–29, 31–33; *CLWJ* 9.99–102, 15.172–73. For Sun Shi's biography, see *SS* 431.12801–808.
24 *CLWJ* 15.172.
25 Ibid., 13.153–54.
26 Ibid., 19.228–29.
27 Chen Zhi'e, *Shi Jie shiji*, 45.
28 *LJZY* 12.398–99. For a translation, see Shao-yun Yang, "'Their Lands Are Peripheral and Their *Qi* Is Blocked Up,'" 392. This chapter is conventionally dated to the early Western Han; an earlier, more rudimentary version of this passage may be found in a chapter of *Dai the Elder's Record of Rites* (Dadai liji) that has been dated to the Warring States: Hu, *Neng Xia ze da yu jianmu Huafeng*, 120–24.
29 *CLWJ* 10.116.
30 Ibid., 10.116–17.
31 The literal-minded Southern Song thinker Huang Zhen (1213–1281) found it ludicrous, pointing out that it was the Buddha's disciples who came from the west and faulting Shi Jie for believing Buddhist claims about the Buddha's exceptional height (according to one text, seven cubits rather than the normal four). See Chen Zhi'e, *Shi Jie shiji*, 45.
32 Huang Zhen noted this reversal and commented skeptically, "I do not know what basis there is for it." Ibid.
33 Chen Zhi'e ignored this problem when explaining Shi Jie's claim about Laozi as a case of Han Yu's "Tracing the Way" formula for interpreting barbarism: "When one uses barbarian rites, then one is regarded as a barbarian." Chen Zhi'e, *Beisong wenhuashi shulun*, 31.
34 My interpretation of Han Yu's use of *ren qiren* follows the commentator Shen Qinhan (1775–1831): *HCLW* 21.
35 *CLWJ* 10.117.
36 Ibid., 6.71.
37 E.g., Ge Zhaoguang, "Songdai 'Zhongguo' yishi de tuxian," 135.
38 Chen Zhi'e, *Beisong wenhuashi shulun*, 32 (cf. 26–29). For a similar view, see Li Xiaohong and Liu Pei, "'Zhongguo' guannian de chongsu."
39 *CLWJ* 2.17–18.
40 Chen Zhi'e dates this poem to 1029 on the grounds that it says Liu Kai has been dead for thirty years. However, another poem that can be dated to 1040 also states the time elapsed since Liu Kai's death as thirty years. It is thus likely that in both poems, "thirty years" is only serving as a rough estimate. See *CLWJ* 2.17, 2.20–21; Chen Zhi'e, *Shi Jie shiji*, 19–20, 96.
41 *CLWJ* 3.24–25.

42 Fang, "Cong herong dao tuobian," 39–43.
43 It was customary in war for rulers surrendering their states in person to bring an empty coffin as a symbol that they were prepared to be put to death by their conquerors but were pleading for mercy. For the *locus classicus*, see *ZZZY* 13.348.
44 Chen Zhi'e dates this poem to 1039, on the eve of the first Song-Xi Xia war, but it is also possible that Shi wrote it after the war began. *CLWJ* 2.22–23; Chen Zhi'e, *Shi Jie shiji*, 87.
45 *CLWJ* 15.182.
46 Chen Zhi'e assumes that the two priests became Shi Jie's students during his stint as an instructor at the Imperial University (Taixue) in 1042–44. However, the use of "returning to Lu" as an analogy in the letter to Zhang Guilu suggests that this letter dates from Shi Jie's time at Mount Tai. Chen Zhi'e, *Shi Jie shiji*, 111; *CLWJ* 7.82.
47 *CLWJ* 14.163–64, 14.170–71.
48 Ibid., 7.82.
49 *QSW* 401.314.
50 Sun Fu also amplifies the bestialization metaphor with a paraphrase of a comment attributed to Lord Ding of Liu (fl. 559–541 BCE) in the *Zuo Tradition*: "If not for [the flood-taming] Yu, we would all be fish!" *QSW* 401.314–15; *ZZZY* 41.1150.
51 One of Sun Fu's essays argues that Dong Zhongshu merits inclusion in the list as well. See *QSW* 401.302–4 (cf. 401.294).
52 Ibid., 401.292–93.
53 *QSW* 401.309.
54 *Pace* Chen Zhi'e, *Beisong wenhuashi shulun*, 31–32.
55 *QSW* 401.310.
56 *JSWJ* 16.1764–67.
57 *CLWJ* 15.175–77.
58 *JSWJ* 16.1767–68.
59 My reading of Ouyang's position is slightly different from Peter Bol's. Bol reads him as a pragmatist who felt that "merely claiming to be right was not quite enough" unless one could also achieve the political power to realize one's ideals. Bol, *"This Culture of Ours,"* 182–83.
60 *JSJ* 2.56–57, 3.68–69, 3.75–76, 34.895–98; *JSWJ* 47.1179–81; Chen Zhi'e, *Shi Jie shiji*, 61–62, 127–30.
61 On the Imperial University style and Shi Jie's role in its emergence, see Higashi, *Fugu yu chuangxin*, 125–41; Feng, *Beisong guwen yundong de xingcheng*, 196–209; Niu, "Beisong Renzong chao de taixue ti jiqi xuefeng, wenfeng."
62 In the twelfth century, Ye Mengde (1077–1148) claimed that Ouyang Xiu was not originally anti-Buddhist but eventually adopted that position under Shi Jie's influence and that Ouyang and Shi were "probably both inspired by Han Tuizhi." On the contrary, Ouyang's preferred response to Buddhism was quite different from those of Han Yu and Shi Jie. See Chen Zhi'e, *Beisong wenhuashi shulun*, 334. For two good analyses of Ouyang Xiu's views on Buddhism, see Chang, *Beisong Qisong de rushi ronghui sixiang*, 97–106; Zhang Peifeng, *Songdai shidafu foxue yu wenxue*, 145–53.
63 *JSJ* 17.513, 17.516–17.

64 Ibid., 17.516.
65 *HCLW* 17–19; *CLWJ* 10.117.
66 *JSJ* 17.511.
67 In 256 BCE, Qin annexed the Eastern Zhou capital and put an end to the Zhou dynasty, as a prelude to unifying the Warring States. On the Warring States image of Qin as a barbarian state, see Pines, "The Question of Interpretation."
68 This incident occurred in 641 BCE, after the state of Zhu took the Zeng ruler captive at a treaty conference. The *Gongyang* and *Guliang* commentaries claim that the sacrifice consisted of striking the Zeng ruler's nose to draw blood and dripping that blood on the altar, implying that the Zeng ruler was not killed. The *Zuo Tradition*, however, claims that the men of Zhu killed the Zeng ruler and sacrificed him on the altar to a local god and that the Song ruler, who had suzerainty over Zhu, connived in this act to gain the loyalty of the "eastern Yi." Note that whereas the *Zuo Tradition* refers to the people of Zhu as "barbarians" (Yi or Man-Yi), the *Gongyang* and *Guliang* commentaries do not. Du Yu's *Zuo Tradition* commentary argues that Zhu, originally a Chinese state, was identified with the eastern Yi because it lay adjacent to them and had adopted some of their rites and customs. Li Wai-yee suggests that the real reason has to do with geopolitical enmity between Lu and Zhu, since the *Zuo Tradition* is based on Lu historical records. ZZZY 14.393, 14.399–400, 50.1431; GYZS 11.240; GLZS 9.160; Li Wai-yee, "Hua-Yi zhi bian yu yizu tonghun."
69 A reference to the Xin You anecdote in the *Zuo Tradition* (see chapter 3).
70 *JSJ* 17.517.
71 In this regard, see also a 1034 letter from Shi Jie to Kong Daofu, in which Shi uses the Lu region as a touchstone for the state of civilization and exclaims: "Passing from the Qin through the Jin, Song, Liang, and Sui, up to the Five Dynasties, how much longer could it have gone on before [the people of] Lu were wearing their hair untied and folding their robes to the left?" In the very next line, Shi blames Laozi, Zhuangzi, Han Fei, Yang Zhu, Mozi, Buddhism, and the Daoist religion for this barbarizing effect on the Chinese. *CLWJ* 14.170–71; Chen Zhi'e, *Shi Jie shiji*, 46.
72 *Pace* Halperin, who claims Ouyang was arguing that the Song's current circumstances "resembled those of the Eastern Zhou, when foreign tribes lived throughout the country." Halperin, *Out of the Cloister*, 161.
73 By noting this similarity between Ouyang and Li, I do not mean to downplay their intellectual differences in other aspects, on which see, e.g., Zuo, "'Ru' versus 'Li.'"
74 *LGJ* 16.140.
75 Ibid., 23.252.
76 Ibid., 28.321–24.
77 Chang, *Beisong Qisong de rushi ronghui sixiang*, 92–96; Li Chenggui, "Shilun Li Gou fojiaoguan de shuangchongxing"; Halperin, *Out of the Cloister*, 62–63, 93, 160, 189–90.
78 *LGJ* 27.299–301, 28.305.
79 On the Song–Xi Xia war's impact on the reform program, see Smith, "A Crisis in the Literati State."
80 *LGJ* 22.242–43.

81 Quoting a famous line from the "Mougong" chapter of *Master Sun's Art of War* (Sunzi bingfa).
82 Another quotation from *Master Sun's Art of War*, this time from the chapter "Xing."
83 *LGJ* 22.242–43.
84 Xiong Mingqin cites "The Enemy Threat" as evidence of the primacy of "culture" over ethnicity in Northern Song understandings of the Chinese-barbarian dichotomy, but this underestimates the essay's deliberate provocativeness: Xiong, "Chaoyue 'Yi-Xia,'" 127. It is possible, however, that "The Enemy Threat" provided some rhetorical inspiration for a memorial that Fu Bi submitted to the throne in 1044; see the conclusion for discussion of the relevant passage.

CHAPTER 5: IDEAS OF BARBARIZATION IN ELEVENTH-CENTURY *ANNALS* EXEGESIS

1 *Uncovering the Intricacies* is mentioned as one of Sun Fu's works in Shi Jie's commemorative inscription for the Mount Tai Academy, which is dated August 28, 1040. *CLWJ* 19.223.
2 The argument that *Uncovering the Intricacies* did not circulate beyond the circle of the Mount Tai Academy until shortly before Sun Fu's death is based on a longstanding assumption that a revised version of *Uncovering the Intricacies* comprised the bulk of the fifteen chapters (*pian*) of writing that—according to Ouyang Xiu's epitaph for Sun—the Song court obtained from Sun during his final illness and added to the imperial library. *JSJ* 27.747; Ge Huanli, *Zunjing zhongyi*, 126–29, 187–89.
3 Note also that in the epitaph that Ouyang composed for Sun Fu twenty years later, he praised Sun's *Annals* scholarship for being "undeluded by the [traditional] commentaries." *JSJ* 18.545–54, 27.747.
4 *CLWJ* 7.81, 15.173.
5 These fragments are analyzed in Huang Juehong, *Tang Song "Chunqiu" yizhu yanjiu*, 99–110.
6 *GYZS* 10.213–14.
7 *ZWFW* 3.10751.
8 Ibid., 5.10763. These lines are missing from the heavily censored *Siku quanshu* edition of *Uncovering the Intricacies*, but can be found in the earlier *Tongzhitang jingjie* edition. Huang Juehong mistakenly identifies them as a fragment from a lost work by Sun Fu: Huang Juehong, *Tang Song "Chunqiu" yizhu yanjiu*, 83–84. Note also that extant editions of *Uncovering the Intricacies* refer to Lord Huan as "Lord Wei" because Southern Song editors had to observe the taboo on Emperor Qinzong's (r. 1126–27) given name, Huan.
9 *ZWFW* 5.10771. This entire passage is missing from the *Siku quanshu* edition, but can be found in the *Tongzhitang jingjie* edition. Again, Huang Juehong misidentifies the passage as a fragment from a lost work: Huang Juehong, *Tang Song "Chunqiu" yizhu yanjiu*, 84–85.
10 Contra Wood, *Limits to Autocracy*, xi, 21, 72–73, 159–60. Wood, having based his study of Song *Annals* exegesis on the widely held assumption that Song thinkers like

Sun Fu interpreted *zunwang rangyi* as the "principal meaning" of the *Annals*, professes surprise that no modern work of history has acknowledged the Song provenance of the nineteenth-century Japanese political slogan *sonnō jōi* and that the *Kodansha Encyclopedia of Japan* claims the Chinese never used the expression *zunwang rangyi* before modern times. The encyclopedia is, in fact, essentially correct: the exact expression appears in no extant Chinese text written prior to the Qing dynasty, although wordier equivalents like *rang Yi-Di, zun tianwang* ("repel the barbarians and respect the Heaven-ordained king") can be found in Song texts (e.g., HSZ 108, 179). *Zunwang rangyi* appears in at least one early Qing text, authored by a Ming loyalist, but then vanishes until reintroduced from Japan during the late Qing. It subsequently became so pervasive in Chinese nationalist discourse that most Chinese historians now assume that a political ideal called *zunwang rangyi* already existed in Eastern Zhou times (with Guan Zhong often misidentified as its originator) and formed the central theme of the *Annals*. For the Ming loyalist Zhu Chaoying's (1605–1670) use of *zunwang rangyi*, see DCQ 141. On the evolution of Japanese *sonnō jōi* discourse, see Wakabayashi, *Anti-Foreignism and Western Learning in Early-Modern Japan*.

11   Pace Ge Huanli, *Zunjing zhongyi*, 134–35, 141. Ge disagrees with Mou Runsun's argument that when Sun Fu wrote about "repelling the barbarians," he "gave priority to respecting the king" and "did not go beyond the boundaries of respecting the king": Mou, "Liang Song Chunqiuxue zhi zhuliu," 106–7. I think Mou is essentially correct, albeit without adequately explaining Sun's understanding of the relationship between the two concepts.

12   JSWJ 9.1563. This argument is truncated in the revised 1071–72 version: JSJ 16.503. On the textual history of "On Legitimate Dynasties," see Higashi, *Fugu yu chuangxin*, 239–47.

13   ZWFW 5.10771.

14   Ge Huanli, *Zunjing zhongyi*, 191–92.

15   This interpretation seems tortured, since one would think that the presence of the Jin and Lu rulers at Huangchi was more, not less, of a humiliation to the Central Lands. After all, they could have boycotted the conference to avoid recognizing the Wu ruler's hegemony. Indeed, the *Gongyang Commentary* implies just that when it argues that Confucius, despite not approving of "barbarians leading the Central Lands" (*Yi-Di zhu Zhongguo*), nonetheless honored Wu by naming the Jin and Wu rulers as joint hegemons at Huangchi because "with [the ruler of] Wu there, not one of the lords in the realm dared not to go [to the conference]." GYZS 28.615–16.

16   ZWFW 12.10828. Wood's translation mispunctuates this line and thus misses the trope of barbarization. Ge Huanli misses the line altogether because of his reliance on the censored *Siku quanshu* edition of *Uncovering the Intricacies*, rather than the uncensored *Tongzhitang jingjie* edition. Wood, *Limits to Autocracy*, 87; Ge Huanli, *Zunjing zhongyi*, 133–34.

17   ZWFW 12.10828.

18   The *Annals* states cryptically that eleven lords met at the Juliang conference, but it was their ministers who made a covenant. Both the *Gongyang* and *Guliang*

commentaries interpret this as a message that the lords had by then become mere puppets in their ministers' hands. The *Zuo Tradition* states the context for the covenant, however: the Qi ruler had sent his minister Gao Hou to the conference as a representative, but Gao came under suspicion of attempting to subvert the Jin ruler's hegemony. A Jin minister then called for Gao to prove his goodwill by making a covenant with the ministers from other states who were present, since it would be ritually inappropriate for a minister to make a covenant with lords. Gao Hou thereupon fled the conference, and the ministers from other states reaffirmed their alignment with Jin by making a covenant to join hands against any state that challenged the Jin-led coalition. See *GYZS* 20.441–42; *GLZS* 16.297; *ZZZY* 33.939–40.

19 In 538 BCE, the Chu king sought to regain hegemony over the Central Lands by convening a multistate conference at Shen. The Jin ruler, choosing not to challenge the Chu bid for hegemony, found an excuse not to attend. This marked the beginning of Jin's decline from being Chu's strongest rival. See *ZZZY* 42.1190–94, 42.1199–203; for Sun Fu's commentary on the Shen conference, see *ZWFW* 10.10809.

20 *ZWFW* 12.10828.

21 One other interpretive difference between Ouyang Xiu and Sun Fu is worth mentioning in this context. In 1037, Ouyang wrote an essay advancing the iconoclastic argument that there was no special significance in Confucius's choice to start the *Annals* from 722 BCE and conclude it at the capture of a *qilin* in 481 BCE. Ouyang argued that Confucius, not being a historian by profession, simply based the *Annals* on a Lu official chronicle that happened to begin and end in those years. Whereas the *Gongyang Commentary* and later *Annals* exegetes tended to ascribe a symbolic meaning to the text's beginning and end, Ouyang Xiu criticized these theories for "bringing confusion to the *Annals*." See *JSJ* 18.556.

22 *ZWFW* 2.10737.

23 Ibid., 2.10744.

24 Cf. the four similar categories of reasons for editorial demotion of "barbarians and lords" in Ge Huanli, *Zunjing zhongyi*, 142–43. Unfortunately, Ge's use of the censored *Siku quanshu* edition prevented him from recognizing these categories' relevance to "barbarizing" demotion.

25 The *Guliang* interpretation of the Jin attack on Xianyu as aiding Chu's encroachment on "the Central Lands" overlooks the fact that the Xianyu people were themselves Di "barbarians" who had established a state in Hebei. Fan Ning's *Guliang* subcommentary tries to resolve this problem by claiming that since Xianyu was on the North China Plain, it counted as part of the Central Lands. Sun Fu instead interprets Xianyu as a Chinese state on the grounds that its rulers had the same surname as the Jin rulers and Zhou kings. *ZWFW* 8.10790, 10.10812, 10.10815; *GYZS* 17.379, 24.517–18; *GLZS* 17.332.

26 *ZWFW* 3.10754, 3.10756; *GLZS* 6.112.

27 The *Gongyang* and *Guliang* commentaries have no comment on this line in the *Annals*, but He Xiu's *Gongyang* subcommentary argues that Confucius regarded the Qin ruler as a barbarian (Yi-Di) because he exceeded reasonable limits in his aggression toward Jin. Interestingly, Sun Fu does not regard the only "barbarizing"

demotion of Qin identified in the *Gongyang* and *Guliang* commentaries per se—namely, the Battle of Xiao—as a demotion of Qin at all. He holds that the only demotion is that of the Jin ruler for ambushing the Qin army and violating the mourning period for his father. *ZWFW* 5.10773–74, 6.10778; *GYZS* 14.296.

28 He Xiu argues that Confucius refers to the Wu ruler as "Wu" in order to make it easier to "promote him gradually" later in the *Annals*—a counterintuitive interpretation similar to his reading of the first mention of the Chu state in the record for 684 BCE. *ZWFW* 8.10791; *GLZS* 6.112; *GYZS* 17.384 (cf. 7.143–46).

29 *ZWFW* 5.10768.

30 Alluding to *Analects* 13.4.

31 *ZWFW* 12.10828.

32 Ibid.

33 *GLZS* 5.89 (cf. *GYZS* 10.213, which also emphasizes Chu's rebelliousness but presents its "barbarian" status as a given rather than a product of rebellion).

34 For a good general account of Liu Chang's career and scholarship, see Ge Huanli, *Zunjing zhongyi*, 154–93. Unfortunately, Ge made the mistake of relying on the *Siku quanshu* editions of Liu Chang's commentaries, which were heavily censored to remove derogatory language about barbarians. This led him to underestimate the significance of the Chinese-barbarian dichotomy in Liu's commentaries.

35 *QSW* 1505.205, 1505.218. Ge Huanli refutes a common belief that Liu was a student of Ouyang Xiu: Ge Huanli, *Zunjing zhongyi*, 155–58.

36 *JSJ* 35.928–29; *QSW* 1505.220.

37 *LSZ* 7.10910. Cf. 6.10904–905, in which Liu Chang (unlike Sun Fu) agrees with the *Gongyang* and *Guliang* commentaries that Confucius saw the Qin ruler as behaving like a barbarian during the events leading up to his army's being ambushed and defeated by Jin at the Battle of Xiao.

38 *LSZ* 9.10924, 12.10946.

39 *CQFL* 2.63–64; *CQWZ* 3.1187.

40 The Ming edition cited here was published in 1559. Guoli gugong bowuyuan, *Siku quanshu buzheng: Zibu*, 78–79.

41 Two of these are cases in which the *Annals* refers to rulers by name rather than by their titles when recording their visits to the Lu court. In the first case, Liu Chang follows Zhao Kuang's interpretation. *LSZ* 2.10873, 6.10903; *CQQH* 2.10982, 11.11069; cf. *JZZL* 4.1051.

42 *LSZ* 6.10900; *CQYL* 1.11144. Ge Huanli argues from this that Liu Chang's emphasis on "respecting the king" was as strong as Sun Fu's: Ge Huanli, *Zunjing zhongyi*, 173–74.

43 *CQYL* 1.11131–32. In this case, Liu Chang was following *Luxuriant Gems*, which did (like the *Gongyang Commentary* itself) interpret the Zhu, Mou, and Ge demotion as "barbarizing": *CQFL* 4.118. As we saw earlier, Sun Fu followed He Xiu's explanation for the demotion, but also did not regard it as "barbarizing."

44 Ge Huanli agrees with earlier arguments that *The Weighing Balance* was Liu Chang's first commentary and that *The Forest of Meanings* was a late work that remained unpublished at the time of Liu Chang's death. Ge further theorizes that *The Forest of*

Meanings consists of lectures on the *Annals* that Liu Chang delivered to the emperor. Ge Huanli, *Zunjing zhongyi*, 160–61.

45 The earliest extant texts identifying Boyi as the ancestor of the Xú ruling house date from the Tang period and include an inscription by Han Yu: *HCLW* 6.460.
46 *CQYL* 1.11135.
47 Ibid., 2.11155–56.
48 Ibid., 1.11148.
49 Ibid.
50 *CQQH* 17.11123. Cf. 15.11100, where Liu Chang asserts that the Chu rulers were not "real barbarians." On Yuxiong, a Chu ancestor who was purportedly a companion of King Wen of Zhou, see *SJ* 40.1691.
51 *GLZS* 14.263.
52 *CQYL* 2.11153–54.
53 This text is preserved in two Southern Song anthologies: *MXWC* 39.630–31; *SWJ* 96.3a–3b. For a similar argument that quotes *Analects* 3.5, see *CQYL* 1.11127.
54 "The True King does not govern the barbarians" is a line in He Xiu's *Gongyang* subcommentary, relating to Lord Yin of Lu's conference with a leader or representative of a group of Rong at Qian in the spring of 721 BCE: *GYZS* 2.29. For the second round of the 1061 decree examination, the examiners chose it as the subject of one of six essays that the candidates were required to write within one day. The five other essay topics, all chosen by the examiners as well, were similarly obscure quotations or allusions from classical and historical texts. Only three candidates passed this examination, including Su Shi and his brother Su Zhe.
55 *SSQJ* 2.184–85.
56 Ibid., 2.185–86.
57 The petition was successful: Chang, *Beisong Qisong de rushi ronghui sixiang*, 50–52.
58 Skonicki, "A Buddhist Response to Ancient-Style Learning."
59 *Analects* 4.10.
60 *TJWJ* 8.153.
61 Ibid., 7.127–28. For *li* in Huayan philosophy, see Ziporyn, *Beyond Oneness and Difference*, 261–68.
62 Although "pattern" and "coherence" are currently the most popular translations, I have chosen to leave *li* untranslated in this book. On the earlier history of *li* as a concept, including its uses in Chinese Buddhist philosophy, see Chan, "Evolution of the Neo-Confucian Concept *Li* as Principle," and, more recently, Ziporyn, *Beyond Oneness and Difference*.
63 For the date of "Refuting Han Yu," see Chang, *Beisong Qisong de rushi ronghui sixiang*, 67.
64 *TJWJ* 14.300–301.
65 He Xiu believed that referring to the Xú ruler only by the name of his state was a "barbarizing" demotion for having joined in the destruction of Qǐ (note that He, being a Gongyang specialist, did not follow the *Zuo Tradition* interpretation of Qǐ as a barbarized state), while referring to the Di ruler as "a man" was promoting him for "frequently aligning himself with the Central Lands": *GYZS* 11.242, 13.289. Sun

Fu agreed with He Xiu's interpretation of the Di case, but interpreted the Xú case as simply indicating that Xú was a barbarian state, rather than an instance of "barbarizing" demotion: *ZWFW* 5.10768, 6.10777. In *The Forest of Meanings*, as we have seen, Liu Chang saw the Xú rulers as barbarized Chinese but traced the barbarization to their using the royal title illegitimately; according to Liu, they were the first Chinese state to be thus barbarized. *The Weighing Balance* directly disagrees with He Xiu, arguing that Xú was a barbarian state long before the attack on Qí, as seen from references to the "Rong of Xú" in the *Documents*: *CQQH* 11.11071 (cf. *SSZY* 20.562).

66 *TJWJ* 14.301.
67 Ibid., 2.45. This essay was written as a sequel to an essay titled "Tracing the [Buddhist] Teaching to Its Source" (Yuanjiao); the resemblance to the title of Han Yu's "Tracing the Way" is deliberate. For its date of composition, see Chang, *Beisong Qisong de rushi ronghui sixiang*, 47, 65.
68 Shao-yun Yang, "Shi Xiaozhang's Spirit Road Stele," 76–77, 80.
69 *WLJ* 2.29, 13.247, 14.254.
70 Late in life, Liu Chang was known to argue that Han Yu's efforts to secure a high post at the imperial court through self-promotion showed that he did not really understand the Way. Su Shi's "On Han Yu" (Han Yu lun), one of fifty essays submitted to the court for the first round of the 1061 decree examination, sharply criticizes Han Yu's theories about humaneness, human nature, and the emotions and concludes that Han loved the "name" (*ming*) of the Way of the Sages but not its "essence" (*shi*). *QSW* 1505.205–6; *DJZ* 40–41; *SSQJ* 4.385–86.
71 Yang Guo'an, "Shilun Beisong ruxue de yanjin."
72 Zhang Peifeng, *Songdai shidafu foxue yu wenxue*, 153–85; Bol, "Government, Society, and the State," 132–33. For Sima Guang's criticism of Han Yu, see *ZZTJ* 240.7759. On Su Shi's practice of Buddhism, see also Egan, *Word, Image, and Deed*, 134–68; Grant, *Mount Lu Revisited*.
73 *ECJ* 38, 50.
74 Much recent scholarship has disproved the myth that Chinese Buddhism underwent a permanent decline during the Song period as the result of a "Confucian revival": e.g., Gregory, "The Vitality of Buddhism in the Sung"; Halperin, *Out of the Cloister*.
75 Guo, "Songdai rushi hudong de yige anli."
76 Huang Juehong's analysis of the surviving fragments of *Expounding the Annals* does not note any arguments based on ethnicized orthodoxy and finds that many (but not all) of Shi Jie's interpretations are similar to Sun Fu's: Huang Juehong, *Tang Song "Chunqiu" yizhu yanjiu*, 104–10.
77 *QSW* 1478.151–52.

CHAPTER 6: CHINESENESS AND BARBARISM IN EARLY DAOXUE PHILOSOPHY

1 *ECJ* 542, 640, 643; Bol, "This Culture of Ours," 302–3; also Bol, *Neo-Confucianism in History*, 78–86.
2 *ECJ* 122.

3   Ibid., 4.
4   Shao-yun Yang, "'Their Lands Are Peripheral and Their *Qi* Is Blocked Up.'"
5   *HCLW* 28.
6   *ECJ* 177.
7   E.g., Yong Huang, *Why Be Moral?*, 56.
8   *ECJ* 43. Hu Anguo's (1074–1138) *Annals* commentary and *Collected Explanations of the Annals* (Chunqiu jijie), attributed to either Lü Benzhong (1084–1145) or Lü Zuqian (1137–1181), both attribute versions of this passage to Cheng Yi: *HSZ* 10; *LZQ* vol. 5, 16.442. But Li Mingfu's (1174–1234) "Guiding Principles for the *Collected Meanings of the Annals*" (Chunqiu jiyi gangling) attributes a version of the passage (with clear signs of Qing-period censorship) to Cheng Hao and merges it with a passage also found in *Supplementary Collection of the Cheng Brothers' Works* (Chengshi waishu) compiled by Zhu Xi: *CQJYGL* 1.1a–1b; cf. *ECJ* 401. On the disputed authorship of *Collected Explanations*, see Huang Juehong, *Tang Song "Chunqiu" yizhu yanjiu*, 261–75.
9   *ECJ* 1201. Yang Shi does not specify which of the Cheng brothers is quoted.
10 For the relevant passage, see *HCLW* 51.
11 *ECJ* 5, 37, 232, 1195, 1201–2.
12 Guoli gugong bowuyuan, *Siku quanshu buzheng: Zibu*, 78.
13 *ECJ* 33, 54.
14 Ibid., 106, 1136; *ZZQS* vol. 6, 2.85; vol. 7, 2a.104.
15 Yang Liu'an has demonstrated that *buru* normally means "inferior to" or "not as good as" in Classical Chinese texts, including the *Analects* itself. Earlier, Simon Leys came to the same conclusion in his 1997 translation of the *Analects*. Note that Yang misattributes Cheng Yi's interpretation of *Analects* 3.5 to Cheng Hao. Yang Liu'an, "'Yan Yi-Xia dafang' yihuo 'zhong junchen dayi'?"; Leys, *The Analects of Confucius*, 123.
16 For example, Alan T. Wood attributes Cheng Yi's self-critical interpretation to Confucius himself, as evidence that "tolerance [toward barbarians] was not new in the Chinese tradition." Wood, *Limits to Autocracy*, 101, 209n75.
17 Zheng Xuan's commentary to *Analects* 3.5 is known only from a manuscript excavated from a Tang-period grave at Astana, near Turfan. The manuscript reads *renxin* 仁心 ("humane hearts"), which experts read as a transcription error for the homophonous *renxin* 人心 ("people's hearts"). Chen Jinmu, *Tang xieben Lunyu Zhengshi zhu yanjiu*, 356; Wang Su, *Tang xieben Lunyu Zhengshi zhu jiqi yanjiu*, 19.
18 *LH* 9.416–17.
19 *GYZS* 19.425.
20 Makeham, "The Earliest Extant Commentary on *Lunyu*," 298.
21 *HMJ juan* 1. On the dating of the *Master Mou's Discourse*, see Beecroft, "When Cosmopolitanisms Intersect," 269–70; Li Xiaorong, *"Hongming ji" "Guang Hongming ji" shulun gao*, 1–45.
22 The *Analects* commentaries by Sun Chuo and Huilin were probably lost before the Song, and only a small number of fragments remain. Huang Kan's subcommentary, which quotes Sun Chuo and Huilin, fell out of circulation during the Southern Song and was reintroduced to China from Japan in the 1760s. The eighteenth-century

editors of the *Siku quanshu* then censored the subcommentary by removing the interpretations of *Analects* 3.5 by Sun Chuo and Huilin and replacing Huang Kan's interpretation with one that accorded with Cheng Yi's; fortunately, uncensored versions of the text have survived. Xu Wangjia, "Huang Kan 'Lunyu jijie yishu' banben yanjiu shuping"; Li Ling, *Sangjia gou*, 91.

23   For Sun's essay, see *HMJ juan* 3. For possible Buddhist influences on Huang Kan, see Makeham, *Transmitters and Creators*, 148–56.

24   My quotations from Sun Chuo, Huilin, and Huang Kan follow the earliest extant version of Huang Kan's subcommentary, an incomplete manuscript recovered from Dunhuang. A 1921 print edition from Shanghai, based on the Japanese text reintroduced in the 1760s, differs slightly from the Dunhuang manuscript. Xu Wangjia assumes that the 1921 edition reflects the original text and that the Dunhuang manuscript deviated from the original. But the opposite may be true, given the longer history of the 1921 text's transmission in Japan. Xu Wangjia, "Huang Kan 'Lunyu jijie yishu' banben yanjiu shuping," 89.

25   Qian Mu, *Lunyu xinjie*, 52.

26   *WS* 101.2242.

27   Ibid., 96.2110.

28   Ibid., 96.2092–93, 97.2117, 97.2129, 97.2153, 98.2161, 98.2172, 98.2188. Li Ling claims that Wei Shou uses *Analects* 3.5 to "criticize the Central Lands for having weak rulers and powerful ministers" and that this is self-criticism comparing the Chinese states unfavorably with the barbarians, the very opposite of Xiaowendi's denigration of the Dangchang king. However, Li's analysis rests on the incorrect assumption that Wei Shou identified the Eastern Jin as "the Central Lands." Li Ling, *Sangjia gou*, 90.

29   Han Yu is known to have worked on an *Analects* commentary that remained unfinished at the time of his death. A commentary known as *Brush-Written Explanations of the Analects* (Lunyu bijie) has been attributed to Han Yu and his student Li Ao since the Northern Song, but the authenticity of the attribution, the commentary's textual history, and its relationship to Han Yu's unfinished commentary remain controversial. Most extant editions of *Brush-Written Explanations* do not contain original commentary on *Analects* 3.5, but the 1771 Itō Kinen edition from Japan (based on an earlier, now probably lost, Korean edition) contains the following: "This shows how deeply Confucius abhorred the barbarians" (Cijian Zhongni wu Yi-Di zhi shen yi). Jin Peiyi suggests that the Itō edition reflects the earliest manuscript of *Brush-Written Explanations*, which he regards as an authentic work by Han Yu. I agree, however, with David McMullen and Chen Jo-shui that there are still strong reasons to avoid using *Brush-Written Explanations* as evidence of Han Yu's ideas. Jin, "Cong wenxian chuanbo liubian tan jinben *Lunyu bijie*"; McMullen, "Han Yü: An Alternative Picture," 640–42; Chen Jo-shui, *Liu Tsung-yüan*, 124n92; Chen Jo-shu, *Tangdai wenshi yu Zhongguo sixiang de zhuanxing*, 425–31.

30   Zheng Xuan's commentary fell into relative obscurity after the An Lushan Rebellion and ceased to be circulated or preserved after the Five Dynasties period, although a copy may have resurfaced briefly in the late tenth century. Some fragments survived in other texts, but none includes the section on 3.5. Numerous incomplete

31 Tang-period manuscript copies of the commentary were recovered at Dunhuang and Turfan in the twentieth century, and only one of these includes 3.5. Chen Jinmu, *Tang xieben Lunyu Zhengshi zhu yanjiu*, 3; Wang Su, *Tang xieben Lunyu Zhengshi zhu jiqi yanjiu*, 1–2; Makeham, "The Earliest Extant Commentary on *Lunyu*," 262–67, 273–74. Qian Mu, *Lunyu xinjie*, 52. For later studies and commentaries that have followed Qian, see, e.g., Yang Liu'an, "'Yan Yi-Xia dafang' yihuo 'zhong junchen dayi'?," 59; Li Zehou, *Lunyu jindu*, 79–80; Leys, *The Analects of Confucius*, 121–22. Li Ling paraphrased Qian's theory incorrectly, making it look as if Song commentators preferred the ethnocentric interpretation while Eastern Jin and Southern Dynasties commentators preferred the self-critical interpretation: Li Ling, *Sangjia gou*, 89.
32 *LYZS* 3.33.
33 *SJ* 4.144.
34 The Kitan occupation resulted from the Later Jin dynasty's sudden collapse under Kitan attack. For evidence of Kitan pillaging in Caozhou, see *ZZTJ* 286.9334–35. For Xing Bing's biography, see *SS* 431.12797–801.
35 *LYZS* 9.132.
36 This is a quotation from Jia Yi's (200–168 BCE) *New Writings* (Xinshu): *XS* 2.68; cf. *HS* 48.2138.
37 Lü Dalin's commentary is lost but can be partially reconstructed from quotations in Zhu Xi's *Essential Meanings*. Different versions of *Essential Meanings* vary, however, over what Lü says the barbarians cannot be allowed to do. A Ming manuscript edition has *xie* ("go together with"), probably a mistranscription of *jian* ("usurp"). A Japanese print edition, dated to 1727, has *ru* ("enter"). The *Siku quanshu* edition has *qi* ("abandon"), probably because of Qing censorship to turn the line into a more innocuous allusion to Confucius's words in *Analects* 13.19: i.e., "Even among the barbarians, you cannot abandon [ritual propriety and moral duty]." *ZZQS* vol. 7, 2a.132; *LTLS* 20, 431.
38 For Cheng Yi's influence on Fan Zuyu's interpretations of Tang history, see *ECJ* 416, 439.
39 At one point in his historical commentary *Mirror of the Tang* (Tangjian), Fan Zuyu makes a similar claim that *Analects* 3.5 is a statement about the barbarians' "not practicing ritual propriety in relations between rulers and subjects": see *TJ* 33.
40 *ZZQS* vol. 7, 2a.104–5.
41 The date of composition for Xie Liangzuo's commentary is indicated in Hu Yin's (1098–1156) postface to the text (dated 1122): *FRJ* 394. On Xie and his commentary, see Selover, *Hsieh Liang-tso*.
42 The quotation is from a description of "the Central Lands" in Yang Xiong's *Exemplary Figures*. According to a fourth-century CE commentary, the "five means of [moral] government" (*wuzheng*) are the Five Constants (*wuchang*) of humaneness, moral duty, ritual propriety, wisdom, and trustworthiness; the "seven crops" (*qifu*) include rice, two kinds of millet, wheat, soybeans, mulberry, and hemp. The *Siku quanshu* edition of *Essential Meanings* changes three characters in the quotation, altering the meaning to "where laws and ordinances (*xingzheng*) are enforced and taxes (*caifu*) are paid." See *FYYS* 6.119; *ZZQS* vol. 7, 2a.132.

43 Alluding to *Analects* 16.2 and 16.3.
44 The wording of the question "who was in charge" (*shui qi shizhi*) is borrowed from the ode "Caiping."
45 *ZZQS* vol. 7, 2a.105.
46 This appears to be alluding to the head of the Ji family, who infringed on the Zhou king's ritual prerogatives by using eight rows of court dancers and performing a sacrifice on Mount Tai: see *Analects* 3.1, 3.6. But the Ji were technically ministers of the Lu ruler, not stewards of ministers.
47 *ZZQS* vol. 7, 2a.105.
48 Ibid.
49 *ZZYL* 25.611. The text mistranscribes "Mister Yin" 尹氏 as "Mister Jun" 君氏. This conversation was recorded by Huang Yigang, whose notes are dated 1193 or later.
50 *ZZQS* vol. 6, 3.662.
51 *ZZYL* 25.611–12.
52 *ECJ* 236 (cf. 1212). Note that this narrative of history has previously been misattributed to Su Shi: see *SSQJ* 65.7322; Su, "'Lidai shibian' fei Su Shi suozuo kao."
53 This comment seems to have inspired Zhu Xi's oft-quoted later comment (made in 1197), "The Tang had its origins among the barbarians, so they did not think it strange when their women violated ritual propriety" (*ZZYL* 136.3245). Many modern historians (e.g., Chen Yinke, *Tangdai zhengzhishi shulun gao*, 1; Sanping Chen, *Multicultural China*, 11–12) have interpreted this as a claim that the Tang emperors' ancestors were Xianbi, but that may be reading Zhu Xi too literally. The first three Tang emperors are known to have had Xianbi mothers, but Song historians generally assumed the Li imperial clan itself was Chinese in origin. That assumption has only been called into question in modern times: see, e.g., Sanping Chen, *Multicultural China*, 4–38.
54 *ECJ* 236. *ECJ* 1212–13 omits mention of the Tang dynasty's "barbarian customs" but supplies examples of incestuous behavior by various Tang emperors and blames the dynasty's immorality for its troubles with "barbarians."
55 On this shift in attitudes toward the Tang and Taizong, see Leung, "Fan Zuyu dui Tang Taizong xingxiang de chongsu."
56 Hu Hong's memorial can be dated from its claim that nine years have elapsed since the fall of Kaifeng to the Jurchens, as well as its mention of an ongoing rebellion in Hunan led by Yang Yao. Southern Song armies defeated Yang Yao's rebellion in mid-1135. *HHJ* 84, 87, 101–2.
57 Ibid., 87–88.
58 *HSZ* 2, 7.
59 *FRJ* 552 (cf. *SS* 435.12916, which misquotes *yong Yi bian Xia* as the more familiar Mencian phrase *yong Xia bian Yi*, "using Chinese [ways] to change the barbarians"). Hsia Chang-Pwu has recently reevaluated the claim made by various early Southern Song literati (including Hu Yin) that Wang Anshi denigrated the *Annals* and sought to suppress its study. Hsia argues that although stories of Wang Anshi dismissing the *Annals* as a "tattered and rotten court bulletin" are probably false, Wang did make efforts at sidelining the study of the *Annals* because of a preference for other classical texts. Hsia, "Cong 'duanlan chaobao' dao bafei shixue."

60 This view originated with Mou Runsun's use of the modern *zunwang rangyi* formula to compare the *Annals* exegesis of Sun Fu and Hu Anguo: Mou, "Liang Song Chunqiuxue zhi zhuliu," 104, 116–19. For another influential example, see Jao, *Zhongguo shixue shang zhi zhengtong lun*, 75.
61 Wang Leisong, *Hu Anguo "Chunqiu zhuan" jiaoshi yu yanjiu*, 379–86.
62 *ECJ* 432–33, 436. On Liu Xun's commentary, only fragments of which are extant, see Huang Juehong, *Tang Song "Chunqiu" yizhu yanjiu*, 155–79.
63 *ECJ* 1107, 1125.
64 Hans Van Ess has challenged the traditional account of Hu Anguo as a student of Xie Liangzuo and suggested that Hu did not become a committed follower of Daoxue until the early 1130s. *HSZ* 512, 528–29; Van Ess, "Compilation of the Works of the Ch'eng Brothers," 264–77.
65 Sun Fu, highlighting the theme of "respecting the king," argued that Confucius was condemning Lord Yin because lords were not supposed to have conferences with one another except when the Zhou king ordered them to—let alone have conferences with barbarians. Liu Chang, in line with an isolationist approach to foreign relations that runs throughout his commentaries, argued that Confucius did not acknowledge the presence of a Rong leader at the conference because "[he] does not approve of diplomatic visits to the court by [peoples] who have not been granted the standard calendar and lie beyond the reach of rites and music." Interestingly, although Su Shi's "On 'The True King Does Not Govern the Barbarians'" agreed with Liu Chang's isolationist approach in principle, it also argued that Confucius did not object to the Qian conference because he approved of the Rong people's interest in negotiating peace agreements rather than waging wars with the Chinese. *ZWFW* 1.10728; *LSZ* 1.10866; *SSQJ* 2.185–86.
66 This is a phrase from the *Documents* chapter "Biming," now known to be a fourth-century CE forgery: *SSZY* 19.524.
67 Alluding to the ode "Bigong."
68 An abbreviated and slightly rephrased version is found in *Select Sayings*, framed as an answer to the question, "When barbarians bring disorder to the Chinese, what is the right way to deal with them?" *ECJ* 1089, 1214.
69 Ibid., 1090.
70 Xiong Mingqin, selectively quoting the line on barbarians who "stayed in their own lands (*ju qidi*) and were friendly to the Central Lands," claims that Cheng Yi did not advocate "repelling the barbarians." This is wide of the mark and probably misreads *ju qidi* as meaning "living in the lands of the Chinese." *ZZZY* 2.67; Xiong, "Chaoyue 'Yi-Xia,'" 128.
71 *SSWJ* 8.62.
72 *CQJYZJ* 1b.
73 This is probably why Li Mingfu attributes this interpretation of the Qian conference to Cheng Yi, while also attributing a similar but much shorter interpretation to Cheng Hao: *CQJYGL* 1.1a; *CQJY* 2.12a–12b; cf. Ge Huanli, *Zunjing zhongyi*, 230–31.
74 Ge Huanli does not address the contrast between these two interpretations of the *Annals*, finding them to be merely complementary: Ge Huanli, *Zunjing zhongyi*,

252–54. Ge also overstates the originality of Cheng Yi's notion of barbarization, seeing it as a deviation from "traditional *Annals* scholarship's emphasis on commending and promoting barbarians."

75 *HSZ* 6. The notion that the *Annals* speaks for the king (the Son of Heaven) comes from *Mencius* 3B.14.
76 *GYZS* 18.400–401.
77 Hon, *The Yijing and Chinese Politics*, 124–26.
78 *HSZ* 6.
79 Chung-ying Cheng, "On the Metaphysical Significance of *Ti*."
80 *HSZ* 6.
81 Here, Hu Anguo uses a metaphor of a person standing upside down, which alludes to Jia Yi's second-century BCE arguments against the Han dynasty's diplomatic practice of sending annual gifts to the Xiongnu, on the grounds that it is tantamount to tribute: *XS* 3.127, 3.131.
82 Hu alludes here to a Xiongnu leader's visit to the Western Han court after submitting to Han suzerainty in 51 BCE. Such a visit was unprecedented and provoked a debate at court over whether the Xiongnu ruler should be accorded a protocol befitting a head of state or treated like one of the Han aristocracy. The former position eventually won out, but Hu Anguo agrees with the Eastern Han historian Xun Yue (148–209 CE) that it was ritually improper. See *ZZTJ* 27.885–86 and the recent analysis of the debate in Habberstad, *Forming the Early Chinese Court*, 61–84.
83 *HSZ* 6. For the quotation, see *ZZZY* 26.717. Lydia H. Liu and Yuri Pines have rejected an ethnic or racialist interpretation of this *Zuo Tradition* quotation, pointing out that in its original context *zulei* referred to clan lineage, not ethnic or racial group: Lydia H. Liu, *The Clash of Empires*, 72–73; Pines, "Beasts or Humans," 88–89n94. Although this is a valid criticism when it comes to interpreting the *Zuo Tradition* itself, it is nonetheless important to recognize that the Chinese have a long history (possibly going back to the third century CE) of misinterpreting or reinterpreting the quotation to justify ethnic prejudice: *JS* 56.1531–32, 101.2646; also Chin, "Antiquarian as Ethnographer," 130–35.
84 *SSZY* 20.562.
85 *HSZ* 7.
86 Ibid.
87 Incidentally, this is another example of Cheng Yi's unusual habit of reading *buru* as "not as bad as."
88 *ECJ* 1102.
89 This interpretation of 9.14 did not come to be questioned until the Song period, first by Liu Chang and later by Zhu Xi. *HS* 28.1658; *QJXZ* 3.9b; *ZZYL* 36.972; *ZZQS* vol. 6, 773.
90 *HSZ* 49.
91 Ibid., 7. Wood writes: "One might even say that [Hu Anguo's] purpose was not so much to root out the barbarians as it was to root out barbarism, whether practiced by Chinese or by the barbarians." This is much more perceptive than the typical view

of Hu as obsessed with repelling barbarians, but it is more likely that both purposes were of equal importance to him. Wood, *Limits to Autocracy*, 122.

92   *HSZ* 6, 7, 108, 128, 147, 177, 180, 182, 183, 191, 193, 199, 204, 224, 234, 251, 253, 266 (two sections), 275, 299, 302, 312, 321, 345–46, 361, 423, 499–500.

93   Ibid., 46, 47, 49, 76, 120, 146–47, 182, 184, 205–6, 229, 230, 250, 275, 293, 306, 307, 310, 311, 384, 397, 399–400, 408, 421, 459, 495, 496–97.

94   Ibid., 182, 230, 306, 408; cf. *ECJ* 1112, 1115, 1117, 1122.

95   *HSZ* 182. In two other sections, Hu Anguo modifies the same theory to argue that losing "trustworthiness" (*xin*) just once turns human beings into barbarians and losing it again turns them into animals: *HSZ* 205–6, 408.

96   Cheng Yi's is not the only discernible influence on Hu Anguo's reading of barbarization in the *Annals*. Four of Hu's sections follow Sun Fu's argument that Chu and Wu were demoted to barbarism for using the royal title: ibid., 146–47, 184, 310, 311. Three other sections follow Liu Chang's theory that Confucius placed Chu and Wu at an intermediate point between full Chineseness and full barbarism, promoting them back toward Chineseness when they relearned the practice of Chinese norms: ibid., 120, 229, 399–400.

97   Tillman also argued, however, that Chen Liang's shift to thinking in terms of a world consisting of "ethnically determined nation-states" remained incomplete because he still saw "the way of the Central Lands" as both superior to "the way of the barbarians" and universally applicable, rather than the exclusive property of the Chinese. Tillman, "Proto-Nationalism in Twelfth-Century China?," 404-6, 424–28; Tillman, *Utilitarian Confucianism*, 167–68.

98   *HSZ* 205–6, 399–400, 421, 459, 495.

99   *GLZS* 19.367; *ECJ* 1115, 1122, 1201.

100   E.g., Yue, "Barbarians and Monstrosity," 237; Ge Zhaoguang, "Songdai 'Zhongguo' yishi de tuxian," 147–48.

CONCLUSION

Epigraph: Cavafy wrote this poem in Greek in 1898 and first had it printed in 1904. Cavafy, *Collected Poems*, 19.

1   Shao-yun Yang, "'Their Lands Are Peripheral and Their *Qi* Is Blocked Up.'"

2   Sun's preface has been dated to 838. *SKZ* 7.1a–1b; Li Guangfu, "Sun Qiao shengping ji Sun wen xinian," 65.

3   Kane, "The Great Central Liao Kitan State," 32–39; *LS* 104.1455; *LDSK* 668.

4   *Analects* 2.1.

5   *SMJW* 22. On Hong Hao's life and work, see Sloane, "Ethnography, Environment, and Empire"; Lin, "A Journey to the Barbarians."

6   *HMJ juan* 1.

7   *SMJW* 22. In premodern usage, the phrase *wenwu* typically means "ritual institutions" or "ritual paraphernalia," not its modern meaning of "cultural artifacts": see Lü, "'Wenwu' yici qianxi."

8   See *SJ* 110.2879 and the accompanying commentary, which states the *communis opinio* that the Xunyu lived in the time of the sage-kings and became the Xianyun of Western Zhou times, who in turn eventually became the Xiongnu.
9   The Tang and Song Chinese habitually referred to enemies of the imperial state, including both rebels and foreign opponents, by the derogatory label *lu*, literally "captive/slave" and often translated as "caitiff." See Shao-yun Yang, "Shi Xiaozhang's Spirit Road Stele," 70–71.
10 Quoted in Zhang Qifan and Xiong Mingqin, "Liao Daozong 'yuan houshi sheng Zhongguo' zhushuo kaobian," 84. For the date of Chao's embassy, see Tackett, *Origins of the Chinese Nation*, 53. The myth of Daozong's admiration for Renzong persisted into the Southern Song, as seen from *SSWJ* 1.4.
11 Zhang Qifan and Xiong Mingqin, "Liao Daozong 'yuan houshi sheng Zhongguo' zhushuo kaobian." On the challenge that India-centered Buddhist cosmology posed to Chinese ethnocentrism in pre-Tang and Tang times, see Abramson, *Ethnic Identity in Tang China*, 75–76; Anne Cheng, "Central India Is What Is Called the Middle Kingdom."
12 Guo, "Liaochao Yi-Xia guan de yanbian," 93–94.
13 *LS* 21.255.
14 The poem uses the toponyms Luli and Jilin, alluding to the Xiongnu and the kingdom of Silla, respectively. For a translation, see Aidong Zhang and Wayne Schlepp, "Xiao Guanyin," 214–15.
15 The *Liaoshi* quotes another Kitan aristocrat denigrating Koryŏ as "a little country of island barbarians (*daoyi*)" in 1010, but this is suspiciously early and may be language added by a later biographer (*pace* Guo, "Liaochao Yi-Xia guan de yanbian," 94). *LDSK* 623; *LS* 88.1339.
16 But see Tackett, *Origins of the Chinese Nation*, 282.
17 Recall also Zhu's blatantly false claim that "from here out to the remote lands, all are subjects [of the Song emperor]," which reflects a similar tendency toward self-deception. *PZKT(2)* 2.142.
18 *ZCZY* 135.1502.
19 Liu Chang served on an embassy to the Liao in 1055, the first year of Daozong's reign: *QSW* 1505.208–9.
20 *HCLW* 28.
21 *SSQJ* 4.385–86.
22 *Pace* Tackett, *Origins of the Chinese Nation*, 190–92. Tackett overstates the salience of ethnicity to Song assessments of the Northern Dynasties and the Five Dynasties. For a more balanced analysis, see Liu Pujiang, *Zhengtong yu Hua-Yi*, 28–31, 35–56.
23 *JSWJ* 9.1561–63; *JSJ* 16.502–5.
24 *JSWJ* 9.1563 (cf. *JSJ* 16.503–4).
25 From early Han times on, inaccurate allusions to *Mencius* 4B.1 more commonly identified Yu's origins as Qiang and misidentified King Wen as an eastern Yi: *XY* 2.43; *JS* 52.1452, 63.1705, 101.2649, 108.2813.

26 *LQJ* 5; see also the discussion of this essay in Puning Liu, "Song Scholars' Views on the Northern Wei Legitimacy Dispute."
27 For Wang Tong's views on the Northern Wei's legitimacy, see *ZS* 1.14, 5.149, 7.181–84, 10.251; Liu Pujiang, *Zhengtong yu Hua-Yi*, 14–15.
28 Jao, *Zhongguo shixue shang zhi zhengtong lun*, 107–9; cf. Puning Liu, "Song Scholars' Views on the Northern Wei Legitimacy Dispute."
29 *JSWJ* 9.1564. This comment appears in two extant Southern Song editions of Ouyang's collected works, held by the National Library of China and the Tenri Library in Japan. Higashi Hidetoshi identifies it as a commentarial note rather than a part of Ouyang Xiu's original essay (e-mail communication with the author, June 1, 2016). The commentator probably belonged to the editorial team led by Zhou Bida (1126–1204) that published an 1196 edition of Ouyang's literary collection: Higashi, *Fugu yu chuangxin*, 181–87.
30 On the date of Zhang Di's defection, see Sun, "Guanyu Zhang Di 'Jinlu tujing' de jige wenti."
31 *SCBM* 242.9b.
32 After a humiliating defeat by Song naval forces on the Yangzi River, Wanyan Liang was assassinated by disgruntled subordinates. An unsuccessful Song counteroffensive then led to stalemate and renegotiation of the 1141 peace agreement on terms that redefined the relationship between the Song and Jin emperors as one of kinship (with the Song as junior), rather than suzerainty.
33 E.g., the 1138 memorial by Fan Rugui (1102–1160) preserved in *SCBM* 187.6a–14a. Fan was a nephew of Hu Anguo and had studied the *Annals* under him.
34 *HHJ* 44. This treatise remained unfinished and unpublished at the time of Hu Hong's death in 1161.
35 Ibid., 14.
36 *DSGJ* 10.373. Cf. 29.1072, which blames Chinese immorality for the barbarian incursions that toppled the Western Jin and plagued the Tang.
37 Ibid., 29.1046–51, 29.1053, 29.1065, 29.1067, 29.1069–70, 29.1073.
38 Ibid., 7.245–46.
39 For exemplary barbarians, see ibid., 8.279, 9.324, 10.374.
40 Ibid., 12.432.
41 Fang, "Yi-Di wu bainian zhi yun." Hu Yin had already used earlier history and *qi* determinism to make an argument to this effect in *Limited Views*: *DSGJ* 29.1072–73.
42 Zhang Jia, *Xin tianxia zhi hua*, esp. 307–23. The points raised briefly in this paragraph are the subject of my ongoing research.
43 Brook, Van Walt van Praag, and Boltjes, *Sacred Mandates*, 146–48. Note that on p. 148, Yongzheng's analogy of Manchuria to a Chinese *jiguan* is misinterpreted to mean "China is our place of residence." The Manchu homeland was also that of the Jurchens, since they were Jurchens who had adopted a new ethnonym in 1636.
44 On this subject, see now Huang, *Chongsu Zhonghua*.

Bibliography

ABBREVIATIONS

Note: Full citations for titles marked with an asterisk can be found under "Works Cited."

BHT	Ban Gu 班固. *Bohutong shuzheng* 白虎通疏證. Beijing: Zhongshua Shuju, 1994.
CLWJ	Shi Jie 石介. *Culai Shi xiansheng wenji* 徂徠石先生文集. Beijing: Zhonghua Shuju, 1984.
CQFL	Attributed to Dong Zhongshu 董仲舒. *Chunqiu fanlu yizheng* 春秋繁露義證. Beijing: Zhonghua Shuju, 1992.
CQJY	Li Mingfu 李明復. *Chunqiu jiyi* 春秋集義. Taipei: Shangwu Yinshuguan, 1969. Reprint of the *Siku quanshu* edition.
CQJYGL	Li Mingfu 李明復. "Chunqiu jiyi gangling" 春秋集義綱領. In *Chunqiu jiyi* 春秋集義. Taipei: Shangwu Yinshuguan, 1969.
CQJYZJ	Li Mingfu 李明復. "Zhujia xingshi shilue" 諸家姓氏事略. In *Chunqiu jiyi* 春秋集義. Taipei: Shangwu Yinshuguan, 1969.
CQQH	Liu Chang 劉敞. *Chunqiu quanheng* 春秋權衡. In Nalan et al., eds., *Tongzhitang jingjie*, vol. 19.*
CQWZ	Lu Chun 陸淳. *Chunqiu weizhi* 春秋微旨. In Zhong, ed., *Gu jingjie huihan*, vol. 2.*
CQYL	Liu Chang 劉敞. *Chunqiu yilin* 春秋意林. In Nalan et al., eds., *Tongzhitang jingjie*, vol. 19.*
DCQ	Zhu Chaoying 朱朝瑛. *Du Chunqiu lueji* 讀春秋略記. In *Yingyin wenyuange siku quanshu* 景印文淵閣四庫全書, vol. 171. Taipei: Shangwu Yinshuguan, 1986.
DJZ	Liu Chang 劉敞. *Gongshi xiansheng dizi ji* 公是先生弟子記. Shanghai: Huadong Shifan Daxue Chubanshe, 2010.
DSGJ	Hu Yin 胡寅. *Dushi guanjian* 讀史管見. Changsha: Yuelu Shushe, 2011.
ECJ	Cheng Hao 程顥 and Cheng Yi 程頤. *Ercheng ji* 二程集. 1981. Beijing: Zhonghua Shuju, 2004.
FRJ	Hu Yin 胡寅. *Feiran ji* 斐然集. Beijing: Zhonghua Shuju, 1993.
FYYS	Yang Xiong 揚雄. *Fayan yishu* 法言義疏. Beijing: Zhonghua Shuju, 1987.

FZ	Liu Zhili 劉治立, ed. *Fuzi pingzhu* 傅子評注. Tianjin: Tianjin Guji Chubanshe, 2010.
GLZS	Fan Ning 范寧, with subcommentary by Yang Shixun 楊士勛. *Chunqiu Guliang zhuan zhushu* 春秋穀梁傳註疏. Beijing: Beijing Daxue Chubanshe, 2000.
GXZS	Zhou Mi 周密. *Guixin zashi* 癸辛雜識. Beijing: Zhonghua Shuju, 1988.
GYZS	He Xiu 何休, with subcommentary by Xu Yan 徐彥. *Chunqiu Gongyang zhuan zhushu* 春秋公羊傳註疏. Beijing: Beijing Daxue Chubanshe, 1999.
HCLS	Qian Zhonglian 錢仲聯, ed. *Han Changli shi xinian jishi* 韓昌黎詩繫年集釋. Shanghai: Shanghai Guji Chubanshe, 1984.
HCLW	Ma Qichang 馬其昶, ed. *Han Changli wenji jiaozhu* 韓昌黎文集校註. Shanghai: Shanghai Guji Chubanshe, 2014.
HFCZ	Huangfu Shi 皇甫湜. *Huangfu Chizheng wenji* 皇甫持正文集. Shanghai: Shanghai Guji Chubanshe, 1994.
HHJ	Hu Hong 胡宏. *Hu Hong ji* 胡宏集. Beijing: Zhonghua Shuju, 1987.
HHS	Fan Ye 范曄. *Hou Hanshu* 後漢書. Beijing: Zhonghua Shuju, 1965.
HJJZ	Liu Zhenlun 劉真倫, ed. *Hanji juzheng huijiao* 韓集舉正彙校. Nanjing: Fenghuang Chubanshe, 2007.
HMJ	Sengyou 僧祐, ed. *Hongming ji* 弘明集. In Takakusu Junjirō 高楠順次郎 and Watanabe Kaikyoku 渡邊海旭, eds., *Taishō Shinshū Daizōkyō* 大正新修大藏経. Tokyo: Taishō Issaikyō Kankōkai, 1924–32. Serial number T 2102.
HS	Ban Gu 班固. *Hanshu* 漢書. Beijing: Zhonghua Shuju, 1962.
HSZ	Hu Anguo 胡安國. *Chunqiu Hushi zhuan* 春秋胡氏傳. Hangzhou: Zhejiang Guji Chubanshe, 2010.
HYSJ	Huang Tao 黃滔. *Puyang Huang Yushi ji* 莆陽黃御史集. Shanghai: Shangwu Yinshuguan, 1936.
JS	Fang Xuanling 房玄齡. *Jinshu* 晉書. Beijing: Zhonghua Shuju, 1974.
JSJ	Ouyang Xiu 歐陽修. *Jushi ji* 居士集. In Hong, ed., *Ouyang Xiu shiwen ji jiaojian*.*
JSWJ	Ouyang Xiu 歐陽修. *Jushi waiji* 居士外集. In Hong, ed., *Ouyang Xiu shiwen ji jiaojian*.*
JTS	Liu Xu 劉煦 et al. *Jiu Tangshu* 舊唐書. Beijing: Zhonghua Shuju, 1975.
JWDS	Xue Juzheng 薛居正 et al. *Jiu Wudai shi* 舊五代史. Beijing: Zhonghua Shuju, 1976.
JZBY	Lu Chun 陸淳. *Chunqiu Dan Zhao er xiansheng jizhuan bianyi* 春秋啖趙二先生集傳辨疑. In Zhong, ed., *Gu jingjie huihan*, vol. 2.*
JZZL	Lu Chun 陸淳. *Chunqiu Dan Zhao jizhuan zuanli* 春秋啖趙集傳纂例. In Zhong, ed., *Gu jingjie huihan*, vol. 2.*
LDSK	Xiang Nan 向南, ed. *Liaodai shikewen bian* 遼代石刻文編. Shijiazhuang: Hebei Jiaoyu Chubanshe, 1995.
LGJ	Li Gou 李覯. *Li Gou ji* 李覯集. Beijing: Zhonghua Shuju, 1981.
LH	Huang Hui 黃暉, ed. *Lunheng jiaoshi* 論衡校釋. Beijing: Zhonghua Shuju, 1990.

LJZY	Zheng Xuan 鄭玄, with subcommentary by Kong Yingda 孔穎達. *Liji zhengyi* 禮記正義. Beijing: Beijing Daxue Chubanshe, 1999.
LKJ	Liu Kai 柳開. *Liu Kai ji* 柳開集. Beijing: Zhonghua Shuju, 2015.
LQJ	Zhang Fangping 張方平. *Lequan xiansheng wenji* 樂全先生文集. In Beijing tushuguan guji chuban bianjizu 北京圖書館古籍出版編輯組, ed., *Beijing tushuguan guji zhenben congkan* 北京圖書館古籍珍本叢刊, vol. 89. Beijing: Shumu Wenxian Chubanshe, 1998.
LS	Toghto 脫脫 et al. *Liaoshi* 遼史. Beijing: Zhonghua Shuju, 1974.
LSZ	Liu Chang 劉敞. *Chunqiu Liushi zhuan* 春秋劉氏傳. In Nalan et al., eds., *Tongzhitang jingjie*, vol. 19.*
LTLS	Chen Junmin 陳俊民, ed. *Lantian Lüshi yizhu jijiao* 藍田呂氏遺著輯校. Beijing: Zhonghua Shuju, 1993.
LYZS	He Yan 何晏, with subcommentary by Xing Bing 邢昺. *Lunyu zhushu* 論語註疏. Beijing: Beijing Daxue Chubanshe, 2000.
LZ	Yang Bojun 楊伯峻, ed. *Liezi jishi* 列子集釋. Beijing: Zhonghua Shuju, 1979.
LZQ	Huang Linggeng 黃靈庚 and Wu Zhanlei 吳戰壘, eds. *Lü Zuqian quanji* 呂祖謙全集. Hangzhou: Zhejiang Guji Chubanshe, 2008.
LZY	Liu Zongyuan 柳宗元. *Liu Zongyuan ji* 柳宗元集. Beijing: Zhonghua Shuju, 1979.
MXWC	Anonymous, ed. *Xinkan guochao erbaijia mingxian wencui* 新刊國朝二百家名賢文粹. In *Xuxiu siku quanshu* 續修四庫全書, vol. 1652. Shanghai: Shanghai Guji Chubanshe, 2002.
PZKT(1)	Zhu Yu 朱彧. *Pingzhou ketan* 萍州可談. In Wang Yunwu 王雲五, ed., *Siku quanshu zhenben bieji* 四庫全書珍本別集, vol. 235. Taipei: Shangwu Yinshuguan, 1975.
PZKT(2)	Zhu Yu 朱彧. *Pingzhou ketan* 萍州可談. Beijing: Zhonghua Shuju, 2007.
PZWS	Pi Rixiu 皮日休. *Pizi wensou* 皮子文藪. Shanghai: Shanghai Guji Chubanshe, 1981.
QJXZ	Liu Chang 劉敞. *Gongshi xiansheng qijing xiaozhuan* 公是先生七經小傳. Shanghai: Shangwu Yinshuguan, 1934.
QSW	Zeng Zaozhuang 曾棗莊 and Liu Lin 劉琳, eds. *Quan Songwen* 全宋文. Shanghai: Shanghai Cishu Chubanshe; Hefei: Anhui Jiaoyu Chubanshe, 2006.
QTW	Dong Gao 董誥, ed. *Quan Tangwen* 全唐文. Beijing: Zhonghua Shuju, 1983.
SCBM	Xu Mengxin 徐夢莘, ed. *Sanchao beimeng huibian* 三朝北盟會編. Shanghai: Shanghai Guji Chubanshe, 1987.
SJ	Sima Qian 司馬遷. *Shiji* 史記. Beijing: Zhonghua Shuju, 1959.
SJZ	Cai Shen 蔡沈. *Shu jizhuan* 書集傳. Beijing: Zhonghua Shuju, 2017.
SKZ	Sun Qiao 孫樵. *Sun Kezhi wenji* 孫可之文集. Shanghai: Shanghai Guji Chubanshe, 1979.
SMJW	Hong Hao 洪皓. *Songmo jiwen* 松漠紀聞. In Li Shutian 李樹田, ed., *Changbai congshu chuji* 長白叢書初集, 1–54. Changchun: Jilin Wenshi Chubanshe, 1986.
SS	Toghto 脫脫 et al. *Songshi* 宋史. Beijing: Zhonghua Shuju, 1977.

SSQJ	Zhang Zhilie 張志烈 et al., eds. *Su Shi quanji jiaozhu* 蘇軾全集校註. Shijiazhuang: Hebei Renmin Chubanshe, 2010.
SSWJ	Shao Bo 邵博. *Shaoshi wenjian houlu* 邵氏聞見後錄. Beijing: Zhonghua Shuju, 1983.
SSZY	Kong Anguo 孔安國, with subcommentary by Kong Yingda 孔穎達. *Shangshu zhengyi* 尚書正義. Beijing: Beijing Daxue Chubanshe, 2000.
SWJ	Lü Zuqian 呂祖謙, ed. *Song wenjian* 宋文鑒. Taipei: Shijie Shuju, 1962.
TD	Du You 杜佑. *Tongdian* 通典. Beijing: Zhonghua Shuju, 1988.
THY	Wang Pu 王溥. *Tang huiyao* 唐會要. Taipei: Shijie Shuju, 1989.
TJ	Fan Zuyu 范祖禹. *Tangjian* 唐鑑. Shanghai: Shanghai Guji Chubanshe, 1984.
TJWJ	Qisong 契嵩. *Tanjin wenji* 鐔津文集. Shanghai: Shanghai Guji Chubanshe, 2016.
TZY	Wang Dingbao 王定保. *Tang zhiyan* 唐摭言. Beijing: Zhonghua Shuju, 1959.
WLJ	Wang Ling 王令. *Wang Ling ji* 王令集. Shanghai Guji Chubanshe, 1980.
WS	Wei Shou 魏收. *Weishu* 魏書. Beijing: Zhonghua Shuju, 1974.
XS	Jia Yi 賈誼. *Xinshu jiaozhu* 新書校註. Beijing: Zhonghua Shuju, 2000.
XTS	Song Qi 宋祁 et al. *Xin Tangshu* 新唐書. Beijing: Zhonghua Shuju, 1975.
XWDS	Ouyang Xiu 歐陽修. *Xin Wudai shi* 新五代史. Beijing: Zhonghua Shuju, 1974.
XY	Wang Liqi 王利器, ed. *Xinyu jiaozhu* 新語校注. Beijing: Zhonghua Shuju, 1986.
ZCZY	Zhao Ruyu 趙汝愚, ed. *Songchao zhuchen zouyi* 宋朝諸臣奏議. Shanghai: Shanghai Guji Chubanshe, 1999.
ZS	Zhang Pei 張沛, ed. *Zhongshuo jiaozhu* 中説校注. Beijing: Zhonghua Shuju, 2013.
ZWFW	Sun Fu 孫復. *Chunqiu zunwang fawei* 春秋尊王發微. In Nalan et al., eds., *Tongzhitang jingjie*, vol. 19.*
ZZQS	Zhu Jieren 朱傑人 et al., eds. *Zhuzi quanshu* 朱子全書. Shanghai: Shanghai Guji Chubanshe; Hefei: Anhui Jiaoyu Chubanshe, 2002.
ZZTJ	Sima Guang 司馬光 et al., with commentary by Hu Sanxing 胡三省. *Zizhi tongjian* 資治通鑑. Beijing: Zhonghua Shuju, 1956.
ZZYL	Li Jingde 黎靖德, ed. *Zhuzi yulei* 朱子語類. Beijing: Zhonghua Shuju, 1994.
ZZZY	Zuo Qiuming 左丘明 (attributed), with commentary by Du Yu 杜預 and subcommentary by Kong Yingda 孔穎達. *Chunqiu Zuozhuan zhengyi* 春秋左傳正義. Beijing: Beijing Daxue Chubanshe, 1999.

WORKS CITED

Abramson, Marc. *Ethnic Identity in Tang China*. Philadelphia: University of Pennsylvania Press, 2008.

Andreini, Attilio. "The Yang Mo Dualism and the Rhetorical Construction of Heterodoxy." *Asiatische Studien / Études Asiatiques* 68.4 (2014): 1115–74.

Basu, Dilip K. "Chinese Xenology and the Opium War: Reflections on Sinocentrism." *Journal of Asian Studies* 73.4 (2014): 92740.

Beckwith, Christopher I. "The Earliest Chinese Words for 'the Chinese': The Phonology, Meaning, and Origin of the Epithet ḥarya ~ ārya in East Asia." *Journal Asiatique* 304.2 (2016): 231–48.

———. *Empires of the Silk Road: A History of Central Eurasia from the Bronze Age to the Present.* Princeton, NJ: Princeton University Press, 2009.

Beecroft, Alexander. "When Cosmopolitanisms Intersect: An Early Chinese Buddhist Apologetic and World Literature." *Comparative Literature Studies* 47.3 (2010): 266–89.

Bergeton, Uffe. *The Emergence of Civilizational Consciousness in Early China: History Word by Word.* New York: Routledge, 2018.

———. "From Pattern to 'Culture'? Emergence and Transformations of Metacultural *Wen.*" PhD dissertation, University of Michigan, 2013.

Berkson, Mark. "Xunzi as a Theorist and Defender of Ritual." In Hutton, ed., *Dao Companion to the Philosophy of Xunzi*, 229–67.

Berlin, Isaiah. *The Hedgehog and the Fox: An Essay on Tolstoy's View of History.* 1953. Princeton, NJ: Princeton University Press, 2013.

Bi Bo 畢波. *Zhonggu Zhongguo de Sute Huren—yi Chang'an wei zhongxin* 中古中國的粟特胡人—以長安爲中心. Beijing: Zhongguo Renmin Daxue Chubanshe, 2011.

Bol, Peter. "Geography and Culture: The Middle-Period Discourse on the *Zhong guo*—the Central Country." In Huang Ying-kuei 黃應貴, ed., *Kongjian yu wenhua changyu: Kongjian zhi yixiang, shijian yu shehui de shengchan* 空間與文化場域：空間之意象、實踐與社會的生產, 61–105. Taipei: Hanxue Yanjiu Zhongxin, 2009.

———. "Government, Society, and the State: On the Political Visions of Ssu-ma Kuang and Wang An-shih." In Robert P. Hymes and Conrad Schirokauer, eds., *Ordering the World: Approaches to State and Society in Sung Dynasty China*, 128–92. Berkeley: University of California Press, 1993.

———. *Neo-Confucianism in History.* Cambridge, MA: Harvard University Asia Center, 2008.

———. Review of Chen Jo-shui, *Liu Tsung-yüan and Intellectual Change in T'ang China, 773–819. Harvard Journal of Asiatic Studies* 56.1 (1996): 165–81.

———. *"This Culture of Ours": Intellectual Transitions in T'ang and Sung China.* Stanford, CA: Stanford University Press, 1992.

Brook, Timothy, Michael van Walt van Praag, and Miek Boltjes, eds. *Sacred Mandates: Asian International Relations since Chinggis Khan.* Chicago: University of Chicago Press, 2018.

Campany, Robert Ford. "On the Very Idea of Religions (in the Modern West and in Early Medieval China)." *History of Religions* 42.4 (2003): 287–319.

Cavafy, C. P. *Collected Poems.* Trans. Edmund Keeley and Philip Sherrard. Princeton, NJ: Princeton University Press, 1992.

Chan, Wing-tsit. "The Evolution of the Neo-Confucian Concept *Li* as Principle." *Tsing Hua Journal of Chinese Studies* 4.2 (1964): 123–47.

Chang Ching-chüan (Zhang Qingquan) 張清泉. *Beisong Qisong de rushi ronghui sixiang* 北宋契嵩的儒釋融會思想. Taipei: Wenjin Chubanshe, 1998.

Chen, Sanping. *Multicultural China in the Early Middle Ages*. Philadelphia: University of Pennsylvania Press, 2012.

Chen Feng 陳峰. "Liu Kai shiji yu Songchu shilin de haoheng zhi qi" 柳開事迹與宋初士林的豪橫之氣. *Renwen zazhi* 人文雜誌 2012(4), 123–30.

Chen Jinmu 陳金木. *Tang xieben Lunyu Zhengshi zhu yanjiu—yi kaoju, fuyuan, quanshi wei zhongxin de kaocha* 唐寫本論語鄭氏注研究—以考據、復原、詮釋爲中心的考察. Taipei: Wenjin Chubanshe, 1996.

Chen Jo-shui (Chen Ruoshui) 陳弱水. *Liu Tsung-yüan and Intellectual Change in T'ang China, 773–819*. Cambridge: Cambridge University Press, 1992.

———. *Tangdai wenshi yu Zhongguo sixiang de zhuanxing* 唐代文士與中國思想的轉型. Rev. ed. Taipei: Taida Chuban Zhongxin, 2016.

Chen Yinke 陳寅恪. *Jinmingguan conggao chubian* 金明館叢稿初編. Beijing: Sanlian, 2001.

———. *Tangdai zhengzhishi shulun gao* 唐代政治史述論稿. 1943. Taipei: Taiwan Shangwu Yinshuguan, 1994.

———. *Yuan Bai shi jianzheng gao* 元白詩箋證稿. 1950. Beijing: Sanlian, 2001.

Chen Yuan 陳垣. *Yuan xiyu ren huahua kao* 元西域人華化考. 1923. Shanghai: Shanghai Guji Chubanshe, 2000.

Chen Zhi'e 陳植鍔. *Beisong wenhuashi shulun* 北宋文化史述論. Beijing: Zhongguo Shehui Kexue Chubanshe, 1992.

———. *Shi Jie shiji zhuzuo biannian* 石介事迹著作編年. Beijing: Zhonghua Shuju, 2003.

Cheng, Anne. "Central India Is What Is Called the Middle Kingdom." In Anjana Sharma, ed., *Records, Recoveries, Remnants and Inter-Asian Interconnections*, 141–59. Singapore: ISEAS Publishing, 2018.

Cheng, Chung-ying. "On the Metaphysical Significance of *Ti* (Body-Embodiment) in Chinese Philosophy: *Benti* (Origin-Substance) and *Ti-Yong* (Substance and Function)." *Journal of Chinese Philosophy* 29.2 (2002): 145–61.

Cheng Yuzhui 程鬱綴. "Wudai ciren Li Xun shengping jiqi ci chutan" 五代詞人李珣生平及其詞初探. *Beijing daxue xuebao* 北京大學學報 1992(5), 7–14.

Chin, Tamara T. "Antiquarian as Ethnographer: Han Ethnicity in Early China Studies." In Mullaney, Leibold, Gros, and Vanden Bussche, eds., *Critical Han Studies*, 128–46.

Chow, Kai-wing. "Imagining Boundaries of Blood: Zhang Binglin and the Invention of the Han 'Race' in Modern China." In Frank Dikötter, ed., *The Construction of Racial Identities in China and Japan*, 34–52. Hong Kong: Hong Kong University Press, 1997.

———. "Narrating Nation, Race, and National Culture: Imagining the Hanzu Identity in Modern China." In Kai-wing Chow, Kevin M. Doak, and Poshek Fu, eds., *Constructing Nationhood in Modern East Asia*, 47–83. Ann Arbor: University of Michigan Press, 2001.

Clark, Hugh R. *The Sinitic Encounter in Southeast China through the First Millennium CE*. Honolulu: University of Hawaii Press, 2016.

Crossley, Pamela Kyle. *A Translucent Mirror: History and Identity in Qing Imperial Ideology*. Berkeley, CA: University of California Press, 1999.

Dang Yinping 黨銀平. *Tang yu Xinluo wenhua guanxi yanjiu* 唐與新羅文化關係研究. Beijing: Zhonghua Shuju, 2008.

De Meyer, Jan. *Wu Yun's Way: Life and Works of an Eighth-Century Daoist Master.* Leiden: Brill, 2006.

De Weerdt, Hilde. *Information, Territory, and Networks: The Crisis and Maintenance of Empire in Song China.* Cambridge, MA: Harvard University Asia Center, 2015.

DeBlasi, Anthony. *Reform in the Balance: The Defense of Literary Culture in Mid-Tang China.* Albany: State University of New York Press, 2002.

Deng Xiaonan 鄧小南. "Shitan Wudai Songchu 'Hu/Han' yujing de xiaojie" 試談五代宋初"胡/漢"語境的消解. In Zhang Xiqing 張希清 et al., eds., *10–13 shiji Zhongguo wenhua de pengzhuang yu ronghe* 10~13 世紀中國文化的碰撞與融合, 114–37. Shanghai: Shanghai Renmin Chubanshe, 2006.

Dikötter, Frank. *The Discourse of Race in Modern China.* 1992. Oxford: Oxford University Press, 2015.

Duara, Prasenjit. *Rescuing History from the Nation: Questioning Narratives of Modern China.* Chicago: University of Chicago Press, 1996.

Durrant, Stephen, Li Wai-yee, and David Schaberg, trans. *Zuo Tradition / Zuozhuan.* Seattle: University of Washington Press, 2016.

Egan, Ronald C. *Word, Image, and Deed in the Life of Su Shi.* Cambridge, MA: Harvard University Asia Center, 1994.

Eisenberg, Andrew. "Collapse of a Eurasian Hybrid: The Case of the Northern Wei." In Nicola Di Cosmo and Michael Maas, eds., *Empires and Exchanges in Eurasian Late Antiquity: Rome, China, Iran, and the Steppe, ca. 250–750,* 369–85. Cambridge: Cambridge University Press, 2018.

Elliott, Mark C. "*Hushuo*: The Northern Other and the Naming of the Han Chinese." In Mullaney, Leibold, Gros, and Vanden Bussche, eds., *Critical Han Studies,* 173–90.

Fan Wenli 樊文禮. *Rujia minzu sixiang yanjiu—xianqin zhi Sui-Tang* 儒家民族思想研究—先秦至隋唐. Jinan: Qilu Shushe, 2011.

———. "Songdai Gaoli bingong jinshi kao" 宋代高麗賓貢進士考. *Shilin* 史林 2002(2), 42–45.

Fang Cheng-hua (Fang Zhenhua) 方震華. "Cong herong dao tuobian—Beisong zhongqi duiwai zhengce de zhuanzhe" 從和戎到拓邊—北宋中期對外政策的轉折. *Xin shixue* 新史學 24.2 (2013): 35–69.

———. "Yi-Di wu bainian zhi yun—yunshu lun yu Yi-Xia guan de fenxi" 夷狄無百年之運—運數論與夷夏觀的分析. *Taida lishi xuebao* 臺大歷史學報 60 (2017): 159–91.

Feng Zhihong 馮志弘. *Beisong guwen yundong de xingcheng* 北宋古文運動的形成. Shanghai: Shanghai Guji Chubanshe, 2009.

Fincher, John. "China as a Race, Culture, and Nation: Notes on Fang Hsiao-ju's Discussion of Dynastic Legitimacy." In David C. Buxbaum and Frederick W. Mote, eds., *Transition and Permanence: Chinese History and Culture,* 59–69. Hong Kong: Cathay Press, 1972.

Fredrickson, George M. *Racism: A Short History.* Princeton, NJ: Princeton University Press, 2002.

Fu Lecheng 傅樂成. "Tang xing wenhua yu Song xing wenhua" 唐型文化與宋型文化 (1972). Reprinted in *Han Tang shi lunji* 漢唐史論集, 339–82. Taipei: Lianjing Chuban Shiye Gongsi, 1977.

———. "Tangdai yixiaguan zhi yanbian" 唐代夷夏觀之演變. 1962. Reprinted in *Han Tang shi lunji*, 209–26.

Gao Mingshi 高明士. "Sui Tang gongju zhidu dui Riben, Xinluo de yingxiang—jianlun Sui Tang bingong ke de chengli" 隋唐貢舉制度對日本、新羅的影響—兼論隋唐賓貢科的成立. In Lin Tien-wai 林天蔚 and Joseph Wong 黃約瑟, eds., *Gudai Zhong Han Ri guanxi yanjiu* 古代中韓日關係研究, 65–102. Hong Kong: Centre of Asian Studies, University of Hong Kong, 1987.

Ge Huanli 葛煥禮. "Dan Zhu, Zhao Kuang he Lu Chun 'Chunqiu' xue zhuzuo kaobian" 啖助、趙匡和陸淳《春秋》學著作考辨. *Xibu xuekan* 西部學刊 2015(4), 17–29.

———. *Zunjing zhongyi: Tangdai zhongye zhi Beisong monian de xin "Chunqiu" xue* 尊經重義：唐代中葉至北宋末年的新《春秋》學. Jinan: Shandong Daxue Chubanshe, 2011.

Ge Zhaoguang 葛兆光. *Lishi Zhongguo de nei yu wai: Youguan "Zhongguo" yu "zhoubian" gainian de zai chengqing* 歷史中國的內與外：有關"中國"與"周邊"概念的再澄清. Hong Kong: Chinese University Press, 2017.

———. "Songdai 'Zhongguo' yishi de tuxian—guanyu jinshi minzu zhuyi sixiang de yige yuanyuan" 宋代'中國'意識的凸現—關於近世民族主義思想的一個遠源. 2004. Reprinted in *Gudai Zhongguo de lishi, sixiang yu zongjiao* 古代中國的歷史、思想與宗教, 135–51. Beijing: Beijing Shifan Daxue Chubanshe, 2006.

———. "Xiangxiang tianxia diguo—yi (chuan) Li Gonglin 'Wanfang zhigong tu' wei zhongxin" 想象天下帝國—以(傳)李公麟《萬方職貢圖》為中心. *Fudan xuebao* 復旦學報 2018(3), 36–48.

———. *Zhaizi Zhongguo: Chongjian youguan "Zhongguo" de lishi lunshu* 宅茲中國：重建有關"中國"的歷史論述. Beijing: Zhonghua Shuju, 2011.

———. *Zhongguo sixiangshi* 中國思想史. Vol. 2: *Qi zhi shijiu shiji Zhongguo de zhishi, sixiang yu xinyang* 七至十九世紀中國的知識、思想與信仰. Shanghai: Fudan Daxue Chubanshe, 2000.

Gernet, Jacques. *A History of Chinese Civilization*. 1972. Trans. J. R. Foster and Charles Hartman. 2nd ed. Cambridge: Cambridge University Press, 1996.

Gillett, Andrew. "The Mirror of Jordanes: Concepts of the Barbarian, Then and Now." In Philip Rousseau, ed., *A Companion to Late Antiquity*, 393–408. Chichester, West Sussex: Wiley Blackwell, 2009.

Goh, Meow Hui. "The Art of Wartime Propaganda: Chen Lin's *Xi* Written on Behalf of Yuan Shao and Cao Cao." *Early Medieval China* 23 (2017): 42–66.

Grant, Beata. *Mount Lu Revisited: Buddhism in the Life and Writings of Su Shih*. Honolulu: University of Hawaii Press, 1994.

Gregory, Peter N. "The Vitality of Buddhism in the Sung." In Gregory and Getz, eds., *Buddhism in the Sung*, 1–20.

Gregory, Peter N., and Daniel A. Getz Jr., eds. *Buddhism in the Sung*. Honolulu: University of Hawaii Press, 1999.

Guo Kangsong 郭康松. "Liaochao Yi-Xia guan de yanbian" 遼朝夷夏觀的演變. *Zhongguoshi yanjiu* 中國史研究 2001(2), 89–95.

Guo Tian 郭畑. "Songdai rushi hudong de yige anli—Qisong fei Han yu Han Yu diwei de zhuanzhe" 宋代儒釋互動的一個案例—契嵩非韓與韓愈地位的轉折. *Chuanshan xuekan* 船山學刊 2011(4), 117–21.

Guoli gugong bowuyuan 國立故宮博物院. *Siku quanshu buzheng: Zibu* 四庫全書補正：子部. Taipei: Taiwan Shangwu Yinshuguan, 1999.

Habberstad, Luke. *Forming the Early Chinese Court: Rituals, Spaces, Roles.* Seattle: University of Washington Press, 2017.

Hall, Edith. *Inventing the Barbarian: Greek Self-Definition through Tragedy.* Oxford: Clarendon Press, 1989.

Halperin, Mark. *Out of the Cloister: Literati Perspectives on Buddhism in Sung China, 960-1279.* Cambridge, MA: Harvard University Asia Center, 2006.

Harris, Eirik Lang. "Xunzi's Political Philosophy." In Hutton, ed., *Dao Companion to the Philosophy of Xunzi*, 95-138.

Hartman, Charles. *Han Yü and the T'ang Search for Unity.* Princeton, NJ: Princeton University Press, 1986.

Higashi Hidetoshi 東英壽. *Fugu yu chuangxin—Ouyang Xiu sanwen yu guwen fuxing* 復古與創新—歐陽修散文與古文復興. Trans. Wang Zhenyu 王振宇, Li Li 李莉, et al. Shanghai: Shanghai Guji Chubanshe, 2005.

Holcombe, Charles. "Immigrants and Strangers: From Cosmopolitanism to Confucian Universalism in Tang China." *T'ang Studies* 20-21 (2002-3): 71-112.

Hon, Tze-ki. *The Yijing and Chinese Politics: Classical Commentary and Literati Activism in the Northern Song Period, 960-1127.* Albany: State University of New York Press, 2005.

Hong Benjian 洪本健, ed. *Ouyang Xiu shiwen ji jiaojian* 歐陽修詩文集校箋. Shanghai: Shanghai Guji Chubanshe, 2009.

———. "Ouyang Xiu Tiansheng xue Han: Beisong 'wenxue zijue' de zhongyao biaozhi" 歐陽修天盛學韓：北宋"文學自覺"的重要標志. *Huadong shifan daxue xuebao* 華東師範大學學報 2009(3), 116-20.

Hsia Chang-Pwu (Xia Changpu) 夏長樸. "Cong 'duanlan chaobao' dao bafei shixue—Wang Anshi xinxue dui Songdai xueshu de yige yingxiang" 從「斷爛朝報」到罷廢史學—王安石新學對宋代學術的一個影響. In He Chengzhou 何成洲, ed., *Kuaxueke shiye xia de wenhua shenfen rentong: Piping yu tansuo* 跨學科視野下的文化身份認同：批評與探索, 322-42. Beijing: Beijing Daxue Chubanshe, 2011.

Hu Hong 胡鴻. *Neng Xia ze da yu jianmu Huafeng—Zhengzhiti shijiao xia de Huaxia yu Huaxiahua* 能夏則大與漸慕華風—政治體視角下的華夏與華夏化. Beijing: Beijing Shifan Daxue Chubanshe, 2017.

Huang, Yong. *Why Be Moral? Learning from the Neo-Confucian Cheng Brothers.* Albany: State University of New York Press, 2014.

Huang Chunyan 黃純艷. "'Han Tang jiujiang' huayu xia de Song Shenzong kaibian" "漢唐舊疆域"話語下的宋神宗開邊. *Lishi yanjiu* 歷史研究 2016(1), 24-39.

Huang Juehong 黃覺弘. *Tang Song "Chunqiu" yizhu yanjiu* 唐宋《春秋》佚著研究. Beijing: Zhonghua Shuju, 2014.

Huang Xingtao 黃興濤. *Chongsu Zhonghua: Jindai Zhongguo "Zhonghua minzu" guannian yanjiu* 重塑中華：近代中國"中華民族"觀念研究. Beijing: Beijing Shifan Daxue Chubanshe, 2017.

———. "Wanqing minchu xiandai 'wenming' he 'wenhua' gainian de xingcheng jiqi lishi shijian" 晚清民初現代"文明"和"文化"概念的形成及其歷史實踐. *Jindaishi yanjiu* 近代史研究 2006(6), 1-34.

Huang Yongnian 黃永年. "'Jiehu,' 'Zhejie,' 'Zazhong Hu' kaobian" "羯胡"、"柘羯"、"雜種胡" 考辨. 1980. Reprinted in *Huang Yongnian wenshi lunwenji* 黃永年文史論文集, vol. 2, 384–97. Beijing: Zhonghua Shuju, 2015.

Huang Yunmei 黃雲眉. "Du Chen Yinke xiansheng lun Han Yu" 讀陳寅恪先生論韓愈. *Wenshizhe* 文史哲 1955(8), 23–36.

Hu-Sterk, Florence. "Entre fascination et repulsion: Regards des poetes des Tang sur les 'barbares.'" *Monumenta Serica* 48 (2000): 19–38.

Hutchinson, John, and Anthony D. Smith, eds. *Ethnicity*. Oxford: Oxford University Press, 1996.

Hutton, Eric L., ed. *Dao Companion to the Philosophy of Xunzi*. New York: Springer, 2016.

———. "Ethics in the *Xunzi*." In Hutton, ed., *Dao Companion to the Philosophy of Xunzi*, 67–93.

———, trans. *Xunzi: The Complete Text*. Princeton, NJ: Princeton University Press, 2014.

Jao Tsung-I (Rao Zongyi) 饒宗頤. *Zhongguo shixue shang zhi zhengtong lun* 中國史學上之正統論. Shanghai: Shanghai Yuandong Chubanshe, 1996.

Jiang Yonglin. "Thinking about 'Ming *China*' Anew: The Ethnocultural Space in a Diverse Empire—with Special Reference to the 'Miao Territory.'" *Journal of Chinese History* 2 (2018): 27–78.

Jin Peiyi 金培懿. "Cong wenxian chuanbo liubian tan jinben *Lunyu bijie*—yi Yidong Guinian *Jiaoke Han Wengong Lunyu bijie* suozuo de kaocha" 從文獻傳播流變談今本《論語筆解》—以伊東龜年《挍刻韓文公論語筆解》所作的考察. *Zhongguo wenzhe yanjiu jikan* 中國文哲研究集刊 37 (2010): 153–202.

Kaldellis, Anthony. "Did the Byzantine Empire Have 'Ecumenical' or 'Universal' Aspirations?" In Clifford Ando and Seth Richardson, eds., *Ancient States and Infrastructural Power: Europe, Asia, and America*, 272–300. Philadelphia: University of Pennsylvania Press, 2017.

———. "From Rome to New Rome, from Empire to Nation-State: Reopening the Question of Byzantium's Roman Identity." In Lucy Grig and Gavin Kelly, eds., *Two Romes: Rome and Constantinople in Late Antiquity*, 387–404. Oxford: Oxford University Press, 2012.

———. "The Social Scope of Roman Identity in Byzantium: An Evidence-Based Approach." *Byzantina Symmeikta* 27 (2017): 173–210.

Kane, Daniel. "The Great Central Liao Kitan State." *Journal of Song-Yuan Studies* 43 (2013): 27–50.

Kern, Martin. "Ritual, Text, and the Formation of the Canon: Historical Transitions of *Wen* in Early China." *T'oung Pao* 87.1 (2001): 43–91.

Kim Sang-Bum 金相範. "Tangdai houqi Yangzhou de fazhan yu waiguoren shehui" 唐代後期揚州的發展與外國人社會. *Taiwan shida lishi xuebao* 臺灣師大歷史學報 44 (2010): 37–66.

Kong, Xurong. "Fuzi." *Early Medieval China* 22 (2016): 65–68.

La Vaissière, Étienne de. *Sogdian Traders: A History*. Trans. James Ward. Leiden: Brill, 2005.

Leung Sze-lok (Liang Sile) 梁思樂. "Fan Zuyu dui Tang Taizong xingxiang de chongsu" 范祖禹對唐太宗形象的重塑. *Jungguksa yeongu* 중국사연구/中國史研究 70 (2011): 25–45.

Lewis, Mark Edward. *The Construction of Space in Early China*. Albany: State University of New York Press, 2006.

Leys, Simon, trans. *The Analects of Confucius*. New York: W. W. Norton, 1997.

Li Chenggui 李承贵. "Shilun Li Gou fojiaoguan de shuangchongxing" 試論李覯佛教觀的雙重性. *Jiangxi shifan daxue xuebao* 江西師範大學學報 38.1 (2005): 31–36.

Li Chuanjun 李傳軍. *Han Tang fengtu ji yanjiu* 漢唐風土記研究. Beijing: Zhongguo Shehui Kexue Chubanshe, 2015.

Li Guangfu 李光富. "Sun Qiao shengping ji Sun wen xinian" 孫樵生平及孫文繫年. *Sichuan daxue xuebao* 四川大學學報 1987(1), 64–67.

Li Junxiu 李峻岫. "Shilun Han Yu de daotong shuo ji qi Mengxue sixiang" 試論韓愈的道統說及其孟學思想. *Kongzi yanjiu* 孔子研究 2004(6), 77–86.

Li Ling 李零. *Sangjia gou—wo du "Lunyu"* 喪家狗—我讀《論語》. Taiyuan: Shanxi Renmin Chubanshe, 2007.

Li Wai-yee (Li Huiyi) 李惠儀. "Anecdotal Barbarians in Early China." In Paul van Els and Sarah A. Queen, eds., *Between History and Philosophy: Anecdotes in Early China*, 113–44. Albany: State University of New York Press, 2017.

———. "Hua-Yi zhi bian yu yizu tonghun" 華夷之辨與異族通婚. In Chiao Chien 喬健, Chiu Tien-chu 邱天助, and Luo Hsiao-nan 羅曉南, eds., *Tanqing shuoyi: Qing, hunyin ji yi wenhua de kuajie lunshu* 談情說異：情、婚姻暨異文化的跨界論述, 45–63. Taipei: Center for the Study of Foreign Cultures, Shih Hsin University, 2012.

———. *The Readability of the Past in Early Chinese Historiography*. Cambridge, MA: Harvard University Asia Center, 2007.

Li Xiaohong 李曉虹 and Liu Pei 劉培. "'Zhongguo' guannian de chongsu—Lun Songchu de jinbian Hua-Yi yu difo zunjing" "中國" 觀念的重塑—論宋初的謹辨華夷與詆佛尊經. *Lilun xuekan* 理論學刊 2016(1), 152–60.

Li Xiaorong 李小榮. "*Hongming ji*" "*Guang Hongming ji*" shulun gao 《弘明集》《廣弘明集》述論稿. Chengdu: Bashu Shushe, 2005.

Li Zehou 李澤厚. *Lunyu jindu* 論語今讀. Hefei: Anhui Wenyi Chubanshe, 1998.

Liao Yi-fang 廖宜方. *Tangdai de lishi jiyi* 唐代的歷史記憶. Taipei: Guoli Taiwan Daxue Chuban Zhongxin, 2011.

Lin Hang. "A Journey to the Barbarians: Hong Hao's Travel to the Jurchen Jin and His Travelogue *Songmo jiwen* from Twelfth Century China." *Revista de estudos chineses—Zhongguo yanjiu* 9 (2013): 89–104.

Liu, Lydia H. *The Clash of Empires: The Invention of China in Modern World Making*. Cambridge, MA: Harvard University Press, 2004.

Liu, Puning. "Song Scholars' Views on the Northern Wei Legitimacy Dispute." *Archiv Orientální* 86 (2018): 105–35.

Liu Chengguo 劉成國. "9–12 shiji chu de daotong 'qianshi' kaoshu" 9~12 世紀初的道統 "前史" 考述. *Shixue yuekan* 史學月刊 2013(12), 108–19.

Liu Pujiang 劉浦江. *Zhengtong yu Hua-Yi: Zhongguo chuantong zhengzhi wenhua yanjiu* 正統與華夷：中國傳統政治文化研究. Beijing: Zhonghua Shuju, 2017.

Liu Qingbo 劉晴波, ed. *Yang Du ji* 楊度集. Changsha: Hunan Renmin Chubanshe, 1986.

Liu Wenming 劉文明. "Shijiu shiji Ouzhou 'wenming' huayu yu wanqing 'wenming' guan de yanbian" 十九世紀歐洲 "文明" 話語與晚清 "文明" 觀的演變. *Shoudu shifan daxue xuebao* 首都師範大學學報 2011(6), 16–25.

Liu Zhenlun 劉真倫. "Wu 'yuan' de chuangzuo yu daotong de queli—jianlun Han Yu Yangshan zhi bian yu wenfeng zhi bian" 五《原》的創作與道統的確立—兼論韓愈陽山之貶與文風之變. *Zhoukou shifan xueyuan xuebao* 周口師範學院學報 23.1 (2006): 1–6.

Loewe, Michael. "'Confucian' Values and Practices in Han China." *T'oung Pao* 98 (2012): 1–30.

———. *Dong Zhongshu, a "Confucian" Heritage and the "Chunqiu Fanlu."* Leiden: Brill, 2011.

———. "Huang Lao Thought and the *Huainanzi*." *Journal of the Royal Asiatic Society* 4.3 (1994): 377–95.

Lorge, Peter. *The Reunification of China: Peace through War under the Song Dynasty*. Cambridge: Cambridge University Press, 2015.

Lü Jun 呂軍. "'Wenwu' yici qianxi" 文物一詞淺析. *Wenwu Chunqiu* 文物春秋 1992(1), 46–47.

Luo Liantian 羅聯添. *Han Yu yanjiu* 韓愈研究. 1981. Tianjin: Tianjin Jiaoyu Chubanshe, 2012.

———. *Tangdai wenxue lunji* 唐代文學論集. Taipei: Taiwan Xuesheng Shuju, 1989.

Luo Zhengming 羅爭鳴. "'Dongtian lingbao sanshi ji bingxu' zuozhe guishu ji xianguan de Huichang miefo wenti kaolun" 《洞天靈寶三師記并序》作者歸屬及相關的會昌滅佛問題考論. *Zongjiaoxue yanjiu* 宗教學研究 2013(1), 46–50.

Makeham, John. "The Earliest Extant Commentary on *Lunyu*: *Lunyu Zhengshi zhu*." *T'oung Pao* 83.4 (1997): 260–99.

———. *Transmitters and Creators: Chinese Commentators and Commentaries on the "Analects."* Cambridge, MA: Harvard University Asia Center, 2003.

McMullen, David. "Han Yü: An Alternative Picture." *Harvard Journal of Asiatic Studies* 49.2 (1989): 603–57.

———. *State and Scholars in T'ang China*. Cambridge: Cambridge University Press, 1988.

Mo Qiong 莫瓊. "Han Yu 'Yuandao' pian xiezuo shijian xinzheng" 韓愈《原道》篇寫作時間新證. *Kongzi yanjiu* 孔子研究 2016(4), 77–86.

Moore, Oliver. *Rituals of Recruitment in Tang China: Reading an Annual Programme in the "Collected Statements" by Wang Dingbao (870–940)*. Leiden: Brill, 2004.

Moriyasu Takao 森安孝夫. *Shirukurōdo to Tō teikoku* シルクロードと唐帝国. Tokyo: Kodansha, 2016.

Mou Runsun 牟潤孫. "Liang Song Chunqiuxue zhi zhuliu" 兩宋春秋學之主流. 1952. Reprinted in *Songshi yanjiuji* 宋史研究集, vol. 3, 103–21. Taipei: Zhonghua Congshu Bianshen Weiyuanhui, 1966.

Mullaney, Thomas S., James Leibold, Stéphane Gros, and Eric Vanden Bussche, eds. *Critical Han Studies: The History, Representation, and Identity of China's Majority*. Berkeley: University of California Press, 2012.

Nalan Xingde 納蘭性德 et al., eds. *Tongzhitang jingjie* 通志堂經解. Taipei: Datong Shuju, 1969.

Ng Pak-sheung (Wu Bochang) 伍伯常. "Beisong chunian de beifang wenshi yu haoxia—yi Liu Kai de shigong ji zuofeng xingxiang wei zhongxin" 北宋初年的北方文士與豪俠—以柳開的事功及作風形象爲中心. *Qinghua xuebao* 清華學報 36.2 (2006): 295–344.

Niu Siren 牛思仁. "Beisong Renzong chao de taixue ti jiqi xuefeng, wenfeng" 北宋仁宗朝的太學體及其學風、文風. *Xibei shida xuebao* 西北師大學報 52.4 (2015): 33–40.

Owen, Stephen. *The End of the Chinese "Middle Ages": Essays in Mid-Tang Literary Culture*. Stanford, CA: Stanford University Press, 1996.

Paper, Jordan D. *The Fu-tzu: A Post-Han Confucian Text*. Leiden: Brill, 1987.

Perdue, Peter C. "Nature and Nurture on Imperial China's Frontiers." *Modern Asian Studies* 43.1 (2009): 245–67.

Pines, Yuri. "Beasts or Humans: Pre-imperial Origins of the 'Sino-Barbarian' Dichotomy." In Reuven Amitai and Michal Biran, eds., *Mongols, Turks, and Others: Eurasian Nomads and the Sedentary World*, 59–102. Leiden: Brill, 2004.

———. "Chu Identity as Seen from Its Manuscripts: A Reevaluation." *Journal of Chinese History* 2 (2018): 1–26.

———. "Confucius' Elitism: The Concepts of *Junzi* and *Xiaoren* Revisited." In Paul R. Goldin, ed., *A Concise Companion to Confucius*, 164–84. Hoboken, NJ: Wiley-Blackwell, 2017.

———. "The Question of Interpretation: Qin History in Light of New Epigraphic Sources." *Early China* 24 (2004): 1–44.

Pulleyblank, E. G. "Neo-Confucianism and Neo-Legalism in T'ang Intellectual Life, 755–805." In Arthur F. Wright, ed., *The Confucian Persuasion*, 77–114. Stanford, CA: Stanford University Press, 1960.

Qian Mu 錢穆. *Lunyu xinjie* 論語新解. 1963. Chengdu: Bashu Shushe, 1985.

———. *Zhongguo wenhuashi daolun* 中國文化史導論. 1948. Shanghai: Sanlian shudian, 1988.

Qian Zhongshu 錢鍾書. *Guanzhui bian* 管錐編. 1979. Beijing: Sanlian, 2007.

Queen, Sarah A., and John S. Major, trans. *Luxuriant Gems of the "Spring and Autumn."* New York: Columbia University Press, 2016.

Raz, Gil. "Buddhism Challenged, Adopted, and in Disguise: Daoist and Buddhist Interactions in Medieval China." In Mu-chou Poo, H. A. Drake, and Lisa Raphals, eds., *Old Society, New Belief: Religious Transformation of China and Rome, ca. 1st–6th Centuries*, 109–27. Oxford: Oxford University Press, 2017.

———. "'Conversion of the Barbarians' [*Huahu*] Discourse as Proto Han Nationalism." *Medieval History Journal* 17.2 (2014): 255–94.

Rong Xinjiang 榮新江. "An-Shi zhi luan hou Sute Huren de dongxiang" 安史之亂後粟特胡人的動向. 2003. Reprinted in *Zhonggu Zhongguo yu Sute wenming*, 79–113. Beijing: Sanlian, 2014.

Rouzer, Paul. "Early Buddhist Kanshi: Court, Country, and Kūkai." *Monumenta Nipponica* 59.4 (2004): 431–61.

Saiki Tetsurō 齊木哲郎. "Eitei kakushin to shunjūgaku: Tōdai shin shunjūgaku no seijiteki tenkai" 永貞革新と春秋学: 唐代新春秋学の政治的展開. *Naruto kyōiku daigaku kenkyū kiyō* 鳴門教育大学研究紀要 22 (2007): 261–73.

———. "Kan Yu to 'Shunjū'—Eitei kakushin wo megutte" 韓愈と「春秋」—永貞革新をめぐって. *Chūgoku tetsugaku* 中国哲学 35 (2007): 137–65.

Sarkissian, Hagop. "Ritual and Rightness in the *Analects*." In Amy Olberding, ed., *Dao Companion to the Analects*, 95–116. New York: Springer, 2014.

Sato, Masayuki. *The Confucian Quest for Order: The Origin and Formation of the Political Thought of Xunzi*. Leiden: Brill, 2003.

Schneider, Julia. *Nation and Ethnicity: Chinese Discourses on History, Historiography, and Nationalism (1900s–1920s)*. Leiden: Brill, 2017.

Selover, Thomas W. *Hsieh Liang-tso and the "Analects" of Confucius: Humane Learning as a Religious Quest*. New York: Oxford University Press, 2005.

Shi, Longdu. "Buddhism and the State in Medieval China: Case Studies of Three Persecutions of Buddhism, 444–846." PhD thesis, SOAS, University of London, 2016.

Shi Xiulian 史秀蓮. "Tangdai de 'bingong ke' yu bingong zhi zhi" 唐代的"賓貢科"與賓貢之制. *Yantai daxue xuebao* 煙臺大學學報 17.3 (2004): 338–41.

Shields, Anna M. "Gossip, Anecdote, and Literary History: Representations of the Yuanhe Era in Tang Anecdote Collections." In Jack W. Chen and David Schaberg, eds., *Idle Talk: Gossip and Anecdote in Traditional China*, 107–31. Berkeley: University of California Press, 2014.

———. *One Who Knows Me: Friendship and Literary Culture in Mid-Tang China*. Cambridge, MA: Harvard University Asia Center, 2015.

Skaff, Jonathan Karam. *Sui-Tang China and Its Turko-Mongol Neighbors: Culture, Power, and Connections, 580–800*. Oxford: Oxford University Press, 2012.

Skonicki, Douglas. "A Buddhist Response to Ancient-Style Learning: Qisong's Conception of Political Order." *T'oung Pao* 97 (2011): 1–36.

———. "'Guwen' Lineage Discourse in the Northern Song." *Journal of Song-Yuan Studies* 44 (2014): 1–32.

Sloane, Jesse. "Ethnography, Environment, and Empire: Foreign and Domestic Travel Accounts of the Jin Dynasty Northern Frontier." *Korean Journal of Chinese Language and Literature* 2013(8), 121–59.

Smith, Paul Jakov. "A Crisis in the Literati State: The Sino-Tangut War and the Qingli-Era Reforms of Fan Zhongyan, 1040–1045." *Journal of Song-Yuan Studies* 45 (2015): 59–137.

Soffel, Christian, and Hoyt Tillman. *Cultural Authority and Political Culture in China: Exploring Issues with the Zhongyong and the Daotong during the Song, Jin and Yuan Dynasties*. Stuttgart: Franz Steiner Verlag, 2012.

Standen, Naomi. *Unbounded Loyalty: Frontier Crossing in Liao China*. Honolulu: University of Hawaii Press, 2007.

Stouraitis, Yannis. "Reinventing Roman Ethnicity in High and Late Medieval Byzantium." *Medieval Worlds* 5 (2017): 70–94.

———. "Roman Identity in Byzantium: A Critical Approach." *Byzantinische Zeitschrift* 107.1 (2014): 175–220.

Su Pinxiao 粟品孝. "'Lidai shibian' fei Su Shi suozuo kao"《歷代世變》非蘇軾所作考. *Sichuan daxue xuebao* 四川大學學報 2003(4), 124.

Sumner, William Graham. *Folkways: A Study of the Sociological Importance of Usages, Manners, Customs, Mores, and Morals*. Boston: Ginn and Company, 1906.

Sun Jianquan 孫建權. "Guanyu Zhang Di 'Jinlu tujing' de jige wenti" 關於張棣《金虜圖經》的幾個問題. *Wenxian* 文獻 2013(2), 131–37.

Tackett, Nicolas. *The Origins of the Chinese Nation: Song China and the Forging of an East Asian World Order*. Cambridge: Cambridge University Press, 2017.

———. "A Tang-Song Turning Point." In Michael Szonyi, ed., *A Companion to Chinese History*, 118–28. Chichester, Sussex: Wiley-Blackwell, 2017.

Tai, Eika. "Rethinking Culture, National Culture, and Japanese Culture." *Japanese Language and Literature* 37.1 (2003): 1–26.

Teng, Emma Jinhua. *Taiwan's Imagined Geography: Chinese Colonial Travel Writing and Pictures, 1683–1895*. Cambridge, MA: Harvard University Asia Center, 2004.

Tillman, Hoyt. "Proto-Nationalism in Twelfth-Century China? The Case of Ch'en Liang." *Harvard Journal of Asiatic Studies* 39.2 (1979): 403–28.

———. *Utilitarian Confucianism: Ch'en Liang's Challenge to Chu Hsi*. Cambridge, MA: Council on East Asian Studies, Harvard University, 1982.

Townsend, James. "Chinese Nationalism." *Australian Journal of Chinese Affairs* 27 (1992) 97–130.

Trauzettel, Rolf. "Sung Patriotism as a First Step toward Chinese Nationalism." In John Winthrop Haeger, ed., *Crisis and Prosperity in Sung China*, 199–213. Tucson: University of Arizona Press, 1975.

Twitchett, Denis. *The Writing of Official History under the T'ang*. Cambridge: Cambridge University Press, 1992.

Van Auken, Newell Ann. *The Commentarial Transformation of the "Spring and Autumn."* Albany: State University of New York Press, 2016.

———. "Who Is a *Rén*? The Use of *Rén* in *Spring and Autumn* Records and Its Interpretation in the *Zuǒ*, *Gōngyáng*, and *Gǔliáng* Commentaries." *Journal of the American Oriental Society* 131.4 (2011): 555–90.

Van Ess, Hans. "The Compilation of the Works of the Ch'eng Brothers and Its Significance for the Learning of the Right Way of the Southern Sung Period." *T'oung Pao* 90.4 (2005): 264–98.

Wakabayashi, Bob Tadashi. *Anti-Foreignism and Western Learning in Early-Modern Japan: The New Theses of 1825*. Cambridge, MA: Council on East Asian Studies, Harvard University, 1986.

Wang Gungwu. "The Rhetoric of a Lesser Empire: Early Sung Relations with Its Neighbors." In Morris Rossabi, ed., *China among Equals: The Middle Kingdom and Its Neighbors, 10th–14th Centuries*, 47–65. Berkeley: University of California Press, 1983.

Wang Leisong 王雷松. *Hu Anguo "Chunqiu zhuan" jiaoshi yu yanjiu* 胡安國《春秋傳》校釋與研究. Beijing: Beijing Shifan Daxue Chubanshe, 2016.

Wang Mingsun 王明蓀. "Sanguo shidai de guojia yu Zhongguo guan" 三國時代的國家與中國觀. *Shixue jikan* 史學集刊 2013(2), 47–58.

Wang Nengxian 王能憲. "'Liyi zhi bang' kaobian" "禮義之邦" 考. *Wenyi yanjiu* 文藝研究 2013(2), 55–62.

Wang Rui 王睿. *Tangdai Suteren Huahua wenti shulun* 唐代粟特人華化問題述論. Beijing: Shehui Kexue Wenxian Chubanshe, 2016.

Wang Su 王素. *Tang xieben Lunyu Zhengshi zhu jiqi yanjiu* 唐寫本論語鄭氏注及其研究. Beijing: Wenwu Chubanshe, 1991.

Welter, Albert. "A Buddhist Response to the Confucian Revival: Tsan-ning and the Debate over *Wen* in the Early Sung." In Gregory and Getz, eds., *Buddhism in the Sung*, 21–61.

———. "Confucian Monks and Buddhist *Junzi*: Zanning's *Topical Compendium of the Buddhist Clergy* (Da Song seng shi lüe) and the Politics of Buddhist Accommodation at the Song Court." In Thomas Jülch, ed., *The Middle Kingdom and the Dharma Wheel: Aspects of the Relationship between the Buddhist Saṃgha and the State in Chinese History*, 222–77. Leiden: Brill, 2016.

Wilkinson, Endymion. *Chinese History: A New Manual.* 4th ed. Cambridge, MA: Harvard University Asia Center, 2015.

Wilson, Thomas A. *Genealogy of the Way: The Construction and Uses of the Confucian Tradition in Late Imperial China.* Stanford, CA: Stanford University Press, 1995.

Wong Kwok-yiu. "Between Politics and Metaphysics: On the Changing Reception of Wang T'ung in the T'ang-Sung Intellectual Transitions." *Monumenta Serica* 55 (2007): 61–97.

Wood, Alan T. *Limits to Autocracy: From Sung Neo-Confucianism to a Doctrine of Political Rights.* Honolulu: University of Hawaii Press, 1995.

Wright, Arthur F. *Buddhism in Chinese History.* Stanford, CA: Stanford University Press, 1959.

Wu Zaiqing 吳在慶. *Tingtao zhai zhonggu wenshi lungao* 聽濤齋中古文史論稿. Hefei: Huangshan Shushe, 2011.

Wyatt, Don J. "Unsung Men of War: Acculturated Embodiments of the Martial Ethos in the Song Dynasty." In Nicola Di Cosmo, ed., *Military Culture in Imperial China*, 192–218. Cambridge, MA: Harvard University Press, 2009.

Xie Haiping 謝海平. *Tangdai liuhua waiguoren shenghuo kaoshu* 唐代留華外國人生活考述. Taipei: Shangwu Yinshuguan, 1978.

Xiong Mingqin 熊鳴琴. "Chaoyue 'Yi-Xia': Beisong 'Zhongguo' guan chutan" 超越"夷夏"：北宋"中國"觀初探. *Zhongzhou xuekan* 中州學刊 2013(4), 124–29.

Xu Huafeng 許華峰. "Cai Shen 'Shu jizhuan' suo yinju de ziliao fenxi" 蔡沈《書集傳》所引據的資料分析. *Donghua Hanxue* 東華漢學 16 (2012): 183–218.

Xu Jieshun. "Understanding the Snowball Theory of the Han Nationality." In Mullaney, Leibold, Gros, and Vanden Bussche, eds., *Critical Han Studies*, 113–27.

Xu Song 徐松 and Meng Erdong 孟二冬. *Dengke jikao buzheng* 登科記考補正. Beijing: Beijing Yanshan Chubanshe, 2003.

Xu Wangjia 徐望駕. "Huang Kan 'Lunyu jijie yishu' banben yanjiu shuping" 皇侃《論語集解義疏》版本研究述評. *Guji zhengli yanjiu xuekan* 古籍整理研究學刊 2002(2), 88–91.

Yan Gengwang 嚴耕望. *Tangshi yanjiu luncong* 唐史研究論叢. Hong Kong: Xinya Yanjiusuo, 1968.

Yang, Shao-yun. "*Fan* and *Han*: The Origins and Uses of a Conceptual Dichotomy in Mid-Imperial China, ca. 500–1200." In Francesca Fiaschetti and Julia Schneider, eds., *Political Strategies of Identity-Building in Non-Han Empires in China*, 9–35. Wiesbaden: Harrassowitz Verlag, 2014.

———. "Letting the Troops Loose: Pillage, Massacres, and Enslavement in Early Tang Warfare." *Journal of Chinese Military History* 6 (2017): 1–52.

———. "Shi Xiaozhang's Spirit Road Stele and the Rhetorical 'Barbarization' of Late Tang Hebei." *Tang Studies* 36 (2018): 57–81.

———. "'Their Lands Are Peripheral and Their *Qi* Is Blocked Up': The Uses of Environmental Determinism in Han (206 BCE–220 CE) and Tang (618–907 CE) Chinese Interpretations of the 'Barbarians.'" In Rebecca Futo Kennedy and Molly Jones-Lewis, eds., *The Routledge Handbook of Identity and the Environment in the Classical and Medieval Worlds*, 390–412. Abingdon, Oxon: Routledge, 2016.

Yang Guo'an 楊國安. "Shilun Beisong ruxue de yanjin yu Han Yu diwei de bianhua" 試論北宋儒學的演進與韓愈地位的變化. *Zhongzhou xuekan* 中州學刊 2002(5), 142–47.

Yang Liu'an 楊柳岸. "'Yan Yi-Xia dafang' yihuo 'zhong junchen dayi'?—'Lunyu' 'Yi-Di zhi youjun, buru zhuxia zhi wu' jie" "嚴夷夏大防" 抑或 "重君臣大義"?—《論語》"夷狄之有君，不如諸夏之亡"解. *Zhongguo zhexue shi* 中國哲學史 2009(4), 58–63.

Yang Zhigang 楊志剛. "Lisu yu Zhongguo wenhua" 禮俗與中國文化. *Fudan xuebao* 復旦學報 1990(3), 77–82.

Yao Dali 姚大力. "Zhongguo lishi shang de liangzhong guojia jiangou moshi" 中國歷史上的兩種國家建構模式. 2014. Reprinted in *Zhuixun "women" de genyuan: Zhongguo lishi shang de minzu yu guojia yishi* 追尋 "我們" 的根源：中國歷史上的民族與國家意識, 141–60. Beijing: Sanlian, 2018.

———. "Zhongguo lishi shang de minzu guanxi yu guojia rentong" 中國歷史上的民族關係與國家認同. 2002. Reprinted in *Zhuixun "women" de genyuan*, 3–24.

Yoshimoto Michimasa 吉本道雅. "Shūshitsu tōsen saikō" 周室東遷再考. *Kyōto daigaku bungaku bu kenkyū kiyō* 京都大學文學部研究紀要 56 (2017): 1–58.

Yue, Isaac. "Barbarians and Monstrosity: A Thematic Study of the Representation of Foreignness in Early Chinese Vernacular Stories." *Études chinoises* 29 (2010): 221–41.

Zhang, Aidong, and Wayne Schlepp. "Xiao Guanyin: Her Tragic Life and Melancholy Poems." *Journal of Song-Yuan Studies* 28 (1998): 213–21.

Zhang Jia 張佳. *Xin tianxia zhi hua—Mingchu lisu gaige yanjiu* 新天下之化—明初禮俗改革研究. Shanghai: Fudan Daxue Chubanshe, 2014.

Zhang Peifeng 張培鋒. *Songdai shidafu foxue yu wenxue* 宋代士大夫佛學與文學. Beijing: Zongjiao Wenhua Chubanshe, 2007.

Zhang Qifan 張其凡 and Xiong Mingqin 熊鳴琴. "Liao Daozong 'yuan houshi sheng Zhongguo' zhushuo kaobian" 遼道宗 "愿後世生中國" 諸說考辨. *Wenshizhe* 文史哲 2010(5), 84–93.

Zhang Qinghua 張清華. "Han Yu de dao, daotong shuo ji 'Wuyuan' de xiezuo shijian bianxi" 韓愈的道、道統說及《五原》的寫作時間辨析. *Hanshan shifan xueyuan xuebao* 26.4 (2005): 1–6.

———. *Han Yu nianpu huizheng* 韓愈年譜匯證. Nanjing: Jiangsu Jiaoyu Chubanshe, 1998.

Zhang Shizhao 章士釗. *Liuwen zhiyao* 柳文指要. Beijing: Zhonghua Shuju, 1971.

Zhang Weiran 張偉然. "Tangren xinmuzhong de wenhua quyu ji dili yixiang" 唐人心目中的文化區域及地理意象. In Li Xiaocong 李孝聰, ed., *Tangdai diyu jiegou yu yunzuo kongjian* 唐代地域結構與運作空間, 307–412. Shanghai: Shanghai Cishu Chubanshe, 2003.

Zhao, Gang. "Reinventing *China*: Imperial Qing Ideology and the Rise of Modern Chinese National Identity in the Early Twentieth Century." *Modern China* 32.1 (2006): 3–30.

Zhong Qianjun 鍾謙鈞, ed. *Gu jingjie huihan* 古經解彙函. Yangzhou: Guangling Shushe, 2012.

Zhu Shangshu 祝尚書. "Liu Kai nianpu" 柳開年譜. In *Songdai wenhua yanjiu* 宋代文化研究, vol. 3, 113–47. Chengdu: Sichuan Daxue Chubanshe, 1993.

Zhu Shengming 朱聖明. *Hua-Yi zhi jian: Qin-Han shiqi zuqun de shenfen yu rentong* 華夷之間：秦漢時期族群的身份與認同. Xiamen: Xiamen Daxue Chubanshe, 2017.

Ziporyn, Brook. *Beyond Oneness and Difference: Li and Coherence in Chinese Buddhist Thought and Its Antecedents*. Albany: State University of New York Press, 2013.

Zuo, Ya. "'Ru' versus 'Li': The Divergence between the Generalist and the Specialist in the Northern Song." *Journal of Song-Yuan Studies* 44 (2014): 85–137.

Index

A

An Lushan Rebellion, 3–6, 19, 25–26, 132, 137, 164–65n14
Analects (Lunyu): *Analects* 2.1, 198n4; *Analects* 2.23, 130; *Analects* 3.1 and 3.6, 195n46; *Analects* 3.5, 7, 9, 34, 49, 109, 122–30, 133, 139, 143–44, 149; *Analects* 4.10, 190n59; *Analects* 5.7, 138; *Analects* 6.18, 13; *Analects* 7.29, 176n15; *Analects* 9.5, 76; *Analects* 9.14, 34, 64–65, 123, 126, 138, 172–73n41, 197n89; *Analects* 13.4, 189n30; *Analects* 13.19, 14, 173n42, 194n37; *Analects* 14.13, 152; *Analects* 14.17, 35, 100; *Analects* 15.5, 173n42; *Analects* 15.11 and 17.18, 175n10; *Analects* 16.2 and 16.3, 195n43; commentaries, 14, 122–29, 193n29. *See also* Confucius
Ancient-Style Prose. *See* Guwen
animality, 21, 54, 73, 88–89, 120, 139, 170n78, 198n95
Annals (Chunqiu): Confucius, attribution to, 5, 29–30, 163n4; *Gongyang Commentary*, 30–42, 66–67, 98–99, 101–103, 135; *Guliang Commentary*, 30–41, 66, 98, 103–5, 110, 140; and interpretations of Chinese identity, 5, 7–8, 24–25, 29–42, 57, 67, 98–121, 123, 131–40, 148; *Luxuriant Gems of the Annals* (Chunqiu fanlu), 31–32, 38, 106, 172n29, 189n43; new commentaries, 37, 42, 98–99, 106, 132–33; "respecting the king and repelling the barbarians"

(zunwang rangyi/*sonnō jōi*) (phrase), 101, 132, 186nn10,11, 196n60; terminology pertaining to warfare between Chinese and barbarians, 110–11; *Zuo Tradition* (Zuozhuan), 32–33, 35–37, 39–40, 49, 64–65, 93, 98, 121, 134, 143. *See also* barbarians; barbarization
Arabs, 6, 59–61

B

Bai Juyi (Bo Juyi), 6, 164n7, 176n17
Bamboo Annals (Zhushu jinian), 126
barbarians: clothing and hairstyle, 35–36, 54, 64–65, 81–83, 93, 95–96, 185n71; Greco-Roman analogues, 9, 166n27; *Hua-Yi zhi bian* (the difference between Chinese and barbarians), 133–35, 137, 139, 151; ignorance, associated with, 34, 64–65, 123, 172–73n41; immorality, associated with, 9, 14–15, 22–23, 49–50, 54, 63–67, 97, 110–13; praiseworthy barbarians, 48–51, 60, 66, 151; primitivity, associated with, 13, 49, 53, 96; promoted in the *Annals*, 7, 10–11, 33–35, 40, 66, 87, 104–5, 107–9, 148–49; terminology and translation, 3, 5, 8–9, 53, 165n20, 166n27, 181n39, 185n68; transformation into Chinese ("Sinicization"), 10–11, 22, 34–36, 65, 95, 109, 122, 142–48,

219

barbarians (*cont.*)
173n42; "Way of the Barbarians," 22, 34, 81, 103–4, 106–7, 121–22, 139–41, 150; *Yi-Xia zhi bian* (the difference between barbarians and Chinese), 134. *See also* barbarization; Di "barbarians"; ethnocentrism; *liyi* (ritual propriety and moral duty); Man "barbarians"; Rong "barbarians"; Yi "barbarians"

barbarization: due to conquest or domination by barbarians, 92–93, 100–102, 111, 131; as editorial demotion in the *Annals*, 29–34, 36–38, 57, 107, 188n24; by heterodoxy (ethnicized orthodoxy), 16, 24–25, 35–36, 75, 81–83, 88–90, 92, 118, 185n71; by immorality (ethnocentric moralism), 21, 57–58, 66–69, 103–5, 108–9, 112, 121–22, 130–32, 139, 150; due to ritual or ethnocultural change, 31–33, 35–40, 64–66. *See also* animality; *Annals* (Chunqiu); Confucius

bestialization. *See* animality

Bi, battle of, 31–32, 172n29

"Bigong" (ode). *See Odes* (Shijing)

bingong (recommended guest) examination candidates, 61–62, 178n11, 179n18

Bohai (Parhae), 61

Boxer Uprising, 5

Buddhism: accepted by Guwen writers, 6, 76, 106, 117; attacked by Guwen writers, 5–7, 24–29, 47–48, 50–51, 74–84, 89–94, 116, 118; the Buddha's great height, 183n31; Chan Buddhism, 27, 113–14, 170n11; and Daoxue philosophy, 114, 117; defended by Liu Zongyuan, 43–50; defended by Qisong, 113–15; Huayan Buddhism, 114; monasticism, 50, 94; myth of decline under the Song, 191n74; state persecution of, 6, 29, 83–84, 91–94. *See also* "Master Mou's Discourse on Resolving Doubts" (Mouzi lihuo lun);

Laozi huahu jing (Scripture on Laozi Transforming the Westerners)

Byzantine empire, 168n60, 169n68

C

Cai Shen, 13, 167n47

Cavafy, C. P., 141, 198

Central Asia and Central Asians (Hu), 6, 36, 164n7, 166n28

Central Lands (Zhongguo): in Buddhist cosmology, 144; Central Lands of the Chinese (Zhonghua), 8, 83, 143, 153; as a civilization, nation, or imperial core region, 16–19; defined by Yang Xiong, 194n42; different meanings of, 8–9, 63–64; and Kitan Liao empire, 142–44; origins of the concept, 7; "Way of the Central Lands" (Zhongguo zhi dao), 82, 84, 106, 141, 198n97; "Way of the Central Plains" (Zhongyuan zhi dao), 150; and *wen*, 13

Changes (Yijing), 48, 50, 86, 94, 121; hexagrams *tai* and *pi*, 135–36

Chanyuan covenant, 80, 145

Chao Yuezhi, 144–46

Chen An, 57–59, 105, 142; "Chinese at Heart" (Huaxin), 13–14, 59–67, 69, 71–74, 109, 116, 179n11, 181n39

Chen dynasty, 63, 147–48

Chen Liang, 139–40, 198n97

Chen Shidao, 147–48

Chen Yinke, 6, 10, 27, 170nn1,7, 195n53

Chen Zhaohua, 78–79, 81

Cheng Hao: *Annals* exegesis, 134–35, 192n8, 196n73; Chinese-barbarian dichotomy, views on, 119–20, 134–35; Daoxue, founder of, 119; *Hua-Yi zhi bian* (phrase), 134–35; and *li*, 114

Cheng Yan, 57–59, 105; "A Call to Arms Against the Inner Barbarian" (Neiyi xi, "Call to Arms"), 67–72, 74, 78, 109, 116, 178n1

220 INDEX

Cheng Yi: *Analects* 3.5, reinterpretation of, 122–30; *Annals* exegesis, 133–40, 192n8, 196n70, 196–97n74; barbarization, views on, 120–40; Buddhism and Daoism, views on, 117; Daoxue, founder of, 119; *Hua-Yi zhi bian* (phrase), 134–35; ethnocentric moralism, 107, 120–22, 130–31; Han Yu, views on, 56, 120–21, 136; history, interpretation of, 127, 130–31; and *li*, 114; Wang Anshi, views on, 117

Chengpu, battle of, 99–101

Chinese (ethnocultural group): Han (as ethnonym), 9–11, 17, 19–20, 58, 143, 153, 166n24, 168n63; Hua, 8–11, 13, 18–19, 132–35, 137, 139, 144, 151, 181n39; Hua-Xia, 165n20; as a multi-ethnic nation, 153; Xia, 9–11, 13, 18, 34, 65, 134, 142, 145.

"Chinese at Heart" (Huaxin). *See* Chen An

Chinese-barbarian dichotomy.

See barbarians

Christianity, 6

Chu (state), 30–36, 87, 92–93, 99–101, 103–12, 123, 125, 148; as barbarized Chinese state, 39–40, 107–10, 112, 171n22; as "Jing," 8, 39–40, 54, 92, 99, 165n18; Yuxiong descent, 110, 190n50; Zhurong descent, 40, 108

Chunqiu. *See Annals* (Chunqiu)

Classicism. *See* Ru

Confucianism. *See* Ru

Confucius: *Annals*, attributed author of, 5, 29–30, 163n4; barbarians, attitudes towards, 7–9, 14, 31, 35–40, 64–67, 99–115, 122–30, 133–39, 148, 151. *See also Analects* (Lunyu); *Annals* (Chunqiu)

Cui Yin, 69–70

culturalism. *See* culture

culture: "culturalism" (concept), 3, 7–11, 15–16, 19–24, 65, 141, 164–65n14, 169n70, 178n3; "this literary culture of ours" (*siwen*), 76, 182n7; as *wen*, 12–13, 167nn39,43; as *wenhua* (transformation by *wen*), 10–11, 13–15, 20, 167n46. *See also feng* and *su* (*fengsu*, customs/folkways); *li* (ritual or ritual propriety) customs. *See feng* and *su*

D

Dan Zhu, 37, 42, 98–99, 106, 173n52

Dao (the Way): as a Classicist concept, 13, 29, 114, 139–40

Daoism: accepted by Guwen writers, 106, 117; and anti-Buddhist persecution, 6; anti-Buddhist polemic, 36; barbarism, associated with, 16, 53–55, 75, 77–83, 86–90, 116, 121; Guwen calls for persecution by the state, 6, 29, 83–84, 117; and Huang-Lao philosophy, 26, 28, 77; as Chinese, 94. *See also* Laozi; *Laozi daodejing* (Classic of the Way and Its Power)

Daotong (Transmission/Succession of the Way), 29; and Chan Buddhism, 27, 170–71n11

Daoxue (Neo-Confucianism), 4; and anti-foreign sentiment, 140; and cultural/moral universalism, 16, 139–40, 169n70; and Han Yu, 55–56, 120–21; and ethnocentric moralism, 73, 118, 121–40; and moral self-cultivation, 22, 122; origins, 114, 119. *See also* Daotong (Transmission/Succession of the Way); *li* (philosophical concept); *qi* (cosmological concept)

Daozong (Liao emperor), 142–45, 149

Dezong (Tang emperor), 137

Di "barbarians," 8–9, 40, 49, 54, 99, 114, 133, 165n18, 190n65; Red Di, 110; White Di, 92, 110; Xianyu (state), 32, 103, 106, 172n29, 173n52, 188n25

Documents (Shangshu), 13, 136–37, 147, 191n65, 196n66

Dong Zhongshu, 31, 184n51

Du You, 53

Du Yu, 32–33, 36, 38, 98, 185n68

INDEX 221

Duke of Zhou, 27–28, 49, 54, 86, 89, 143, 165n18, 177n45

E

Eastern Jin. See Jin dynasty
environmental determinism. See *qi* (cosmological concept)
ethnocentrism, 14, 66–67, 130, 136, 146–47, 153, 168n59
eunuchs, 69–71
exceptionalism, 153

F

Fairbank, John K., 10, 166n30
Fan Ning, 31, 33, 37–38, 40, 98, 104, 107, 110, 188n25
Fan Rugui, 200n33
Fan Zhongyan, 95
Fan Zuyu, 127, 129, 156, 194n38
Fang Songqing, 52, 165n16, 181n50
Fang Xiaoru, 20
feng and *su* (*fengsu*, customs/folkways), 11–12, 14, 21, 167n36. See also culture; *li* (ritual or ritual propriety)
Feng Ao, 61
Feng Su. See Han Yu
Five Dynasties, 18, 147, 169n67, 185n71
folkways. See *feng* and *su*
Fu Bi, 95, 145–46, 186n84
Fu Xuan, 36

G

Gaozong (Song emperor), 132, 127, 150
Ge (state), 38–39, 103, 107, 172n29, 174n55, 189n43
Gongyang Commentary. See *Annals* (Chunqiu)
Guan Zhong, 35, 54, 100, 187n10
Guliang Commentary. See *Annals* (Chunqiu)
Guwen (Ancient-Style Prose), 4–6, 13, 19, 21, 24–25, 41, 63, 72, 101, 142; and Buddhism, 6, 16, 43, 75–77, 81–84, 89–91, 93, 95, 113, 116–18; and Daoism, 6, 16, 53–55, 75–79, 80–88, 94, 116–17; Guwen moderates, 77, 90–96, 116–17; "Guwen movement," 76, 182n6; Guwen radicals, 77–80, 96–97, 106, 116–18, 121; Guwen revival, 16, 75–98, 113, 117–18, 141

H

Han (as ethnonym). See Chinese (ethnocultural group)
Han dynasty, 4, 8, 12–14, 29, 60, 63, 142, 199n25; Eastern Han, 26, 36, 123–24, 130; Western Han, 8, 26, 130, 137, 197nn81,82
Han Fei (Han Feizi), 45–46, 48, 176n23, 185n71
Han Jian, 69–71
Han Wudi, 60
Han Yu: and *Annals* exegesis, 8, 24–25, 29, 34–42, 174n66; *Brush-written Explanations of the Analects* (Lunyu bijie), 193n29; and Buddhist monks, 27, 44–46, 175n13; as "culturalist," 7–8, 15; Feng Su, letter to, 25; fox and hedgehog analogy, 55; ideological exclusivity, 6–7, 43–44, 55–56, 76–77; literary influence, 8, 24, 29, 40, 57, 75, 80–81, 116–17; and Liu Zongyuan, 41–53, 55–56, 63, 115, 176n16; "Memorial on the Buddha Relic" (Lun fogu biao), 5, 53, 81, 164n13, 173n46; Meng Jian, letter to, 53–55; Third Miscellaneous Discourse (Zashuo san), 73, 181m50; "Tracing Humanity to Its Source" (Yuanren), 120, 146; "Tracing the Way to Its Source" (Yuandao, "Tracing the Way"), 6, 28–29, 33–35, 51–55, 72–73, 112, 121, 125, 165n16; Mencius, Xunzi, and Yang Xiong, view on, 25–28, 55–56; Veritable Records for Shunzong's reign, 41, 43, 174nn65, 66; Wenchang preface, 27–28, 44–46, 48, 50, 53, 73, 177n39

Haochu, 47–48
He Xiu, 30, 38, 42, 98, 103–4, 115, 123–24
hegemons (*ba*), 38–39, 99–101, 107, 133–34
Hong Hao, 143
Hu. *See* Central Asia and Central Asians (Hu)
Hu Anguo, 132–33, 135–40, 150, 157, 192n8, 198nn95,96, 200n33
Hu Hong, 132, 150, 172n32, 195n56, 200n34
Hu Yin, 132, 150–52, 200n41
Hua (as ethnonym). *See* Chinese (ethnocultural group)
Huang Chao Rebellion, 71
Huang Hanjie, 94
Huang Kan, 124, 192–93n22, 193nn23,24
Huang Tao, 58–59, 69
Huang Zhen, 183nn31,32
Huangchi conference, 102, 104–5, 174n57, 181n39, 187n15
Huangfu Shi, 63–65, 180nn29,33,34
Huilin, 124, 192n22
Huizong (Song emperor), 132, 135

I

India, 36, 144, 199n11
Inner Asians, 17–18, 142, 145, 181n45
inscriptions, 48, 76, 88, 94–95, 142, 144, 172n32, 178n2, 186n1, 190n45
Iranians, 6, 61
irredentism, 16–18, 78–79, 84–86, 135, 149

J

Jia Yi, 194n36, 197n81
Jie (ethnonym used as epithet), 71, 181n45
Jifu, battle of, 30, 34
Jin (state), 28, 30–32, 64–65, 102–4, 106, 110, 112, 143, 171n21, 172n29, 173n52, 187n15, 188n18, 189n27; Lord Wen of Jin, 99–101
Jin dynasty (266–420 CE), 185n71; Eastern Jin, 63–64, 124–25, 132, 193n28, 194n31; Western Jin, 63, 130–32, 147, 200n36
Jin dynasty (1115–1234). *See* Jurchen Jin dynasty
Jin Midi, 60
jinshi examinations, 59–62, 75, 86, 91, 93–94, 179n18
Jizha, 48–49, 51, 115
Juliang conference, 102, 187n18
junzi (noble/superior men) and *xiaoren* (inferior men), 13–15, 135–36, 168n54
Jurchen Jin dynasty, 4, 16, 23, 131–33, 135–37, 139–40, 143, 149–52, 195n56

K

King Li (of Zhou), 126
"Kingly Institutions" (Wangzhi). *See* Record of Rites.
King Wen (of Zhou), 27–28, 39, 89; barbarian, identified as, 34, 147–48, 173n42, 199n25
King Wu (of Zhou), 27–28, 89
Kitan empire. *See* Liao dynasty
Kong Daofu, 88–89, 100, 102, 185n71
Koryŏ, 85, 145

L

Laozi, 26, 28, 36, 47, 53, 78–83, 87–89, 94, 106, 117, 185n71; barbarian, identified as, 78, 82–83, 116
Laozi daodejing (Classic of the Way and Its Power), 26, 28, 53, 106, 117
Laozi huahu jing (Scripture on Laozi Transforming the Westerners), 36, 82
Later Han dynasty, 147
Later Jin dynasty, 147, 150–51, 194n34
Later Liang dynasty, 70
Later Tang dynasty, 147
Later Zhou dynasty, 85
Levenson, Joseph, 10, 17, 168n59, 169n74
li (philosophical concept): in Buddhist philosophy, 114, 190nn61,62; use by Daoxue, 114, 119, 122; use by Qisong, 113–14

li (ritual or ritual propriety), 11–16, 21, 60, 64–65, 72, 113, 120, 122, 126. See also *liyi* (ritual propriety and moral duty)
Li Ao, 25, 193n29
Li Chu, 47–48
Li Gou, 75–77, 93; and Buddhism, 94–95, 117; as Guwen moderate, 77; ethnocentric moralism, 97; "The Enemy Threat" (Dihuan), 95–96, 116, 145–46
Li Han, 175n2
Li Keyong, 70–72, 181n43
Li Ling, 60
Li Maozhen, 69–72
Li Mingfu, 134–35, 192n8, 196n73
Li Xun, 61
Li Yansheng, 59–62, 69, 142
Liang dynasty, 28, 63, 124, 147–48, 180n33, 185n71
Liang Wudi, 180n33
Liao dynasty (Kitan empire), 3–4, 16–17, 84; centrality, claims of, 23, 142–45; use of the Chinese-barbarian dichotomy, 143–45; fall to the Jurchens, 23; north China invasion (947 CE), 126; Song dynasty, war with, 78–80; Song perceptions, 144–46;
Liji. See Record of Rites
Lingzong, 46
Liu Chang, 106–12, 122, 133; and Cheng Yi, 106–7; ethnocentric moralism, 111, 118; *Forest of Meanings in the Annals* (Chunqiu yilin), 107–11; "On Governing the Barbarians" (Zhirong lun), 111; and Guwen radicals, 106; Han Yu, criticism of, 116, 191n70; and Ouyang Xiu, 106; on "real barbarians," 107–12, 146; *Weighing Balance of the Annals* (Chunqiu quanheng), 107, 109–10
Liu Kai, 75–81, 91–92, 116–17, 182n10; cannibalism (alleged), 78, 80, 182n20; ethnicized orthodoxy, 77, 80–81, 88, 131; irredentism, 79, 84–86; military career, 79–80, 85–86; sagehood, claims to, 77

Liu Sui, 81
Liu Xun, 133
Liu Yuxi, 178n2
Liu Zongyuan, 41–53, 63, 66; and Buddhism, 43–50, 175n4; and Han Yu, 43–52, 55–56, 115, 175n1, 176n16; intellectual pluralism, 47–48, 55, 74, 177n34; and new *Annals* exegesis, 41–42; and "Tracing the Way to Its Source," 50–53, 177n34
Liu-Song dynasty, 63, 147, 185n71
liyi (ritual propriety and moral duty): barbarians seen as lacking in, 9, 13–15, 21, 36, 60, 64–65, 110, 126–27, 139, 148; origins of the phrase, 14, 167n52; in Ouyang Xiu's "On Fundamentals," 92
Lu (state), 32–33, 102–4, 107, 128; as Confucius's birthplace and home state, 67, 86; Ji (Jisun) ministerial family, 124, 195n46; Lord Huan of Lu, 38, 103, 137–38; Lord Yin of Lu, 38, 133–34, 137–38
Lu Chun (Lu Zhi), 37–40, 98–99, 103, 107, 174n55; change of name, 174n65; Han Yu, influence on, 40–41, 174n66; Wang Shuwen faction, influence on, 41, 174n63
Lü Dalin, 127, 129, 194n37
Lu Guimeng, 182n13
Lu Jun, 61–63, 69, 179n21
Lu Tong, 41–42
Lu Wan, 60
Luhun, Rong of. See Rong "barbarians"
Lunyu. See Analects
Luxuriant Gems of the Annals (Chunqiu fanlu). See *Annals* (Chunqiu)

M

Man "barbarians," 8, 40, 92, 148. See also Chu (state); Shu (statelets); Wu (state); Yue (state)
Manchus, 152–53, 167n46, 200n43. See also Qing dynasty
Manicheism, 6

"Master Mou's Discourse on Resolving Doubts" (Mouzi lihuo lun), 49, 124–25, 143, 192n21
Master Sun's Art of War (Sunzi bingfa), 186nn81,82
Mencius, 14, 26–29, 54, 76, 80, 88–90, 102, 119, 121; Han Yu, influence on, 27–29, 34, 44, 55–56, 171n16; *Mencius* 3A.4, 34, 36, 49, 173n43, 177n45; *Mencius* 3B.9, 26, 54–55, 88, 170n7, 177n45; *Mencius* 4B.1, 34, 147, 173n42, 199n25; *Mencius* 7B.38, 26–27; Way of the Sages, narratives of, 26–29, 170n6, 171n17
Meng Jian. *See* Han Yu
Minister Yu, 52
ming (name) and *shi* (essence), 48–52, 115, 191n70
Ming dynasty, 20, 106, 166n23, 167n47, 169n71, 187n10, 194n37
Mo "barbarians," 9
Mongol empire. *See* Yuan dynasty
moral duty. *See liyi* (ritual propriety and moral duty)
mores, 12, 14, 112, 148
Mozi, 26, 28, 47–48, 54–55, 79–80, 88–90, 116, 176n23, 185n71
Mou (state), 38–39, 103, 107, 172n29, 174n55, 189n43
Mouzi. *See* "Master Mou's Discourse on Resolving Doubts"
Mount Tai Academy. *See* Sun Fu
Mu Xiu, 75–76

N

Nanzhao, 142
nationalism, 3–5, 10–11, 16–21, 84–86, 139, 141, 153, 164–65n14, 168nn59,60,64, 198n97; modern Chinese nationalism, 10, 153, 167n46
nativism, 5, 7, 62, 164–65n14
Neo-Confucianism. *See* Daoxue
Nine Provinces (synonym for the Central Lands), 92–93, 105

Northern and Southern Dynasties, 18, 25, 63–65, 147–49, 151–52, 180n33
Northern Wei dynasty, 63–65, 125; Song perceptions, 147–48, 150–51. *See also* Xiaowendi
Northern Zhou dynasty, 63, 65, 180n33. *See also* Zhou Wudi

O

Odes (Shijing), 8, 121, 147, 195n44; "Bigong" (ode), 8, 54, 133, 165n18, 177n45, 196n67
Opium War, 4
Ouyang Xiu, 75, 88, 90–96, 131, 169n67, 186n2; on *Annals* exegesis, 93, 98, 101–2, 186n3, 188n21; and Buddhism, 90–93, 95, 116–17, 184n62; ethnicized orthodoxy, rejection of, 77, 92; "On Fundamentals" (Benlun), 91, 95, 100, 102; as Guwen moderate, 77; "On Legitimate Dynasties" (Zhengtong lun), 101, 147–48; literary influence, 75, 91, 106; and Shi Jie, 90–93, 184n62

P

parallel prose, 25, 75, 90
Parhae. *See* Bohai
Pi Rixiu, 181n39, 182n13
political legitimacy (zhengtong), 63–65, 125, 147–49, 151–52, 180nn29,33
Protestant Reformation, 7, 164n13

Q

qi (cosmological concept), 19–20, 120, 151; use by Daoxue, 20, 119–22, 151
Qi (state), 99, 112, 114, 138–39, 148, 172n32, 190n65; Lord Huan of Qi, 99–101, 186n8
Qǐ (state), 32–33, 37–39, 51, 64–65, 103, 107, 172n32, 190–91n65
Qian conference, 133–35, 151, 181n39, 190n54, 196n65

INDEX 225

Qian Mu, 10, 27, 124–26, 169n76
Qiang (ethnonym), 49, 125, 176n28, 199n25
qilin, 101–2, 188n21
Qisong: as Buddhist apologist, 113; ethnocentric moralism, 113–18; "Expanding Upon 'Tracing the [Buddhist] Teaching to Its Source'" (Guang Yuanjiao), 115; and Great Centrality, 113–14; "Refuting Han Yu" (Fei Han), 114
Qin (state), 49, 101; as a barbarian state, 30, 92–93, 104, 106, 148, 171n21, 185n67, 188–89n27, 189n37
Qin dynasty, 8, 26, 28, 30–31, 130
Qing dynasty, 106, 152–53, 169n69, 187n10, 192n8, 194n37. *See also* Manchus
Qinzong (Song emperor), 186n8
Qiu Jun, 106, 167n47; *Supplement to the Extended Meaning of the Great Learning* (Dayue yanyi bu), 106, 122
Quanzhou, 58–59

R

racism/racialism, 10–11, 19–21, 167n46, 169n74, 197n83
Record of Rites (Liji), 82, 94, 183n28; *Dai the Elder's Record of Rites* (Dadai liji), 183n28; "Kingly Institutions" (Wangzhi), 82, 96
Record of the Historian (Shiji). *See* Sima Qian
Reformation. *See* Protestant Reformation
Renaissance humanism, 7
Renzong (Song emperor), 132–33
"Respecting the king and repelling the barbarians" (zunwang rangyi). *See Annals* (Chunqiu)
revanchism, 140, 144–45, 149, 150–51
ritual. *See li* (ritual or ritual propriety); *liyi* (ritual propriety and moral duty)
ritual propriety and moral duty. *See liyi* (ritual propriety and moral duty)

Rong "barbarians," 8–9, 30, 40, 49, 54, 113; used against the Khitans, 85; used against Li Keyong, 71; and the Lu state, 133–34, 136–38, 165n18, 181n39, 190n54, 196n65; Rong-Man, 110; Rong of Luhun, 64–65; Rong of the Mountains, 110; Rong of Xú, 92, 136–37, 190–91n65
Ru (Classicism/Confucianism), 4, 16, 43–44, 48, 56, 74, 92, 94, 113; "Confucian revival," 44, 191n74; "Confucian" translation, 163n3; as identity, 16, 21, 24, 42, 55–56, 74, 76, 152. *See also* Daoxue (Neo-Confucianism); Way of the Sages

S

Shang dynasty, 49, 64, 170n6, 180n28
Shang Yang, 101
Shangshu. *See Documents* (Shangshu)
Shao Bo, 134, 175n1
Shaoling covenant, 99–101
Shatuo Türks, 70, 72, 147
Shen Buhai, 48, 176n23
Shen conference, 102, 188n19
Shenzong (Song emperor), 132, 135
Shi Jie: *Annals* exegesis, 87, 99, 118, 191n76; "The Central Lands" (Zhongguo lun), 81–84, 86–90; ethnicized orthodoxy, 80–88, 116–18, 131, 185n71; as Guwen radical, 77, 80; "Imperial University" literary style, 90–91; irredentism, 84–86; and Lu region, 86–87, 185n71; and Ouyang Xiu, 90–93; physical stature, 86; and Sun Fu, 86, 89, 99, 106, 186n1, 191n76
Shi Jingtang, 150
Shijing. *See Odes* (Shijing)
Shizong (Later Zhou emperor), 85
Shu (statelets), 8, 54, 165n18
Shun (sage-king), 26–28, 49, 89, 143, 170n6, 177n34; as barbarian, 34
Shunzong (Tang emperor), 41, 43
Silla, 61, 142, 199n14

Siku quanshu: censorship, 106, 169n69, 186nn8, 9, 187n16, 188n24, 189n34, 192–93n22, 194nn37,42

Sima Guang, 117, 191n72

Sima Qian, 39, 107, 179n12; *Record of the Historian* (Shiji), 39–40, 49

Sinicization. *See* barbarians

Sogdians, 6, 163n6

Song (Eastern Zhou state), 185n68

Song dynasty: and *Annals* exegesis, 97–99, 111–12, 118; as empire or nation-state, 16–19, 84–86, 169nn70,72; factionalized politics, 117; foreign relations, 3–4, 16–20, 23, 79–80, 84–86, 142–52; Southern Song, 4, 16–17, 19, 23, 132, 139–40, 148–52; Tang dynasty, perception of, 131

Song Qi, 116

sonnō jōi ("respecting the king and repelling the barbarians"). *See Annals* (Chunqiu)

Southern Qi dynasty, 63, 147–48

Su Shi, 91; and Buddhism, 117; ethnocentric moralism, 118; Han Yu, criticism of, 116, 146, 191n70; "On 'The True King Does Not Govern the Barbarians'" (Wangzhe buzhi Yi-Di lun), 112–13, 148, 196n65

Su Zhe, 91

Sui dynasty, 18, 28, 63, 77, 131, 185n71

Sumner, William Graham, 12, 14

Sun Chuo, 124, 126, 192n22

Sun Fu: on barbarians, 100–102, 131; ethnicized orthodoxy, 77, 86, 88–89, 102, 116, 184n50, 191n76; ethnocentric moralism, 97, 112, 118; as Guwen radical, 77; "The Humiliation of the Classicists" (Ruru), 89, 100, 102; influence as an *Annals* exegete, 97–99, 107, 140, 198n96; Mount Tai Academy, 88, 99, 186nn1,2; and Shi Jie, 86, 88–89, 106; *Uncovering the Intricacies of Respecting the King in the Annals* (Chunqiu zunwang fawei, *Uncovering the Intricacies*), 98–105, 186n10, 196n65

Sun He, 75

Sun Qiao, 142

Sun Shi, 80–81, 88, 99

Supplement to the Extended Meaning of the Great Learning (Dayue yanyi bu). *See* Qiu Jun

supremacism, 152–53

synecdoche, 8–9

T

Taizong (Tang emperor), 83, 131–32

Tang (sage-king and founder of the Shang dynasty), 27–28

Tang covenants, 134, 136–39

Tang dynasty: cosmopolitanism and pluralism, 3, 7, 17–18, 29, 43–44, 56, 141, 175n3; end of the dynasty, 69–70; foreign relations, 5–6, 61, 142; late Tang xenophobia, 3, 5–7, 58, 65, 141, 164n13, 164–65n14, 168n62; new *Annals* exegesis, 37, 41–42. *See also* An Lushan Rebellion; Huang Chao Rebellion

Tang-Song transition, 3, 5, 22, 24, 268n64

Tanguts. *See* Xi Xia

Tatars, 145

Ten Kingdoms, 169n67

Third Miscellaneous Discourse. *See* Han Yu

Three Kingdoms, 63

"three teachings" (Classicism, Buddhism, and Daoism), 43

ti (essence/substance) and *yong* (application/function/manifestation), 136

Tibetan empire, 5, 132, 137, 142

Tongzhitang jingjie, 186nn8,9, 187n16

"Tracing the Way to Its Source." *See* Han Yu

U

Uighur empire, 5, 137, 142, 163n6

universalism (cultural, moral, or political), 3, 7, 16–19, 24, 66–67, 136, 139–40, 142, 152–53, 169n70

V

valedictory prefaces, 27, 44–48, 59, 79, 116
Vietnam, 8, 85, 168n66

W

Wang Anshi, 117, 132; alleged suppression of *Annals* exegesis, 195n59
Wang Chao, 59, 178n7
Wang Chong, 123
Wang Ling: and the debate between Han Yu and Liu Zongyuan, 50–52; emulation of Shi Jie, 116; ethnicized orthodoxy, 116
Wang Mang, 130
Wang Shuwen faction, 41, 47
Wang Tong, 77, 80, 89, 147, 182n13, 200n27
Wang Xingyu, 71–72
Wang Yucheng, 75–76, 182n10
Wanyan Liang, 149, 151, 200n32
Warring States. *See* Zhou dynasty
Way of the Barbarians. *See* barbarians
Way of the Sages: Cheng Yi's use of the term, 119; Han Yu's use of the term, 15, 22, 26–29, 44–45, 54–56, 74; Liu Kai's use of the term, 77; Liu Zongyuan's understanding of the term, 177n34; Mencius's use of the term, 26, 170n6; Shi Jie's use of the term, 76, 80, 84, 86–90, 141, 170n6, "Way of Confucius," 26, 54, 89. *See also* Han Yu; Mencius; Ru (Classicism/Confucianism)
Wei Shou, 125, 193n28
wen. See culture
Wenchang. *See* Han Yu
wenhua (transformation by *wen*). *See* culture
wenming (illumination by *wen*), 13–15, 60, 66
Western Jin. *See* Jin dynasty
Wu (state), 31, 33–34, 49, 93, 102–5, 125, 187n15; as barbarized Chinese state, 39–40, 107–12, 181n39; Taibo descent, claim of, 39, 108, 110, 174n57

Wuding (Shang king), 180n28
Wuzong (Tang emperor), 6

X

Xi Xia, 17, 84–85, 95–96, 105, 135, 145–46; war with the Song dynasty, 95, 184n44
Xia (as ethnonym). *See* Chinese (ethnocultural group)
Xia dynasty, 32, 147–48, 172n32
Xianbi (Xianbei), 64–65, 148, 180n31, 195n54
Xianyu. *See* Di "barbarians"
Xianyun, 143–44, 199n8
Xiao (or Yao), battle of, 30, 171n21, 189nn27,37
Xiaowendi (Northern Wei emperor), 63, 65, 125, 147, 151–52, 180n26, 193n28
Xie Liangzuo, 128, 194n41, 196n64
Xin dynasty, 130
Xin You, 64–65, 96, 185n69
Xing Bing, 126–27
Xiongnu, 60, 130, 137, 197nn81,82, 199nn8,14; as an epithet for the Khitans, 85
Xú (state), 39–40, 92, 108, 114, 136–37, 173n53, 190n45, 190–91n65. *See also* Rong "barbarians"
Xun Yue, 197n82
Xunyu, 143–44, 199n8
Xunzi, 14, 28, 56, 80, 89, 171n16, 172n41

Y

Yan region (Youzhou), 17, 79, 84–85, 150
Yang Du, 167n46
Yang Fugong, 71
Yang Huizhi, 177n34
Yang Shi, 121, 128, 133
Yang Xiong, 24–28, 44–48, 56, 77, 80, 89–90, 170n3, 171n16, 176n23, 194n42
Yang Yi, 75, 90, 181n2
Yang Zhu, 26, 28, 47, 54–55, 79–80, 88–90, 116, 185n71
Yangzhou massacre, 6
Yao (sage-king), 26–28, 49, 89, 143, 177n34

Yao Xuan, 75
Ye Mengde, 184n62
yi (moral duty). See *liyi* (ritual propriety and moral duty)
Yi "barbarians" (non-generic/non-synecdochic usage), 8, 32–33, 64–65, 92, 138, 185n68; associated with Korea, 8, 138. *See also* Qĭ (state); Zhu (state)
Yi-Di. *See* barbarians
Yijing. See *Changes* (Yijing)
Yin Tun, 128–29
Yin You, 42
Yongzheng emperor, 153
You Yu, 48–49, 51, 96, 115, 176n27
Yu (sage-king), 27–28, 89; as barbarian, 147, 199n25; as Yue rulers' ancestors, 108;
Yuan dynasty, 152
Yuan Jixu (Yuan the Eighteenth), 47, 176n17
Yuan Zhen, 6, 164n7
Yuanhao, 85
Yue (state), 39–40, 108
Yue Fei, 23

Z

Zang Bing, 77–78, 182n14
Zanning, 76
Zeng (state), 185n68
Zeng Gong, 91
Zeng Min, 13
Zhang Di, 149
Zhang Fangping, 147–48
Zhang Guilu, 86–88, 184n46

Zhang Ji, 25–28, 170n4
Zhang Jun, 71
Zhao Kuang, 37–39, 42, 98–99, 103, 107
Zhaozong (Tang emperor), 59, 69–70
Zheng (state), 30, 32, 45, 103, 106, 138, 171n28, 172n29
Zheng Xie, 118
Zheng Xuan, 123–25, 192n17, 193–94n30
Zhenzong (Song emperor), 80
Zhongguo. *See* Central Lands
Zhonghua. *See* Central Lands
Zhou (last Shang king), 64, 180n28
Zhou Bida, 200n29
Zhou dynasty: Eastern Zhou, 8–10, 28, 64, 82, 90–93, 99–100, 126, 133, 170n6, 185n67; Warring States, 9, 12, 14, 30, 167n36; Western Zhou, 126, 172n32, 199n8
Zhou Mi, 176n22
Zhou Wudi, 180n33
Zhu (state), 38–39, 103, 107, 172n29, 174n55, 185n68, 189n43
Zhu Wen, 69–72
Zhu Xi, 52, 123, 127, 165n16, 167n47, 195n53, 197n89; on *Analects* 3.5, 129
Zhu Yu, 18, 145, 169n69
Zhuangzi, 45–46, 48–49, 94, 106, 176n23, 185n71
Zoroastrianism, 6
zunwang rangyi ("respecting the king and repelling the barbarians"). See *Annals* (Chunqiu)
Zuo Tradition (Zuozhuan). See *Annals* (Chunqiu)